P9-EJT-571

Download Forms on Nolo.com

You can download the forms in this book at:

 www.nolo.com/back-of-book/COHA.html

We'll also post updates whenever there's an important change to the law affecting this book—as well as articles and other related materials.

More Resources from Nolo.com

 Legal Forms, Books, & Software
Hundreds of do-it-yourself products—all written in plain English, approved, and updated by our in-house legal editors.

 Legal Articles
Get informed with thousands of free articles on everyday legal topics. Our articles are accurate, up to date, and reader friendly.

 Find a Lawyer
Want to talk to a lawyer? Use Nolo to find a lawyer who can help you with your case.

NOLO
LAW for ALL

14th Edition

The Copyright Handbook

What Every Writer Needs to Know

Stephen Fishman, J.D.

FOURTEENTH EDITION	JANUARY 2021
Editor	REBECCA PIRIUS
Book Design	SUSAN PUTNEY
Proofreading	SUSAN CARLSON GREENE
Index	VICTORIA BAKER
Printing	BANG PRINTING

ISSN: 2325-4564 (print)
ISSN: 2325-4572 (online)

ISBN: 978-1-4133-2783-0 (pbk)
ISBN: 978-1-4133-2784-7 (ebook)

This book covers only United States law, unless it specifically states otherwise.

Please note

We know that accurate, plain-English legal information can help you solve many of your own legal problems. But this text is not a substitute for personalized advice from a knowledgeable lawyer. If you want the help of a trained professional—and we'll always point out situations in which we think that's a good idea—consult an attorney licensed to practice in your state.

Acknowledgments

Many thanks to:

Jake Warner for giving me the opportunity to write a book on such an interesting subject and for his editorial contributions.

Richard Stim and Steve Elias, whose ideas and superb editing made this a much better book. Rebecca Pirius and David Goguen for their editing.

Kent Dunlap, Assistant General Counsel, U.S. Copyright Office, and Lisa Goldoftas for reviewing the chapter on copyright registration.

Dedication

This book is dedicated to my mother, Helen F. Poellot.

About the Author

Stephen Fishman has been writing about the law for over 25 years. He received his law degree from the University of Southern California in 1979. He has published 20 books and hundreds of articles, and has been quoted in *The New York Times, Wall Street Journal, Chicago Tribune,* and many other publications. He is the author of the treatise *Copyright and the Public Domain* (Law Journal Press). His Nolo publications include:

- *The Public Domain: How to Find Copyright-Free Writings, Music, Art & More*
- *Consultant & Independent Contractor Agreements*
- *Deduct It! Lower Your Small Business Taxes*
- *Every Landlord's Tax Deduction Guide*
- *Home Business Tax Deductions: Keep What You Earn*
- *Tax Deductions for Professionals*
- *Working for Yourself: Law & Taxes for Independent Contractors, Freelancers & Gig Workers of All Types,* and
- *Working With Independent Contractors.*

Table of Contents

Your Legal Companion

In 2007, Amazon, the nation's largest online seller of print books, unveiled the Kindle, an electronic book reader that allows users to download books from almost anywhere in the United States (and within minutes). Unlike the books that have been sold for the past six centuries, the Kindle does not require ink to be placed on paper, glue to be applied to a binding, or books to be shipped from publisher to a store. But the Kindle does have one thing in common with the millions of books that came before it: It offers the written word to readers ... and most of the works sold for the Kindle are—like most of the books sold at Amazon—protected by copyright.

That's what this book is about: copyright for the written word.

If you're a writer—whether a novelist, short story writer, poet, playwright, screenwriter, biographer, historian, author of how-to books, writer of scientific and technical works and other works of nonfiction, published or unpublished author, journalist, blogger, freelance writer, person employed by others to create written works, person who employs others to create written works, editor who works for a magazine or a book publisher, established publisher, self-publisher, librarian, teacher, or literary agent—this book is for you.

This book is composed of two parts:
- The first part (Chapters 1–3) consists of a short overview of copyright law (Chapter 1, "Copyright Basics"), and a how-to guide on copyright notice and registration with the Copyright Office.
- The second part (Chapters 4–14) serves as your copyright resource; it discusses the most important aspects of copyright law in detail. If you are unable to find the answers to your questions in earlier chapters, the final chapter tells you how to do further research on your own and, if necessary, find a copyright attorney.

Not everyone will want to read the whole book. The parts you do want to read will, of course, depend on why you bought the book; most likely for one of these three reasons:

- **You want to know how to correctly fulfill the procedural requirements necessary to obtain maximum copyright protection for a written work.** If you want to know how to place a valid copyright notice on your work (that's the © followed by a date and name you usually see on published works), read Chapter 2, "Copyright Notice." Placing a valid copyright notice on your work will make it easier to enforce your copyright. If you want to register your work with the Copyright Office, refer to Chapter 3 for a step-by-step explanation.

- **You have a specific copyright question or problem.** If you have a specific question or problem, start with the table of contents at the front of the book. For example, suppose you want to know whether you need permission to use a quotation from Abraham Lincoln that you found in a recent Civil War history. By scanning the table of contents, you would discover that Chapter 9, "Using Other Authors' Words," is probably the place to start. If you didn't find a helpful topic in the table of contents, you could use the index at the back of the book and search under terms such as "quotations" or "public domain."

- **You want a general education about copyright law.** If you simply want to learn more about copyright, read Chapter 1, "Copyright Basics," and then read as much of Chapters 4 through 14 as you wish. You can skip Chapter 3, because this chapter is intended for people who want to take specific steps to obtain maximum copyright protection for a written work.

This book only covers copyright for written works—meaning, this book is not about:

- copyright protection for music, artwork, photography, or audiovisual works; for a detailed discussion of legal protection for music, see *Music Law: How to Run Your Band's Business,* by Richard Stim (Nolo).

- publishing contracts; although we discuss the copyright aspects of publishing contracts, this is not a book about how to negotiate or draft contracts.

- protecting inventions; see *Patent It Yourself,* by David Pressman and David E. Blau (Nolo), if you want to know about patent protections.

- protecting titles, logos, or slogans; because these items may be protected under the federal and state trademark laws, which have nothing to do with copyright, see *Trademark: Legal Care for Your Business & Product Name,* by Stephen Fishman (Nolo).

- protecting ideas; copyright only protects words, not ideas. Ideas can be protected as trade secrets, which involves committing anyone who learns of the ideas to secrecy and maintaining security procedures to prevent the ideas from leaking out.

Get Forms, Updates, and More at *The Copyright Handbook*'s Companion Page

You can download all of the forms in this book at *The Copyright Handbook*'s companion page on Nolo's website (free for readers of this book) at:

www.nolo.com/back-of-book/COHA.html

In addition, when there are important changes to the information in this book, we'll post updates at the companion page, as well as podcasts from the author, Stephen Fishman.

Copyright Basics

This chapter introduces some basic copyright concepts and vocabulary. It is designed to pave the way for more detailed discussions in later chapters. So, we urge you not to use material in this chapter to reach a final conclusion about any particular issue. Only after reading one or more of the later chapters will you be in a position to make a judgment about a particular question or course of action.

Why Have a Copyright Law?

The Founding Fathers recognized that everyone would benefit if creative people were encouraged to create new intellectual and artistic works. When the United States Constitution was written in 1787, the framers took care to include a copyright clause (Article I, Section 8) stating that "The Congress shall have Power ... To promote the Progress of Science and useful Arts, by securing for limited times to Authors ... the exclusive Right to their ... writings."

The primary purpose of copyright, then, is not to enrich authors; rather, it is to promote the progress of science and the useful arts—that is, human knowledge. To pursue this goal, copyright encourages authors in their creative efforts by giving them a mini-monopoly over their works— termed a "copyright." But this monopoly is limited when it appears to conflict with the overriding public interest in encouraging creation of new intellectual and artistic works generally.

What Is Copyright?

Copyright is a legal device that provides the creator of a work of art or literature, or a work that conveys information or ideas, the right to control how the work is used. The Copyright Act of 1976—the federal law providing for copyright protection—grants authors a bundle of intangible, exclusive rights over their work. These rights include:

- reproduction right—the right to make copies of a protected work
- distribution right—the right to sell or otherwise distribute copies to the public
- right to create adaptations (or derivative works)—the right to prepare new works based on the protected work, and
- performance and display rights— the right to perform a protected work, such as a stage play, or to display a work in public.

An author's copyright rights may be exercised only by the author (or by a person or an entity to whom the author has transferred all or part of his or her rights). If someone wrongfully uses the material covered by the copyright, the copyright owner can sue and obtain compensation for any losses suffered.

In this sense, a copyright is a type of property—it belongs to its owner (usually the author), and the courts can be asked to intervene if anyone uses a copyrighted work without permission. And, like other forms of property, a copyright may be sold by its owner or otherwise exploited for his or her economic benefit.

Some Common Copyright Misconceptions

Copyright is a confusing and fast-changing area of the law. Many people have ideas about copyright that are simply not true. For example:

- "A work must be registered with the U.S. Copyright Office to be protected by copyright."

  Copyright protection begins automatically the moment a work is set to paper or otherwise fixed in a tangible form.

- "Only works that have a copyright notice on them are protected by copyright."

  Use of copyright notices has been optional since March 1, 1989.

- "No one can use a protected work without the owner's permission."

  This has never been true. You can use protected works so long as the action falls within the bounds of fair use—that is, does not diminish the value of the protected work.

- "You can copyright your great ideas."

  This also has never been true. Copyright only protects the expression of an idea, not the idea itself.

How Is a Copyright Created and Protected?

A copyright automatically comes into existence the moment an author fixes his or her words in some tangible form—for instance, the moment a book or an article is inputted into a computer, handwritten, or dictated. No further action need be taken. However, it is wise to place a valid copyright notice on all published works and to register these works in the U.S. Copyright Office shortly after publication.

What Constitutes Publication

Because many important copyright rules differ for published and unpublished works, knowing whether a work has been published or not can be important. A work is published for copyright purposes when copies are sold, rented, lent, given away, or otherwise distributed to the public by the copyright owner or by others acting with the owner's permission—for example, a publisher. It is not necessary to sell thousands of copies of a work for it to be considered published. So long as copies of a work are made available to the public, the work is "published" for copyright purposes, even if no copies are actually sold or otherwise distributed.

Notice

In the past, all published works had to contain a copyright notice (the © symbol followed by the publication date and copyright owner's name) to be protected by copyright. This is no longer true. Use of copyright notices is optional. Even so, it is always a good idea to include a copyright notice on all published works so that potential copiers will be informed of the underlying claim to copyright ownership.

Registration

Prompt registration in the U.S. Copyright Office makes your copyright a matter of public record. Moreover, you must register your work before you are allowed to file a copyright infringement lawsuit in federal court to enforce your rights. To register a work you must complete a registration application (normally online) and deposit online or physical copies of your work with the Copyright Office.

What Copyright Protects

Copyright protects an author's words if and to the extent they are original—that is, not copied from other authors' works. Because the main goal of copyright is to encourage creation of new intellectual and artistic works, it follows that copyright protection extends only to material authors write themselves.

There is also no reason to protect works that are purely mechanical or clerical acts.

Protecting works, such as phone books or certain blank forms, would not help develop the arts and sciences. An author must employ a minimal amount of creativity in creating the work. This does not mean that to be protectable a work has to be a great work of art, but a minimal amount of thought or judgment must be involved in its creation.

Also, a work need not be entirely new to be protectable. Copyright protects new material an author adds to a previously existing work. For example, copyright protects derivative works. A derivative work is created by adapting or transforming previously written material into a new work of authorship. Examples include a screenplay or stage play based on a novel, an English translation of a work written in a foreign language, and condensed versions of articles. Copyright can also protect "compilations." These are works in which preexisting materials are selected, coordinated, and arranged so that a new work of authorship is created—for example, anthologies or catalogs.

Limitations on Copyright Protection

We've seen that the purpose of copyright is to encourage intellectual and artistic creation. But at the same time, giving authors too much copyright protection can inhibit rather than enhance creative growth. To avoid this, some important limitations on copyright protection have been developed.

Ideas and Facts Are Not Protected

Copyright only protects the words with which a writer expresses facts and ideas. Copyright does not protect the facts or ideas themselves; facts and ideas are free for anyone to use. To give an author a monopoly over the facts and ideas contained in his or her work would hinder intellectual and artistic progress, not encourage it. For example, imagine how scientific progress would have suffered if Charles Darwin could have prevented anyone else from writing about evolution after he published *On the Origin of Species.*

Because copyright only extends its protection to words rather than the underlying facts and ideas, works in which the particular words used by the author are important and distinctive—such as poems, novels, and plays—enjoy the most copyright protection. Works that readers buy primarily for the ideas and facts they contain, not their language, receive less protection. This includes most types of factual works, such as histories, biographies, how-to books, news stories, and so forth.

Fair Use

To foster the advancement of the arts and sciences, a free flow of information and ideas must exist. If no one could quote from a protected work without the author's permission (which could be withheld or given only upon payment of a permission fee), the free flow of ideas would be stopped dead.

To avoid this, a special fair use exception to authors' copyright rights was created. An author is free to copy from a protected work for purposes such as criticism, news reporting, teaching, or research so long as the value of the copyrighted work is not diminished.

Works in the Public Domain

Any work that is not protected by copyright is said to be in the public domain. This includes works where the copyright was lost or has expired and works authored or created by the federal government. Public domain means what it says—such works belong to the public as a whole. Anyone is free to use them any way he or she wishes without asking anyone's permission. And no one can ever obtain copyright protection for public domain material, no matter how the person transforms it. Everything published in the United States more than 95 years ago now exists in the public domain, freely available to us all.

Copyright Ownership and Transfer of Ownership

Initially, the work's author or authors own the copyright in a protectable work. But a person need not actually create the work to be its "author" for copyright purposes. A protectable work written by an employee as part of a job is initially owned by the employer—that is, the employer is considered to be the work's author. Such works are called "works made for hire." Works created by nonemployees who sign work-made-for-hire agreements may also be works made for hire.

Like any other property, a copyright can be bought and sold. This is the way authors other than self-publishers profit from their work. Typically, authors sell their work to publishers for a fee or royalty. However, transfers of copyright ownership are unique in one respect: Authors or their heirs have the right to terminate any transfer of copyright ownership 35 years after it is made.

How Long a Copyright Lasts

Few things in this world last as long as copyright protection. Indeed, an author's work is likely to be long forgotten before the copyright in it expires. The copyright in works created after 1977 by individuals usually lasts for the life of the author plus an additional 70 years. The copyright in works created by employees for their employers lasts for 95 years from the date of publication or 120 years from the date of creation, whichever occurs first.

The copyright in works created and published between 1923 and 1963 lasts for 95 years from the date of publication, if the copyright was timely renewed by the copyright owner 28 years after publication. It might be necessary to do some legwork to determine whether a renewal was filed for

a work. The copyright in works published between 1964 and 1977 lasts for 95 years regardless of whether a renewal was filed. The copyright in works created but not published before 1978 lasts at least until 70 years after the author dies.

Copyright Infringement

Copyright infringement occurs when a person other than the copyright owner exploits one or more of the copyright owner's exclusive rights without the owner's permission. This type of theft is also commonly termed "copyright piracy."

The Copyright Act doesn't prevent copyright infringement from occurring, just as the laws against auto theft do not prevent cars from being stolen. However, the Copyright Act does give an author a legal remedy after an infringement has occurred: The author may sue the infringer in federal court.

An author who wins an infringement suit can stop any further infringement, get infringing copies destroyed, obtain damages from the infringer (often the amount of any profits obtained from the infringement), and recover other monetary losses. This means, in effect, that an author can make the "copyright pirate" restore the author to the same economic position as if the infringement had never occurred. And, in some cases, the copyright owner might even be able to obtain monetary penalties that far exceed actual losses.

Other Protections for Intellectual Property

The copyright law is not the only means available to protect economically valuable products of human intellect. State and federal trademark laws protect distinctive words, phrases, logos, and other symbols used to identify products and services in the marketplace. The federal patent law protects new inventions. State trade secret laws may protect novel and generally unknown ideas, processes, or technical designs that provide a commercial advantage in the marketplace.

Trademarks

The copyright laws do not protect names, titles, or short phrases. This is where trademark protection comes in. Under both federal and state laws a manufacturer, merchant, or group associated with a product or service can obtain protection for a word, phrase, logo, or other symbol used to distinguish that product or service from others. If a competitor uses a protected trademark, the trademark holder can obtain a court injunction (an order to stop the unlawful use) and monetary damages.

EXAMPLE: The word "Kleenex" is a registered trademark of Kimberly-Clark Worldwide, Inc. None of Kimberly-Clark's competitors can use this word on a box of facial tissues without Kimberly-Clark's consent. If they do, Kimberly-Clark could get a court to order them to stop and could sue for damages.

Trademark laws are often used in conjunction with copyright laws to protect advertising copy. The trademark laws protect the product or service name and any slogans used in the advertising, and the copyright laws protect any additional literal expression that the ad contains.

Patents

By filing for and obtaining a patent from the U.S. Patent and Trademark Office, an inventor is granted a monopoly on the use and commercial exploitation of an invention for a limited time. A patent may protect the functional features of a machine, process, manufactured item, method of doing business, composition of matter, ornamental design, or asexually reproduced plant. A patent also protects new uses for any such items. However, to obtain a patent, the invention must be novel and nonobvious.

EXAMPLE: Mickey invents an entirely new and nonobvious type of mousetrap. He applies for a patent on his invention. If and when the patent is issued, no one can make, use, or sell Mickey's invention without his permission for the term (length) of the patent (20 years from the date the patent application was filed). If they do, Mickey can sue them for patent infringement.

The basic difference between a patent and a copyright is that a patent protects ideas as expressed in an invention, whether a machine or process of some type. Copyright protects only the words an author uses to express an idea, not the idea itself.

> EXAMPLE: Mary invented the widget, a device only dreamed about for decades. She obtains a patent for her invention. She manufactures and sells the widget herself. She also writes and publishes a technical manual, *The Widget Owner's Survival Guide.* The patent law prevents anyone from manufacturing and selling widgets without Mary's permission. The copyright law prevents anyone from copying the manual without Mary's permission.

Obtaining a patent can be a difficult and time-consuming process (it usually takes years). See *Patent It Yourself,* by David Pressman and David E. Blau (Nolo), for a detailed discussion.

Trade Secrets

A trade secret is information or know-how that is not generally known in the community and that provides its owner with a competitive advantage in the marketplace. The information can be an idea, written words, a formula, a process or procedure, a technical design, a list, a marketing plan, or any other secret that gives the owner an economic advantage.

If a trade secret's owner takes reasonable steps to keep the confidential information or know-how secret, the courts of most states will protect the owner from disclosures of the secret by:

- the owner's employees
- other persons with a duty not to make such disclosures
- industrial spies, and
- competitors who wrongfully acquire the information.

That is, the trade secret's owner may be able to sue the infringer and obtain an injunction or damages. However, once information becomes widely known—for example, through publication—it loses its trade secret status and courts will not protect it.

> EXAMPLE: Recall that Mary, in the second patent law example above, wrote a training manual for her widget invention. This manual was automatically protected by copyright. If the manual is also kept confidential (Mary only allows her employees to read it and makes them sign agreements to keep it confidential), it might also be entitled to trade secret protection. However, once Mary publishes and distributes the manual widely to the public, any trade secret protection would cease.

Because most authors want their work to be published and as widely read as possible, trade secret laws usually have little application to written works. However, trade secret protection can be important to authors of written works containing competitively advantageous information that has been kept confidential. Trade secret protection is provided primarily under state law and varies from state to state.

Contract Protection for Ideas

Consider this example: Manny, a TV producer, agrees to pay Sally $100,000 for telling him an idea she has for a new TV show. Sally tells Manny the idea, but he fails to pay. Does Sally have any recourse against Manny?

We know that copyright does not protect ideas, so Sally cannot sue Manny for copyright infringement. Her idea is not for a new invention, so she gets no help from the patent laws. And let's assume the idea is not a trade secret.

All is not lost for Sally, because some courts have held that if a person agrees to pay another person for disclosing an idea, the agreement constitutes an enforceable contract.

This means that if the person fails to pay as promised, the person who disclosed the idea might be able to sue and collect the promised payment. This might mean that Sally can sue Manny for breach of contract and collect the $100,000. Some courts would permit Sally the $100,000 only if her idea was novel and concrete and Manny actually used it. Others would not require novelty and use.

However, very few Mannys or Sallys exist in the real world. Rarely, if ever, will a producer, a publisher, an editor, or another person agree to pay an author for a mere idea. Thus, contract protection for ideas is usually more theoretical than real. The best way to protect your ideas is to disclose them only to people whose integrity can be trusted.

Copyright Notice

Introduction:
The Little "c" in a Circle

I n this chapter, you'll learn about copyright notice. That's the "c" in a circle, followed by a publication date and name, usually seen on published works. The purpose of such a notice is to inform the public that a work is copyrighted and provide notice of when it was published and who owns the copyright. Before March 1, 1989, a notice was required on all published works as a condition of keeping the copyright. For works published after that date, a notice is not required. Nonetheless, it's a very good idea to provide a notice on all your published works.

The use of a copyright notice is the responsibility of the copyright owner and does not require any advance permission from, or registration with, the Copyright Office.

The extent to which you need to be concerned with the material in this chapter depends upon your particular situation.

Authors of books published by established companies. As a practical matter, you don't have to worry much about the copyright notice if you're being published by an established publisher. The publisher, as a matter of course, will include copyright notices on all copies of the books it distributes. The author just needs to make sure that the information in the notice is correct.

Freelance writers. Freelance writers whose work appears in print or online magazines and other periodicals or on established websites or blogs are protected by the notice the publisher provides for the periodical as a whole. But some freelancers choose to include a separate notice on their work.

Self-published authors. Persons who self publish their work—whether in print, online, or as electronic books—must compose and format their copyright notices themselves. Self-published authors should carefully read this chapter, as should anyone who works in the publishing field.

When Copyright Notice Is Required

Copyright notice is mandatory for some works and not for others, depending upon the date of publication.

Works Published Before 1978

Until 1978, all works published in the United States had to contain a valid copyright notice in order to be protected by copyright. Failure to provide the notice resulted in loss of the copyright in the work—that is, the work was injected into the public domain where anyone could copy or otherwise use it without the author's permission.

EXAMPLE: Bernie self-published his poetry collection in 1977. He knew nothing about copyright law and failed to provide a copyright notice on the work. Shirley finds a copy of the collection in a used bookstore in 2020 and decides to include several of Bernie's poems in a compilation of modern American poetry. Because the book did not contain a copyright notice, it is considered to be in the public domain and Shirley may reproduce all or part of it without Bernie's permission.

Works Published Between January 1, 1978 and March 1, 1989

As the example above illustrates, the pre-1978 notice requirement often had draconian results—authors could lose their copyright protection just because they failed to comply with a mere technical formality. The harshness of this rule was moderated somewhat by the Copyright Act of 1976. The act provided that a work published after January 1, 1978 without a valid notice did not enter the public domain, if—within five years after the publication—the work was registered with the Copyright Office and a reasonable effort was made to add a valid notice to all copies of the work distributed after the omission was discovered. (See Chapter 3, "Copyright Registration," for a detailed discussion.)

Works Published After March 1, 1989

The copyright notice requirement for published works ended altogether when the United States signed the Berne Convention, an international copyright treaty. The Berne Convention is discussed in detail in Chapter 11, "International Copyright Protection." All you need to know about it now is that it required the United States to get rid of its notice requirement, which happened on March 1, 1989. Any work printed after that date need not contain a copyright notice, even if it was originally published prior to that date.

EXAMPLE: George self-publishes a book in 1988. The work had to contain a valid copyright notice to be protected by copyright. He then reissues the book in 2020. The newly printed copies need not contain a copyright notice, but it is a good idea to provide one, anyway (see below).

Special Rules for Foreign Works

Works by foreign citizens or residents that were published in foreign countries without a copyright notice before March 1, 1989 entered the U.S. public domain under the law then in effect, just like any other work. However, as a result of an international trade agreement (called the GATT Agreement), the U.S. copyright in these works was automatically restored effective January 1, 1996 and they receive a full term of U.S. copyright protection. (See Chapter 11.)

Why Provide a Copyright Notice on Published Works?

Even though a notice is not required for works published after March 1, 1989, you should still make sure that a valid copyright notice appears on every copy of every work you publish. There are several excellent reasons for this.

Notice Helps Make Infringement Suits Economically Feasible

Authors and other copyright owners enforce their copyright rights by suing persons who copy their work or otherwise infringe on their copyright rights without permission. Unfortunately, copyright infringement litigation is usually very expensive (copyright attorneys typically charge $250 to $500 an hour). As a result, copyright infringement lawsuits tend to be economically feasible only if the author can obtain substantial damages (money) from the infringer.

The way to get substantial damages is to prove that the infringement was *willful*—that is, that the infringer knew that he or she was breaking the law but did so anyway. Courts usually award far more damages where the infringement

was willful than where the infringer didn't realize what he or she was doing was wrong. (See Chapter 10, "Copyright Infringement," for a detailed discussion of infringement suits.)

Proving willfulness can be difficult if a work lacks a valid copyright notice. Why? It's due to what's known as the innocent infringement defense. If a person copies a published work that does not contain a copyright notice, the copier can claim in court that the infringement was innocent— that is, the copier didn't know the work was protected by copyright. If the judge or jury believes this defense, the copier may still be liable for infringement, but the damages (monetary compensation) may be drastically reduced from what they otherwise would have been. On the other hand, if the work contains a valid copyright notice, the infringer cannot claim innocence and will be treated as a willful infringer.

EXAMPLE 1: Mary self-publishes a book without a copyright notice. Izzy copies a substantial amount of it in a book of his own. Mary sues Izzy for copyright infringement. Mary proves to the court that she suffered $25,000 in damages due to the infringement. However, Izzy, while admitting that he copied Mary's work, claims that he did not realize it was copyrighted because it lacked a copyright notice. The judge buys Izzy's story and, as a result, rules that Izzy need pay Mary only $5,000 in damages rather than the $25,000 required to fully compensate her.

EXAMPLE 2: Assume instead that Mary included a valid copyright notice in her book. She sues Izzy for copyright infringement. Since her book contained a valid notice, Izzy cannot argue that he did not realize the book was protected by copyright. As a result, Mary is awarded the full amount of damages required to fully compensate her: $25,000.

Copyright Notice Might Deter Potential Infringers

Another important reason to place a copyright notice on all copies of your published work is to help deter copyright infringement. The notice lets readers know that the work is protected by copyright and may not be copied without the owner's permission. Moreover, because copyright notices appear on the vast majority of published works, a reader of a work not containing a notice might mistakenly assume that the work is not copyrighted and feel free to copy it.

TIP

Placing a copyright notice on your published work costs nothing and may end up saving you thousands of dollars by deterring others from copying your work and enabling you to recover your full measure of damages against those who do copy it. Always, always, always place a valid copyright notice on your published work!

When to Provide Notice

A copyright notice should be included on a work when it is first published and on every subsequent published edition. For copyright purposes, a work is published when it is made generally available to the public by the copyright owner or others acting with the owner's permission—a publisher, for example. It is not necessary to sell or otherwise transfer any copies of the work—publication occurs if the work is made available to the public without restriction. For example, leaving copies of a work in a public place would constitute publication, as would distributing copies on a busy street. But distributing copies to a restricted group would not constitute publication. Sending five copies of a manuscript to five publishers would not be a publication, nor would circulating copies to colleagues (a restricted group) for comment.

A copyright notice has never been required for unpublished works, and it will not bar an infringer from raising the innocent infringement defense. But, under certain circumstances, providing a notice on an unpublished manuscript might be desirable.

Notices for Online Works

It's not altogether clear whether making a copy of a work available online constitutes a publication. However, you should assume that it does. Place a copyright notice on anything you don't want copied.

Form of Notice

There are strict technical requirements as to what a copyright notice must contain. Follow these rules exactly or your notice could be found to be invalid and not accomplish its intended purpose. A valid copyright notice contains three elements:

- the copyright symbol
- the year in which the work was published, and
- the name of the copyright owner.

It is not required that these elements appear in any particular order in the notice, but most notices are written in the order set forth above. We'll discuss each element in turn.

Adding the Word "Copyright" to the Notice

Often, you'll see the word "Copyright" or the abbreviation "Copr." followed by or preceding the © symbol—for instance, "Copyright ©." Technically, this is not required—the © symbol alone is sufficient. However, it is a good idea to include the words anyway, because they will further clarify that the work is protected by copyright.

Copyright Symbol

You should use the familiar © symbol—a lowercase letter "c" completely surrounded by a circle. The word "Copyright" or the abbreviation "Copr." are also acceptable in the United States but not in many foreign countries. So, if your work might be distributed outside the United States, be sure to always use the © symbol.

Year of Publication

The copyright notice must also state the year the work was published. For first editions, this is easy. Put the year the work was actually published. (See "When to Provide Notice," above.)

New Versions

The copyright notice for a new version of a work must contain the date that version was published. (See Chapter 5, "Adaptations and Compilations," for when changes in a work make it a new version for copyright purposes.) The notice need not contain the date or dates of the prior version or versions. However, it is common practice to include such dates in the copyright notice. One reason to do this is to let the reader know when the earlier versions were created. Another reason is that it's sometimes difficult to determine if a work qualifies as a new version under Copyright Office rules.

EXAMPLE: Sally Bowles published the first edition of her high school textbook on French in 2020. The copyright notice reads "Copyright © 2020 by Sally Bowles." The book is revised and republished as a second edition in 2022. If the second edition qualifies as a new version,

the notice need only state "Copyright ©
2022 by Sally Bowles." However, Sally is not
sure whether the changes she made were
substantial enough to make the second edition
a new version. She decides to err on the side
of caution and writes the notice like this:
"Copyright © 2020, 2022 by Sally Bowles."

Form of Date

The date is usually written in Arabic numerals
—for instance, "2022." But you can also
use abbreviations of Arabic numerals—for
instance, "'22"; Roman numerals—for
instance, "MMXXII"; or spelled-out words
instead of numerals—for instance, "Two
Thousand Twenty-Two."

TIP

Copyright tip. Copyright owners
sometimes state the year of publication in
Roman numerals in the hope readers won't be
able to decipher it and will think the work more
recent than it really is. However, in some foreign
countries, dates must be written in Arabic
numerals to be acceptable.

Copyright Owner's Name

The name of the copyright owner must
also be included in the notice. Briefly, the
owner is:

- the author or authors of the work
- the legal owner of a work made for
  hire, or

- the person or entity (partnership or
  corporation) to whom all the author's
  exclusive copyright rights have been
  transferred.

Author or Authors

Unless a work is made for hire (see below),
the original author or authors own all the
copyright rights. Where all these rights are
retained, the author's name should appear
in the copyright notice.

> **EXAMPLE:** Eli Yale self-publishes a book on
> ivy gardening in 2022. Eli wrote the book
> himself and owns all the copyright rights. The
> copyright notice should state: "Copyright ©
> 2022 by Eli Yale."

If there are multiple authors, they should
all be listed in the copyright notice. The
authors' names can appear in any order.

> **EXAMPLE:** Joe Sixpack, Louis Loser, and
> Benny Bigmouth write a book together
> about nuclear physics. All their names
> should appear in the copyright notice. For
> example: "Copyright © 2022 by Joe Sixpack,
> Louis Loser, and Benny Bigmouth."

Works Made for Hire

A work made for hire is a work made by
an employee as part of his or her job or a
work specially ordered or commissioned
under a written work-made-for-hire
contract. (See Chapter 6, "Initial Copyright
Ownership.") The writer's employer or
another person for whom the work was

prepared is the copyright owner, and that person's (or entity's) name should appear in the copyright notice. The writer-employee's name should not be included in the notice.

> EXAMPLE: Archie and Marion are technical writers employed by Datavue Publications, Inc. As part of their job, they write a technical manual that Datavue publishes. Only Datavue's name should appear in the copyright notice: "Copyright © 2022 by Datavue Publications."

Transferees

If all of an owner's copyright rights are transferred to another person or entity, that person's or entity's name should appear in the copyright notice on all copies printed and distributed after the transfer. However, any copies published before the transfer occurred may be distributed without updating the notice.

> EXAMPLE: Eli Yale self-publishes his book on ivy gardening in 2021. His name alone appears on the copyright notice. He prints 1,000 copies and, by January 2022, 500 have been sold. In February 2022, Eli transfers his entire copyright in the book to Joe Harvard, the owner of a small bookstore. Joe is now the copyright owner. However, Joe can distribute the 500 unsold copies without updating the copyright notice they contain, even though the notice states that Eli is the copyright owner. But, if Joe prints and distributes any new copies, his name alone should appear in the copyright notice.

If You Want to Remain Anonymous

The word "anonymous" should not be used in a copyright notice, because an author is obviously not generally known by that name. Likewise, it is not advisable to use a pseudonym by which you are not generally known. You can avoid revealing your name in a copyright notice, and still ensure the notice's validity, by transferring all of your copyright rights to your publisher. This way, the publisher's name may appear in the notice. Another approach would be to form a corporation, transfer your entire copyright to it, and then use the corporation's name in the notice.

The most common form of transfer of rights is by a writer to his or her publisher. A writer can sell all or part of his or her copyright rights to a publisher. The extent of the transfer is a matter for negotiation. Trade book publishing contracts typically provide the publisher with an exclusive license to exercise the rights the publisher needs (for example, the right to publish the book in all English speaking countries). In this event, the author's name should appear in the copyright notice, not the publisher's name, because the author has retained some of the copyright rights. Another approach, commonly used in textbook publishing, is for the author to transfer all copyright rights to his publisher. Where this occurs, the publisher's name should appear in the notice.

Form of Name

Usually, the owner's full legal name is used. However, it is permissible to use an abbreviation of the owner's name; a last name alone; a trade name, nickname, fictitious name, or pseudonym; initials; or some other designation, as long as the copyright owner is *generally known* by the name or other words or letters used in the notice. However, if the author is generally known only by his or her full name, only that name should be used in the notice.

If the copyright owner is a corporation, it is not necessary to include the word "Inc." in the name, even if this is part of the corporation's full legal name. Nor is it necessary for the word "by" to precede the copyright owner's name, although it is commonly used—for example, a notice can be written as "Copyright © 2022 by Joe Blow" or "Copyright © 2022 Joe Blow."

Notice on Compilations and Adaptations

Compilations and adaptations are formed all or in part from preexisting material. Even so, it is usually not necessary that the copyright notice for this type of work refer to the preexisting material.

Compilations

A compilation can be a collective work—that is, a work that consists of separate and independent works assembled into a collective whole, such as encyclopedias, anthologies, and serial works like magazines, periodicals, newspapers, newsletters, and journals. A compilation can also be a work in which preexisting materials—usually data of various types—are selected, coordinated, and arranged so that a new work is created—for example, a catalog. (See Chapter 5, "Adaptations and Compilations," for a detailed discussion.)

Unless a person who creates a compilation uses material in the public domain, the compiler must either own the preexisting material used in the work or obtain the permission of those who do own it. If the creator of a compilation does not own the preexisting material, all he or she owns is the copyright in the compilation as a whole—that is, the copyright in the creative work involved in selecting, combining, and assembling the material into a whole work. Regardless of what rights the creator of a compilation has, a compilation need only contain one copyright notice in the name of that copyright owner.

EXAMPLE: James Henry compiles and publishes an anthology of the best American short stories of 2022. The anthology contains 12 stories. The authors of the stories gave Henry permission to publish them in the anthology but still retain all their copyright rights. The anthology need contain only one copyright notice in Henry's name: "Copyright © 2022 by James Henry." Separate copyright notices need not be provided for the 12 contributions owned by persons other than Henry.

Although an individual contribution to a compilation does not have to have its own copyright notice, a notice is permissible where the copyright in the contribution is owned by someone other than the owner of the compilation as a whole. This may help deter a potential infringer and make clear that the owner of the copyright in the compilation does not own that particular contribution.

Publication Date for Compilations

The copyright notice for a compilation need only list the year the compilation itself is published, not the date or dates the preexisting material was published.

EXAMPLE: Josephine self-publishes an anthology of her short stories in 2022. The stories were published in various literary journals between 2010 and 2020. The notice on the anthology need only state 2022 as the publication date.

Online Works

Websites, blogs, and other online works are usually collective works. As with any collective work, a single notice in the name of the copyright owner of the collective work as a whole is sufficient. Notices are not required for each individual contribution to a website or blog. However, there is no harm in doing so anyway if you want to make clear that the materials are copyrighted and may not be used without permission.

Advertisements

The rule that a single notice for a compilation as a whole covers all the material in the work does not apply to advertisements. Advertisements in serial publications such as periodicals, magazines, and newspapers must carry their own copyright notice. However, an advertisement inserted in a compilation on behalf of the copyright owner of the compilation need not contain its own notice—for example, an ad inserted in *Time* magazine by its owners urging readers to subscribe would not need its own notice.

Adaptations (Derivative Works)

An adaptation—called a derivative work in copyright jargon—is a work that is created by recasting, transforming, or adapting a previously published work into a new work of authorship. Examples include a screenplay or play based on a novel, an English translation of a work written in a foreign language, condensed versions of articles, such as those found in *Reader's Digest*, and annotations to literary works.

Unless the preexisting material used by a derivative work is in the public domain or is owned by the creator of the derivative work, the creator must obtain the copyright owner's permission to use it. (See Chapter 5, "Adaptations and Compilations.")

As with compilations, the copyright notice for a derivative work need only contain the name of the owner of the copyright to the derivative work itself, not the owner of the preexisting material upon which the derivative work is based.

> **EXAMPLE:** Sally obtains Sue's permission to write a screenplay based on a novel written by Sue. Only Sally's name need appear in the copyright notice to the screenplay.

Publication Date

As with collective works, the publication date in the notice for a derivative work should be the year the derivative work was published, not the year or years the preexisting material was published.

> **EXAMPLE:** Joe writes a play based on his previously published novel. The novel was published in 2021, the play in 2022. The copyright notice on the published copies of the play need only state 2022 as the publication date.

The publication date for a website is the date you uploaded the work. If the work being uploaded has already been published in a different medium, include that publication date as well.

Works Containing United States Government Materials

The rule that a single general notice is sufficient for a compilation or derivative work does not always apply to publications incorporating U.S. government works. U.S. government publications are in the public domain—that is, they are not copyrighted and anyone can use them without asking the federal government's permission. However, if a work consists preponderantly of one or more works by the U.S. government, the copyright notice must affirmatively or negatively identify those portions of the work in which copyright is claimed—that is, that part of the work not consisting of U.S. government materials. This enables readers of such works to know which portions of the work are government materials in the public domain.

It's up to you to decide if your work consists preponderantly (largely) of U.S. government materials. Certainly, if more than half of your book or other work consists of federal government materials, your notice should enable readers to determine which portions of the work are copyrighted and which are in the public domain.

EXAMPLE: Databest Incorporated publishes a book containing analyses of U.S. census data and including several appendixes containing U.S. Census Bureau material. The book is a collective work in which independently created contributions have been combined to form a collective whole. The appendixes amount to over half the book. The copyright notice for the work could state: "Copyright © 2022 by Databest Incorporated. No protection is claimed in works of the United States government as set forth in Appendixes 1, 2, 3, 4, 6." Alternatively, the notice could affirmatively identify those portions of the work in which copyright is claimed—that is, those portions not containing government materials, say Chapters 1–10. In this event, the notice might look like this: "Copyright © 2022 by Databest Incorporated. Copyright claimed in Chapters 1 through 10."

Failure to follow this rule will result in the copyright notice being found invalid. This means that an infringer of the material in which you claim a copyright would be allowed to raise the innocent infringement defense at trial.

In addition, federal regulations require that when a contractor obtains ownership of a work created under a contract with a U.S. government civilian agency or NASA, the copyright notice must acknowledge U.S. government sponsorship (including the contract number). The notice must be on the work when it is delivered to the government, published, or deposited for registration with the U.S. Copyright Office. (Federal Acquisition Regulation (FAR) 52.227-14; www.acquisition.gov/Far.) Here's a suggested format for such a notice:

COPYRIGHT STATUS: This work, authored by _____ employees , was funded in whole or in part by _____ under U.S. Government contract _____ , and is, therefore, subject to the following license: The Government is granted for itself and others acting on its behalf a paid-up, nonexclusive, irrevocable worldwide license in this work to reproduce, prepare derivative works, distribute copies to the public, and perform publicly and display publicly, by or on behalf of the Government. All other rights are reserved by the copyright owner.

Where to Place Copyright Notice

Where to place your copyright notice depends on the nature of the work. The main idea is to make it legible and readable without the aid of a magnifying glass. Remember, you want the notice to be seen by the readers so that they will know that the work is protected by copyright and who owns the copyright.

Paper Books

If the work is a paper book (bound or unbound), booklet, pamphlet, or multipage folder, place the copyright notice in one of the following locations:

- the title page
- the page immediately following the title page (this is the most commonly used location for books)
- either side of the front cover
- if there is no front cover, either side of the back leaf of the copies—that is, the hinged piece of paper at the end of a book or pamphlet consisting of at least two pages
- the first or last page of the main body of the work
- if there are no more than ten pages between the front page and the first page of the main body of the work, on any page between the front page and the first page of the main body of the work, provided that the notice is reproduced prominently and is set apart from other matter on the page where it appears, or
- if there are no more than ten pages between the last page and the main body of the work, on any page between the last page of the main body of the work and the back page, provided that the notice is reproduced prominently and is set apart from other matter on the page where it appears.

Electronic Books

The copyright notice for an electronic book (that is, a digital book that must be read on a Kindle, an iPad, or another device) may be placed:

- with or near the title
- at or near the beginning of the work, or
- at or near the end of the work.

Magazines and Periodicals

The copyright notice for a magazine, periodical, newsletter, or journal, or another serial publication may be placed in any of the locations provided for books (above), or:

- as part of, or adjacent to, the masthead (the masthead typically contains such information as the periodical's title, information about the staff, frequency of issuance, and subscription policies)
- on the same page as the masthead, but not as part of the masthead itself, provided that the notice is reproduced

prominently and set apart from the other matter appearing on the page, or

- adjacent to a prominent heading appearing at or near the front of the issue containing the periodical's title and any combination of the volume and issue number and date of the issue.

Websites and Other Online Works

No special rules exist about where notices should be placed on websites, blogs, or other online works. If a website contains copyrighted materials, a copyright notice should, at the very least, be placed on the site's home page. However, although likely not required by law, it's not a bad idea to place a notice on every page of a website.

Individual Contributions to Compilations

As explained earlier, individual contributions to compilations normally do not need to contain their own copyright notices; however, it is permissible to provide one.

Contributions of One Page or Less

If the contribution consists of a single page or less, the optional copyright notice may be placed:

- under the title of the contribution on that page
- adjacent to the contribution, or

- on the same page if, through format or wording, it is clear that the notice applies only to that particular contribution.

Contributions Containing More Than One Page

If the contribution contains more than one page, the optional copyright notice may be placed:

- under a title appearing at or near the beginning of the contribution
- on the first page of the main body of the contribution
- immediately following the end of the contribution, or
- on any of the pages where the contribution appears, if it is less than 20 pages and the notice is prominent and set apart from the other matter on that page.

On Same Page as Copyright Notice for Compilation

Regardless of the individual contribution's length, the copyright notice may always be placed on the same page as the copyright notice for the compilation as a whole, in a table of contents, or in a list of acknowledgments appearing near the front or back of the compilation. However, the contribution must be listed separately by title or, if it's untitled, by a description reasonably identifying it. These locations may be the most convenient if you need to include a large number of copyright notices.

EXAMPLE 1: The *Nutne Reader*, a literary magazine, publishes an article called "Deconstructionism at a Crossroads" written by Joe Fogel, a freelance literary critic. Joe owns all the copyright rights in the article. Although the *Nutne Reader* contains its own copyright notice, at Joe's insistence, it prints the following notice on the same page containing the copyright notice for the *Nutne Reader* as a whole: "'Deconstructionism at a Crossroads' Copyright © 2022 by Joe Fogel."

EXAMPLE 2: Praetorian Publishing, Inc., publishes a new translation of Caesar's *Gallic Wars*. The book also contains many new illustrations. The translation was done by Gus Augustus and the illustrations by Rene Renoir. Gus and Rene have sold Praetorian only the right to publish their work in the United States and have retained their other copyright rights. The copyright notice for this compilation, combining Gus's translation with Rene's illustrations to form a collective whole, could simply state "Copyright © 2022 by Praetorian Publishing." However, if they so wish and Praetorian agrees, separate notices can also be provided for Gus's and Rene's contributions. If these notices were placed on the same page as Praetorian's notice, the copyright notice would look like this:

> Copyright © 2022 by Praetorian Publishing. Translation copyright © 2022 by Gus Augustus. Illustrations copyright © 2022 by Rene Renoir.

Single-Leaf Works

A single-leaf work is a work consisting of one page, whether printed on one or both sides. A book dust jacket is a good example. The copyright notice for a single-leaf work may be placed anywhere on the front or back of the work.

Other Information Near the Notice

Certain other information, in addition to the copyright notice itself, is commonly included on the same page as the notice.

"All Rights Reserved"

The words "All rights reserved" used to be necessary in a copyright notice to obtain copyright protection in Bolivia and Honduras. This is no longer the case. You do not need to include these words in a copyright notice. However, some publishers include them anyway out of force of habit. This does no harm.

Warning Statements

Because many people do not really understand what a copyright notice means, many publishers include various types of warning or explanatory statements on the same page as the copyright notice. The purpose is to make clear to readers that the work is copyrighted and may not be reproduced without the copyright owner's permission. It does not cost anything (apart from page space) to place this type of statement near the copyright notice, and it might help deter copyright infringement. But remember, such statements do not take the place of a valid copyright notice as described earlier in this chapter

Statements Commonly Used in Books

Here are some examples of warning statements that are commonly used in books:

> Except as permitted under the Copyright Act of 1976, no part of this book may be reproduced in any form or by any electronic or mechanical means, including the use of information storage and retrieval systems, without permission in writing from the copyright owner. [*Some publishers add:* Requests for permissions should be addressed in writing to [*publisher's name and address and/or website*].]

Or, more simply:

> Except as permitted under the Copyright Act of 1976, this book may not be reproduced in whole or in part in any manner.

Screenplays and Stage Plays

Here is an example of a warning statement that might be used on a published version of a stage play or screenplay:

> **Caution:** Professionals and amateurs are hereby warned that this material is fully protected by copyright and is subject to royalty. This play may not be used for stage production (professional or amateur), motion pictures, radio, television, public reading, or mechanical or electronic reproduction, or for any other purpose without written permission of the copyright owner. Contact [*publisher's name*] at [*address*] for information concerning licenses to dramatize this material.

Granting Permission to Use Excerpts

If you don't mind portions of your work being copied and want to avoid the need to formally grant a license each time someone requests to do so, you can include a statement after the copyright notice granting permission to copy the work. This permission can be as broad or narrow as you wish. For example:

> Permission is hereby granted to reprint quotations from this work up to [*number*] words in length provided that such quotations are not altered or edited in any way and provided that an appropriate credit line and copyright notice are included.

Online Works

There are no special requirements for the content of a website notice. It need only consist of the word "Copyright" or the © symbol, followed by the copyright owner's name and publication year—for example:

> Copyright © Jack Webby 2022.

However, if you really want to make it clear that all aspects of your site are copyrighted, you could use a notice like this: "All website design, text, graphics, selection, arrangement, and software are the copyrighted works of Jack Webby, © Copyright 2022."

Some website owners are happy to permit certain types of unauthorized copying while prohibiting others. To make it clear to Web users what types of copying are permissible, you can include a Creative Commons license allowing the public to make free use of your material for certain purposes—for example, noncommercial purposes with attribution. To do this, you're supposed to include a Creative Commons logo on your site, consisting of two "C"s within a circle. Clicking on the logo or a plain text hyperlink sends the user to a page on the Creative Commons website explaining how the license works. This is explained in detail on the Creative Commons website at https://creativecommons.org/license. These Creative Commons licenses are discussed in more detail in Chapter 13.

Other Material on Copyright Page

Particularly in books, certain other types of material are commonly placed on the same page as the copyright notice, even though they have nothing to do with copyright.

ISBN or ISSN Number

An International Standard Book Number (ISBN) is a number preceded by the letters ISBN. An ISBN is assigned to each book by its publisher under a system administered by the R.R. Bowker Co. The number identifies the country of publication, the publisher, and the title of the book itself. It is designed to facilitate handling orders and keeping track of inventory by computer. The number has nothing to do with copyright and has no official legal status. Although not legally required, the ISBN is important for cataloging and order fulfillment.

If you intend to sell your book or other book-like publication in physical bookstores, on Amazon.com or other online stores, through wholesalers, or to libraries, you need to obtain an ISBN. On the other hand, if you don't intend to distribute your book in any of these ways, you don't need an ISBN. For example, you wouldn't need to obtain an ISBN if you wrote a book you planned to distribute solely at seminars or other events.

If you're a self-publisher, you'll need to obtain an ISBN yourself. You will need one ISBN for each edition and format of your book—for example, hardback, paperback, EPUB, PDF, MOBI, and audio. You can apply for ISBNs online at the ISBN agency's website (www.isbn.org). You must pay a fee to obtain an ISBN number. The fee amount depends on how many numbers you order at one time. You can purchase ISBNs in advance and register your titles any time after they are obtained. ISBNs never expire and have no renewal fees.

You cannot reuse an ISBN once you've assigned it to a publication. You can save any ISBNs you don't use for future books. The fee you pay for your ISBNs is usually a tax-deductible business expense. It is the publisher's responsibility to assign numbers to each published title and enter them on the Bowker website. The ISBN should be printed on the lower right-hand corner of the back of the book and on the book's copyright page.

With your ISBN, you'll also be able to get a bar code, which graphically represents the ISBN number in a computer-readable format. It is required by bookstores and other book distributors. It may be obtained from Bowker or many other sources.

An eight-digit International Standard Serial Number (ISSN) is utilized for serial publications such as magazines, periodicals, journals, newsletters, numbered monograph series, and so on. ISSNs are also appropriate for electronic serials. An ISSN is like a Social Security number for a serial publication. It helps libraries and their patrons find and identify titles in automated systems more quickly and easily. You only need one ISSN for an entire serial publication—they do not change from issue to issue.

The ISSN should be placed on the same page as the copyright notice, in the masthead area, or on the page containing instructions for ordering the publication. For online serials, the ISSN should appear on the title screen or home page and/or in the masthead or other areas where information about publisher, frequency, subscribing, or copyright, is given.

The ISSN program is administered by the National Serials Data Program of the Library of Congress. There is no charge to obtain an ISSN. For more information about how to obtain an ISSN, visit the Library of Congress ISSN website at www.loc.gov/issn, call 202-707-6452, or email issn@loc.gov.

Library of Congress Control Number

The Library of Congress will preassign a Library of Congress Control Number (LCCN) upon request. The LCCN is the stock control number for the Library of Congress's records. The number is used by librarians for classification and ordering purposes. According to the Library of Congress, the LCCN benefits publishers because books with LCCNs are listed on a computer database that alerts librarians of forthcoming publications and enables them to select and promptly order new books.

How Many ISBNs Do You Need?

Ideally, each edition of a book or another publication should have a unique ISBN number. According to Bowker, this allows for more efficient marketing of products by booksellers, libraries, universities, wholesalers, and distributors. Online retailers, such as Amazon.com, want publishers to provide unique ISBNs for the print and electronic editions of the books they sell. Moreover, if a book is published and distributed in two or more different file formats—like EPUB and MOBI—each format should have its own ISBN.

Thus, for example, a book that is issued in five formats—hardback, paperback, EPUB, MOBI, and audio—should have five different ISBN numbers. Future editions of the same book should also be given unique ISBNs.

You can obtain an LCCN in advance of publication of a book through the Library of Congress Preassigned Control Number (PCN) program. Only U.S. book publishers, including self-publishers, are eligible to participate in the PCN program. You cannot obtain an LCCN for books published only in electronic format. To obtain an LCCN, you must first establish an account with the Library of Congress. You can do so online at www.loc.gov/publish/prepubbooklink.

The LCCN should be printed on the reverse of the title page, which is usually the page where the copyright notice is placed on books. There is no charge for an LCCN, but a complimentary copy of the book must be sent to the Cataloging in Publication program after it is published. This is in addition to the copies furnished to the Copyright Office as part of the registration process. (See Chapter 3, "Copyright Registration.")

Copyright Notice on Unpublished Manuscripts

It has never been necessary to place a copyright notice on an unpublished manuscript, and doing so will not prevent an infringer from raising the innocent infringement defense. However, it does not seem likely that a copier could convince a judge or jury that his or her infringement of an unpublished manuscript was innocent if the manuscript contained a copyright notice. In addition, as with published works, placing a copyright notice on an unpublished manuscript might help to deter potential infringers.

Manuscripts Sent to Book and Magazine Publishers

Literary agents and editors advise against placing a copyright notice on a manuscript you submit to a book or magazine publisher. Publishers and editors are aware of the copyright laws and know that unpublished manuscripts are copyrighted whether or not they have a notice. Placing a notice on your manuscript makes you look like an amateur who doesn't understand the rules of the publishing game.

The one exception to this rule is where all or part of the material in the manuscript has been previously published or will be published. In this event, you should state at the bottom of the title page where the publication took place and include a notice for that publication.

> **EXAMPLE:** Nora Zorba has written a book on Greek cooking. A portion of chapter three was previously published as an article in *Culinary Magazine*. Nora should state at the bottom of the title page of her manuscript: "Portions of Chapter Three originally published in *Culinary Magazine*, December 2020. Copyright © 2020 by Culinary Publications."

Other Distributions of Unpublished Manuscripts

It is sensible to place a copyright notice on your unpublished manuscript before sending it to persons other than publishers or editors. For example, you might want to include a notice on a manuscript that you intend to send to a colleague (or colleagues) to read. It is impossible to know just who will get their hands on your manuscript once it leaves your possession. The notice might deter a potential infringer.

Form of Notice

A copyright notice for an unpublished manuscript should be in one of the following forms:

> Copyright © by John Smith (This work is unpublished.)

or

> Copyright © by John Smith (Work in progress)

You should not include a date in such a notice, because the date on a copyright notice denotes the date of publication.

Copyright Registration

This chapter explains how to register your work with the Copyright Office. It covers the reasons why you should register, what types of works can be registered, and who can accomplish the registration. The chapter also explains step by step how to complete the application forms, deposit the correct material with the Copyright Office, and take the other necessary steps to complete the registration process.

What Is Copyright Registration?

Copyright registration is a legal formality by which a copyright owner makes a public record in the U.S. Copyright Office in Washington, DC, of some basic information about a copyrighted work, such as the title of the work, who wrote it and when, and who owns the copyright. When people speak of copyrighting a book or other work, they usually mean registering it with the Copyright Office.

To register, you must fill out and send an application form, pay an application fee, and send the application and fee to the Copyright Office along with one or two copies of the copyrighted work. Works can be registered online through the Copyright Office website, although you also have the option of registering by postal mail.

Contrary to what many people think, registering a copyright is not necessary to create or establish a copyright. An author's copyright comes into existence *automatically* the moment an original work of authorship is written down or otherwise fixed in a tangible form. (See Chapter 1, "Copyright Basics.")

Why Register?

If registration is not required, why bother? There are several excellent reasons.

Registration Is a Prerequisite to Infringement Suits

If you're an American citizen or legal resident and your work is first published in the United States (or simultaneously in the U.S. and another country), you may not file a copyright infringement suit in this country until your work has been registered with the Copyright Office. You may be thinking, "Big deal, I'll register if and when someone infringes on my work and I need to file a lawsuit." If you adopt this strategy, you might end up having to register in a hurry so you can file suit quickly. You'll have to pay an extra $800 for such expedited registration.

> ### Compare—Works First Published Abroad
>
> Copyright owners who are not U.S. citizens or residents and whose work is first published in most foreign countries need not register to sue for infringement in the United States. (See Chapter 11, "International Copyright Protection.") But, if they do timely register their copyrights, they will receive the important benefits discussed in the next section.

Registration Must Be Completed

The copyright law says that a copyright infringement lawsuit can't be filed unless "registration of the copyright claim has been made." (17 U.S.C. § 411(a).)

In the past, some courts held that a copyright owner could bring an infringement lawsuit so long as an application for registration had been filed with Copyright Office. However, the U.S. Supreme Court ruled that filing for registration is not enough. Before a copyright infringement lawsuit may be filed, the registration process must be completed with either a registration certificate issued or denied by the Copyright Office. (*Fourth Estate Pub. Benefit Corp. v. Wall-Street.com, LLC*, 139 S. Ct. 881 (2019).)

Benefits of Timely Registration

You can register your work any time you want. However, there are significant benefits if you do so within the time limits discussed below. For one thing, you won't ever need to pay the extra $800 for expedited registration. Far more important, however, if you register within the time limits, you will receive a huge bonus: the right to receive special statutory damages and possibly reimbursement of your attorneys' fees if you successfully sue someone for infringing upon your work.

Normally, a copyright owner who registers a work and successfully sues an infringer is entitled to receive actual damages—the amount of losses caused by the infringement (for example, lost sales), plus any profits the infringer (and the infringer's publisher, if there is one) earned. See Chapter 10, "Copyright Infringement," for detailed discussion. Unfortunately, this remedy is not usually as good as it sounds. Because an infringer's profits are often small and the copyright owner's losses equally modest, actual damages are often quite small in comparison with the costs of copyright litigation (copyright lawyers typically charge between $250 and $500 per hour).

To give copyright owners a strong incentive to register their works and to help make copyright infringement suits economically feasible, the Copyright Act permits copyright owners who *timely* register their work and later successfully sue an infringer to be awarded statutory damages, which range from $750 to $150,000 per infringed work, plus attorneys' fees and court costs.

Statutory damages are special damages a copyright owner may elect to receive instead of actual damages. The amount of statutory damages awarded depends on the nature of the infringement—the more deliberate and harmful the infringement, the better the chance of obtaining a large award. (See detailed discussion in Chapter 10, "Copyright Infringement.")

In one case, for example, *Playboy Magazine* was awarded statutory damages of $1.1 million against a publisher who downloaded 52 *Playboy* photos from the Internet and published them on a CD-ROM. The court awarded *Playboy* $20,000 in statutory damages for each copied photo. (*Playboy Enter., Inc. v. Starware Publ'g Corp.*, 900 F. Supp. 433 (S.D. Fla. 1995).) It's likely *Playboy* would not have been awarded nearly as much had the photos not been timely registered and damages were limited to *Playboy*'s actual provable monetary losses.

What Date Is a Work Registered?

A work is registered for purposes of obtaining statutory damages and attorneys' fees on the day that an acceptable application, deposit, and filing fee are received by the Copyright Office—usually long before the application is actually processed by the Copyright Office.

This date is called the "Effective Date of Registration" or EDR. The EDR is shown on the copyright registration certificate issued by the Copyright Office and in the online record for the registration.

Special Relief for Works Not Timely Registered Due to Coronavirus Pandemic

Special relief from the timely registration requirements is available if you were unable to file an electronic or physical copyright registration application due to the coronavirus (COVID-19) pandemic. You may submit an application after the Copyright Office announced the end of the disruption. Include with your application a Section 710 declaration certifying, under penalty of perjury, that you were unable to submit an application electronically or physically and would have done so but for the coronavirus emergency. In the declaration, you need to explain why you were unable to submit the application—for example, you were subject to a stay-at-home order.

If you file your registration application within 60 days after the coronavirus disruption period officially ends, your application will be deemed to have been filed within three months after publication of the work(s) covered by the registration. This way, you can collect statutory damages and attorneys' fees in a copyright infringement suit. A Section 710 declaration form is available at www.copyright.gov/coronavirus/710-declaration-form.pdf.

Check the Copyright Office website at www.copyright.gov/coronavirus, for the current status of these emergency rules.

> ### Importance of Timely Registration to Value of Copyright
>
> If you fail to qualify for an award of statutory damages and attorneys' fees—by not timely registering your copyright—the costs of a copyright infringement lawsuit could easily outweigh any potential award of actual damages. And, even if you file a lawsuit as a warning to infringers, it's unlikely the amount you will be able to collect would serve as a disincentive to infringement, as actual damages are hard to prove.
>
> As a practical matter, a lack of timely registration makes it difficult (if not impossible) to enforce a copyright and, accordingly, reduces its value.

What Is Timely Registration?

We said above that copyright owners can collect statutory damages and attorneys' fees if they *timely* register their work—that is, register within the time period prescribed by the Copyright Act. There are different time periods for published and unpublished works.

Published Works

A published work is considered to be timely registered, entitling the copyright owner to statutory damages and attorneys' fees, only if it was registered:

- within *three months* of the date of the *first* publication, or
- *before* the date the copyright infringement began.

A work is published for copyright purposes when copies are made available to the public on an unrestricted basis. (See Chapter 1, "Copyright Basics," for detailed discussion of what constitutes publication.)

EXAMPLE 1: Assume that Kay's novel was registered by her publisher two months after it was published. Kay is then entitled to elect to receive statutory damages and attorneys' fees if she sues Copycat (or anyone else) for copyright infringement.

EXAMPLE 2: Assume that Kay's publisher neglected to register Kay's novel. Kay finds out about this and registers it herself nine months after publication. Copycat published his copycat novel three months later. Kay is entitled to statutory damages and fees if she sues Copycat and his publisher, because she registered her work before Copycat copied it.

EXAMPLE 3: Assume instead that Kay's novel was never registered. After discovering Copycat's infringing novel, Kay registers her novel with the Copyright Office. If Kay sues Copycat and his publisher, she may not elect to receive statutory damages and attorneys' fees and costs. Reason: Kay's novel was registered neither within three months of publication nor before Copycat copied her work.

Unpublished Works

The ordinary rule is that if an unpublished work is infringed upon, its author or another copyright owner is entitled to obtain statutory damages and attorneys' fees from the infringer only if the work was registered *before the infringement occurred.*

You cannot get around this requirement by publishing the manuscript and then registering it within three months of the publication date. The three-month rule discussed above applies only if the infringement began after first publication.

The Copyright Office allows some unpublished works to be preregistered. The owner of a preregistered work can obtain statutory damages and attorneys' fees against a copyright infringer even if the work was not fully registered until after the infringement occurred. Only unpublished books, movies, music, sound recordings, computer programs, or advertising photographs may be preregistered, and only if the work is being prepared for commercial distribution.

Websites

The Copyright Office says that placing text, photos, videos, graphics, music and other works online does not, by itself, constitute publication of the work for copyright purposes. *U.S. Copyright Office, Compendium of U.S. Copyright Office Practices,* § 1008.3(B) (3d ed. 2017).) This is so even if millions of people view the work.

This might seem odd, but public display of a work does not constitute publication.

For a publication to occur, the copyright owner must make copies of the work available to the public. So, an online work is published if the copyright owner permits users to download copies. Such permission can be express—for example, where a website includes a "download now" button or similar link, or the site's terms of service provide that the work may be downloaded, copied, or forwarded. Permission can also be implied in the absence of any clear permission from the copyright owner—for example, where downloading is facilitated in some way by the website. However, in some cases, it can be difficult to tell if implied permission is granted or not, making it unclear whether material on some websites has been published. In such cases, the Copyright Office leaves it largely up to you to decide whether the work is published for copyright registration purposes. But keep in mind that if the same work is posted online and distributed in tangible copies, such as CDs, DVDs, or in printed form, the work is published, even if it has not been published online.

If there is a notice on a website or in the terms of service stating that the work and/or all content on the site may not be downloaded, printed, or copied (or another statement to that effect), the work is deemed unpublished, because any copying done by users is not authorized by the copyright owner.

Registration Deters Infringement

Another reason to register is that it causes the work to be indexed in the Copyright Office's records under the title and author's name. These records are open to the public and frequently searched by persons or organizations seeking to find out whether a particular known work has been registered and, if so, who currently owns the copyright. If you have registered your work, these people may contact you and be willing to pay you a permission fee or royalty to use it. If you haven't registered, they may conclude that you're not very serious about enforcing your copyright rights. As a result, they may be inclined to use your work without asking your permission (that is, they may be more inclined to commit copyright infringement).

What Can and Should Be Registered

Any work containing material that is protected by copyright may be registered. A work need not consist entirely of protected material to be registrable. So long as a part of a work is protectable, it can be registered. The registration covers those portions of the work that are protected. (See Chapter 4, "What Copyright Protects.")

Published Works

As a general rule, any published work of value should be registered within three months of publication. You can probably forget about registration, however, if your work is not worth copying (which is usually the case where the work will become outdated shortly after publication or where it is not especially new or creative), or if you aren't concerned about someone copying your work.

Unpublished Works

In deciding whether to register your unpublished work, you need to consider how many people will see it, who they are, how valuable you feel the work is, and how likely it is that someone would want to copy it.

The potential for copying exists whenever you circulate a manuscript to publishers, literary agents, personal contacts, and others. When you submit a manuscript to publishers or others, you have no control over how many people are going to read it.

However, don't be unduly paranoid about others stealing your work. The fact is that very few manuscripts are ever copied by publishers. It is usually easier and cheaper for a publisher to purchase the right to publish a manuscript than go to the trouble of copying it and risk an infringement suit.

Ideas Are Not Protected by Registration

Copyright does not protect facts or ideas, only their expression in a tangible form. (See Chapter 4, "What Copyright Protects.") This means you cannot register a book or an article idea. And registering a book or article proposal, outline, or sample chapters before submission to a publisher will not extend copyright protection to your idea.

EXAMPLE: Leslie writes a detailed outline and sample chapters for a proposed book on nude skydiving. She registers the outline and chapters, and then sends them to several publishers. Larry, a freelance writer, hears about Leslie's submission from an editor acquaintance at one of these publishers and decides to write a book of his own on nude skydiving. In doing so, however, Larry does not copy anything from Leslie's outline or sample chapters (indeed, he never saw them). Leslie cannot successfully sue Larry for copyright infringement for stealing her idea for a book on nude skydiving. The fact that she registered her outline and sample chapters did not extend copyright protection to the ideas they contained.

Who Can Register?

Anyone who owns all or part of the rights that make up a work's copyright may register that work, as can that person's authorized agent (representative). This means registration may be accomplished by:

- the author or authors of a work
- anyone who has acquired one or more of the author or authors' exclusive copyright rights, or
- the authorized agent of any of the above.

Ownership of copyrights is discussed in detail in Chapter 6, "Initial Copyright Ownership," and Chapter 7, "Transferring Copyright Ownership." The following discussion briefly describes ownership solely for registration purposes.

Ownership by the Author(s)

Unless a work is a work made for hire (see below), the copyright initially belongs to the person or persons who created it.

Individually Authored Works

The copyright in a work created by a single individual is owned by that individual. An individually authored work can be registered by the author or an authorized agent (that is, someone the author asks to register on the author's behalf).

EXAMPLE: Shelby has written a history of the Civil War. The book can be registered by Shelby (himself) or by his authorized agent—for example, his publisher—on Shelby's behalf.

Works Made for Hire

A work made for hire is a work created by an employee as part of a job, or a work that has been specially commissioned under a written work-made-for-hire agreement. For registration purposes, the author of a work made for hire is the writer's employer or another person for whom the work was prepared. It is normally the employer who registers a work made for hire, not the employee-writer.

EXAMPLE: Bruno is a technical writer/translator employed by BigTech, Inc. His latest project was translating a technical manual into German. The manual is a work made for hire and should be registered by BigTech, Bruno's employer.

RESOURCE

If you create a protectable work on a freelance basis for someone else, the question of ownership can be complex. Read Chapter 6, "Initial Copyright Ownership," before completing the registration.

Joint Works

If two or more persons who are not employees create a protectable work together, the work so created is called a joint work. A joint work is co-owned by its creators and can be registered by one, some, or all of the authors or by their agent.

EXAMPLE: Bob, Carol, Ted, and Alice decide to write a nonfiction book entitled *The New Celibacy*. They each agree to write one-quarter of the entire work and agree that they will each own 25% of the entire copyright. After it is written, *The New Celibacy* may be registered by any combination of Bob, Carol, Ted, and Alice or their authorized agent(s).

Again, for a detailed discussion of these categories, see Chapter 6, "Initial Copyright Ownership."

Registration by Publishers and Other Transferees

As discussed in Chapter 1, "Copyright Basics," an author's copyright is really a bundle of separate, exclusive rights. These exclusive rights include the right to make copies of an original work, the right to distribute or sell the work, the right to display the work, and the right to adapt—that is, make derivative works out of—the work. A copyright owner can sell or otherwise transfer all or part of his or her exclusive copyright rights. Indeed, this is usually how an author benefits economically from work.

Transferees need to be concerned about registration, because if the work is not timely registered, they will not be entitled to obtain statutory damages and attorneys' fees if they successfully sue a person who infringes on the rights they purchased. (Again, registration is timely only if its effective date is within three months of publication or before an infringement occurred.) Fortunately, transferees do not have to rely on authors to timely register. Anyone who obtains one or more of an author's exclusive rights is entitled to register the author's work.

EXAMPLE 1: In return for a 12% royalty on each copy sold, Darlene transfers to Able Publishers all of her exclusive rights to her bowling instruction guide. Able may register the book.

EXAMPLE 2: Assume instead that Darlene transfers to Able the exclusive right to sell, display, and make copies of the book, but retains her other copyright rights. As a holder of some of Darlene's exclusive rights, Able is still entitled to register the book.

If only a portion of a work's copyright is transferred, it is possible that several different persons or entities qualify to register the copyright.

EXAMPLE: Bill writes a novel and grants Scrivener & Sons the exclusive right to publish it in the United States. He also grants Repulsive Pictures the exclusive right to author and produce a screenplay based on the novel. Scrivener and Repulsive each hold one of the exclusive rights that are part of Bill's overall copyright, and Bill holds the rest. This means the novel could be registered by Bill, Scrivener, or Repulsive.

Letting Your Publisher Register the Copyright

In the past, publishers always registered the books they published with the Copyright Office. Many still do and, even if you retain some of your rights, your publisher should accomplish the registration as an owner of an exclusive right or rights (such as the right to make copies and sell the book) or as your authorized agent.

However, today some smaller independent publishers avoid registering a work, as a means of saving money. Be sure to check your publishing agreement to see what it says about registering your work. If it's silent on the matter, you may wish to add a clause requiring the publisher to register, or you may prefer to avoid the hassle and just do it yourself.

If your publisher is supposed to perform this task, you should check in one or two months after publication to make sure your book has been registered, especially if you're dealing with a very small or inexperienced publisher that may be lax about such matters. (Recall that to obtain statutory damages and attorneys' fees, your work must be registered within three months of publication or before the infringement begins.)

Of course, the situation is very different if you are self-publishing your work. In this scenario, you must handle the registration yourself. This is also usually the case if you are paying a vanity press to publish your book.

Although several people may be entitled to register a work, normally only one registration is allowed for each version of a published work. It makes absolutely no difference who gets the job done. The single registration protects every copyright owner.

> **EXAMPLE:** Assume that Scrivener & Sons registered Bill's novel in the example above. This means that neither Bill nor Repulsive Pictures can register it. Nor do they need to. The single registration by Scrivener covers them all—that is, they are all entitled to the benefits of registration.

Again, for a detailed discussion of the rights of copyright transferees, see Chapter 7, "Transferring Copyright Ownership."

Registration as a Single Unit

A work of authorship often consists of many separate works that are combined to form a unitary whole. For example, a book will normally consist of a main text written by an author or authors. But it may also contain photographs or artwork supplied by the author or others. It may have a dust jacket containing artwork or promotional copy written by someone other than the author(s) of the text. Or, if the book is a paperback, the cover may contain artwork and copy. And it may contain an introduction or other material written by someone other than the author(s) of the main text.

The question naturally arises, "Must I register each type of authorship separately, or can I register everything together at the same time?" If your work satisfies the requirements listed below, you can register the whole work at one time. This will take less time and save on application fees. However, it could result in a smaller financial award if you sue for copyright infringement. (See "When You Register Multiple Works as a Single Unit," below.)

You can register any number of *separate* works of authorship together on one application if all of the following are true:

- They are being published for the *first* time.
- They constitute a *single unit of publication*—that is, they're sold together as a single unit with each work an integral part of the whole unit.
- The same person(s) created *all* the works in the unit, or the same person or entity has acquired ownership of *all* the copyright rights in all of the works in the unit.

Let's apply this rule to some real-life situations.

Works Containing Photographs or Artwork

The artwork or photographs a written work contains can be registered together with the text only if both of the following are true:

- They have never been published before.
- They were created by the author of the text, or the same person or entity owns the copyright to the artwork or photos and text.

When You Register Multiple Works as a Single Unit

If your work qualifies as a single unit of publication, you can register the whole thing at one time and save on registration fees. However, by doing so, you may lose the right to obtain multiple awards of statutory damages. Statutory damages are awarded by the jury or judge instead of any actual monetary losses suffered from a copyright infringement and usually range from $750 to $30,000 (but can go all the way up to $150,000 in cases of willful infringement). (See Chapter 10, "Copyright Infringement.")

Statutory damages sometimes far exceed the actual monetary losses from infringement. In the largest statutory damages award to date, a television production company was awarded $9 million in statutory damages against a television station owner who aired 900 television programs without permission; $10,000 in statutory damages was awarded for each program—each of which was separately registered with the Copyright Office. (*MCA Television Ltd. v. Feltner*, 89 F.3d 766 (11th Cir. 1996).)

If you register a work containing multiple works of authorship as a single unit of publication, you may be restricted to a single award of statutory damages in a copyright infringement lawsuit. If you register each type of authorship separately, you will be entitled to a separate statutory damages award for each type of infringed authorship. Here's a hypothetical example.

EXAMPLE: Mary creates and publishes a book about the Dalai Lama that contains text, photos, and drawings. Because she owns the copyright in each type of authorship, she could register it all together at one time for one $65 fee. Instead, Mary decides to register the text, photos, and drawings separately at a cost of $195 in registration fees. Mary subsequently files and wins a copyright infringement lawsuit against a website that copied the entire book without her permission. Because her actual dollar losses from the infringement were negligible, Mary asks for statutory damages. The jury awards her $15,000 ($5,000 for the infringement of the text, $5,000 for the photos, and $5,000 for the drawings). Had Mary registered the entire book together as a single unit of publication, she may have been restricted to a single statutory damages award of $5,000. By paying an extra $130 to the Copyright Office, Mary recovered an extra $10,000 in damages.

Keep in mind that most registered works are never infringed. So, one strategy you might want to consider is to register each element separately only if you believe a work is likely to be infringed. For works less likely to be copied, register all of the elements— text, photos, and artwork—as a single unit of publication.

EXAMPLE 1: Jackie is a poet and Bill is a photographer. Jackie and Bill collaborate to publish a book combining Bill's photographs and Jackie's poetry. They agree to co-own the entire copyright in the work. Normally, poetry and photographs are registered separately on different application forms. However, because the work is a single unit of publication and the text and photos are owned by the same persons, Jackie and Bill may register the entire book at the same time for one application fee and on one application form.

EXAMPLE 2: Jim and Jean agree to produce a book on how to operate a toxic waste dump. Jim writes the text, and Jean provides the pictorial illustrations for the book. Jim and Jean decide that each is the sole owner of their respective contributions. The single registration rule does not apply here. The photos and text were not created by the same persons, and they are not owned by the same persons. They were created and are owned separately by Jim and Jean. This means that Jim and Jean must each register their work separately, and each pay an application fee.

Artwork, Photos, and Promotional Copy on Book Dust Jackets or Covers

The artwork, photos, or promotional copy on a book dust jacket or cover may be registered together with the text only if both of the following are true:

- The artwork and copy have never been published before.
- The same person or entity owns the copyright to the text, cover art, and promotional copy.

How to Register Artwork and Photographs

If you have to register artwork or photographs separately from the main text of a written work, you must do so with a separate online application or on paper Form VA.

Because cover art and promotional copy are normally owned by the publisher (whether created by the publisher's employees or independent contractors hired by the publisher), these items usually can be registered together with the text of the book only if the publisher acquired all the author's rights in the text.

EXAMPLE 1: Jane Milsap writes a novel and sells all her copyright rights to Acme Press. Acme employees prepare artwork and text for the cover. The text of the novel and artwork and text for the cover can be registered together on one Form TX, because Acme owns them all.

Some Freelance Writers Must Register Separately

If you're a freelance writer and sell an article or other work to a magazine or similar publication that does not purchase copyright in the work, you must separately register it. This situation might not apply to you as most publications do purchase all rights (or sign work-made-for-hire agreements). However, some do not. So, examine your publishing agreement to determine what rights you're selling. If you have an oral agreement with an editor to provide an article or other work, you're not selling all your rights. (You can only transfer copyright by a signed written agreement. See Chapter 7, "Transferring Copyright Ownership.") If you don't timely register such articles, you'll lose the right to obtain statutory damages and attorneys' fees in an infringement suit. In any event, you must register your works in order to file a copyright infringement lawsuit.

Consider Lois Morris, a freelancer who wrote a series of columns for *Allure Magazine*. She did not transfer her copyright to *Allure* and failed to separately register the columns. When she discovered two dozen columns had been reprinted in a newsletter without her permission, she sued for copyright infringement, relying on the magazine's copyright application. Her case was dismissed because she had never filed her own copyright registrations for the articles. (*Morris v. Bus. Concepts, Inc.*, 283 F.3d 502 (2d Cir. 2001).) Although she was entitled to later register the works and refile the lawsuit, her failure to timely file registrations resulted in a loss of potential financial damages. Therefore, to guarantee your rights, a prompt registration is recommended. Freelancers can save money by registering groups of articles at one time.

EXAMPLE 2: Bart Milsap, Jane's brother, writes a novel and grants Acme Press only the exclusive right to publish it in North America. Bart retains all his other copyright rights. Acme employees prepare artwork and text for the cover. The text of the novel and the artwork and text for the cover must be registered separately, because they are separately owned. Acme may register the artwork and cover copy together on the same form.

Introductions, Prefaces, Bibliographies, Indexes, and Similar Items

An introduction, preface, bibliography, or index or similar material may be registered together with a work's main text only if it is being published for the first time and the person or entity that owns the copyright in the main text also owns the introduction, bibliography, index, or other item.

Registering a Group of Unpublished Works for a Single Application Fee

You can register up to 10 unpublished works together at one time on one application form for one $85 application fee. This option is available even if the works are self-contained (that is, do not constitute a single unit of publication) and would normally be registered separately. This procedure can save you a great deal of money. Four requirements must be met:

- All the works must be unpublished.
- You must submit the same type of work (such as literary works).
- All the works must be created by the same author or coauthors, and the author and claimant for each work must be same person or entity.
- You must electronically upload or send by mail a copy of each work to complete the deposit requirement.

EXAMPLE: Joe Sixpack has written 10 unpublished short stories. Joe may register all 10 stories together, using the Copyright Office's online registration system, for one $85 application fee. Note: If Joe had registered each story separately, it would have cost him $450—that is, 10 registrations times $45.

To register an unpublished group, go to the Copyright Office registration webpage and select the link for "Register a Group of Unpublished Works."

You can also register a group of up to 750 published or 750 unpublished photographs together for one $55 fee. The photographs must be by the same author. Go to the Copyright Office registration page and click the link for "Register a Group of Photographs."

EXAMPLE 1: Sam writes a book on the Civil War and gets the well-known Civil War expert Marcus Hand to write an introduction. Hand gives Sam's publisher the right to use the introduction only in Sam's book and retains all his other copyright rights. The introduction would have to be registered separately from the book.

EXAMPLE 2: Assume instead that Acme Press, Sam's publisher, paid Hand for all his rights in the introduction and that Acme also acquired all of Sam's copyright rights in the main text. Acme could register both the text and the introduction together as a single unit. Reason: The same entity owns the copyright in both the main text and the introduction.

Different Editions With the Same Content

It is common for the same work to be published in different editions—for example, in hardcover, paperback, and electronic book editions. Where the content of the different editions is identical, only one need be registered. This would normally be the first published edition.

EXAMPLE 1: Acme Publications publishes and promptly registers a hardcover edition of a book on car repair. One year later, Acme publishes the book in an identical paperback edition. The paperback need not be registered. The registration of the hardcover edition protects all the material the paperback contains.

EXAMPLE 2: Assume the same facts as Example 1, except that the paperback has new cover art and copy. Acme should register the artwork and copy. But again, there is no need to reregister the text of the book.

If multiple identical editions of the same work are published simultaneously, again, only one registration need be made. In such cases, however, the applicant should deposit with the Copyright Office the edition that is the best edition. (See below for detailed discussion of deposits.)

Anthologies, Newspapers, Magazines, and Other Serials

Anthologies, newspapers, magazines, and similar works usually contain a number of separate articles, photos, artwork, and other material. Each individual contribution must be registered by the person or entity that owns it. If the same person or entity owns all the contributions, only one registration is required. The anthology or magazine should also be registered once as a whole, usually by its publisher. Registration of newspapers, magazines, and other serial publications is discussed below.

How Many Times to Register a Single Unit of Publication

Subject to the exceptions noted below, a single unit of publication need be and can be registered only once.

Published Works

As a general rule, a published work constituting a single unit of publication can only be registered once. If the facts stated in the registration application change after the work has been registered—for instance, the work's title is changed—an application for supplementary registration should be filed with the Copyright Office to correct them.

However, there are exceptions to the general rule. If someone other than the author is identified as the copyright claimant on a registration application, the author may register the same work again in his or her own name as copyright claimant. (The "claimant" is either the author or person who acquires all copyright rights in the work; see "Claimants" below.)

A second registration may also be made if the prior registration was unauthorized or legally invalid—for instance, where registration was effected by someone other than the author, the owner of exclusive rights, or an authorized representative.

Unpublished Works

A work originally registered as unpublished may be registered again after publication, even if the published and unpublished versions are identical. Even if they are identical, it is a good idea to register the published version of a previously registered unpublished work. If you ever become involved in an infringement suit, it may be very helpful to have the published version of the book on deposit with the Copyright Office. The second registration also establishes the date of publication, which may later aid you in proving that an infringer had access to your work. (See Chapter 10, "Copyright Infringement.")

Registering Derivative Works and Compilations

Derivative Works

A derivative work is one created by transforming or adapting previously existing material. This includes:

- new editions of previously published works, including condensed or abridged editions or editions containing new material (new chapters, for example)
- dramatizations or fictionalizations, such as screenplays or stage plays based on novels, histories, biographies, or other works
- translations, and
- annotations, such as *CliffsNotes*.

These types of works are discussed in detail in Chapter 5, "Adaptations and Compilations." If you're not sure whether your work is a derivative work, read that chapter before attempting to register it.

When Can a Derivative Work Be Registered?

For a derivative work to be registrable, the new expression created by the work's author must:

- be owned by the copyright claimant for the derivative work
- contain sufficient original authorship to be copyrightable as an independent work

- not be in the public domain in the United States
- be new—that is, not previously published, and
- not have been previously registered in unpublished form.

Preexisting Expression Should Have Already Been Registered

Assuming it's protectable, the preexisting expression used to create the derivative work, whether a novel, a factual work, or another work, should already be registered with the Copyright Office. If not, it should be registered. The preexisting expression can be registered together with the new expression if they constitute a single unit of publication and the copyright claimant is the same. Otherwise, the preexisting expression should be registered separately by its owner.

EXAMPLE: Tom writes a play based on his novel. The play is a new work based on and adapted from the novel. Tom owns the play, and it has never previously been published or registered. The play can and should be registered separately. If he doesn't register the play, Tom will not be entitled to statutory damages and attorneys' fees if he sues someone for copying those aspects of the play not already protected by the copyright in the novel.

Registering New Editions of Factual Works

Authors of factual works such as scientific treatises, histories, and textbooks often revise their works and publish new editions. Not all new editions can or should be registered. Look at the protected content of the various versions. If the first version you registered contains substantially the same protected content as a later version, there is no reason to register the later version—its content is protected by the initial registration. But if substantial new protectable material is added to another version, it's wise to register that version.

As a general rule, your changes are substantial enough to merit registration only if enough new expression has been added so that it is possible to tell the difference between the previous edition and the new edition. Trivial changes—such as spelling corrections—are not enough.

EXAMPLE 1: Augusta writes and publishes a college-level textbook on ancient Roman art. Two years later, she publishes a new edition of the work. The new edition is identical to the first except that Augusta corrected several spelling and punctuation errors. The Copyright Office probably will not register such a work. And, indeed, there is no reason to do so because the new edition does not contain any new expression that needs to be protected by registration.

EXAMPLE 2: Assume that five years later, Augusta substantially revises her book on Roman art. She adds three new chapters and makes numerous substantive changes in the other chapters. This new edition is clearly different from the original edition in a meaningful way. Augusta should register the work to protect the changes she made to her preexisting material.

As a practical matter, you don't need to go to the trouble and expense of registration merely to protect minor changes that have no value independent from the original work. However, if you've added considerable new material to your work that has substantial value and that someone may want to copy for its own sake, registration might be prudent.

Compare—More Complete Version Published First

If two versions of a work are published at different times, and the more complete version is published first, the less complete version may not be registered. The Copyright Office will not knowingly register a claim in a work where all of the copyrightable content has previously been published.

EXAMPLE: Schooldays Publications publishes two editions of a Spanish textbook—one version is for teachers and the other for students. The teacher's edition contains all of the text and pictorial material in the student's edition, plus additional instructions, questions, and answers. The teacher's edition was published one week before the student edition. The student edition may not be registered; all the material it contains is already protected by the registration of the teacher's edition.

Compilations

A compilation is a work created by selecting, organizing, and arranging facts or data in such a way that the resulting work as a whole constitutes an original work of authorship. Examples include anthologies, bibliographies, and catalogs of all types.

Some compilations are not considered to be sufficiently creative to merit copyright protection and may not be registered. Refer to Chapter 5, "Adaptations and Compilations," for a detailed discussion of how to tell if your compilation is registrable (and ways to help make it so).

How to Register

Copyright registration involves three steps:
1. Complete an application form.
2. Submit the form and registration fee to the Copyright Office.
3. Send the required deposit to the Copyright Office.

Below, we describe your options for accomplishing these steps.

Option 1: Online Registration

Almost all types of written works can be registered online at the Copyright Office website, although you might have to mail a copy of your work (called a "deposit"). The Copyright Office strongly prefers that you register online. It is also the cheapest and fastest way to register.

The fee is $45 for electronic registration of a "single application"—this is a registration for one work by a single author (not a work made for hire) who owns all the rights in the work. Electronic registration of other works costs $65. Such works are registered using a "standard application" and include:

- works by more than one author
- deposits containing elements by more than one author (for example, a comic book with text and illustrations by two authors)
- works with more than one owner
- joint works
- works made for hire
- multiple works (for example, unpublished and published collections)
- multiple versions of a work
- collective works (for example, serial publications, anthologies)
- units of publication
- group registrations
- databases
- websites, and
- choreography.

> ### Where to Get Help
>
> If any aspect of the registration process becomes difficult to understand, you can get help by calling the Copyright Office at 877-476-0778 between 8:30 a.m. and 5:00 p.m. Eastern time, Monday through Friday. You can also request help by email at www.copyright.gov/help/general-form.html. Questions about online registration should be emailed to: www.copyright.gov/help/contact-eco.html.
>
> You can also contact the Copyright Office by mail at:
> Library of Congress
> Copyright Office-COPUBS
> 101 Independence Avenue SE
> Washington, DC 20559
> Copyright Office Information Specialists are knowledgeable and helpful, but they're not allowed to give legal advice. If you have a particularly complex problem that calls for interpretation of the copyright laws, consult a copyright attorney; see Chapter 14, "Help Beyond This Book."

Option 2: Registration Using Paper Forms

You can still use the old paper application forms: Form TX (literary works); Form VA (visual arts works); Form PA (performing arts works, including motion pictures); Form SR (sound recordings); and Form SE (single serials). For the Copyright Office, a paper application is the least preferred way to register, and you'll have to pay the highest fee—a whopping $125 per registration. It also takes the Copyright Office much longer to process paper registration applications (they were not processed at all while the Copyright Office was closed during the coronavirus pandemic). There appears to be no good reason to use this method of registration.

Online Copyright Registration

Almost all types of works can be registered online through the Copyright Office website. This Web-based copyright registration system is called the Electronic Copyright Office (eCO). You'll complete the application at the eCO website and pay your fee electronically. Certain types of deposits can also be made online. However, other types must be sent in hard-copy form to the Copyright Office by mail.

Online registration is the fastest and cheapest way to go.

Which Works Qualify for Online Registration?

Online registration may be used to register all "basic claims" in literary works, visual arts works, performing arts works (including motion pictures), sound recordings, or single serial publications (including periodicals, newspapers, magazines, bulletins, newsletters, annuals, journals, and similar publications). Basic claims include:

- any single work
- multiple unpublished works, if they qualify for a single registration under the rules discussed above (see "Registering a Group of Unpublished Works for a Single Application Fee" above), or
- multiple published works, if they are all published together in the same publication on the same date and are all owned by the same claimant.

In other words, the online registration system may be used to register any single written work, published or not.

How to Register Online

To register using eCO, go to the Copyright Office website at www.copyright.gov and click the "Register" link. You'll be taken directly to the eCO online system. Look for links to the (very thorough) eCO tutorial, which you should read before tackling your online application.

You'll need to create an account with a user ID and password. You must have an email address to do this. Then start the registration process. The eCO system includes a special "Save for Later" feature that will preserve your work in the event you sign off and then sign on at a later time. Your registration will be assigned a case number. Your first task will be to complete the online application form, which consists of the following 11 sections.

Type of Work

First, you must select the type of work you're registering. Most written works are "literary works" for registration purposes. Literary works include: fiction, nonfiction, poetry, textbooks, reference works, directories, catalogs, advertising copy, compilations of information, computer programs, and databases. This category also includes single articles published in a magazine, a newspaper, or another serial publication, but not an entire issue of a magazine, a newspaper or another serial publication (works published on an established periodic schedule).

If you're registering more than one type of authorship in a work, your "type of work" selection should be the material that predominates. For example, if you are registering a book that's mostly text and also contains a few photographs, select "Literary Work."

Titles

The Copyright Office uses the title for indexing and identifying your work. If your work contains a title, fill in that wording. It should be the same title that appears on your deposit. If your work is untitled, either state "untitled" or give an identifying phrase. You need not include this phrase on your untitled work. If you're registering a work written in a foreign language, you don't have to translate the title into English.

Publication/Completion

Publication occurs for copyright purposes when a work is made widely available to the public. (See Chapter 1, "Copyright Basics.") Enter the month, day, year, and country when or where your work was first published. Give only one date. If you're not sure of the exact publication date, state your best guess. If your book has been published and has an ISBN number, provide the number in the space indicated. If you preregistered the work, provide the preregistration number as well.

If the work is unpublished, fill in the year in which the work you're registering first became fixed in its final form, disregarding minor editorial changes. This year has nothing do to with publication, which could occur long after creation. Deciding what constitutes the year of creation might prove difficult if the work was created over a long period of time. Give the year in which the author completed the particular version of the work for which registration is now being sought, even if other versions exist or if further changes or additions are planned.

Authors

List the names of all the authors of the work being registered. We discussed who the author is for registration purposes under "Who Can Register?" above. If you need more information, read Chapter 6, "Initial Copyright Ownership," and Chapter 7,

"Transferring Copyright Ownership." Unless the work was made for hire, the person or people who created the work are the authors. However, if the work to be registered is a work made for hire, the "author" for registration purposes is the employer or person or entity that commissioned the work. The full legal name of the employer or commissioning party must be provided as the "Name of Author" instead of the name of the person who actually wrote the work.

The requested information on the author's "Citizenship" or "Domicile" must always be provided, even if the author is a business, chooses to remain anonymous, or used a pseudonym. An author's "citizenship" (nationality) and "domicile" could be different. An author's domicile generally is the country where the author maintains a principal residence and intends to remain indefinitely. An author is a citizen of the country in which he or she was either born or later moved to and became a citizen of by complying with its naturalization requirements.

EXAMPLE: Evelyn is a Canadian citizen, but has U.S. permanent resident status and has lived year-round in Boston since 1980 with the intention of remaining there for the indefinite future. She is domiciled in the United States. She can state "Canada" in the citizenship field or United States in the domicile field.

The citizenship of a domestic corporation, a partnership, or another organization should be given as United States, regardless of the state or states in which it is organized and does business.

As the last part of the "Authors" section, you must check the appropriate box(es) to indicate the author's contribution, such as the work's text, photography, or artwork.

What if the author wishes to remain anonymous or use a pseudonym? An author's contribution to a work is "anonymous" if the author is not identified on the copies of the work. A contribution is "pseudonymous" if the author is identified under a fictitious name (pen name).

If the work is anonymous, you may leave the author name fields blank, state "anonymous" in the "Last Name" field, or reveal the author's identity.

If the work is pseudonymous, you may either leave the author field blank or reveal the author's name. In either case, you should check the pseudonymous box and give the pseudonym in the space provided.

Of course, if the author's identity is revealed on the application, it will be a simple matter for others to discover, because the application becomes a public document available for inspection at the Copyright Office.

Claimants

Next, you must provide the name and address of the copyright claimant(s), which must be one of the following:

- the persons or organizations that have, on or before the date the application is filed, obtained ownership of *all* the exclusive U.S. copyright rights that initially belonged to the author
- the author or authors of the work (including the owner of a work made for hire, if applicable), or
- the person or organization contractually authorized by the author or owner of all U.S. copyright rights to act as the claimant for copyright registration. (While there is no legal requirement that such contract be in writing, it's not a bad idea.) (See 37 C.F.R. § 202.3(a)(3) (1984).)

We discuss in Chapter 1, "Copyright Basics," the fact that under the copyright laws an author automatically holds several different exclusive rights in the work—the right to reproduce the work, to distribute it, to perform or publicly display it, and to prepare derivative works based upon it. The author is entitled to transfer one or more—or any portion—of these rights in any way desired. But, if another person or organization acquires all these exclusive rights in a work, that person or organization is considered the copyright "claimant" for registration purposes, and the author is no longer the claimant.

EXAMPLE: Joe, an experienced mountaineer, self-publishes a pamphlet on advanced rock-climbing techniques. The Colorado Rock Climbing Club purchases Joe's entire copyright in the pamphlet and republishes it. Joe never registered the pamphlet, so the club does so. The club should be listed as the copyright claimant, not Joe.

Frequently, no one owns all the exclusive rights in the work. This might occur where an author transfers less than all exclusive rights to a publisher, or where a person or an entity that acquired all the author's rights transfers some, but not all, of the rights to a third party. In this event, the author must be listed as the copyright claimant, even if someone else owns most of the exclusive copyright rights.

EXAMPLE 1: Assume that Joe transferred to the Colorado Rock Climbing Club only the right to publish a new edition of the pamphlet for its members and other Colorado residents. Joe retained all of his other exclusive rights. Joe is the copyright claimant.

EXAMPLE 2: Assume again that the Colorado Rock Climbing Club acquired all of Joe's exclusive rights in his pamphlet. Before the pamphlet is registered, the club transfers to the Southern California Climber's Federation the right to publish and distribute the pamphlet in California. No one now owns all the exclusive rights in the pamphlet—not Joe (who owns no rights), not the club, and not the federation. When the club registers the pamphlet, Joe must be listed as the copyright claimant because he is the author and the exclusive rights are not concentrated in one pair of hands.

In the case of a work made for hire, the "author" is the creator's employer or the person or entity that commissioned the work under a written work-made-for-hire agreement. This means the copyright claimant is either (1) the employer or commissioning party; or (2) the person or entity to whom the employer or commissioning party has transferred all of its exclusive rights in the work.

> EXAMPLE 1: Assume that Joe was an employee of the Colorado Rock Climbing Club and wrote the pamphlet as part of his job. The club is the copyright owner of this work made for hire and the club should be listed as the copyright claimant.

> EXAMPLE 2: Assume that the club dissolved not long after Joe finished writing the pamphlet. Kate purchased all the club's exclusive rights in the pamphlet. When Kate registers the work, she should list herself as the copyright claimant.

Notice that the section on Claimants also provides space to deal with transferred claims. If the copyright claimant listed is not the author or authors named in the "Authors" section, you must indicate how ownership of the copyright was obtained. (However, don't attach the transfer documents to the application.) The transfer statement must show the copyright examiner that *all* the author's

U.S. copyright rights have been transferred by a *written agreement* or by operation of law. Two alternatives are provided in the "Transfer Statement" field: "By written agreement" or "By inheritance." If these don't describe how the rights were acquired, you must fill in the "Transfer Statement Other" box to explain—for example, "By operation of state community property law." Examples of *unacceptable* statements include:

- words indicating that possibly less than all the author's U.S. copyright rights have been transferred to the claimant—for example: "By license," "By permission," or "Transfer of right of first publication"

- statements suggesting that the person named as the claimant simply owns a physical copy of the work being registered, not the author's copyright rights—for example: "Author gave me this copy," "Found in attic trunk," or "Author asked me to keep it for him," and

- statements indicating that the named claimant has a special relationship to the author, but that don't show any actual transfer of ownership— for example: "Claimant is author's publisher," "Claimant is author's agent," or "Author is president of claimant corporation."

Again, see Chapter 7, "Transferring Copyright Ownership," for a detailed discussion of copyright transfers.

If the author or owner of all rights has authorized another person or organization to act as the claimant, include language like the following: "Pursuant to the contractual right from [author *or* owner of all U.S. copyright rights] to claim legal title to the copyright in an application for copyright registration."

Limitation of Claim

You must complete the limitation of claim section if the work being registered contains or is based on material that was:

- previously registered
- previously published, or
- in the public domain.

The purpose of this section is to exclude such preexisting material from your claim and identify the new material you're registering.

If the preexisting material in the work being registered was not published, registered, or in the public domain, don't complete this section.

> **EXAMPLE:** Leila writes a screenplay based on her unpublished, unregistered novel. The screenplay is based on preexisting material, but Leila need not complete the limitation of claim section when she registers the screenplay.

Another relevant limitation on the claim is material that you're not asking to have included within it. Check the appropriate box(es) to exclude any preexisting material that the work being registered is based on

or incorporates. You can also add more information in the "Other" space to clarify what exactly is being excluded from the registration. This is often a good idea, because checking the boxes alone may not provide the needed information.

> **EXAMPLE:** Joseph writes a biography of Gypsy Rose Lee that includes photographs and excerpts from letters owned by others. In the "Material Excluded" section, he checks the "Text and Photograph(s)" boxes. He also adds the following explanation in the "Other" space to make it clear what is being excluded from his registration: "letters and photos from different sources."

Also notice there is an option to enter information for "New Material Included." Check the appropriate box(es) to identify all new or revised material being claimed in this registration. The descriptions provided in the "New Material Included" space should be identical to the descriptions provided in the "Author Created" space. You may use the "Other" space to give a more specific description of the new material. In the preceding "Author" section, be sure you've also checked or described the new material and named the author(s) of all the new material checked or described in this section.

> **EXAMPLE:** Joseph from the above example checks the "Text" box in the "New Material Included" section.

Rights and Permissions

Completing this section is optional, but you should do it. It will tell anyone who examines your completed registration who to contact about obtaining rights or permissions to use your work.

Correspondent

Provide the name, postal address, email address, and telephone number (with area code) of the person the Copyright Office should contact if it has questions about your application.

Mail Certificate

Fill in your name and the return mailing address for your copyright registration certificate.

Special Handling

You need to complete this section only if you wish to have your application processed on an expedited basis. This costs $800 extra. See "Expedited Registration," below.

Certification

Check the certification box and provide the name of the certifying individual where indicated. The certifying individual must be:

- the author
- another copyright claimant (a person who has acquired of all the author's rights)
- the owner of one or more—but not all—of the exclusive rights making up the entire copyright, or
- the authorized representative of: the author, another person who is the copyright claimant, or the owner of one or more—but not all—exclusive rights.

Payment

You must pay the registration fee ($45 for single applications, $65 for standard applications) electronically. You can do this by credit or debit card, electronic funds transfer from a bank account, or by setting up a deposit account with the Copyright Office.

Deposit Requirements

The last step is sending the Copyright Office a copy of the work (the deposit). You can upload an electronic copy if the work is unpublished or published only online. You must mail physical copies of works published offline in the physical world. Ordinarily, you must submit two copies of the "best edition" of physically published works.

The system will prompt you to pay before you can upload your work as an electronic file. Otherwise, print out a shipping slip if you plan to submit a physical copy of your work. See "Satisfying Copyright Office Deposit Requirements" below for a detailed discussion of Copyright Office deposit rules.

Certificate of Registration

If your claim is approved, the Copyright Office will mail you a simplified certificate of registration.

Registering Using Form TX and Other Paper Application Forms

You also have the option to register by mail using the old Copyright Office paper application forms: Form TX (literary works); Form VA (visual arts works); Form PA (performing arts works, including motion pictures); Form SR (sound recordings); and Form SE (single serials).

The Copyright Office really doesn't want you to register this way. If you use this method, the registration fee is $125. Also, you can't pay by credit card unless your registration form is hand delivered to the Copyright Office Public Information Office.

It will also take the Copyright Office much longer on average to process your application—six to 16 months compared to three to six months for electronic applications. There will be additional delays for paper applications submitted during the coronavirus (COVID-19) pandemic disruption. The Copyright Office was not processing mail during this time.

You can fill out the paper forms by hand or typewriter. Alternatively, you can fill in online versions of the forms on the Copyright Office website and then print them out to mail.

You can go online at www.copyright.gov/forms/formrequest.html and request that the Copyright Office mail you (up to two) copies of the paper forms. You can also obtain copies 24 hours a day by calling 202-707-9100 and leaving a recorded message. The fill-in forms are on the Copyright Office website at www.copyright.gov. Under "Law and Guidance," click "Forms."

Registering Newspapers, Magazines, Newsletters, and Other Serial Publications

What Is a Serial?

A serial is:
- a "collective work" in which a number of individual contributions, such as articles, stories, cartoons, and photographs, are assembled into a collective whole
- issued on an established schedule in successive issues or parts with a numerical or chronological designation—for example, "July 1" or "Summer," and
- intended to be continued indefinitely.

Newspapers, magazines, periodicals, newsletters, journals, and bulletins are ordinarily considered serials. The Copyright Office sometimes confusingly refers to serials as "periodicals," but periodicals are really just one type of serial.

Serials can be in print or electronic form. For example, an electronic newsletter would qualify as a serial if it (a) contains multiple articles, (b) is distributed to email subscribers as a fixed and self-contained work, (c) is sent on the first Monday of each month, and (d) has no end date. But an email newsletter containing a single article or essay would not qualify as a serial, because it is not a collective work.

Registration and Protection

Importantly, both a serial as a whole and the individual contributions it contains are entitled to full copyright protection.

A magazine or another serial issue is registered as a whole by the person(s) or organization that owns the publication or supervises its creation. When a magazine or another serial issue is registered as a whole, the registration protects:

- the revising, editing, compiling, and similar efforts that went into putting the issue into final form
- any individual contributions (articles and so on) prepared by the publication's employees or by nonemployees who signed work-made-for-hire agreements, and
- any individual contributions by freelancers to which the publication has purchased all rights.

If a serial issue contains any independently authored contributions to which all of the rights have not been acquired by the publication, those contributions are not protected when the issue is registered as a whole. To protect their work, individual contributors who retain some of their rights must register separately.

> **EXAMPLE:** The *Jogger's Journal* is a monthly magazine owned and published by Ededas, Inc. The July issue contains 11 articles: Two articles were written by the journal's editorial staff; two were written by freelance writers who signed work-made-for-hire agreements; four were written by freelancers who assigned to the journal all their rights; and three were written by freelancers who assigned to the journal only the right to publish their articles for the first time in North America. When the July issue is registered, all the material in it will be protected except for the three articles to which the journal did not acquire all rights.

You can register any single serial publication (including a single periodical issue, newspaper, magazine issue, bulletin, newsletter issue, annual, journal, or similar publication) using Form SE. Such registration may be done electronically or by mail, as described above. The registration fee is $45 per issue if registered online. However, it's cheaper and easier to register a group of serial publications together in a single registration as described below.

Group Registration of Serials

The Copyright Office permits multiple issues of the same magazine or another serial publication to be registered together as a group for one application fee. For example, the same monthly magazine may be registered three issues at a time. This way, registration need only be accomplished four times a year instead of 12. The registration fee is $35 per issue for group registration compared with $45 per issue registered online singly.

You must register a group of contributions to serials online and upload digital copies of the serial works as your deposit. Go to the Copyright Office registration portal at www.copyright.gov/registration, and log on to the electronic Copyright Office (eCO). After logging in, click "Register Certain Groups of Published Works." Click "Start Registration" and choose "Serial Issues" from the Type of Group list.

Unfortunately, there are some restrictions on which serials may be registered as a group, and there are special requirements and higher registration fees for group registration of newspapers and newsletters.

Serial Must Be a Work Made for Hire

For group registration, the magazine or other serial must be a work made for hire. This means that the persons who create the periodical as a whole—that is, do the editing, compiling, and similar work necessary to put the issue in its final form—must be employees of the owner of the publication or have been commissioned to do the work under a written contract. (See Chapter 6, "Initial Copyright Ownership," for a detailed discussion of works made for hire.) Most serial publications are works made for hire for which the owner of the publication has hired or commissioned others to compile and edit.

> **EXAMPLE:** *Newspeak Magazine* is a weekly news magazine that is compiled and edited entirely by the publisher's editorial staff. *Newspeak* is a work made for hire, and the weekly issues may be registered together.

However, a serial that is independently owned and created by the same individual(s) who own it—that is, not created by employees or commissioned workers—is not a work made for hire. Such a publication may not be registered as a group. Each issue must be separately registered (see below).

> **EXAMPLE:** Dr. Brown, an eminent urologist, owns, publishes, writes, and edits a monthly online newsletter for urologists called *Urine Analysis*. The newsletter is not a work made for hire. This means that Dr. Brown must register each newsletter issue separately.

Frequency of Publication Restrictions

You may register together two or more issues of the same serial so long as they are published:

- no more frequently than once a week
- at least four times a year, and
- within a 90-day period during the same calendar year.

Collective Work Authorship Must Be Essentially All New

Group registration may be used only if the collective work authorship—that is, the editing, compiling, revising, and other work involved in creating each issue as a whole—of all the issues being registered together is essentially all new in terms of when the work was done. It's not exactly clear how recently created a periodical issue must be to qualify as essentially all new. But as an outside time limit, each issue must have been created no more than one year prior to its publication.

Author and Copyright Claimant Must Be the Same for All Issues

The person(s) or organization responsible for the creation of the issue as a whole, whether it employs an editorial staff or freelance editors or uses volunteers, is the author of a magazine or another serial issue. The author is normally the person(s) or organization that owns the publication.

To use group registration, the author of all the periodical issues being registered and the copyright claimant in the issues must be the same. As discussed above, the author of a publication is also the copyright claimant unless the author transfers all of his or her copyright rights to a third party. This means the author-publisher of a serial issue would normally be the copyright claimant as well. However, if the author-publisher transferred his or her copyright rights to one or more of the serial issues to a third party, those issues could not be registered as a group.

EXAMPLE: *The Toxic Waste Tipster* is a monthly trade journal owned and published by a corporation called Toxic Waste Interment and Transport, Inc. (TWIT). TWIT oversees the creation of each issue through its editorial staff. TWIT is the author and copyright claimant for each issue.

Group Registration for Newspapers

An entire calendar month's worth of daily newspaper issues can be registered at one time for a single $95 fee. You must register online and upload a digital copy of the final edition of each newspaper issue as your deposit.

What Works Qualify as Daily Newspapers

Any daily serial publication mainly designed to be a primary source of written information on current events (local, national, or international) qualifies as a daily newspaper so long as it contains a broad range of news on all subjects and activities and is not limited to any specific subject matter. Publications such as newsletters on particular subjects and daily racing forms do not qualify as daily newspapers.

Newspaper websites are not eligible for group registration because a website is not considered a serial for purposes of registration. But individual electronic newspaper issues can qualify for group registration. Each electronic issue must be a self-contained work, such as a digital version of a print newspaper.

Requirements for Group Registration

Group registration may be used only if the newspaper is an essentially all-new collective work made for hire. Virtually all daily newspapers should be able to satisfy this requirement because they are essentially all new every day and are created by employee-reporters and editors.

In addition, the author and copyright claimant must be the same person or organization. Again, this should pose no problem given the author and claimant will normally be the owner(s) of the newspaper.

An Entire Month's Issues Must Be Registered

To use group registration, an entire calendar month of daily newspaper issues must be registered—no more and no less. This means you'll have to register 12 times a year.

Time Limit for Registration

Your group registration must be filed with the Copyright Office within three months after the publication date of the last newspaper issue included in the group.

Group Registration for Newsletters

Newsletters may also be registered as a group online with a digital deposit. For registration purposes, a daily newsletter is a serial published and distributed by mail or electronic media. Publication must occur at least two days per week, and the newsletter must contain news or information of interest chiefly to a special group—for example, trade and professional associations, corporations, schools, colleges, and churches. Daily newsletters are customarily available by subscription and not sold on newsstands.

The requirements for group registration of newsletters are the same as those for newspapers covered in the preceding section, except:

- You must register at least two issues that were published within one calendar month in the same year.
- The application must be filed within three months of the last publication date of the newsletter issues included in the group.

Registering a Group of Contributions to Serials

As discussed above, authors who retain some of the rights in their contributions to serial publications need to register them to obtain the benefits of registration for their work. This requirement applies regardless of whether the publisher of the serial registers the issue as a whole.

EXAMPLE: Arnie, a freelance writer, sells an article to *Newspeak Magazine*. He grants the magazine only the right to publish the article the first time in North America and retains his other copyright rights. When the publisher of *Newspeak* registers the issue containing Arnie's article, the article will not be covered by the serial registration. Arnie must register the article himself for it to be fully protected.

You can register each article you write individually using the Copyright Office's online registration system. However, at $45 per registration, individually registering a substantial number of articles or other serial contributions each year can be very expensive.

Fortunately, a writer may register all of the articles he or she writes in any 12-month period as a group on one application for one $85 application fee. (As an alternative to this annual group registration, you may register a group of up to 50 short articles or other text of not more than 17,500 words published only online during a three-month period. The registration fee is $65. See "Group Registration of Short Online Literary Works.")

Who Qualifies for Group Registration

A single copyright registration for a group of works can be made only if all of the following are true:

- All of the works are by the same author who is an individual—that is, not a work made for hire—or all the works are by the same coauthors.
- All of the works were first published as individual contributions to serials (including newspapers, magazines, newsletters, and journals) within any single 12-month period (not necessarily a calendar year).

- All of the works have the same copyright claimant.

EXAMPLE: Jean published 12 short stories in various literary journals from July 2020 to July 2021. She retained the copyright for all the stories. Jean may register all 12 stories as a group at one time.

How to Apply for Group Registration

To register a group of contributions to serials, you must complete an online application and upload your deposit through the Copyright Office's online registration system. You will only be required to pay a single $85 registration fee.

You begin the registration by clicking "Register a Group Claim," and then select "Contributions to Periodicals TX." When you complete the online application, you will be required to identify each contribution included in the group, including the date of publication for each contribution and the serial issue in which it was first published.

Effect of Group Registration

All of your articles or other contributions are protected by registration on the date the Copyright Office receives your application. If any of the registered articles are copied after that date, you are entitled to all the benefits of timely copyright registration (that is, statutory damages and attorneys' fees). However, if any of the contributions were copied before the registration date, you will not be entitled to statutory damages and attorneys' fees unless the registration was made within three months after the first publication of the contribution.

 CAUTION

The one drawback of group registration: If you wait more than three months after an article is published so that you can register it together with other articles for one fee, you will lose the benefits of timely registration of that article for any infringement occurring before the Copyright Office receives your application. If you feel that an article or other serial contribution is extremely valuable, make sure that it is registered within three months of publication, even if you have to register it by itself. If you publish a large number of articles every year, you should make a group registration every three months.

Registering Websites

You can register a website as a collective work or compilation. This method registers the website as a whole and the individual works that appear on the website. But, you may register as a collective work or compilation only if the same claimant owns the copyright in the website as a whole and in the individual works it contains.

You can always separately register individual works contained on a website, such as text, photos, and audiovisual works.

For example, you can register a blog post consisting of text as a literary work.

If the website is unpublished, you can register a group of contributions together using the group registration of unpublished works option discussed in the sidebar above.

You can't register uncopyrightable elements of websites, such as:

- ideas or plans for future websites
- functional design elements
- domain names or URLs
- the layout, format, or "look and feel" of a webpage, and
- other common, unoriginal material like names, icons, or familiar symbols.

You can register hypertext markup language (HTML), but only if it was created by a human, not by website design software. A registration for HTML will not cover any formatting and layout that may be dictated by the HTML or style sheets. Nor will registration cover any audio, visual, or audiovisual content that might appear on a website and is not perceptible in the HTML.

It is a good idea to register a website at least every three months. If you sue someone for copyright infringement, this three-month registration regimen avoids any possibility that the alleged infringer could claim your registration was not timely.

In some cases, a frequently updated online work may constitute an automated database. A group of updates to a database, published or unpublished, covering up to a three-month period within the same calendar year, may be combined in a single registration. All updates from a three-month period may be registered with a single application and filing fee. See below for instructions on registering databases. If you're not sure whether your website qualifies as a database, contact the Copyright Office and ask them.

In addition, if your website is an online daily blog, newsletter, newspaper, magazine, or other serial publication, you can register several weeks' or months' worth of issues together at one time for one application fee by using the Copyright Office's group registration procedure discussed above.

Registering Online

Websites are registered using the Copyright Office's online registration system. Registration is completed in the same manner as for any other work, with the following exceptions.

Authors

Websites often include contributions by many authors. You can register all the content to which you own all the copyright rights. This includes content created by employees and independent contractors who sign over their rights.

Many websites also contain user-generated content. You can register this material if the copyright in it was transferred to you through your website's terms of service. The Copyright Office will accept an application that asserts a claim in user-generated content as long as you identify the authors of that content and confirm that the copyright in that content has been transferred to the claimant named in the application. If there are a large number of authors, the Copyright Office will accept a representative number of author names and the number of authors who contributed to the content.

Authorship

You must also describe the original authorship being registered. Use terms that clearly refer to copyrightable authorship. Examples are "text," "compilation," "music," "artwork," "photographs," "audiovisual material" (including sounds), or "sound recording" (when the sounds do not accompany a series of images).

Do not use terms that refer to elements that are not protected by copyright or may be ambiguous—for example, "website," "interface," "format," "layout," "design," "look of website," "lettering," "game," or "concept."

Date of Publication

As discussed above, it's up to you to decide whether a website or another online work has been published. If you determine that your work is published, give the complete date and nation of first publication. For a revised version, the publication date should be the date the revised version was first published, not the date the original version first appeared online. For registration purposes, give a single nation of first publication, which may be the nation from which the work is uploaded. If the same work is published both online and by the distribution of physical copies, and these events occur on different dates, the publication date should refer to whichever occurred first.

Extent of Registration

When you register a website, the registration extends only to the copyrightable content received by the Copyright Office in your deposit and identified as the subject of the claim. The application for registration should exclude any material that has been previously registered or published or any work that's in the public domain. If you characterize the work as published, the registration only covers the material published on the date of publication given in the application.

Material published before this date will not be covered by the registration—meaning in cases where a website is frequently revised, each revision would have to be separately registered. But this limitation only applies if the online work is characterized as published. If it's unpublished, you can register any amount of material at one time as an unpublished collection for a single application fee.

Group Registration of Short Online Literary Works

The Copyright Office instituted a new registration procedure in late 2020 allowing for group registration of up to 50 short online works. A short online literary work contains at least 50 words and no more than 17,500 words, such as a poem, short story, article, essay, column, blog entry, or social media post. The work must be published as part of a website or an online platform, including online newspapers, social media websites, and social networking platforms. The group may not include computer programs, audiobooks, podcasts, or emails. Claims in any form of authorship other than "text" or claims in the selection, coordination, or arrangement of the group as a whole are not permitted.

To qualify for group registration, all the works must:
- be published within a three-calendar-month period
- be created by the same individual or jointly by the same individuals, and
- not be works made for hire.

You register your group online using the GRTX application. You must upload one electronic copy of each work in a ZIP file. The group registration fee is $65.

Registering Multimedia Works

For copyright registration purposes, a multimedia work is any work which, excluding its container, combines authorship in two or more media.

The authorship can include text, artwork, sculpture, cinematography, photography, sounds, music, or choreography. The media may include printed matter (such as a book), audiovisual material (such as videotape, slides, or filmstrips), a phonorecord (such as an audio tape or audio disk), or any machine-readable copy (such as a computer disk or chip). Any work combining two or more types of authorship in two or more different types of media is a multimedia work and may be registered using the procedures discussed in this section. For example, a book combined with an audio tape would be a multimedia work.

It is always permissible to register each element of a multimedia work separately—manual, text, photos, video, and so on.

However, it might not be necessary to do so. An entire multimedia work can be registered at one time on one registration form for one fee, if both of the following are true:

- The copyright claimant is the same for all elements of the work for which copyright protection is sought.
- All such elements are (1) unpublished or (2) published at the same time as a single unit (excluding preexisting elements, such as photos, music, and video, which will not be covered by the registration).

An example will help make these rules clear. Assume that a company, Scrivener & Sons, has developed an educational application (app) containing a history of the Iraq War. The app consists of text, photos, video, and music. Scrivener is the copyright owner of the text, which was written by its employees and freelancers. All other material was licensed by Scrivener—that is, it obtained permission to copy and distribute it from the copyright owners.

Scrivener does not own the copyright in any of these individual photos, videos, or music. However, Scrivener does own a compilation copyright in the entire app—that is, a copyright in the selection, arrangement, and coordination of all the material in the book, which was performed by Scrivener employees and work-made-for-hire freelancers. The selection, arrangement, and coordination constitutes a work of authorship if original and minimally creative. (See Chapter 5, "Adaptations and Compilations.")

Scrivener may register all the elements to which it claims copyright ownership—the text it owns and the compilation copyright covering all the material—on a single application for a single fee. Why? Because the copyright claimant for all the elements of the multimedia work for which protection is sought by Scrivener is the same—Scrivener—and all these elements are being published together as a single unit at the same time.

What about registering all the individual bits of music, photos, video that Scrivener licensed? That's the province of the copyright owner of each individual licensed item. Scrivener may not register such material because it is not the copyright claimant (owner).

A multimedia work is registered in the same way as any other work.

Database Software Must Also Be Registered

The discussion below is only about how to register the selection and arrangement of the contents of a computer-database. It does not cover registration of computer software designed to be used with databases to facilitate retrieval of the data. Software registration is beyond the scope of this book.

Registering Contents of Databases

A database is a body of facts, data, or other information assembled into an organized format suitable for use on a computer. Since most databases are frequently updated or revised, the Copyright Office has instituted a special group registration procedure whereby a database and all the updates or other revisions made within any three-month period may be registered in one application. This way, a database need only be registered a maximum of four times per year, rather than each time it is updated or revised.

Databases Qualifying for Group Registration

To qualify for group registration, all of the following conditions must be met:
- All of the updates or revisions must be fixed or published only in machine-readable copies.
- All of the updates or revisions must have been created or published within a three-month period, all within the same calendar year.
- All of the updates or revisions must be owned by the same copyright claimant.
- All of the updates or revisions must have the same general title.
- The updates or revisions must be organized in a similar way.

Satisfying Copyright Office Deposit Requirements

You must submit (deposit) one or two copies of the work being registered with your application. The Copyright Office reviews your deposit to make sure that the work is copyrightable and is accurately described on your application. Your registration only covers the material that you deposit with the Copyright Office—except where a special deposit of less than the entire work is made, such as for a multivolume encyclopedia.

Emergency Deposit Rules in Effect During Coronavirus Pandemic Disruption

The Copyright Office buildings were closed during the coronavirus (COVID-19) pandemic. The Copyright Office continued to accept and process certain electronically filed registration applications. Electronic applications that required only electronic deposits were processed normally because the electronic deposits could be examined remotely. However, Copyright Office personnel were unable to examine physical deposits, which were placed in storage. The Copyright Office implemented emergency deposit rules permitting electronic deposits in cases where the normal rules require physical deposits. This way, the registration process could be completed before the Copyright Office resumed in-office examinations of physical deposits.

These emergency rules were effective only during the officially declared coronavirus disruption period.

Electronic deposit plus physical deposit. Under these emergency rules, if you submit an electronic application for a published work that requires submission of the "best edition" physical copies of the work as described below, you have the option of uploading an electronic copy of the work in addition to mailing the required physical copies. You must submit both an electronic deposit copy and a declaration form, under penalty of perjury, stating that the electronic copy is identical to the required physical copies that you will mail within three days to the Copyright Office together with the shipping slip. You can find the declaration form here: www.copyright.gov/coronavirus/declaration-form.pdf. If these emergency rules are still in effect at the time of your application, submitting an electronic deposit will result in much faster processing.

No physical deposit submitted. If you were unable to submit the required physical deposit during the coronavirus disruption period but could submit the rest of your application, you may send the Copyright Office a Section 710 declaration. This declaration states under penalty of perjury that you were unable to submit your physical deposit due to the COVID-19 pandemic. If you then mail your physical deposit within 30 days after the coronavirus disruption period officially ends, your application will be deemed to have been filed within three months after publication. This way, you can collect statutory damages and attorneys' fees in a copyright infringement suit. A Section 710 declaration form is available at www.copyright.gov/coronavirus/710-declaration-form.pdf.

Before you do anything, check the Copyright Office website at www.copyright.gov/coronavirus for the current status of these emergency rules.

Electronic Deposits

If you use the Copyright Office's electronic registration system to submit your registration application, you may make your deposit electronically as well if the work is:

- unpublished
- published only electronically
- a published work for which the deposit requirement is identifying material (see below), or
- a published work for which there is a special agreement requiring the hard-copy deposits to be sent separately to the Library of Congress.

When you register electronically, you'll be prompted to choose your deposit method. Submitting an electronic deposit is optional. You can submit a physical (hard-copy) deposit if you want. But there is no advantage to doing so.

To deposit electronically, you'll upload one electronic copy to the Copyright Office website when you complete your application. The online application form explains what types of files are accepted and how to upload them.

Websites

The deposit requirements for websites and website content are generally the same as for any other work. If the website is unpublished or if it has been published solely online, you must electronically submit a complete copy. For example, if you want to register an entire website, you must submit all of the pages as they actually appear on the site.

If you want to register an individual work that appears on the website, the deposit must depict the work in the context in which it appears on the website or webpage. In other words, the deposit should show how the content would be perceived when a user accesses that content online.

The Copyright Office prefers you submit your deposit in a portable document format (PDF) file. The Office will not accept a link to a website or other online sources. Do not submit HTML for a website unless you specifically want to register it.

Note that your registration does not cover any content that can't be viewed in the deposit, such as audio or audiovisual works embedded within the website.

Group Registration of Serial Issues

If you register a group of newspapers, magazines, or newsletters online, you must deposit a PDF file of each issue identified in the application.

Group Registration of Individual Contributions to Serials

If you are registering a group of individual contributions to a serial publication, such as a magazine or newspaper, you must upload one electronic copy of each contribution as it appeared when published. You may submit:

- the entire issue of the periodical where the contribution was first published
- the entire section of the newspaper where it was first published, or
- the specific pages from the periodical where the contribution was first published.

Each individual contribution must be contained in its own separate electronic file.

Short Online Literary Works

If you register on Form GRTX a group of up to 50 text works published only online, you must upload an electronic copy of each work in a single compressed ZIP file. You must also submit a sequentially numbered list containing a title/file name for each work in the group. The list must also include the publication date and word count for each work. The numbered list must be contained in an electronic file in *Excel* format (.xls), a PDF file, or another electronic format approved by the Copyright Office.

Deposits of Physical Copies

You must deposit physical copies of a work that is published in physical (hard-copy) form. This is so even if it is also published online. For example, you must make a physical deposit for a book that is published both as a hard-copy book and an electronic book.

In addition, you usually have the option of submitting a physical deposit, even if it is not required.

The general rule is that you must submit two complete copies of the "best edition" of a published work. However, you need only submit single copies of:

- unpublished works (but you have the option of making an electronic deposit for an unpublished work)
- multimedia works
- works first published outside the United States (only one copy of the first foreign edition needs to be deposited and it does not need to be the best edition)
- advertising materials (you need to send only one copy of the page in which an advertisement appeared in a periodical, not the entire periodical issue)
- lectures, sermons, speeches, and addresses published separately (that is, not as part of a collection), and
- tests and test answers published separately from each other.

Best edition. When you make a physical deposit, you must submit the "best edition" of the work. The best edition is the work of the highest quality, in terms of printing and binding. For example, you would deposit a hardcover edition rather than the paperback version of a work. If there are two hardcover versions, you would deposit the edition that is the better bound, larger in size, or printed on the better paper. It's up to you to decide which edition is the best.

TIP
The Copyright Office publishes a circular describing in detail all the criteria used to determine what constitutes the best edition of a work. If you're in the publishing business, you may find it useful. You can download Circular 7b from the Copyright Office website at www.copyright.gov or obtain it by calling or writing the Copyright Office.

You only need to deposit the best edition of the work in existence at the time you register. If a better edition is published after you have already registered, you do not need to deposit it with the Copyright Office.

Make sure, however, that each of the editions has substantially the same content. If the second edition contains enough new material to be considered a new version, it must be registered separately to protect the new material.

Depositing Identifying Material

Depositing complete physical copies of some works could prove burdensome both for the applicant and the Copyright Office. For example, you would not wish to mail (and the Copyright Office would not want to store) a 30-volume encyclopedia. Indeed, the Copyright Office will not accept any item that exceeds 96 inches in any dimension.

If your work exceeds 96 inches, you'll have to deposit identifying material rather than the entire work. For example, instead of depositing every volume of an encyclopedia that takes up ten feet of shelf space, you might be able to submit photos of every volume. To prepare identifying material, first call the Copyright Office at 202-707-3000 or 877-476-0778 (toll free), describe your work, and find out what type of identifying material is acceptable.

Deposits for Multimedia Works

The Copyright Office has imposed special deposit requirements for multimedia works. One complete copy of the best edition of a multimedia work first published in the United States must be deposited with the Copyright Office. Everything that is marketed or distributed together must be deposited, whether or not you're the copyright claimant for each element. For details, see the Copyright Office brochure entitled *Circular 55: Copyright Registration for Multimedia Works.*

Deposits for Electronic Databases

The rules for electronic database deposits depend on whether you are making a group registration or nongroup registration.

Deposit Requirements for Group Registration

You must submit the following deposit with your registration application.

Identifying material. Identifying material meeting the following requirements:

- 50 representative pages of printout (or equivalent units, if reproduced in microfilm) from a single-file database, or

• 50 representative complete data records (not pages) from each updated data file in a multiple-file database.

The printout or data records must be marked to show the copyrightable revisions or updates from one representative publication date (if the database is published) or from one representative creation date (if the database is unpublished) within the three-month period covered by the registration; or, alternatively, you may deposit a copy of the actual updates or revisions made on a representative date.

Descriptive statement. In addition, you must submit a brief, typed descriptive statement providing the following information:

• the title of the database
• the name and address of the copyright claimant
• the name and content of each separate file in a multiple-file database, including its subject, the origin(s) of the data, and the approximate number of data records it contains
• information about the nature, location, and frequency of the changes within the database or within the separate data files in multiple-file databases, and
• information about the copyright notice, if one is used, as follows:
  ▪ For a machine-readable notice, transcribe the contents of the notice and indicate the manner and frequency with which it's displayed—for example, at a user's terminal only, at sign-on, continuously on terminal display, or on printouts.
  ▪ For a visually perceptible notice on any copies of the work (or on tape reels or containers), include a photocopy or another sample of the notice.

Nongroup Registration

If your database doesn't qualify for group registration or you do not wish to use that procedure, you should deposit the first and last 25 pages of a single-file database. If the database consists of separate and distinct data files, deposit one copy of 50 complete data records (not pages) from each file or the entire file, whichever is less. You must also include a descriptive statement for a multiple-file database containing the same information.

If the database is fixed in a CD-ROM, deposit one complete copy of the CD-ROM package, any instructional manual, and a printed version of the work that is fixed on the CD-ROM, if such an exact print version exists. The deposit must also include any software that is included as part of the package. A printout of the first and last 25 pages of the software source code is acceptable.

Library of Congress Deposit Requirements

The Library of Congress has its own deposit requirements for published works, which are separate from those of the Copyright Office. However, the library's deposit requirements are deemed satisfied when a work is registered and a deposit made with the Copyright Office. In other words, you don't have to worry about the Library of Congress if you register your work with the Copyright Office. The one exception to this rule is deposits for machine-readable works such as automated databases. The library may demand deposit of the machine-readable copies distributed after registration has been made.

If you don't register your published work with the Copyright Office, you are supposed to deposit two copies with the Library of Congress. If you don't, the library is entitled to demand that you do so, and you are subject to monetary penalties if you do not comply. However, in practice this rarely happens. Contrary to popular belief, the Library of Congress does not collect copies of everything published in the United States.

Your Registration Is Effective When the Application Is Received

Your registration is effective on the date the Copyright Office receives all three elements: application, deposit, and application fee in proper form. This is so regardless of how long it takes the Copyright Office to process the application and send you your certificate of registration. Your certificate will list the effective date, called the "Effective Date of Registration" or EDR. This means you don't need to worry about not being able to obtain statutory damages or attorneys' fees from anyone who copies your work while your application is being processed. (Remember,

you can obtain such fees and damages only if the work was registered before the infringement occurred or within three months of publication.)

Expedited Registration

A work's registration must be completed and a certificate of registration issued by the Copyright Office before a copyright infringement lawsuit can be filed for the work. Or the Copyright Office must refuse to register the work after a complete application was submitted. In this event, the Copyright Office will send you a rejection letter explaining the grounds for its refusal to register your work.

When you submit your registration application, you may request that your application be given special handling by the Copyright Office. Special handling applications are processed in five to ten days, rather than the normal three to six months or more.

Special handling is available only if needed for copyright litigation, to meet a contractual or publishing deadline, or for some other urgent need.

You must pay an additional $800 fee for special handling. The fastest way to obtain special handling is to register the work online. The online registration system allows you to include a request for special handling and either to upload a digital copy or mail in a hard copy to the special handling address below. You'll need to do the following:

- Check the "Special Handling" box in the online application.
- Select at least one of the "Compelling Reasons" why expedited processing is needed.
- Check "I certify" to confirm that the information contained in the request is correct to the best of your knowledge.

Enter comments or special instructions, including certificate delivery preferences, in the "Explanation" box.

If you need special handling for an application that has already made with the Copyright Office, you need to submit a written request in the form of a letter containing the following information:

- the service request number/case number for the work (if known)
- the exact title appearing on the application
- the names of the author(s) and claimant(s)
- a full description of the deposit copy or copies
- when and how the application and deposit were delivered to the Copyright Office (in person, by courier, or by mail), and
- if sent by mail, the type of mailing (registered, certified, first class, and so forth).

Send the letter along with the $800 special handling fee to:

Special Handling
Copyright RAC Division
P.O. Box 71380
Washington, DC 20024-1380

Screening Delay Before Mailed Applications Received

Due to the anthrax scare in late 2001, all mail sent to the Copyright Office is screened before delivery at a special facility in Washington, D.C. This screening process causes a three-to-five-day delay before the Copyright Office receives your application. Mail sent by commercial carriers, such as FedEx and UPS, is screened as well as postal mail. This means, for example, that if you send an application by FedEx overnight delivery, the Copyright Office won't receive it overnight—the screening facility will. Because your registration isn't effective until it is received by the Copyright Office, the screening process adds a few days to the lag time before your application becomes effective.

The Copyright Office advises that to avoid damage to your deposit from Copyright Office security measures, you should package the following items in boxes rather than envelopes:

- electronic media such as audiocassettes, videocassettes, CDs, and DVDs
- microfilm
- photographs, and
- slick advertisements, color photocopies, and other print items that are rubber and vegetable based.

Special Handling During Coronavirus Disruption Period

If you apply for special handling during the coronavirus disruption period, you should submit an electronic copy of your deposit so it can be remotely examined by Copyright Office staff. If a physical deposit is required, mail it as well. If you fail to provide an electronic deposit, your application won't be processed until the pandemic disruption ends. Check www. copyright.gov/coronavirus for the latest guidance.

Preregistration of Unpublished Works

In today's digital era, it is common for copies of some works-in-progress to be pirated and published on the Internet and elsewhere before the work has been completed and the authorized publication or distribution has occurred. This is most common with unauthorized prereleases of movies, music, and software. But it can happen to books as well. In one case, for example, portions of former President Gerald Ford's unpublished memoirs were lifted from his publisher and published without permission in *The Nation* magazine. (*Harper & Row v. Nation Enter.*, 471 U.S. 539 (1985).)

The Problem: Infringement Lawsuits Involving Unpublished Works

Prepublication copyright infringement has always posed a problem for copyright owners. As discussed at the start of this chapter, the statutory damages and attorneys' fees obtained against an infringer when a work is timely registered can often make an infringement suit worthwhile. However, the copyright law provided that such damages and fees were available for an infringed unpublished work *only* if the work was registered before the infringement occurred.

It is possible to register an unpublished work, but registration poses problems. For one thing, a copy of the uncompleted work must be provided to the Copyright Office where it becomes available for inspection by the public. Many authors, publishers, and other creators don't want the public—especially the competition—to have access to what they are working on. Also, the registration only covers the work as it existed when registered. Subsequent changes would not be covered by the registration—they would have to be registered in their own right. Thus, to really be protected, a creator might have to register an unpublished work many times as it evolves and changes over time. Obviously, this is a costly and time-consuming proposition.

The Solution: Online Preregistration Without a Deposit

Starting in 2006, copyright law offered a solution to the problem outlined above.

A procedure called preregistration was created. Creators of the works that are prone to infringement before release may preregister their work by filling out an online application at the Copyright Office website. A copy of the unpublished work need not be provided.

The copyright owner of an unpublished work that has been preregistered may file a copyright infringement suit without having to register the work with the Copyright Office. This allows a lawsuit to be filed quickly and might help the owner obtain court action to prevent distribution of the work.

Even more important, the copyright owner may obtain statutory damages and attorneys' fees in a successful infringement suit against anyone who pirated the unfinished work *after the preregistration was made* provided that the work is fully registered with the Copyright Office during the *earlier* of the following times:

- three months after the first publication of the work, or
- one month after the copyright owner learned of the infringement.

EXAMPLE: Copyright pirates obtain a copy of a draft version of Gillian Flynn's sequel to *Gone Girl* and release it on the Internet before the final version is published. Flynn's publisher preregistered the book before the draft was stolen. As a result, the publisher can immediately file a copyright infringement suit against the copyright pirates. The publisher registers the unpublished work three weeks later. If the lawsuit proves successful, the publisher

and Flynn can obtain an award of their attorneys' fees and statutory damages.

If the copyright owner fails to meet the deadline for full registration, a court must dismiss any lawsuit brought by the owner for copyright infringement that occurred before or within the first two months after first publication. In this event, the copyright owner would have to register the work and file a new infringement suit. The late-registering owner may not obtain attorneys' fees and statutory damages if the suit is successful. However, this rule does not apply to infringement lawsuits for infringements occurring more than two months after first publication.

Note that *preregistration is not a substitute for registration*, nor does it provide all the benefits of registration—for example, it doesn't create a legal presumption that the work is protected by a valid copyright. Its purpose is simply to advise the Copyright Office prior to the publication of a work that the work is being prepared for commercial distribution and preserve your right to obtain statutory damages and attorneys' fees in an infringement suit. You must follow through with a full registration of the work shortly after publication or infringement of the work. The fact that a work has been preregistered does not mean that the Copyright Office necessarily will register the work when an application for registration is submitted. Also, you may register an unpublished work without preregistering it.

Is Preregistration for You?

For the vast majority of works, pre-registration is a waste of money. The Copyright Office itself says that "(f)or the vast majority of works, preregistration is not useful." Few works, especially written works, are infringed upon before they are published or otherwise distributed. This type of thing usually occurs with popular movies and songs. However, you may benefit by preregistering your work if you think it's likely someone may infringe your unfinished work before it is released.

How to Preregister

Preregistration is a quick, though expensive, online process.

What Can Be Preregistered?

You can preregister your work *only if all the statements below apply:*

- It is unpublished.
- Its creation has begun.
- It is being prepared for commercial distribution.
- It is one of the following: a motion picture, musical work, sound recording, computer program, book, or advertising photograph.

Written works other than books may not be preregistered—for example, a screenplay not intended to be published in book form. The intended commercial distribution of the work can be in either physical or digital format—for example, e-books or CDs to be sold online.

You can't preregister ideas for new works. You must have begun to actually write the work involved, though it does not have to be finished.

Online Application

You preregister by completing an online application on Electronic Form PRE at the Copyright Office website (www.copyright. gov/prereg). You must provide the following information:

- the work's title (a working title may be used)
- the names of the author and copyright claimant
- the date the actual writing of the book began and the date you anticipate completing it, and
- a description of the work, including the nature of the subject matter (such as biography of a public figure or novel about ghosts), the type of work (such as novel or biography), the version (such as a later edition or revision of a previous work), and any other details which may help identify the work in published book form.

You need not provide the Copyright Office with a copy of your unpublished work or make any other deposit. The nonrefundable filing fee for preregistration is $200.

If you fill out the application correctly, the Copyright Office will email you a notification of preregistration which will include a preregistration number and date. This is the only notice you will receive that preregistration has been made. The Copyright Office does not issue a paper certificate of preregistration.

What Is Publication?

Publication occurs for copyright purposes when the copyright owner, or someone acting with the copyright owner's authority, distributes one or more copies of the work to the general public or offers the work for distribution, public display, or public performance. Copies do not need to be sold for publication to occur—they can be leased, rented, loaned, or even given away, so long as the work has been made available to the general public.

Publication does *not* occur when:

- Copies of the work are made but not distributed.
- The text of the work is performed publicly (for example, a speech is presented).
- The text of the work is displayed (for example, in a slide presentation or on television).

A "limited publication" is also not considered a publication. A limited publication occurs if copies are distributed only:

- to a selected group of people
- for a limited purpose, and
- without the right of further reproduction, distribution, or sale.

For example, it is not a publication when an author sends copies of a manuscript to several publishers seeking publication.

 CAUTION
Your preregistration is a public record. Everything you say in your preregistration application becomes a public record of the Copyright Office that can be read by others. So you might not want to say too much about your work-in-progress. Moreover, if you want to have a website using the book's title as a domain name, you may want to obtain the name before you preregister the book. Otherwise, a "cybersquatter" could learn about your title from your preregistration and register the domain name before you.

Dealing With the Copyright Office

The Copyright Office has an enormous workload (they handle over 700,000 applications per year), so it can take several months for your application to be processed. Indeed, the Copyright Office says that the average processing time is three to six months for online registrations and six to 16 months for paper form registrations. If you apply for copyright registration online, you will receive confirmation by email that your application has been received. You can also monitor the progress of your application online. This is not possible with applications by mail. Be patient and remember that the registration is effective on the date it is received (assuming the forms were filled out properly), not the date you actually receive your registration certificate.

The Copyright Office will eventually respond to your application in one of three ways:

- If your application is acceptable, the Copyright Office will send you a registration certificate, which is merely a copy of your application with the official Copyright Office seal, registration date, and number stamped on it. Be sure to retain it for your records.
- If your application contained errors or omissions the Copyright Office believes are correctable, a copyright examiner might phone or email you for further information. Or he or she may return the application or deposit with a letter explaining what corrections to make.
- If the Copyright Office determines that your work cannot be registered, it will send you a letter explaining why. Neither your deposit nor fee will be returned.

Extent of Copyright Examiner's Review of Your Application

The copyright examiner will examine your deposit to see whether it constitutes copyrightable subject matter and review your application to determine whether the other legal and formal requirements for registration have been met.

Unregistrable Material

The Copyright Office will refuse to register a work that is unprotectable. For example, the Copyright Office would not register:

- a title, since titles are not copyrightable
- a work in the public domain (for instance, the King James version of the Bible) unless the applicant added protectable material to it
- a work lacking human authorship
- a work not fixed in a tangible medium of expression
- a work not independently created, or
- a work unlawfully employing preexisting material.

Presence of Errors or Omissions

The Copyright Office will not issue a certificate if the application contains errors or omissions or is internally inconsistent or ambiguous. Here are some of the more common errors:

- failure to sign the application
- failure to pay the application fee
- failure to provide the required number of deposit copies
- failure to adequately describe the nature of authorship
- deposit does not match description of nature of authorship
- nature of authorship is described by a title or identifying phrase
- failure to provide the publication date

- the work-made-for-hire box is checked, but the employer is not listed as the copyright claimant
- failure to state how ownership was transferred where copyright claimant is not the same as the author
- failure to identify adequately the material added to a new version or derivative work, and
- date application is signed is prior to publication date in application.

The Copyright Office will ordinarily call you or send a letter asking you to fix technical errors such as these. Reread our discussion about how to complete the application forms to help you make your corrections. Send your corrected application or new deposit back to the Copyright Office in one package.

Be sure you respond within 120 days to any correspondence from the Copyright Office concerning your application. Otherwise, your file will be closed, and you'll have to reapply by sending in a new application, deposit, and fee.

Review of Copyright Office's Refusal to Register Application

If you think the copyright examiner has wrongfully refused to register your work, you may submit a written objection to the refusal and request that the Copyright Office reconsider its action. This written objection is called an "appeal."

Filing Suit After Copyright Office Refuses Registration

Filing an appeal with the Copyright Office is purely optional. You can bring a copyright infringement action when the Copyright Office first refuses to register your work. It is not necessary to appeal a refusal to register to file a copyright infringement lawsuit.

However, the fact the Copyright Office refused to register your work will doubtless make it far more difficult to succeed in such a suit. Without a registration certificate, you'll have to prove to the court that your work is copyrightable. The court makes this determination on its own, but the fact the Copyright Office refused to register your work will weigh heavily against you. Also, you must serve a copy of your infringement suit on the Copyright Office, which may join in the suit to explain to the court why it refused registration.

If you wish to appeal, you must do so by letter and pay a hefty fee. The appeal letter should specify the reasons you think the Copyright Office improperly refused the registration. It should also include the Copyright Office ten-digit case number and name of the copyright claimant. The appeal letter should be addressed to:

First Request for Reconsideration
U.S. Copyright Office
RAC Division
P.O. Box 71380
Washington, DC 20024-1380

The first request for reconsideration must be received in the Copyright Office within three months of the date of the office's first refusal to register. A $350 fee is charged to process an appeal; you must include the fee with your appeal letter.

If the claim is refused after reconsideration, the head of the appropriate Examining Division section will send you written notice of the reasons for the refusal. After this, you may again request reconsideration in writing. This second appeal must be received in the Copyright Office within three months of the date of the office's refusal of the first appeal.

A second appeal costs $700 to process and is handled by the Copyright Office Board of Review, which consists of the Register of Copyrights, the general counsel, and a third person. The chair of the Board of Review will send you a letter setting out the reasons for acceptance or denial of your claim. The board's decision constitutes the Copyright Office's final action. You may then bring a legal action in federal district court under the Administrative Procedures Act to have the court review the Copyright Office's decision. But this review is limited to determining whether the Copyright Office abused its discretion. The district court does not determine whether the work is protected by copyright. Such suits are rarely successful.

Full-Term Retention of Physical Deposits and Other Ways to Preserve Deposits

Whether or not your application is accepted, your deposit becomes the property of the U.S. government and will never be returned to you. The Library of Congress may add the deposit to its own collection. If the Library chooses not to do so (which is usually the case), and your application is accepted, the Copyright Office will retain a physical deposit in its own storage facilities for five years. Due to a lack of storage space, the Copyright Office normally destroys all deposits of published works after five years. However, the Copyright Office may not destroy a deposit of an unpublished work without first making a copy of it.

Full-Term Retention of Physical Deposits

People sued for copyright infringement have been known to attempt to turn the tables on their accusers and claim that the accusers actually copied from them or others. Such accusations are easily disproved if the work you claim was infringed upon was deposited with the Copyright Office before the infringing work or other work the infringer claims you copied was written or published. In this event, you just need to submit to the court a certified copy of the deposit you made with the Copyright Office.

The Copyright Office will provide certified copies of deposits of registered works that are involved in litigation. But, of course, such copies can be made only if the Copyright Office still has the deposit. So you might be in for trouble if the infringement litigation takes place more than five years after the work was registered and the deposit has been destroyed by the Copyright Office.

If you want to protect against this possibility, you may request full-term retention of your deposit. Full-term retention means that the Copyright Office will retain one copy of your deposit for 75 years from the date of publication. You must request full-term retention in writing and pay a $540 fee. Only the person who made the deposit, the copyright owner, or an authorized representative may make the request. You can make this request when you register the work or any time thereafter. There is no form for this purpose. Send a letter to:

U.S. Copyright Office
Attn: Director of the Office of Public Records and Depositories
101 Independence Avenue SE
Washington, DC 20559-6000

The letter should state that you desire full-term retention of your deposit. Identify the deposit by title, author, and registration number. If you request full-term retention of your deposit when you make your initial registration, you must send the Copyright Office an additional copy of the deposit—that is, *three* copies of published works and *two* copies of unpublished works.

> **TIP**
>
> **There is no reason to go to the trouble and expense of having the Copyright Office retain your deposit for 75 years** unless the work is very valuable and you think there is a good possibility you could end up in copyright litigation more than five years after you register it—which is when the Copyright Office would normally destroy your deposit. Keep in mind, however, that most infringements occur relatively soon after publication. Because you can make your request for full-term retention at any time, wait until four or four-and-one-half years after registration before making this decision. Things might look very different by then.

Mailing Deposit to Yourself

As an alternative to paying the Copyright Office for full-term retention of your physical deposit, you can mail copies of your deposit to yourself (preferably by certified mail). This way, if you later become involved in infringement litigation, you can present the package in court to help prove that your work existed in a certain form as of the date of the mailing. You must not unseal or otherwise tamper with the envelope. However, this method is not foolproof, because a judge or jury might not believe that you did not tamper with the envelope (this actually happened in one case).

Note that emailing a digital copy to yourself instead of postal mailing a hard copy is not a good option. The reason? Email is not delivered by an independent government agency (the U.S. Post Office) and can easily be altered by the recipient.

Depositing Screenplays With the Writers Guild of America

For screenplays and similar works, registration and deposit with the Writers Guild of America is actually better than full-term retention by the Copyright Office. The Writers Guild is the scriptwriters' union. It represents writers primarily for the purpose of collective bargaining in the motion picture, television, and radio industries. The guild establishes guidelines regarding payment for scripts and stories and giving screen credit to authors. The guild does not obtain employment for writers or accept or handle material for submission to production companies. Scripts, treatments, and so on must be submitted directly to production companies or through an agent.

To help writers establish the completion date and identity of works written for the entertainment industry, the Writers Guild registers scripts deposited by writers and keeps them on file. If a dispute arises as to the authorship of the material, the guild deposit constitutes proof that the material existed in a certain form as of the date of the deposit. You need not be a member of the Writers Guild to deposit a script with the guild (indeed, you can't join until you have sold a script or story idea or performed other writing assignments).

TIP
Depositing a copy of your script with the Writers Guild is not a substitute for registration with the Copyright Office. However, the deposit will help you prove that you wrote the material deposited and when you wrote it if an authorship dispute later arises (such disputes are common in Hollywood). Moreover, many producers will not even read a script unless it has been registered with the Writers Guild.

What Can Be Deposited

The Writers Guild will register scripts, treatments, synopses, outlines, or written ideas specifically intended for radio, television and theatrical motion pictures, and interactive media. It also registers stage plays, novels, books, short stories, poems, commercials, lyrics, drawings, and various media work, such as Web series, code, and other digital content. However, the guild does not register or protect titles. (See Chapter 4 for information about legal protection for titles.)

Each property must be registered separately. However, three episodes, skits, or sketches for an existing television series may be deposited as a single registration.

A Tale of Two Writers Guild Branches

The Writers Guild is divided into two branches: Writers Guild West located in Los Angeles and Writers Guild East headquartered in New York City. Technically, the Guild West covers the area west of the Mississippi River and the Guild East covers the area east of the Mississippi. However, regardless of where you live, you may deposit your work with either branch. Because most of the film and television industries are located in Los Angeles, it's advisable to register a screenplay, teleplay, or other work designed for film or television with the Writers Guild West. This will be more convenient if you sue in Los Angeles for copyright infringement and need to have someone from the guild testify about your deposit. (Such lawsuits must be filed where the alleged infringer resides—meaning they would likely have to be filed in Los Angeles, anyway.)

However, if your work is most likely to be produced in New York or elsewhere east of the Mississippi—for example, a stage play bound for Broadway—you might wish to deposit it with the Writers Guild East. The procedure is much the same as that described here, except you can register by mail or messenger delivery in addition to online. The fee is $25 for nonmembers of the guild and $17 for students. The deposit is retained for ten years instead of five (as is the case for Guild West). For detailed information, visit the Writers Guild East website at www.wgaeast.org or call 212-767-7801.

Deposit Procedure

You must deposit your work electronically over the Internet. Go to the Writers Guild website at www.wgawregistry.org, fill out the online registration form, provide your credit card number to pay the fee, and upload your work to the guild. The registration fee is $20 for nonmembers and $10 for members.

After your deposit is accepted, it is dated and assigned a registration number. (By the way, scriptwriting experts consider it amateurish to put this number on your script when you submit it to agents, producers, or actors.)

Duration of Deposit

The guild retains the deposit for five years. You may renew the registration for an additional five years at the conclusion of the term.

Supplementary Registration

The same published work normally can be registered only once with the Copyright Office. However, a second supplementary registration might be necessary to augment your original basic registration if any of the following are true:

- You later discover that you forgot something important.
- You supplied the Copyright Office with the wrong information.
- Important facts have changed.

Why a Supplementary Registration Should Be Filed (When Appropriate)

If you ever become involved in copyright litigation, your registration certificate (which is simply a copy of your basic registration application form stamped and returned to you by the Copyright Office) will be submitted into evidence to prove the existence of your copyright. It could prove embarrassing, and possibly harmful to your case, if the certificate is found to contain substantial errors, is unclear, or is ambiguous, or if important facts have changed since you registered. For this reason, you should file a supplementary registration to correct significant errors in your certificate or to reflect important factual changes.

Also, remember that your registration is a public record. By keeping your registration accurate and up-to-date, you will make it easier for those searching the Copyright Office records to discover your work and locate you—which might result in new marketing opportunities and help to prevent an infringement.

Corrections

A supplementary registration should be filed to correct *significant* errors that occurred at the time the basic registration was made and were overlooked by the Copyright Office. This includes:

- identifying someone incorrectly as the author or copyright claimant of the work
- registering an unpublished work as published, or
- inaccurately stating the extent of the copyright claim.

Errors in these important facts could cast doubt upon the validity and duration of your copyright and will needlessly confuse and complicate copyright litigation. They will also confuse anyone searching the Copyright Office records. Correct them as soon as you discover them.

Supplementary Registration Not Needed to Correct Obvious Errors the Copyright Office Should Have Caught

It is not necessary to file a formal supplementary registration to correct obvious errors the Copyright Office should have caught when it reviewed your application. This includes, for example, the omission of necessary information, such as the author or claimant's name, and obvious mistakes like listing an impossible publication date—for instance, 1022. When you receive your registration certificate, if you discover that such errors have been overlooked by the copyright examiner, simply notify the Copyright Office and the mistake will be corrected with no need for a supplementary registration and *no* additional fee.

Amplifications

For the same reasons discussed above, file a supplementary registration to:

- reflect important changes in facts that have occurred since the basic registration was made
- provide additional significant information that could have been provided in the original application but was not, or
- clarify or explain information in the basic registration.

Other Important Changes

Other important changes requiring a supplementary registration include the following:

If you have changed your address. File a supplementary registration to change the address listed on your certificate. It is not legally necessary for you to keep your address current in the Copyright Office's records. However, by doing so you will make it easy for people who want to use your work to locate you and arrange for permission and compensation. The harder you are to locate, the more likely it is that your copyright will be infringed.

If an author or copyright claimant was omitted. All the authors and copyright claimants must be listed in the registration. This means a supplementary registration should be filed if an author or copyright claimant's name was omitted.

EXAMPLE: Jack and Jill coauthored a children's book. Jill completed the registration form, but later discovered that she had forgotten to list Jack as a coauthor. A supplementary registration should be filed to add Jack's name.

Change in claimant's name. A supplementary registration should be made where the name of the copyright claimant has changed for reasons other than a transfer of ownership.

Change in title of the registered work. File a supplementary registration if you changed the title of the registered work without changing its content. However, if the content of the work is changed, a new registration will have to be made (see below).

Nature of authorship needs clarification. In some cases, it is a good idea to file a supplementary registration to correct or amplify the nature of authorship statement in the original registration.

EXAMPLE: Karen wrote and published a book on beekeeping in 2019. Karen never registered the book. In 2021, Karen revised and added several new chapters to her book. Karen registered this new edition with the Copyright Office. She stated "revision and chapters 9–12 added" in the nature of authorship section of her registration application. She did not complete the part of the application calling for information regarding derivative works. This registration would only protect the new material Karen added to her book; it would not protect the preexisting material that Karen never previously registered or described in her application.

Karen should file a supplementary registration to change the claim to "entire text." She should also describe the preexisting material and new material added to this derivative work. These changes will ensure that all the work she did will be protected by the registration.

When Supplementary Registration Is Not Appropriate

Some types of errors should not be corrected by supplementary registration. And supplementary registration may not be used to reflect some types of factual changes.

Changes in Copyright Ownership

Supplementary registration cannot be used to notify the Copyright Office of post-registration changes in ownership of a copyright, whether by license, inheritance, or other form of transfer. A special recordation procedure must be completed for changes in ownership. (See discussion in Chapter 7, "Transferring Copyright Ownership.")

Errors or Changes in Content of Registered Work

A supplementary registration cannot be filed to reflect corrections in the content of a registered work or other changes in that work.

Where such changes are so substantial as to make the new work a new version, it must be registered separately and a new deposit made. If the content changes are minor, there is no need to file a new registration because the original registration will provide adequate protection.

Errors in Copyright Notice

There is no need to file a supplementary registration where you discover and correct errors in the copyright notice.

Supplementary Registration Procedure

Filing a supplementary registration is a straightforward procedure.

When to File

You may file a supplementary registration any time during the existence of the copyright for a work that was published or registered after January 1, 1978. However, there is a time limit for works published or registered before that date. See a copyright attorney before filing a supplementary registration for a pre-1978 published work.

Who Can File

After the original basic registration has been completed, a supplementary registration may be filed by:

- any author or other copyright claimant in the work

- the owner of any exclusive right in the work, or
- the authorized agent of any of the above.

Online Application

You must submit your supplementary registration application online if you are correcting or amplifying the information in a registration for any work that was—or may be—registered through the Copyright Office's online system.

Paper Application

Use the Copyright Office's paper Form CA to file a supplementary registration for:

- a renewal registration for works published or registered before January 1, 1978
- a GATT registration (this is registration for a foreign work that was in the U.S. public domain but had its copyright restored under the international General Agreement on Tariffs and Trade (GATT) on January 1, 1996; see Chapter 11), or
- a group registration for a non-photographic database.

Registration Fee

Online supplementary registration costs $100. The fee for a paper filing is $150.

Effect of Supplementary Registration

If your application was completed correctly, the Copyright Office will assign you a new registration number and issue a certificate of supplementary registration under that number. The certificate is simply a copy of your Form CA with the new registration number, date, and certification stamped on it. Be sure to keep it in your records.

The information in a supplementary registration augments, but does not supersede, that contained in the original basic registration. The basic registration is not expunged or cancelled. However, if the person who filed the supplementary registration was the copyright claimant for the original registration (or the claimant's heir or transferee), the Copyright Office will place a note referring to the supplementary registration on its records of the basic registration. This way, anyone needing information regarding the registration will know there is a supplementary registration on file if an inquiry is made regarding the work.

What Copyright Protects

We said in Chapter 1, "Copyright Basics," that the copyright laws give authors and other copyright owners the exclusive right to reproduce, distribute, prepare derivative works based upon, display, and perform their work. This chapter explains that these rights extend only to a work's protected expression. It is vital to clearly understand what parts of a work constitute protected expression—and therefore belong exclusively to the author or another copyright owner—and what parts are not protected at all. Those aspects of a work that are not considered protected expression are in the public domain, free for all to use.

Only works containing protected expression may be registered with the Copyright Office in the manner described in Chapter 3, "Copyright Registration." When copyright owners sell or otherwise transfer their copyright ownership rights as described in Chapter 7, "Transferring Copyright Ownership," what they are selling is the right to use their protected expression. And, as described in Chapter 10, "Copyright Infringement," copyright owners have valid claims for copyright infringement against persons who use their work without permission only if it is protected expression that has been used.

What Copyright Protects: Tangible, Original Expression

Described at its most fundamental level, the creation of a book, an article, or other written work consists of selecting, from all the words in the English (or some other) language, a particular sequence of words and other symbols that communicate what the author wants to convey to his or her readers.

Subject to some important limitations we'll discuss below, copyright protects an author's particular choice of words from unauthorized use by others. But copyright protection does not end with the words an author uses. It also extends to an author's selection and arrangement of material—that is, his or her choices as to what the work should contain and the arrangement of those items.

An author's particular choice of words and selection and arrangement of material is called "expression." This is all that copyright protects.

However, not all expression is protected by copyright. An author's expression is protected only if, and to the extent, it satisfies the following three fundamental requirements.

Requirement #1: Fixation

The most basic requirement that a person's expression must meet to qualify for copyright protection is that it must be fixed in a "tangible medium of expression." The Copyright Act is not picky about how you fix your expression; any medium from which your expression can be read back or heard, either directly or with the aid of a machine, will suffice. In other words, your expression will be protected if you handwrite it on a piece of paper, save it on a computer or an online storage mechanism such as "the cloud," dictate it into a smartphone, act it out in front of a video camera, or use any other means to preserve it.

Copyright protection begins the instant you fix your expression. There is no waiting period, and it is not necessary to register with the Copyright Office (but, as discussed in Chapter 3, "Copyright Registration," very important benefits are obtained by doing so). Copyright protects both drafts and completed works and both published and unpublished works.

The Copyright Act does not protect oral expressions that go unrecorded, because they aren't fixed. Likewise, copyright does not protect expression that exists in your mind but that you have not set to paper or otherwise preserved. For example, if ancient Greece had had a copyright law the same as ours, Homer's *Iliad* (which, according to tradition, Homer composed and recited in public, but never wrote down or otherwise recorded) would not have been protected by the federal Copyright Act. However, such unfixed works may be protected by state copyright laws, also known as common law copyright.

California has a law that broadly recognizes rights in unfixed original works of authorship. (Cal. Civ. Code § 980.) Other states don't have such laws (though several do outlaw unauthorized commercial recording of live performances). Courts in some of these states have given common law copyright

protection to unfixed expressions, but the extent of such protection is far from clear. Several state courts have been reluctant to extend such protection very far. For example, a New York state court refused to give state law protection to a conversation the author Ernest Hemingway had with his biographer, A.E. Hotchner, which Hotchner reproduced years later in the book *Papa Hemingway* after Hemingway's death. The court held that for an oral statement to be protected by state law, the speaker would have to "mark off the utterance in question from the ordinary stream of speech" and indicate that he or she wished to exercise his or her control over its publication. (*Hemingway v. Random House, Inc.*, 296 N.Y.S.2d 771 (1968).)

This means that a person who wants to protect what is said during a conversation would have to say something like, "I reserve all my copyright rights in what I'm about to say." Obviously, people rarely do this during ordinary conversation.

On the other hand, courts may be more willing to give common law copyright protection to words spoken outside of ordinary conversation—for example, to unrecorded lectures and speeches. For instance, one court held that a professor's lectures were protected by common law copyright. (*Williams v. Weisser*, 273 Cal.App.2d 726 (1969).) There are distinct, identifiable boundaries to a speech or lecture—that is, a clear beginning and end—so it is easier for both the public and the courts to understand what is and is not protected.

Still other courts have refused to protect unfixed words at all. A court in New Jersey refused to grant common law copyright protection to the words spoken at a "scared straight" program in which inmates serving life sentences confronted juveniles who had begun experiencing difficulties with the law. (*Rowe v. Golden W. Television Prods.*, 184 N.J. Super. 264, 445 A.2d 1665 (1982).)

Requirement #2: Originality

A work consisting of expression that is written down or otherwise fixed in a tangible form is protected by copyright only if, and to the extent, it is original. But this does not mean that a written work must be novel—that is, new to the world—to be protected. For copyright purposes, a work is original if it—or at least a part of it—owes its origin to the author. A work's quality, ingenuity, aesthetic merit, or uniqueness is not considered. In short, the Copyright Act does not distinguish between the Great American Novel and a six-year-old's letter to her Aunt Sally; both are entitled to copyright protection to the extent they were not copied by the author—whether consciously or unconsciously—from other works. So long as a work was independently created by its author, it is protected even if other similar works already exist.

EXAMPLE: Tom and Tim are identical twins who do everything together. While on a Caribbean cruise, they enjoy a spectacular sunset and are so impressed, they decide to go back to their adjoining staterooms and each write a poem about it. Not surprisingly, the poems turn out to be almost identical—after all, the twins think virtually alike. However, since they were independently created, both poems are entitled to copyright protection despite the similarities.

Derivative Works and Compilations

It is not necessary that an entire work be independently created by its author for it to be protectable. Copyright protects works created by adapting, transforming, or combining previously existing material in new ways. These types of works are called derivative works or compilations and are discussed in Chapter 5, "Adaptations and Compilations." The main point to remember about derivative works and compilations here is that they aren't protected by copyright if they infringe upon a copyright in the original works.

Requirement #3: Minimal Creativity

Finally, a minimal amount of creativity— over and above the independent creation requirement—is necessary for copyright protection. Works completely lacking in creativity are denied copyright protection even if they have been independently created. However, the amount of creativity required is very slight. A work need not be novel, unique, ingenious, or even any good to be sufficiently creative. All that's required is that the work be the product of a very minimal creative spark. The vast majority of written works—including catalog copy, toy instructions, and third-rate poetry—make the grade.

Legal Protection for Cookbooks

If you publish your grandmother's special pie crust recipe in a cookbook, can it be freely copied? Unfortunately, a listing of ingredients for a recipe is not protected by copyright. But this doesn't mean there's no legal protection at all for cookbooks. The text in cookbooks—other than simple listings of ingredients—is protected, as are photographs and drawings. Cooking videos are protected as videos, but the recipes demonstrated in such videos are not protected.

Also, at least in theory, recipes can qualify for patent protection. However, chefs rarely apply for patents, because it's a long and expensive process, and only a small minority of recipes are patentable. To qualify for a patent, a recipe must be (1) novel—unique in some way, and (2) nonobvious—surprising to a chef of ordinary skill. Few recipes are both novel and nonobvious.

But there are some types of works that are usually deemed to contain no creativity at all. For example, a mere listing of ingredients or contents, such as in a recipe, is considered to be completely lacking in creativity and is not protectable (but explanatory material or another original expression in a recipe or another list is protectable). Telephone directory white pages are also deemed to lack even minimal creativity. Likewise, Internet domain names and URLs are not protectable—they are basically the online equivalent of a phone number or mailing address. Other listings of data might also completely lack creativity (see the detailed discussion in Chapter 5, "Adaptations and Compilations"). The Copyright Office will not register these types of works.

Examples of Works Containing Protected Expression

Let's now put these three requirements—fixation, originality, and minimal creativity—together by looking at a list containing examples of the types of works that commonly contain protected expression:

- advertising copy
- blank forms that convey information
- catalogs, directories, price lists, and other compilations of information
- fiction of any length and quality
- instructions
- interviews, lectures, speeches, jokes, and so on that are fixed in a tangible medium of expression
- leaflets and pamphlets
- letters and diaries, whether or not they have any artistic merit or general interest
- magazines, newspapers, newsletters, periodicals, journals, and other serial publications

- nonfiction of any length and quality
- plays
- poetry
- reference books and technical writings
- screenplays
- song lyrics, whether or not combined with music
- textbooks, and
- websites, blogs, and email.

Copyright Protection for Music, Movies, Sound Recordings, Computer Software, and Pictorial, Graphic, and Other Types of Work

This book focuses on copyright protection for works consisting wholly or primarily of words. However, copyright protects more than just words. Provided that the three fundamental requirements—fixation, originality, and minimal creativity—are met, copyright protects all types of expression, including music; pictorial, graphic, and sculptural works; motion pictures and other audiovisual works; sound recordings; pantomimes and choreographic works; and architectural works (architectural drawings and blueprints and the design of actual buildings). If you're interested in copyright protection for these types of works, refer to Chapter 14, "Help Beyond This Book."

Computer software and computer databases are also entitled to copyright protection.

What Copyright Does Not Protect: The Boundaries of the Public Domain

Towns and cities of the 18th and 19th centuries often had a common—a centrally located unfenced area of grassland that was free for all to use. Authors also have a common: It's called the public domain. The public domain contains everything that is not protected by copyright and is therefore free for all to use without permission.

Without the public domain, it would be virtually impossible for anyone to write anything without committing copyright infringement. This is because new expression is not created from thin air; all authors draw on what has been written before. As one copyright expert has noted, "Transformation is the essence of the authorship process. An author transforms her memories, experiences, inspirations, and influences into a new work. That work inevitably echoes expressive elements of prior works." (Jessica Litman, *The Public Domain*, 39 Emory L.J. 965 (Fall 1990).) Without the public domain, these echoes could not exist.

 RESOURCE

For a detailed discussion of all aspects of the public domain, including how to find public domain works, see *The Public Domain: How to Find & Use Copyright-Free Writings, Music, Art & More,* by Stephen Fishman (Nolo).

Ideas and Copyright

Copyright only protects an author's tangible expression of ideas, not the ideas themselves. Ideas, procedures, processes, systems, methods of operation, concepts, principles, and discoveries are all in the public domain, free for all to use. In effect, they're owned by everybody. (17 U.S.C. § 102(b).)

There is a good reason for this: If authors were allowed to obtain a monopoly over their ideas, the copyright laws would end up discouraging new authorship and the progress of knowledge—the two goals that copyright aims to foster.

However, although ideas are not protectable in themselves, an author's particular *selection and arrangement* of ideas can constitute protected expression. For example, an author's selection and arrangement of traits (ideas) that make up a literary character may be protected.

The Unclear Demarcation Between Ideas and Expression

It's easy to say that copyright does not protect ideas, only expression, but how do you tell the difference between an unprotected idea and its protected expression? These are very fuzzy concepts, and, in fact, no one has ever been able to fix an exact boundary between ideas and expression; probably nobody ever can. But after you read the following material, you should gain a better understanding of this dichotomy.

Patent Laws Protect Ideas for Inventions

Ideas embodied in novel and nonobvious inventions can be protected under U.S. and foreign patent laws. For a detailed discussion, see *Patent It Yourself*, by David Pressman and David E. Blau (Nolo).

Facts and Copyright

Copyright does not protect facts—whether scientific, historical, biographical, or news of the day. If the first person to write about a fact had a monopoly over it, the spread of knowledge would be greatly impeded. Another reason why copyright law does not protect facts is that an author does not independently create facts; at most, he or she may discover a previously unknown fact. Census takers, for example, do not create the population figures that emerge from a census; in a sense, they copy these figures from the world around them. The Copyright Act does not protect discoveries. (17 U.S.C. § 102(b).)

So, the facts contained in works such as news stories, histories, biographies, and scientific treatises are not protectable. Subject to the important limitation of the merger doctrine discussed below, all that is protected is the author's original expression of the facts contained in such works.

Legal Protection for "Hot News"

Although facts are not protected by copyright, state unfair competition laws might protect them in certain narrowly defined situations. For example, a court has held that "hot news" is protected under such laws if the following are true:

- A person or company generates highly time-sensitive factual information at some cost or expense.
- Another person's or entity's use of the information constitutes free-riding on the fact gatherer's costly efforts to collect the information.
- The use of the information is in direct competition with a product or service offered by the fact gatherer.
- Other people free-riding on the fact gatherer's efforts would threaten its ability to stay in business.

For example, it would likely be unlawful for a newspaper to copy news stories contained in a competing newspaper and print them as its own. But a company that used pagers to transmit to subscribers real-time NBA game scores and other information tabulated from television and radio broadcasts of basketball games did not commit misappropriation, because there was no free-riding involved. The company collected the scores itself; it didn't steal them from the NBA. (*Nat'l Basketball Assoc. v. Motorola, Inc.*, 105 F.3d 841 (2d Cir. 1997).) Similarly, there was no actionable misappropriation where a website aggregated and published, before the stock market opened each day, the recommendations made by three investment management firms. There was no free-riding because the investment recommendations reported by the defendant were the news itself—the defendant was merely reporting their existence. (*Barclays Capital, Inc. v. Theflyonthewall.com, Inc.*, 650 F.3d 876 (2d Cir. 2011).)

The Merger Doctrine—When Ideas, Facts, and Their Expression Merge

Sometimes there is just one way, or only a few ways, to adequately express a particular idea or fact. If the first person to write about such an idea or fact could copyright the expression, that person would effectively have a monopoly over that idea or fact itself—that is, no one else could write about it without the original author's permission. The copyright law does not permit this, because it would discourage authorship of new works and thereby impede the progress of knowledge. In these cases, the idea or fact and its particular expression are deemed to merge, and the expression—the author's words—is either treated as if it were in the public domain or given very limited copyright protection.

The merger doctrine applies mainly to factual works, such as histories, biographies, and scientific treatises, rather than to works of fancy, such as novels, plays, and poems. This is because the ideas and facts in factual works can often be expressed only in one particular way or only in a few ways, while the ideas contained in novels and similar works can usually be expressed in a wide variety of ways.

For example, assume you wish to write an unadorned factual account of Paul Revere's famous midnight ride during the Revolutionary War. You research Revere's life and create a work containing, in part, the following sequence of words:

On April 18, 1775, the Boston minutemen learned that the British intended to march on Concord with a detachment of 700 men. Paul Revere arranged for a signal to be flashed from the steeple of the Old North Church in Boston. Two lanterns would mean that the British were coming by water, and one, by land.

The particular selection and arrangement of words in the above paragraph appears to satisfy the three requirements for copyright protection: fixation, originality, and minimal creativity. Does this mean that if anyone used these three sentences without your permission they would be liable for copyright infringement? Because of the merger doctrine, the answer is probably not. This is because if anyone else wrote a brief factual account of Paul Revere's ride, it would necessarily have to contain sentences looking very much like those in your paragraph. This would be so even though the author had never read your account—there are just not many different ways to express the facts described in your paragraph. For example, how many different words can an author use to explain that one

lantern meant that the British were coming by land and two by sea? The facts pretty much dictate the form of expression here.

As a result, if your paragraph were protected by copyright, nobody else could ever write a factual account of Paul Revere's ride without your permission. The copyright law cannot permit this result, because it would effectively give you a monopoly over the facts concerning Paul Revere's ride. To prevent this, the facts of Paul Revere's ride and the words you used to express them would be deemed to merge. Some courts would hold that your paragraph was in the public domain and could be copied verbatim (or used in any other way) without your permission. Other courts would not go quite this far; they would give your paragraph limited protection by holding that your paragraph was protected from unauthorized verbatim copying, but nothing else. (See *Landsberg v. Scrabble Crossword Game Players, Inc.,* 736 F.2d 485 (9th Cir. 1984); *Morrissey v. Procter & Gamble Co.,* 379 F.2d 675 (1st Cir. 1967).)

In contrast, the merger doctrine would not be applied to a work of fancy—for example, a poem—about Paul Revere's ride. Consider this:

Listen, my children, and you shall hear
Of the midnight ride of Paul Revere,
On the eighteenth of April, in Seventy-five.
Hardly a man is now alive
Who remembers that famous day and year.
He said to his friend, "If the British march

By land or sea from the town tonight,
Hold a lantern aloft in the belfry arch
Of the North Church tower as a signal light,
One, if by land, and two, if by sea.

These stanzas were written by Henry Wadsworth Longfellow over 100 years ago and are thus in the public domain because the copyright has expired—see Chapter 8, "Copyright Duration." But let's pretend for purposes of our example that they were written just the other day.

This verse conveys almost exactly the same factual information as your paragraph above, yet the facts and expression would not be deemed to merge. Why? Because the author's words are embellished and highly distinctive. The sequence of words has not been dictated solely by the facts. Indeed, it is the unique word sequence itself, not the facts, that is the work's main attraction. No one needs to copy this particular word sequence in order to convey the same facts or to write another work of fancy about Paul Revere's ride. A person who copied even the first two lines would probably be found to have infringed on the copyright in the poem.

> **TIP**
> **Nonfiction writers should not get the idea that they need to start writing in poetic meter to obtain copyright protection.** But the more distinctive their words, the more protection they will receive. An elegantly written

biography of Paul Revere will receive more protection than an unadorned factual account. Similarly, Loren Eiseley, Stephen Jay Gould, and Lewis Thomas have all written books about science whose language transcends the way their subjects are normally handled. The prose in their books receives far more protection than that of a run-of-the-mill scientific treatise. The moral is that the more effort you take to make your writing transcend the mundane and purely functional, the more copyright protection your work will receive.

Words, Names, Titles, Slogans, and Other Short Phrases

Individual words are always in the public domain, even if they are invented by a particular person. Names (whether of individuals, products, or business organizations or groups), titles, slogans, and other short phrases (for example, "I'd walk a mile for a Camel" and "No Smoking") are not protected by copyright law, even if they are highly creative, novel, or distinctive, and will not be registered by the Copyright Office. (37 C.F.R. § 202.1(a).) However, these items—especially slogans—may be protectable under the trademark laws. (See Chapter 1, "Copyright Basics.") Most tweets—messages up to 280 characters long—posted on Twitter.com are not protectable because they are too short. The Copyright Office has refused to register tweets because they are unprotectable short phrases.

Titles May Be Protectable Under State Law

Although titles are not protected by the Copyright Act, they may be protected under state and federal unfair competition laws (that is, laws that prohibit unfair competitive business practices). Under these laws, an author may protect a title from unauthorized use if the following are true:

- The title is strongly identified in the public's mind with the author's work.
- The author proves that the public will be confused if the title is used in another work.

These laws prevent a person from passing off or palming off a work on the public—that is, publishing a work with the same or similar title as a previously published, well-known work in the hope that people will buy it because they confuse it with the well-known work.

> **EXAMPLE:** A successful play called *The Gold Diggers* was made into a film entitled *Gold Diggers of Broadway*. The film's producers sued the producer of a subsequent film called *Gold Diggers of Paris* for passing off. The court held that it was unlawful for *Gold Diggers of Paris* to be marketed under that title, at least without a conspicuous disclaimer that the picture was not based on the play or the earlier picture. The court found that the title "Gold Diggers" was strongly identified in the public's mind with a series of films based on the original play. Moreover, use of the words "Gold Diggers" in the title of the defendants' film was unfair and misleading, because they would represent to the public that the film was produced by Warner Bros. Pictures and based on the play. (*Warner Bros. Pictures, Inc. v. Majestic Pictures Corp.,* 70 F.2d 310 (2d Cir. 1934).)

Titles May Be Protectable as Trademarks

The title of a single book or another written work cannot be protected as a trademark. However, trademark protection may be available for:

- titles for a series of books—for example, the title for a series of fishing guide books called *Fishing Hot Spots* that was protectable as a trademark (*Fishing Hot Spots, Inc. v. Simon & Schuster*, 720 F. Supp. 746 (E.D. Wis. 1989)), and
- titles of newspapers, magazines, and other periodicals—for example, the magazine called *Atlantic Monthly*. (*Atlantic Monthly Co. v. Frederick Ungar Publishing Co.*, 197 F. Supp. 524 (S.D.N.Y. 1961).)

However, if the title describes the contents of the work—which is probably the case with most titles—it must have "secondary meaning" to be eligible for trademark protection. This means that the title must become distinctive in the minds of the public over time through long, widespread use or intensive advertising. For example, the title *Aviation Magazine* was found to be descriptive of the magazine's contents, but the court decided it lacked a secondary meaning required to be protectable as a trademark. (*McGraw-Hill Pub. Co. v. American Aviation Assoc., Inc.*, 117 F.2d 293 (D.C. Cir. 1940).) On the other hand, a court found that the title *Photoplay* magazine, although descriptive, had attained secondary meaning and was entitled to protection. (*Photoplay Pub. Co. v. La Verne Pub. Co.*, 269 F. 730 (3d Cir. 1921).)

For a detailed discussion of trademarks, refer to *Trademark: Legal Care for Your Business & Product Name*, by Stephen Fishman (Nolo).

Quotations

The author of a news story, biography, history, oral history, or similar work may not claim copyright ownership of statements made by others and quoted verbatim in the work. Reason: A verbatim quotation of what someone else says is not original.

> EXAMPLE: The author of a book about motion pictures included, in a section on John Wayne, quotations from third-person interviews and excerpts from two letters never previously published that were unearthed through the author's research. Subsequently, *Newsweek* magazine published an obituary of Wayne that used quotations from the interviews and letters contained in the author's book. The author sued *Newsweek* for copyright infringement and lost. The

court held that the author held no copyright in the quotations because they were not original—that is, the author didn't say them, other people did. (*Suid v. Newsweek Magazine*, 503 F. Supp. 146 (D.D.C. 1980).)

However, this doesn't mean the quotations are always in the public domain. If the quote is written down or otherwise recorded with the speaker's authorization, it is protected by federal copyright law. The copyright is owned by the speaker. Typically, the person who writes down or records the speaker's words will have the speaker's permission to use the quotes. Such permission may be expressed or implied by the fact that the speaker consented to an interview.

In addition, a conversation reconstructed by an author from memory, rather than quoted verbatim from written notes or a recording, may be protectable by the author (not the person who made the original remarks) if some originality was involved in reconstructing the conversation. (*Harris v. Miller*, 50 U.S.P.Q. 306 (S.D.N.Y. 1941).) Moreover, the selection and arrangement of all the quotations in a book of quotations may be a protectable compilation, although the individual quotations are not protected. (*Quinto v. Legal Times of Washington, Inc.*, 506 F. Supp. 554 (D.D.C. 1981).) One or more of the individual quotations in such a book could be copied without the compiler's permission, but verbatim copying of the entire book would infringe on the compiler's copyright.

But there are many instances where quotations *are* in the public domain. For example:

- A quotation by a federal government employee spoken as part of his or her duties is in the public domain. This includes official speeches by the president and Congresspeople.
- Quotations that are written down and published enter the public domain when the copyright in the published work expires. (See Chapter 8, "Copyright Duration.")
- Quotations that are simply short phrases may also be in the public domain.
- Quotations from public domain sources—for example, from a book whose copyright has expired or never existed, such as a Shakespeare play or the King James version of the Bible—are in the public domain. Republishing them in a new work does not revive their copyright.

In addition, for a quotation to be copyrightable, it must be written down or recorded *with the speaker's authorization.* A quotation recorded without the speaker's authorization is not protected by copyright. Good examples are the many phone conversations Linda Tripp had with Monica Lewinsky that Tripp secretly recorded without Lewinsky's permission. Monica's portion of these conversations is not protected by the federal Copyright Act. Unless they can be protected under state law, they are in the public domain.

Blank Forms

Blank forms designed solely to record information are in the public domain. The Copyright Office will not register such items. (37 C.F.R. § 202.1(c).) According to the Copyright Office, this includes such items as time cards, graph paper, account books, bank checks, scorecards, address books, diaries, report forms, and order forms. The rule also applies to digital forms—for example, digital forms used to process automated teller machine (ATM) transactions. (*Datacarrier S.A. v. WOCCU Servs. Group, Inc.*, No. 16-CV-122-JDP (W.D. Wis. Mar. 27, 2018).)

However, forms that themselves convey information are protected and may be registered. The problem with this distinction is determining when a form does and does not convey protectable information. Even a true blank form—that is, a form consisting primarily of blank space to be filled in—can convey information. The columns or headings on a blank form may be interlaced with highly informative verbiage. Moreover, the configuration of columns, headings, and lines may itself convey information.

The courts have been inconsistent in interpreting the blank form rule and its information conveyance exception. Courts have denied copyright protection to such items as:

- charts used to record emergency room patients' symptoms, which consist of blocks to be filled in (*Utopia Provider Systems, Inc. v. Pro-Med Systems, LLC*, 596 F.3d 1313 (11th Cir. 2010))
- a time log chart that graphed hours in the business day on the vertical axis and the day's project and activities on the horizontal axis (*Januz Marketing Communications, Inc. v. Doubleday & Co. Inc.*, 569 F. Supp. 76 (S.D.N.Y. 1982)), and
- a medical "superbill" form containing spaces for patient information and lists of procedures and diagnoses to be performed by doctors (*Bibbero Systems, Inc. v. Colwell Systems, Inc.*, 893 F.2d 1104 (9th Cir. 1990)).

In contrast, other courts have extended copyright protection to a form used to record medical laboratory tests (*Norton Printing Co. v. Augustana Hosp.*, 155 U.S.P.Q. 133 (N.D. Ill. 1967)); record-keeping forms with instructions (*Edwin K. Williams & Co. v. Edwin K. Williams & Co.-East*, 542 F.2d 1053 (9th Cir. 1976)); and an answer sheet for a standard multiple-choice examination, designed to be graded

by an optical scanning machine (*Harcourt, Brace & World, Inc. v. Graphic Controls Corp.*, 329 F. Supp. 517 (S.D.N.Y. 1971).)

The general rule appears to be that the more word sequences (as opposed to simple headings) a form contains, the more likely it is to be protectable. Forms that contain substantial textual material—for example, insurance policies, contracts, and other legal forms—are probably protectable. However, where there are only a few ways to express the facts and ideas contained in such forms, the merger doctrine comes into play to severely limit protection. For example, one court held that insurance bond forms and indemnity agreements were protectable, but because the forms contained standard language that would have to be included in any form designed to accomplish the same purpose, only verbatim copying of the forms' exact wording would constitute infringement. (*Continental Cas. Co. v. Beardsley*, 253 F.2d 702 (2d Cir. 1958).)

TIP

If you have produced any type of form that you want protected by copyright, by all means, register it with the Copyright Office.

Compilations of Forms

To make things even more complicated, works consisting of forms designed solely for recording information may nevertheless be protectable as compilations if originality has been employed in selecting which items of information are to be recorded and in the arrangement of such items. In this event, copyright protection extends only to the compiler's selection or arrangement of all the forms as a group. In one case, for example, a court held that the blank forms contained in an organizer (including calendars, telephone and address pages, and sections for recording daily activities) were not copyrightable. But the organizer as a whole was a protected compilation. However, the defendant was not liable for copyright infringement because it only copied a part of the organizer, not the whole thing. (*Harper House, Inc. v. Thomas Nelson, Inc.*, 889 F.2d 197, (9th Cir. 1989).) See Chapter 5, "Adaptations and Compilations," for a discussion of compilations.

Government Works

Government edicts, such as judicial opinions, legislation, public ordinances, administrative rulings, and similar official legal documents, are all in the public domain. This rule applies to all levels of government—local, state, and federal—and even includes foreign government edicts.

Works by Federal Grantees

Works created for the federal government by independent contractors—that is, persons who are neither U.S. government officers nor employees—can be protected by copyright. However, the government may require these persons to sign work-made-for-hire agreements as a condition of receiving federal money. In this event, the U.S. government, not the individual who actually wrote the work, would be considered the author of the work; this would mean that the work would be in the public domain. See Chapter 6, "Initial Copyright Ownership," for detailed discussion of work-made-for-hire agreements.

Other types of works created by U.S. government officers and employees as part of their jobs are also in the public domain. This includes, for example, everything published by the U.S. Government Publishing Office, Internal Revenue Service, Copyright Office, and Patent and Trademark Office, and all the president's official speeches. But this rule does not apply to works by state and local government employees; those works may be protected by copyright. For example, a state tax pamphlet or booklet on air pollution or water conservation published by a city or county may be protected.

Works in Which Copyright Protection Has Expired or Was Never Obtained

The public domain also includes works whose copyright has expired and some works published without a copyright notice.

Works Whose Copyright Has Expired

Copyright protection does not last forever. When a work's copyright protection expires, it enters the public domain and is freely available to anyone. All works published in the United States over 95 years ago are in the public domain. So are many works published as recently as 1963 if the copyright owner failed to renew the copyright. See the detailed discussion of copyright duration and renewal in Chapter 8, "Copyright Duration."

Works Published Without a Copyright Notice

Works published before March 1, 1989 without a valid copyright notice may also be in the public domain. However, you can never assume that a pre-1989 work that lacks a valid notice is in the public domain, because several exceptions exist to the notice requirement that may have saved the work from entering the public domain. For example, an unnoticed work did not enter the public domain if the notice was omitted from a small number of copies, the omission was corrected, or the notice was removed without the copyright owner's permission. (See 18 U.S.C. § 405.). Because of these exceptions, it can be very difficult—sometimes impossible—to determine whether

a pre-1989 work that lacks a notice is in the public domain.

Distinguishing Between Protected Expression and Material in the Public Domain: Putting It All Together

Now let's review the information we have just covered by looking at examples of protectable and public domain elements in works of fancy and factual works. Works of fancy include novels, short stories, plays, screenplays, and poems. A factual work is a work of nonfiction, such as a biography, history, news story, how-to book, or scientific treatise.

What's Protected in a Work of Fancy

Let's start by evaluating this example for a work of fancy. Sue writes a novel about police work set in the South Bronx. Narrated by a rookie cop named Walker, the novel begins on her first day at the 41st Precinct station house, where she is shocked by its squalor. The book unfolds as a chronicle of police work and daily life in a violent neighborhood. Several chapters focus on specific topics, such as attacks on police officers. Throughout the book, Walker expresses compassion for those she considers the victims of the South Bronx, hopelessness regarding the prospects for basic improvement in the area, and a fear that the officers of the 41st Precinct will continue to fight

Protection for Distinctive Characters

Some courts have held that distinctively "delineated" original characters are protectable. These court rulings appear to suggest that no one can copy the particular original combination and selection of qualities—such as personality traits, physical attributes, and mode of dress—that make the character distinctive. An author's selection and combination of such distinctive qualities (ideas) is deemed to constitute protectable expression.

Unfortunately, there are no uniform standards for judging when a character is or is not sufficiently distinctive to be protectable. Copyright protection has been extended to such disparate characters as Tarzan, Amos 'n' Andy, Hopalong Cassidy, and E.T. but was denied for the characters of Sam Spade and the Lone Ranger.

Is Sam Spade any less distinctive than Hopalong Cassidy? The only general rule is that "the less developed the characters, the less they can be copyrighted." (*Nichols v. Universal Pictures Corp.*, 45 F.2d 119 (2d Cir. 1930).) In addition, the owners of some well-known characters have sought to protect them under state and federal trademark laws. For example, Lois Lane, the Teenage Mutant Ninja Turtles, and Spiderman have all been federally registered as trademarks or service marks. State unfair competition and misappropriation laws have also been used to try to protect characters. For more information on trademarks, see *Trademark: Legal Care for Your Business & Product Name*, by Stephen Fishman (Nolo).

When a fictional work enters the public domain, its characters do as well. However, there can be complications when a character is used in numerous works, some of which are in the public domain and some of which are not. For example, an appeals court ruled that the four novels and 46 short stories containing the characters Sherlock Holmes and Dr. Watson that were published by Arthur Conan Doyle before January 1, 1923, are in the public domain in the United States, because their copyrights have all expired. The characters of Holmes and Watson, as depicted in these novels and stories may be freely used. However, Doyle published ten Holmes stories after 1923 that are still under copyright in the United States. The appeals court held that that the elements first introduced in these post-1923 stories—such as the fact that Watson played rugby for Blackheath and had a second wife—remain under copyright in the United States. The last of these 10 stories will enter the public domain in 2023. (*Klinger v. Conan Doyle Estate, Ltd.*, No. 14-1128, 755 F.3d 496, 761 F.3d 789 (7th Cir. 2014); see also https://freesherlock.com.)

a rearguard action against lawlessness with very limited success. The book ends with her transfer to another precinct.

Unprotectable Aspects of a Work of Fancy

We'll first examine those aspects of Sue's novel that are not protectable under the copyright law.

The idea to create a novel about police officers in the South Bronx. The underlying idea to create a certain type of work is always in the public domain. Thus, the fact that other authors have written many novels about police officers (including some set in the Bronx) does not preclude Sue (or anyone else) from writing another one.

The work's theme. The theme of Sue's novel—the hopelessness of the situation in the South Bronx and, by extension, all urban America—is in the public domain. Another novelist is free to express the same theme in his or her own words. A theme is an unprotectable idea, not a protectable expression.

The work's setting. A fictional work's setting—that is, the time and place in which the story occurs—is not protected by copyright. Anyone can write a story set in the 41st Precinct of the Bronx. But the particular words Sue used to describe this setting are protectable. For example, Sue described one vacant lot as "filled with the refuse of stunted lives; a dead place, with no colors and no smells ... not even the garbage smelled." This sequence of words is protected.

The work's basic plot. A fictional work's plot—that is, the sequence of events by which Sue or any other author expresses his or her theme or idea—is a selection and arrangement of ideas. We know that ideas themselves are not protected, but an author's selection and arrangement of ideas does constitute protected expression to the extent that it's original (independently created). So, Sue's plot constitutes protectable expression only to the extent it was independently created by her.

Plots are rarely protectable, because there are very few independently created plots. One literary critic has noted that "authors spin their plots from a relatively small number of 'basic situations,' changing characters, reversing roles, giving modern twists to classic themes." (*The Thirty-Six Dramatic Situations*, by George Polti (The Writer, Inc.).) For example, the plot of the film *The Dirty Dozen* is basically a World War II updating of *Jason and the Argonauts*. And authors have recycled the time-tested plot of boy gets girl, boy loses girl, boy gets girl back, over and over again throughout the centuries. Naturally, these basic plots are all in the public domain; otherwise, it would be very difficult, if not impossible, for anyone to create a "new" work of fancy.

Independently created variations or twists on basic plots would constitute protected expression. But there aren't very many new plot twists, either. For example, can you think of any variations on the boy meets girl scenario that haven't been done before?

The plot of Sue's novel may be described as follows: Idealistic young person joins urban police force, gets assigned to inner city, sees horrors of life there, and ends up disillusioned. It's hard to see anything original in this. There are doubtless hundreds of other police stories with similar plots.

The work's scenes and situations. There are certain sequences of events, scenes, situations, or details that necessarily follow from a fictional work's given theme or setting. The French call these *scènes à faire* (that which must follow a certain situation). Sue's novel includes scenes involving drunks, prostitutes, stripped cars, rats, and a car chase. Any novel about police work in the South Bronx, West Oakland, East Los Angeles, or any other major city would likely include such elements. Such predictable—or stock—story elements are all unprotectable ideas.

However, to the extent they are original, the particular words an author uses to describe or narrate a *scène à faire* are protected, even though the idea for the scene is not. Thus, although any author can write a police novel that includes a scene involving a high-speed car chase, he or she could not copy the words Sue used to describe the car chase in her novel.

The work's stock characters. Similarly, there are many standard character types that have developed in fiction over time— for example, the eccentric little old lady; the tall, silent, strong cowboy; the two-fisted, hard-drinking private detective; and the streetwise, fast-talking urban hustler.

Because they are not original creations, these character types are not protectable; they are part of the stock of ideas that all fiction writers may draw upon. For example, one of the characters in Sue's novel is police Sergeant Jim McCarthy, a hard-drinking, fourth-generation Irish cop who's seen it all. Such a sketchily drawn stock character, commonly found in police stories, would not be protected. Any author of a police thriller is free to use such a character.

TIP

Never use a well-known character— either by name or detailed description—from a copyrighted work without first consulting a copyright attorney or disguising the character to such an extent that it is not recognizable. Even if the character doesn't seem sufficiently distinctive to you to merit protection, its creator and publisher might feel quite differently and sue you for copyright infringement.

The work's facts. Sue's novel is extremely well researched. She describes what police officers do and how they do it in great detail, and realistically catalogs the conditions of life in the South Bronx. Indeed, her novel is a better source of factual information on the South Bronx than many guidebooks or sociological studies. Of course, facts are not protectable, so all of the factual information contained in Sue's novel is in the public domain.

The work's writing style and individual words and phrases. Sue's novel is written in a highly unusual stream-of-consciousness style. She also invented new slang words and phrases for her characters to use. Neither Sue's style nor her new words and phrases are protectable. The original and creative word sequences in Sue's novel are protected by copyright. But a writing style itself is in the public domain, no matter how original it is. So are the individual words and short phrases a work contains, even if the author invented them. For example, the new words and phrases in George Orwell's *1984*—"newspeak" and "I love Big Brother"—entered the public domain (and enriched our language) the moment Orwell published them.

The work's literary devices. Finally, literary devices such as the story within a story, flashbacks, the epistolary novel, prosodic forms, and rhetorical devices such as alliteration are all unprotectable ideas.

Protected Expression in a Work of Fancy

You might be wondering just what *is* protected by copyright law in a work of fancy. All that is protected is the author's original expression. This includes, of course, the particular sequence of words Sue has chosen to tell her story. But her protected expression does not end there. To create her novel, Sue had to select, arrange, and combine all the unprotected elements listed above—theme, setting, plot, characters, scenes, and situations—into an integrated whole. To the extent it is original (independently created), this selection and combination also constitutes protected expression. For lack of better terms, courts sometimes call this a work's "total concept and feel" or its "overall pattern" or "fundamental essence."

What's Protected in a Factual Work

Let's imagine that Commodore Hornblower spends 12 years researching the sinking of *RMS Titanic*. He scours archives in Britain and America and interviews the remaining survivors. He then writes and publishes a 500-page book describing the *Titanic*'s voyage in minute detail. The book contains many previously unknown facts; for example, that the ship's captain actually survived the sinking and lived out his life as a circus performer under an assumed name. The book ends with a startling new interpretation of the facts: The *Titanic* struck the fatal iceberg because it was sailing too fast, and it was sailing too fast because there was an out-of-control fire in one of its coal bunkers—it was desperately trying to reach port before the fire destroyed the ship.

Unprotectable Elements of Factual Works

The following aspects of Hornblower's book are in the public domain.

Research. The facts that an author discovers in the course of research are in the public domain, free to all. This is so even if an author spends considerable effort conducting the research. Copyright does not protect the fruits of creative research, no matter how grueling or time-consuming the research may have been. Copyright only protects fixed, original, and minimally creative expression. Thus, copyright does not protect the previously unknown facts about the *Titanic*'s voyage that the commodore discovered, even though it took him 12 years to discover them. Anyone is free to use these facts—for example, that the captain actually survived the sinking—in any way desired. But see the discussion of plagiarism in Chapter 10, "Copyright Infringement."

Quotations from public domain materials. Hornblower included in his book numerous quotations from newspaper reports about the sinking. These reports, first published before 1923, are in the public domain. Their inclusion in Hornblower's book does not revive their copyright protection. Anyone can use these quotations in a work of their own. They don't have to go back to the original sources.

Author's interpretation of facts. An author's interpretation of facts is itself a fact (or a purported fact) that is deduced from other facts. Interpretations are therefore also in the public domain. Thus, the commodore's theory as to what caused the *Titanic* to hit the iceberg (the need to reach

port quickly due to the coal bunker fire) is no more protectable than the fact that the *Titanic* hit an iceberg.

Book design. The commodore's publisher spared no expense on his book. It is filled with photos and beautifully designed. Is the book's "look" protected by copyright? No. Book designs—that is, a book's physical and visual attributes—are considered to be unprotectable ideas. This includes the choice of typeface style and size, leading (space between lines of type), arrangement of type on pages and placement, and spacing and juxtaposition of text and illustrations.

Protected Expression in Factual Works

We now turn to those aspects of a factual work that *are* protected by copyright.

Literal expression of facts. An author's literal expression of facts is, theoretically, entitled to protection so long as it is original. Thus, anyone who copied the commodore's words verbatim or closely paraphrased a substantial portion of the language in his book would infringe on his copyright. However, because there are often only a few ways to express the facts contained in factual works, the protection they receive may be greatly limited through application of the merger doctrine. In addition, selected passages of Hornblower's book probably could be quoted under the fair use privilege. (See discussion in Chapter 9, "Using Other Authors' Words.")

Fictional elements in factual works. Hornblower was not only a dogged researcher, but had a vivid imagination as well. He included in his book certain scenes and dialogue among the *Titanic*'s passengers and crew that seemed to him likely to have occurred but were still completely fictional. Fictional expressions in otherwise factual works are entitled to full copyright protection. However, an author who represents his or her work to be completely factual may not bring a copyright infringement suit against someone who, relying on such representations, copies a portion of it thinking it was unprotectable fact when it was really protectable fiction. (*Houts v. Universal City Studios, Inc.*, 603 F. Supp. 26 (C.D. Cal. 1984).)

Selection or arrangement of facts. In writing his book, the commodore had to select which facts to write about and arrange them in a certain order. Is this selection and arrangement protected expression? If the commodore simply arranged the facts of the *Titanic*'s voyage and sinking in chronological order, probably not. A historical chronology is itself a fact that is in the public domain.

But what if the commodore organized the facts contained in his book in an original nonchronological way; shouldn't that original arrangement be protected? Some courts say yes, others disagree. (Compare *Pacific & Southern Co., Inc. v. Duncan*, 744 F.2d 1490 (11th Cir. 1984) ("editorial judgment" makes a new presentation of

facts an "original work of authorship") with *Hoehling v. Universal City Studios, Inc.*, 618 F.2d 972 (2d Cir. 1980) ("there cannot be any such thing as copyright in the order of presentation of the facts, nor, indeed in their selection").)

Copyright in the Online World

Far more written works are available online in digital form, in electronic databases, than in all the libraries of the world. Widespread confusion exists as to whether and how much copyright protects written and other works in the online world, or whether it can protect them at all. The remainder of this chapter explores how copyright applies in the digital world.

What Online Materials Qualify for Copyright

Copyright protects all types of works of authorship, including all kinds of written works, photos, artwork, videos, films, and sound recordings. A digital version of a work of authorship is entitled to copyright protection if the requirements discussed below are satisfied. The fact that a work in its digital form can be read only by computers—because it consists only of ones and zeros—does not affect copyright protection. Computer "language" is protectable under copyright, just like recorded human words and speech.

Under the copyright laws, the moment a work of authorship is created, it is automatically protected by copyright if, and to the extent, it is:

- original—that is, not copied from others
- fixed in a tangible medium of expression, and
- minimally creative. (See above for a detailed discussion.)

All three requirements are easily met in the online world.

Originality and Creativity

The originality and creativity requirements pose no special problems at all. A work is sufficiently original if it was independently created—that is, not copied from other works.

Are RAM Copies Copies?

A digital work doesn't have to be stored on permanent physical media like a hard disk to be used. Instead, it can be stored in temporary computer memory, also known as RAM (short for random access memory). RAM exists only while a computer is turned on. For example, a computer user may download (copy) a work from the Internet to the RAM in a computer. The downloaded copy exists for as long as the computer is on—which could be minutes, hours, weeks, or longer. The computer user can read the copy on the computer display or otherwise use the copy. But after turning off the computer, the copy is lost unless it is first saved to a permanent storage medium, like a hard disk.

Most courts have held that a RAM copy of a work is a copy for copyright purposes. Because a RAM copy can theoretically exist for a very long time (even years, if a user keeps a computer on that long), these courts view it as being sufficiently fixed to merit copyright protection. (*MAI Systems Corp. v. Peak Computer, Inc.*, 991 F.2d 511 (9th Cir. 1993); Quantum Sys. *Integrators, Inc. v. Sprint*

Nextel Corp., 338 Fed. Appx. 329, 336-337 (4th Cir. 2009).)

If a RAM copy of a work is a copy for copyright purposes, simply reading or viewing a work online could technically constitute an infringement of the copyright owner's reproduction right, unless it is done with permission or qualifies as a fair use. It seems likely that simply reading or viewing a work online is a fair use. Or, at the very least, it's likely people who post their works on the Internet and online services give their implied permission for others to read them—after all, why else would they place them online?

In any event, some copyright experts believe that loading a digital copy into computer RAM is not copying as defined in the copyright law, since the "copy" only exists temporarily and is lost when the computer is shut off. Under this view, reading or browsing copyrighted works online is permissible as long as a permanent copy is not made—for example, on a hard disk, flash drive, or hard-copy printout.

The amount of creativity required is very slight. It's sufficient that a work be the product of a very minimal creative spark. It doesn't have to be novel, unique, ingenious, or even any good to be sufficiently creative. But still, some works of expression lack even this minimal level of creativity. One good example of "expression" that was denied copyright protection was telephone directory white pages. (See above for detailed discussion.)

Fixed in a Tangible Medium of Expression

A work that is original and minimally creative must also be fixed in a tangible medium of expression to be protected by copyright—for example, written down on paper or recorded on film or tape. Words that are thought or spoken but never recorded in some tangible medium are not protected.

There are many ways to fix an expression in the online world once it's reduced to digital form. For example, it can be fixed on a computer hard disk, flash drive, CD-ROM, or online storage medium such as "the cloud."

Rights Enjoyed by Copyright Owners Online

Under the general copyright laws, the owner of a work of authorship entitled to copyright protection automatically acquires a bundle of exclusive copyright rights. Exclusive means no one may exercise these rights without the copyright owner's permission.

Anyone who does will be liable to the owner for copyright infringement. These exclusive rights are the:

- reproduction right—that is, the right to make copies of a protected work
- distribution right—that is, the right to initially sell or otherwise distribute copies to the public
- right to create adaptations (or "derivative works")—that is, the right to prepare new works based on the protected work, and
- performance and display rights—that is, the right to perform or display a work in public.

These exclusive copyright rights exist in the online world the same way they do in the physical world. Just as copyright protects words printed in books, available to anyone with access to a bookstore or library, it also protects words which are input into computer systems and made available to people with computers and modems. It's important to remember, however, that although a copyright owner's rights are exclusive, they are subject to some important exceptions, most notably the fair use privilege.

Let's now take a closer look at what these copyright rights are and how they apply in the online world.

Reproduction Right

The reproduction right is the right to make copies of a work. This is the most fundamental copyright right. Subject to the fair use privilege, a copyright owner has the exclusive right to make copies of his or her work online. The exclusive reproduction right extends not only to text but also to graphics, pictures, and sounds.

A copy of a work of expression is made whenever the work is digitized—that is, converted to a series of binary ones and zeros that can be read by a computer—and placed into a permanent computer storage device, such as a hard disk, a CD-ROM, or an online storage medium.

If a person downloads (transfers) this digital copy onto a personal computer and saves it on a permanent storage medium, a second copy is made. If this person prints out a hard copy of the work on paper, a third copy is made, and if the person then transmits digital copies to other computers over a network and such copies are permanently stored, additional copies—perhaps thousands—are made.

Unless this copying is a fair use or done with express or implied permission, it is a violation of the copyright owner's reproduction right. Much of the copying done by individuals in the online world likely qualifies as a fair use.

Distribution Right

A copyright owner has the exclusive right to distribute copies of his or her work to the public by sale, rental, or lending. This includes making a work available to the public on the Internet.

But there is a very important exception to the distribution right: Once a copy is sold or otherwise distributed, the new owner of the copy may sell or otherwise transfer that particular copy without the copyright owner's permission. This is called the first sale rule. For example, if you buy a book in a bookstore, you may sell the book (technically, a copy of the underlying work of expression covered by copyright) to a used bookstore without the copyright owner's permission. But you can't make additional copies of the book. There are two exceptions to the first sale rule: Computer programs and sound recordings can't be rented, leased, or lent to others without the copyright owner's permission. But they may be sold or given away without permission.

The first sale rule could apply to digital works, such as e-books—there is nothing in the copyright law to prevent this. However, the copyright owners of most such works require end users to agree to licenses that limit or eliminate the right of first sale. For example, Amazon.com's end user agreement for its Kindle e-books provides that users "may not sell, rent, lease, distribute, broadcast, sublicense, or otherwise assign any rights to the Kindle Content or any portion of it to any third party." Restrictive licenses like this have been upheld by the courts.

Right to Create Derivative Works

A copyright owner also has the exclusive right to create derivative works from the original work—that is, new works based upon or adapted from the original work. (See Chapter 6 for a detailed discussion.) A user who modifies a downloaded file by annotating, editing, translating, or otherwise significantly changing the contents of the file creates a derivative work. Such a work would be an infringing work unless it was created with the copyright owner's permission or is a fair use.

There is, however, one important exception to the exclusive right to create derivative works: The lawful owner of a copy of a computer program may adapt or modify it solely for personal use. (17 U.S.C. § 117.)

Public Display Rights

Copyright owners not only have the exclusive right to make copies of their works, they also have the exclusive right to publicly display them. A "display" includes showing an image on a computer terminal connected with an information storage and retrieval system.

However, the fact that the display must be in public limits the display right. A public place is a place the public is free to enter without restriction, other than an admission fee or an agreement to adhere to rules of comportment. It is a place where a substantial number of people outside the usual circle of family or social acquaintances are gathered. A digital transmission of a work protected by copyright, which is shown on a computer in a bar, school, conference hall, or other public place, is considered a public display.

A display is also considered to be public when the public can share in it individually at home. For example, a television broadcast is a public display even though each member of the viewing audience might see the broadcast in private. Similarly, a video made publicly available on a website, such as YouTube, would likely be viewed as publicly displayed even though the viewers of the video are at home.

However, it's important to differentiate between a public display and simply making material available for copying. Placing a digitized version of a photograph in a file online that users can download and view on their computers is not a public display—it is simply making a copy available to individual members of the public. But if the same photo automatically appears on the user's computer screen when he or she logged on to an online service, it would be a public display.

Public Performance Rights

The owner of a written work, such as a poem or play, has the exclusive right to perform it in public—for example, to recite or act it in a public place, such as a theater, or to broadcast it to the public on television. What constitutes a public performance is governed by rules used to determine if a display is public, as discussed above.

This means, for example, that a live transmission of a rock concert, movie, or radio show over a computer network would constitute a public performance of the work. Unless permission was obtained, such a transmission would constitute copyright infringement. But simply placing a digitized copy of a rock concert video online for downloading by users would not be a public performance of the concert.

An audiovisual work is "performed" whenever images and sounds are publicly displayed in any sequence. However, a single photo, painting, or sculpture does not "perform." Thus, the public performance right does not extend to pictorial, graphic, and sculptural works. The display right is considered sufficient for such works.

Fair Use Limitation on Copyright Owners' Exclusive Rights

There is an extremely important limitation on the exclusive copyright rights described above: the fair use rule. Anybody can use a copyright owner's protected expression without permission if the use constitutes a fair use. Fair use applies in the online world just as it does in the physical world.

It's difficult to describe any general rules about fair use, because it is always very fact specific. However, private individuals who copy works for their own personal use have much greater fair use rights than those who copy for commercial purposes. Although no court has so ruled, it seems likely that

---

Limiting Liability With Disclaimers

If a website owner is concerned about liability for links but is unable or unwilling to seek permission from the linked website, a prominently placed disclaimer might reduce the likelihood of legal problems. A disclaimer is a statement denying an endorsement or waiving liability for a potentially unauthorized activity. A disclaimer is rarely a cure-all for legal claims, but if a disclaimer is prominently displayed and clearly written, a court may take it into consideration as a factor limiting damages. In some cases, such as trademark disputes, it may help prevent any liability. For example, in a case involving a dispute between websites for two restaurants named Blue Note, one factor that helped the lesser-known restaurant avoid liability was a prominently displayed disclaimer stating that it was not affiliated with the more famous restaurant. (*Benusan Rest. Corp. v. King*, 937 F. Supp. 295 (S.D.N.Y. 1996).) To minimize liability for any activities that occur when a visitor is taken to a linked website, a webmaster may want to include a linking disclaimer on its home page or on any pages with otherwise troublesome links.

Here is a sample linking disclaimer:

> By providing links to other sites, *[name of your website]* does not guarantee, approve, or endorse the information or products available at these sites, nor does a link indicate any association with or endorsement by the linked site to *[name of your website]*.

it is a fair use for private individuals to make temporary RAM copies of online files in order to read or browse them on their computers.

It is likely also a fair use to download online files to a single hard disk or another permanent computer storage device or personal online storage space for personal use only. You can even print a single hard copy of an online file for personal use.

> **EXAMPLE:** Art downloads a copy of a copyrighted article from *The New York Times* website and stores it in his password-restricted online storage space in "the cloud" for future reference. This is probably a fair use.

Other uses can also be a fair use. This is most likely where they are for educational, scholarly, or journalistic purposes. For example, it may be a fair use to quote a portion of an online text file in a newspaper article, college dissertation, or book.

In addition, the more "transformative" a use is, the more likely it will be a fair use. A use is transformative where the material is used to help create a new and different work, not simply copied verbatim. Be careful, however, that you don't take so much material from the original work that your work would constitute a derivative work—that is, a work "based on or adapted from the original work." Taking such a large amount of material can rarely be a fair use.

Linking, Framing, and Inlining

In some cases, online linking, framing, and inlining can violate copyright and other laws and should not be done without obtaining permission.

Linking

Linking is one of the most appealing features of the Internet: The use of hypertext links allows users to instantly navigate from one website to another (or within a website) by clicking on the link.

It is not a violation of copyright to create a hyperlink. But courts have found violations of the law when a party encourages and contributes to unauthorized copying of a copyrighted work by linking material the party knew or should have known was unauthorized.

> **EXAMPLE:** A website posted infringing copies of a church's copyrighted handbook at its site. The website was ordered to remove the handbook, but it subsequently provided links to other sites that contained infringing copies of the handbook. These links were different from traditional hyperlinks because the website knew and encouraged the use of the links to obtain unauthorized copies. The linking activity constituted contributory copyright infringement. (*Intellectual Reserve, Inc. v. Utah Lighthouse Ministry, Inc.*, 75 F. Supp. 2d 1290 (D. Utah 1999).)

Deep Linking

A link that bypasses a website's home page and instead goes to another page within the site is often called a deep link. Some website owners object to the use of deep links. They want all the people who use their website to go first to the home page, usually because advertising is posted there.

The use of deep links can cost websites advertising revenue. In one of the first cases of its kind, Ticketmaster sued a competitor called Tickets.com partly because it linked from its website to pages deep within Ticketmaster's site. The court held that deep linking does not violate the copyright laws, because no copying is involved. However, the court held that Ticketmaster might have a claim against Tickets.com on other legal grounds, such as violation of trademarks or unfair business practices. (*Ticketmaster Corp. v. Tickets.com, Inc.*, 54 U.S.P.Q.2d 1344 (C.D. Cal. 2000).)

Many copyright experts believe that deep linking is not copyright infringement— after all, the author of a novel can't prevent readers from reading the end first if they so desire, so why should a website owner have the right to determine in what order a user can access a website? Nevertheless, it's prudent to be careful before deep linking to advertising-rich commercial sites. Many such sites have linking policies posted. Some well-known websites, such as Amazon. com, welcome deep links. If a commercial website has no posted linking policy or says that deep links are not allowed, it's wise to ask for permission before deep linking. Otherwise, you could end up getting a cease and desist letter from a lawyer.

Framing

Framing means that Website A shows visitors content from Website B—but inside a frame on Website A. Framing can trigger a dispute under copyright and trademark law theories because a framed site arguably alters the appearance of the content and creates the impression that its owner endorses or voluntarily chooses to associate with the framer. In a 1997 lawsuit, TotalNEWS framed news content from media outlets such as CNN, *USA TODAY*, and *Time*. For example, the content of a CNN webpage appeared within a frame packed with advertising and information about TotalNEWS. The lawsuit settled and TotalNEWS agreed to stop framing and use text-only links.

A subsequent court fight involving two dental websites also failed to fully resolve the issue. Applied Anagramic, Inc., a dental services website, framed the content of a competing site—Futuredontics, Inc. The frames included information about Futuredontics, as well as its trademark and links to all webpages. A district court ruled that a website containing a link that reproduced webpages within a frame may constitute an infringing derivative work. The court reasoned that the addition of the frame modified the appearance of the linked site and such modifications could, without authorization, amount to infringement. (*Futuredontics, Inc. v. Applied Anagramic, Inc.*, 46 U.S.P.Q.2d 2005 (C.D. Cal. 1997).)

Inlining

Inlining is the process of displaying a graphic file on one website that originates at another. For example, inlining occurs if a user at Website A can, without leaving Website A, view a "cartoon of the day" featured on Website B. Inlining makes it look like the linked-to file actually originated on Website A, instead of Website B.

Most courts follow the "server test" to determine liability for inlining. Under the server test, you're liable only if you download the image or other content, copy it, and store it on your own server. If the actions don't meet the server test, you haven't violated the copyright owner's exclusive display rights, because the images or other content are hosted on a server owned and operated by an unrelated third party. (*Perfect 10, Inc. v. Amazon.com, Inc.*, 508 F.3d 1146 (9th Cir. 2007).)

However, another court refused to follow the server test in a case where a photo of Tom Brady went viral from Snapchat to Reddit to Twitter. The photo eventually ended up the websites of nine news organizations in a tweet embedded alongside articles they wrote about the quarterback. The court held that the news organizations could be liable for infringement of the photographer's exclusive display rights even though the photo of Tom Brady was hosted on the Twitter server. (*Goldman v. Breitbart News Network, LLC*, 302 F. Supp. 3d 585 (S.D.N.Y. 2018).)

How Copyright Protects Different Types of Online Works

Many different types of copyrighted works are available in the online world, including text, graphics, photos, sounds, and electronic mail. Let's see how copyright protects particular types of online works.

Text Files

Digital copies of text files stored in online databases pose no special copyright problems. They are entitled to the same copyright protection as printed copies of books stored on the shelves of a bookstore. It is illegal for you to go into a bookstore and use a smartphone scanning application to make digital copies of books displayed in the store or to recite a copyrighted book on the radio without permission from the copyright owner. Similarly, you may not copy, distribute, adapt, perform, or display a digital version of a written text without the copyright owner's permission, unless your use constitutes a fair use.

As mentioned above, making a single copy of a text file solely for personal use likely constitutes a fair use. In addition, a copyright owner who uploads a text file to the Internet or online service does so in order that other people can access and read it. Arguably, the act of uploading the work grants other users an implied license to download the work solely for their personal use.

Images and Sounds

Images and sounds—whether photos, graphics, or recordings—are fundamentally no different from text files for copyright purposes. They are protected by copyright if they are original, minimally creative, and fixed in a tangible medium of expression. Subject to the fair use rule, the copyright owner has the exclusive right to copy, distribute, adapt, perform, and display such works.

It is a copyright infringement, for example, to scan a copyrighted photograph and place the image on the Internet without the copyright owner's permission. It is likewise an infringement to download a protected image and use it without permission. Use means copying, distributing, adapting, or publicly performing or displaying the work.

EXAMPLE 1: Starware Publishing Corp. downloaded several graphics files from a computer bulletin board service and published them on CD-ROMs. The files contained 52 copyrighted photos owned by *Playboy Magazine. Playboy* sued Starware for copyright infringement and was awarded $1.1 million. (*Playboy Enter., Inc. v. Starware Publ'g Corp.*, 900 F. Supp. 433 (S.D. Fla. 1995).)

EXAMPLE 2: One hundred forty music publishers sued CompuServe, alleging that the online service had infringed the copyrights in over 550 music compositions that were uploaded and downloaded to and from CompuServe by subscribers. CompuServe agreed to pay $500,000 in damages and to work with the publishers to help them license their work to online users. (*Frank Music Corp. v. CompuServe, Inc.*, No. 93 Civ. 8153 (S.D.N.Y. 1993).)

Is Modifying Images or Sounds Infringement?

It is common practice for graphic artists and others to download images from the Internet and other online sources and then modify or adapt them using computer graphics software. The altered images are often used in magazines, books, and other published works. Similarly, it's possible to download sounds and reuse bits and pieces in new recordings.

One of the exclusive rights a copyright owner has is to create derivative works from his or her own work. A derivative work is one that is based on or recast from an original. (See Chapter 6.) A derivative work is created when an existing image or sound is modified or altered to form part of a new work. Such a work would be a copyright infringement unless permission is obtained to create it or it constitutes a fair use. The only exception to this rule might be where the original image or sound is so completely altered that the original source is no longer recognizable.

However, simply viewing an image or listening to sounds that have been placed online by the copyright owner is not an infringement. Although no court has so ruled, it seems clear that by the act of uploading such a work, the copyright owner has granted other users an implied license to download it to their own computer for personal viewing or listening.

Websites

Websites are protected by copyright if, and to the extent, they are original. If a site contains valuable expressive material, it should contain a copyright notice. Many websites consist largely of collections of hypertext links, similar to an address book. These may be protectable as compilations if a minimal amount of creativity was required to create them. (See Chapter 5, "Adaptations and Compilations.") For example, a collection of links to the best poetry sites on the Internet is likely a protectable compilation—the individual links would not be protected, but copying the entire collection would be a copyright violation. Such link collections are a new form of protectable material produced on the Internet.

However, there is no copyright protection for the format of a frequently asked questions (FAQ) page on a website. The FAQ format is considered common property. (*Mist-On Systems, Inc. v. Gilley's European Tan Spa*, 303 F. Supp. 2d 974 (W.D. Wis. 2002).)

The HTML code used to create a website is protectable as a literary work and will be registered by the Copyright Office if it is created by a human being (rather than a website design program) and is sufficiently original and minimally creative. But such protection does not extend to the website's layout, formatting, or look and feel. So, for example, a cascading style sheet is not protectable because it simply defines the layout of text.

Electronic Databases

An electronic database is a collection of facts, data, or other information assembled into an organized format suitable for use on a computer. The material contained in a database may consist of text files, graphics, images, sounds, and anything else a database creator can think of. Many electronic databases are accessible online— for example, databases of magazine and journal articles can be accessed through commercial online services, like LexisNexis.

The individual works contained in a database may be protected by copyright as described in this section, or they might be unprotectable. Either way, there can also be a compilation or collective work copyright for the database as a whole. (See Chapter 5 for a detailed discussion.)

Public Domain Books Get Digitized

In 2004, Google.com entered into agreements with several major research libraries to digitally scan millions of books from their collections and make them available on the Internet as part of Google's book search service (https://books.google.com).

The Authors Guild filed suit against Google, in late 2005, claiming that Google's plan to make digital copies of copyrighted books without first obtaining permission from their copyright owners constituted copyright infringement. After ten years of litigation and fruitless settlement efforts, the case was finally resolved in 2015 when a federal appeals court held that Google's book scanning program was a fair use of the copyrighted books involved. The appeals court found that "Google's making of a digital copy to provide a search function … augments public knowledge by making available information about [p]laintiffs' books without providing the public with a substantial substitute for matter protected by the [p]laintiffs' copyright interests in the original works or derivatives of them." (*Authors Guild v. Google, Inc.*, 804 F.3d 202, 207 (2d Cir. 2015).) The U.S. Supreme Court declined to review the case.

Google has now digitized over 25 million books. In addition to its book search service (for books protected by copyright), Google allows full access to those published over 95 years ago that are in the public domain.

Google is not the only entity with big plans to digitize books. Others include:

- **Internet Archive.** Although primarily known for its vast collection of websites and other "born digital" content, it also contains digitized versions of over eight million public domain books. See https://archive.org.
- **Project Gutenberg.** Billing itself as the first producer of free electronic books, U.S.-based Project Gutenberg is a private-sector project offering over 57,000 public domain texts, including literature and reference materials available to the general public through e-book downloads to portable devices. It has partners in various countries, including Australia, Canada, the United Kingdom, and France, through which over 100,000 free e-books are available. See www. gutenberg.org.
- **HathiTrust Digital Library.** The Hathi-Trust is a group of 57 libraries, including the Library of Congress, whose goal is to "contribute to the common good" by providing a shared platform for making digital collections available to users. The initial focus of the trust was on preserving and providing access to digitized books and journals in collaboration with Google, the Internet Archive, Microsoft, and in-house digitization initiatives. Over eight million books have been digitized. See www.hathitrust.org.

Public Domain Books Get Digitized (continued)

- **Digital Public Library of America.** The Digital Public Library of America (DPLA) went online in mid-2013. It was created by Harvard University's Berkman Center for the Internet & Society, with financial support from various funders. The DPLA plans to aggregate metadata records for millions of photographs, manuscripts, books, sounds, moving images, and more from hundreds of libraries, archives, and museums around the United States. Each record links to the original object on the content provider's website. Many of the items are in the public domain. Digital copies of some objects are available for download, based on the content provider and the individual rights status of the object. See https://dp.la.

Electronic Mail

Electronic mail (email) is protected the same way as a physical letter. To the extent that it is original—that is, not copied from someone else—it is protected by copyright the instant it is fixed in a storage medium, such as online on "the cloud" or a computer hard disk.

The author of an email message owns the copyright in the message unless it was created by an employee within the scope of employment. In this event, the employer is considered the author for copyright purposes and automatically owns the copyright in the message. (See Chapter 8.)

Email Service Providers

An important exception exists to an email creator's copyright ownership rights when the creator uses certain email service providers to create and send emails. Email service providers, such as Google Gmail and Yahoo, require users to grant them a worldwide, royalty free, and nonexclusive license to make use of their email content. These licenses are spelled out in the providers' terms of service on their websites. They are legally enforceable. For example, Google's terms of service (found at https://policies.google.com/terms) give it a "worldwide license to use, host, store, reproduce, modify, create derivative works (such as those resulting from translations...), communicate, publish, publicly perform, publicly display and distribute" users' content.

Incoming Emails

What about making use of emails others send to you? When you receive a physical letter from someone, you don't have the right to publish it in a newspaper or book, unless such a use constitutes a fair use or the owner of the letter gives you permission. The same holds true for email.

Subject to the fair use rule, it would be copyright infringement for you to forward an email received from someone else without permission. Likewise, modifying an email without the sender's permission would violate the sender's exclusive right to create derivative works from the message.

Of course, email is distributed and modified all the time without obtaining express permission from the copyright owners. So long as this is not done for commercial purposes, it probably constitutes a fair use—for example, it's undoubtedly a fair use to quote portions of an email message for a scholarly, journalistic, or educational purpose.

However, some people who send email might not be aware of this and would be upset if their messages were copied without their permission. Although it's highly unlikely anyone would bother to bring a copyright infringement suit over something as valueless as email, it's good manners to ask permission before distributing another person's email.

In some cases, however, the senders of email may be deemed to have implicitly consented in advance to permit others to distribute their email—for example, when a person sends email to a Usenet newsgroup (a discussion group). The only reason to send such a message is to have it posted on the newsgroup so that others may read it. It's much like sending a letter to the editor

of a newspaper. In such cases, the sender would likely be deemed to have consented in advance to the posting of the message.

Blogs

It is estimated that 75,000 new blogs are created every day. Like any other work of authorship, a blog is protected by copyright to the extent it is original.

Blogs ordinarily present far fewer copyright issues than forums or newsgroups, because they are usually authored primarily by just one person. In this case, that one person owns the copyright in the work. However, blogs often include writings, photos, artwork, music, and other copyrighted work owned by other people. In some cases, these uses might be a fair use; in other cases, permission should be obtained. See Chapter 9, "Using Other Authors' Words," and Chapter 13, "Obtaining Copyright Permissions."

Public Domain Materials

A large and growing number of public domain materials are available on the Internet. For example, Project Gutenberg (www.gutenberg.org) is creating digitized versions of great literary works and making them available for downloading on the Internet. This is perfectly legal. When a work enters the public domain, copyright protection ceases. The work is freely available for all to use.

The Da Vinci Code and the Public Domain

In 2003, Dan Brown published *The Da Vinci Code*, based on a startling idea: Jesus Christ and Mary Magdalene married and had a child whose descendants are alive today. The book became the subject of a lawsuit that resulted in one of the most celebrated copyright infringement trials in history. The British authors of the 1982 nonfiction book *The Holy Blood and the Holy Grail* sued Brown's publisher in Great Britain, claiming that Brown had gotten the idea, and much else, for his novel from their book.

Brown admitted that he had relied on the book for his research, and even mentioned it in his novel. Nevertheless, the judge, applying British copyright law nearly identical to American, held that Brown had not committed copyright infringement. Brown had used many of the ideas, facts, theories, and conjectures in *The Holy Blood and the Holy Grail* to write his book, but these were not copyrightable. The architecture, structure, or way in which these facts and ideas were presented could be protected, but Brown had not appropriated the architecture of the 1982 book. Rather, he "put together these generalized facts and ideas in to a well received thriller." (*Michael Baigent and Richard Leigh v. The Random House Group Ltd.*, [2006] E.W.H.C. 719 (Ch.).)

A work can enter the public domain for many reasons. The most common reason is that the copyright expires. Other types of works receive no copyright protection—for example, works created by the U.S. government. An author—that is, the person who creates a work or the owner of a work made for hire—can also dedicate an otherwise protectable work to the public domain. This can be done by stating, "This work is dedicated to the public domain" on the work. An author can also use a Creative Commons public domain dedication (see https://creativecommons.org/publicdomain/zero/1.0). There is no need to make a filing with the Copyright Office or any other agency to dedicate a work to the public domain. Note carefully, however, that a work is not dedicated to the public domain simply because it is made available online.

Never assume that a work is in the public domain merely because it lacks a copyright notice. Copyright notices are optional for published works and are not required at all for unpublished material. So the fact that a work lacks a notice essentially tells you nothing about whether the work is protected by copyright.

In addition, be aware that some publications available online contain a mix of public domain material and material that is protected by copyright. Protected material does not lose its copyright protection merely because it is mixed with public domain material. Copying an entire file containing such mixed material could constitute copyright infringement of the protected material.

> EXAMPLE: A publisher of legal databases used a computer scanner to make digital copies of legal case reports from West Publishing Company. The legal cases themselves were in the public domain, but the copies also included editorial material prepared by West that was protected by copyright. Although the database publisher deleted the protected editorial material before permanently storing the public domain cases in its database, it was still found guilty of infringement. The court held that the temporary copies of the West editorial materials infringed West's copyrights even though they were subsequently deleted. (*West Publ'g Co. v. On Point Solutions Inc.*, No. CIV.A.1:93-CV2071MHS, 1994 WL 778426 (N.D. Ga. Sept. 1, 1994).)

Adaptations and Compilations

When 'Omer smote 'is bloomin' lyre,
He'd 'eard men sing by land an' sea;
An' what he thought 'e might require,
'E went an' took—the same as me!

—Rudyard Kipling
Barrack Room Ballads

The old saying "there's nothing new under the sun" may be the truest of all platitudes. If Kipling was right, not even the earliest authors created their works out of whole cloth. Since authorship began, authors have been borrowing and adapting what others created before them. This chapter is about works that are created by using previously existing material. It covers derivative works—works created by transforming or adapting preexisting expression—and compilations—works created by selecting and arranging preexisting material in new ways.

Derivative Works

If you take a molten lump of copper and add tin to it, you'll end up with something new: bronze. A similar process of transformation can be used to create new works of authorship. An author can take expression that already exists, add new expression to it, and end up with something new—that is, a new and different work of authorship. Such works are called derivative works.

EXAMPLE: Sheila writes a screenplay based upon a novel. In doing so, she takes the novel's expression (words) and adds her own expression to it—she organizes the material into cinematic scenes, adds dialogue and camera directions, and deletes prose descriptions and other material that can't be filmed. The result is a new work of authorship that can be separately protected by copyright: a screenplay that is clearly different from the novel, yet clearly based upon or derived from it.

Of course, all works are derivative to some extent. As Kipling declared, all authors "take" from each other. Authorship is more often than not a process of translation and recombination of previously existing ideas, facts, and other elements. Rarely, if ever, does an author create a work that is entirely new. For example, writers of fiction often draw bits and pieces of their characters and plots from other fictional works they have read. The same is true of writers of factual works. For example, it's likely that any new book on the impact of the electronic media on society would be derived to some extent from Marshall McLuhan's *The Medium Is the Message* (Random House, 1967).

However, a work is derivative for copyright purposes only if its author has taken a *substantial* amount of a previously existing work's *expression*. As discussed in detail in Chapter 4, "What Copyright Protects," copyright only protects an author's expression: the words used and the selection and arrangement of material, if original. So, a new book on the impact of the media on society would be derivative of *The Medium Is the Message* for copyright purposes only if its author copied or paraphrased substantial portions of the words McLuhan used to express his ideas.

The ideas and facts themselves are not protectable and are therefore free for anyone to use. Likewise, this year's novel about boy meets girl is not derivative of last year's novel on the same theme unless its author copied substantial portions of its expression.

How much is substantial? Enough so that the average intended reader of the work would conclude that it had been adapted from or based upon the previously existing expression.

> EXAMPLE 1: Edna writes a poem about her cat. She includes one line from a poem in T.S. Eliot's cat poetry collection, *Old Possum's Book of Practical Cats*. She probably has not used enough of Eliot's expression for her poem to be considered a derivative work of *Old Possum's Book of Practical Cats*.

> EXAMPLE 2: Andrew Lloyd Webber and Trevor Nunn write a musical entitled *Cats*. The musical is based entirely on the poems in *Old Possum's Book of Practical Cats*. Here and there a word or two is altered to make

the verses fit the music better, but the show is nothing more than Eliot's poems set to music. *Cats* is a derivative work of *Old Possum's Book of Practical Cats*.

Types of Derivative Works

Many different types of derivative works exist. Let's look at those of most interest to writers in terms of the type of expression the author takes from a previously existing work and the expression added to it to create a new, derivative work.

Editorial Revisions and Elaborations

Preexisting expression taken. The entire text of any preexisting work.

New expression added. Editorial revisions or other new material.

> EXAMPLE: Dr. Blood writes a new edition of his ten-year-old textbook on heart surgery. He adds several new chapters on new surgical techniques and revises the other chapters in light of recent developments. The new edition is a derivative work based on, but designed to take the place of, the earlier edition.

Fictionalizations

Preexisting expression taken. A substantial portion of the protected expression contained in a factual work (biography, history, and so on).

New expression added. Editing, reorganization, new dialogue, descriptions, and other new material needed to transform the preexisting nonfiction work into a novel, a play, a screenplay, or another work of fiction.

EXAMPLE: Art takes the nonfiction work *The Diary of Anne Frank* and transforms it into a stage play. To do so, he deletes prose descriptions, adds new dialogue, organizes the work into scenes and acts, and adds new scenes and incidents that weren't in the diary. But he also retains as much of Anne Frank's expression—her words—as possible. The play is a derivative work based on the nonfiction diary.

Dramatizations

Preexisting expression taken. All or a substantial part of the expression in a fictional work not meant to be performed in public—that is, a short story, novel, or poem.

New expression added. Editing, reorganization, new dialogue, and other new material needed to transform the work into a work that can be performed in public—for instance, a stage play or screenplay.

Translations Into a New Medium

Preexisting expression taken. All or a substantial portion of the protected expression of a work in one medium—for instance, a published book.

New expression added. Transfer of the work's protected expression into a new medium.

EXAMPLE: Kitty makes a sound recording of selected highlights from her unauthorized biography of Hillary Clinton. The recording is a derivative work based on the written biography.

Translations Into a New Language

Preexisting expression taken. All the expression contained in a preexisting work.

New expression added. Translation of the work's expression into a new version in another language.

EXAMPLE: Miguel translates Stephen King's latest bestseller into Spanish. To do so, he takes King's expression (the words contained in the novel) and replaces them with Spanish words. The resulting translation is a derivative work based on the original English-language novel.

Abridgements and Condensations of Fiction or Nonfiction Works

Preexisting expression taken. A substantial portion of a work's protectable expression.

New expression added. Editing and other revisions that transform the work into a new, shorter version.

EXAMPLE: The website and mobile application *Blinkist* creates bite-sized summaries of thousands of current nonfiction books and makes them available to subscribers. These summaries are derivative works based on the unabridged editions of the works.

Annotations

Preexisting expression taken. All or a substantial portion of a work's protected expression.

New expression added. Notes or other materials that clarify the meaning of the preexisting text.

> EXAMPLE: The annotated version of Lewis Carroll's *Alice in Wonderland* is a derivative work prepared from the original version of *Alice*.

When You Need Permission to Create a Derivative Work

One of the five exclusive copyright rights that automatically come into existence the moment an original work of authorship is written down or otherwise fixed in a tangible form is the exclusive right to prepare and distribute derivative works based on the work's protected expression. This means you cannot create and publish a derivative work by using someone else's protected expression without obtaining their permission. If you do, you violate that person's copyright and would be subject to a copyright infringement suit.

> EXAMPLE: Rhonda writes a critically acclaimed novel. Rex writes a screenplay based on Rhonda's novel without obtaining her permission to do so. Rex sells the screenplay to a Hollywood studio. Rhonda has a valid claim against Rex for infringing on her right to create derivative works from her novel.

Such permission usually takes the legal form of an exclusive license to prepare a particular derivative work—for example, a screenplay—from the preexisting material. (See Chapter 7, "Transferring Copyright Ownership.")

What Happens If You Fail to Get Permission

If you create a derivative work without obtaining permission from the owner of the copyright in the preexisting work, your original contributions will ordinarily enter the public domain. For example, if you translate a Spanish novel into English without permission, you will lose any claim to copyright protection in the original elements you added in your translation—that is, your choice of English language words to convey the meaning of the Spanish original. Anyone would be free to copy your translation without obtaining your permission, but they would have to obtain permission from the owner of the original Spanish work (but the owner of the Spanish novel would need no permission at all to copy your translation).

If you intend to create a derivative work from preexisting expression that is still under copyright, be sure to get the copyright owner's permission to use the work before you go to the time and trouble of adapting it into a new work.

When You Don't Need Permission to Create a Derivative Work

In some instances, it is not necessary to seek anyone's permission to create a derivative work, and the only legal issue the author must deal with is registering the derivative work with the Copyright Office. Registration of derivative works is discussed in Chapter 3, "Copyright Registration."

Author Owns Right to Prepare Derivative Works From Preexisting Expression

An author doesn't have to get anyone's permission to create a derivative work if the author owns the entire copyright in the preexisting protected expression or the right to prepare derivative works based upon it. Authors start out owning all the copyright rights in their works, including all derivative rights, but they often transfer them to publishers, film producers, and others. An author cannot create a derivative work from his or her own work if he or she has transferred his or her derivative rights to others. (See Chapter 7, "Transferring Copyright Ownership.")

> **EXAMPLE:** Livia writes a novel and sells the exclusive right to prepare a screenplay based upon it to Repulsive Pictures. Livia cannot write a screenplay based upon her novel without Repulsive's permission.

Preexisting Material in the Public Domain

You don't need permission to create a derivative work based on expression that is in the public domain. Public domain material belongs to the world, and anyone is free to use it in any way he or she wishes. (See Chapter 4, "What Copyright Protects," for a detailed discussion of the public domain.) A work may be in the public domain because it was never copyrighted or the copyright expired. The expression in such works may be used in any way without permission.

Fair Use of Protected Expression

Even if a derivative work author uses someone else's protected expression, permission might not be required if the use constitutes a fair use. Pursuant to the fair use privilege, an author may take a *limited* amount of the protected expression in preexisting works without the copyright owner's permission. Whether or not a use is fair is determined according to the facts and circumstances of the particular case. Courts consider the purpose of the use (whether for educational or commercial purposes, for example), the nature of the preexisting expression, the amount of preexisting expression taken, and whether the use reduces the value of the copyright owner's rights in the preexisting expression. A parody of a well-known work might be one example of a derivative work that can be created without obtaining permission from the owner of the preexisting expression pursuant to the fair use privilege. Fair use is discussed in detail in Chapter 9, "Using Other Authors' Words."

EXAMPLE: You can write a screenplay based on Dickens's *Great Expectations* without obtaining anyone's permission, because the novel's copyright expired long ago.

Facts and ideas are always in the public domain. For this reason, an author need not obtain permission to use the facts or ideas contained in an otherwise protected preexisting work.

EXAMPLE: Shirley, a three-year-old girl, falls into a well in Texas and is rescued one week later—miraculously still alive. The entire story was reported live on CNN and extensively covered by other news media as well. Shirley's parents write a book about the episode, which includes extensive quotations from Shirley describing her experiences. The GETFLIX streaming service hires Bart to write a movie about the event. Bart bases the screenplay on the basic facts contained in news accounts and the CNN coverage. He also uses some of the facts contained in the parents' book; but he neither quotes nor paraphrases any of the material in the book. The screenplay is not a derivative work of the book, and GETFLIX need not obtain the permission of Shirley's parents to stream its movie.

Derivative Work Doesn't Affect Existing Copyright Protection

The copyright status of preexisting expression used in a derivative work is unaffected by the derivative work. If the preexisting expression was in the public domain, it remains so and anyone else is free to use it. If the preexisting expression was protected by copyright, that copyright continues just as if the derivative work never existed.

EXAMPLE 1: Jillian wants to write a screenplay based upon a novel published in 1917. She pays the owner of the copyright in the novel to grant her the exclusive right to prepare derivative works based upon it. She writes the screenplay. She now owns the copyright to all the material she added to the preexisting material in order to adapt it into a screenplay. Her copyright in this material will last for the rest of her life plus an additional 70 years. However, the copyright in the novel itself is not extended or otherwise affected by Jillian's screenplay. The novel's copyright expired on December 31, 1992.

EXAMPLE 2: Dr. Huxley writes an updated new edition of Charles Darwin's *The Origin of Species*. The publication of the new edition does not in any way revive the copyright in *The Origin of Species*, which expired long ago. Anyone else is free to write their own updated version of Darwin's great work, or otherwise use the material in the book.

Registering Derivative Works

A derivative work can and should be registered with the Copyright Office. This way, if anyone infringes upon the new material that has been added to the preexisting material, the derivative work author will be able to obtain statutory damages and attorneys' fees in an infringement suit. (See Chapter 3, "Copyright Registration.")

Compilations

A compilation is a work created by selecting, organizing, and arranging previously existing material in such a way that the resulting work as a whole constitutes an original work of authorship. Compilations differ from derivative works because the author of a compilation makes no changes in the preexisting material and need not add any new material of his or her own. Moreover, protectable compilations can be created solely from material that is in the public domain.

Fact Compilations (Databases)

A protectable fact compilation is created by selecting and arranging facts or other items that are in the public domain. (See Chapter 4, "What Copyright Protects," for a detailed discussion of what is and is not in the public domain.)

> EXAMPLE 1: Andrea, a baseball card dealer, compiles an online guide listing the 10,000 cards in existence she deems to be the most valuable for collectors. Andrea sells subscriptions to the continually updated website to collectors across the country. Andrea's guide is a protectable compilation consisting of 10,000 unprotectable facts— the names of 10,000 baseball cards.

> EXAMPLE 2: Mark, an efficiency expert, takes a number of blank forms and other materials in the public domain (datebooks, address books, and a calendar) and arranges them all into a new "executive organizer." Mark's organizer is a protectable compilation consisting of unprotectable forms and calendars.

In addition to baseball card lists and executive organizers, fact compilations can include, but are not limited to, works such as bibliographies, directories, price lists, catalogs of all types, and even databases. Databases are composed of a body of facts, data, or other information assembled into an organized format suitable for use on a computer. The variety of information contained on databases is nearly endless and growing rapidly. Everything from government documents to stock quotes to magazine and journal articles can be accessed.

Collective Works

A compilation can also be created by selecting and arranging into a single whole work preexisting materials that are separate and independent works entitled to copyright protection in their own right. Such compilations are called collective works.

> EXAMPLE: Elliot compiles an anthology of the 25 best American short stories published during the 2010s. Each story is a separate and independent work that was

protected by copyright the moment it was created. However, Elliot has created a new protectable collective work by selecting and arranging the stories into a collective whole—that is, a collection of the best short stories of the 2010s. (Of course, Elliot would have to get permission from the copyright owners of all the stories before publishing the collection.)

Other examples of collective works include newspapers, magazines, and other periodicals in which separately protectable articles are combined into a collective whole, and encyclopedias consisting of independently protectable articles on various topics.

Websites of all kinds are often collective works containing contributions that are separate and independent works in themselves, such as text, photographs, videos, sound recordings, and the like.

Fact Compilation Combined With Collective Work

It is possible to create a compilation that includes both unprotectable facts and other items that are individually protectable.

EXAMPLE: An anthology of selected articles by various historians on ancient Sparta also contains a bibliography listing every article written on Sparta in the 20th century.

Extent of Copyright Protection for Compilations

You might be wondering why a compilation should be protected by copyright. The author of a compilation has not written anything new. For example, how can Andrea's baseball card guide in the example above constitute a protectable original work of authorship? Where is the originality—that is, independent creation plus minimal creativity? Andrea simply compiled a list of the names of baseball cards; none of the names on her list is individually protectable.

What makes Andrea's list protectable are the creativity and judgment she employed in deciding which of the thousands of baseball cards in existence belonged on her list of the 10,000 most desirable cards and in what order the names should appear on the list. Similarly, Elliot in the example above used creativity and judgment in selecting which of the thousands of short stories published during the 2010s belonged in his anthology of the 25 best short stories of that decade and deciding on the arrangement of the stories. It is this selection and arrangement of the material making up a compilation that constitutes protected expression.

The copyright in a protectable fact compilation or collective work extends only to this protected expression not to the pre-existing material itself. This is sometimes referred to as a thin copyright.

EXAMPLE: The copyright in Elliot's short story anthology extends only to Elliot's selection and arrangement of the stories in his anthology, not to the stories themselves. This means that anyone could reprint the stories contained in the collection (with the copyright owners' permission) without violating Elliot's compilation copyright. But another person could not, without Elliot's permission, publish a book of the best short stories of the 2010s using the same stories in Elliot's book, printed in the same order.

Raw Facts in Fact Compilations Not Protected by Copyright

Because the copyright in a fact compilation extends only to the compiler's selection and arrangement of the facts, the raw facts or data themselves are not protected by copyright. The Supreme Court has stated that the raw facts may be copied at will and that a compiler is even free to use the facts contained in another's compilation to aid in preparing a competing compilation (*Feist Publ'ns, Inc. v. Rural Telephone Serv. Co.*, 111 S. Ct. 1282 (1991)); but, as discussed above, the competing work may not feature the same selection and arrangement as the earlier compilation.

EXAMPLE: Assessment Technologies of Wisconsin created a computer program called Market Drive to help Wisconsin county assessors' offices compile real estate data, such as property addresses and the names of the owners, in an electronic database. The counties used the data for tax assessment purposes. A company, WIREdata, attempted to obtain the raw data from the counties to create its own database for use by real estate brokers. A court held that Assessment Technologies could not sue WIREdata for copyright infringement because the raw data WIREdata wanted was in the public domain. (*Assessment Techs. of Wisconsin, LLC v. WIREdata, Inc.*, 350 F.3d 640 (7th Cir. 2003).)

Opinions Are Not Facts

Raw facts cannot be protected by copyright. However, some things you might think are unprotectable facts really aren't. At least, that's what two federal appellate courts have held. These cases involved copying of databases containing price data. In one case, someone copied the price quotations in coin dealer newsletters. In the other, the prices for used cars—listed in a used car price guide called the *Red Book*—were copied. In both cases, the courts held that the individual price quotations were copyrighted because they were entirely subjective—they were simply estimates given by the publishers of the guides. They represented the publishers' opinions of what the coins and used cars were worth, not what someone actually paid for them. The courts held that sufficient creativity was required to devise these estimates for them to be protected by copyright. (*CCC Info. Servs., Inc. v. Maclean Hunter Mkt. Reports*, 44 F.3d 61 (2d Cir. 1994); *CDN Inc. v. Kenneth A. Kapes*, 197 F.3d 1256 (9th Cir. 1999).)

It might seem unfair that the facts contained in a compilation gathered at great trouble and expense may be used by others without compensating the original compiler. However, recall that the purpose of copyright is to advance the progress of knowledge, not to reward authors. If the first person to compile a group of raw facts had a monopoly over them, such progress would be greatly impeded.

The Minimal Creativity Requirement

A work must be the product of a minimal amount of creativity to be protected by copyright. This requirement applies to fact compilations as well as all other works. The data contained in a factual compilation need not be presented in an innovative or surprising way, but the selection or arrangement cannot be so mechanical or routine as to require no creativity whatsoever. If no creativity was employed in selecting or arranging the data, the compilation will not receive copyright protection.

In a landmark decision on fact compilations, the Supreme Court held that the selection and arrangement of white pages in a typical telephone directory fails to satisfy the creativity requirement and is therefore not protected by copyright. (*Feist Publ'ns, Inc. v. Rural Telephone Serv. Co.*, 111 S. Ct. 1282 (1991).) There are doubtless many other types of compilations that are unprotectable for the same reason. For example, the names, phone numbers, and addresses contained in a yellow pages

phone directory organized into an alphabetical list of business classifications have been found to completely lack creativity and therefore not to qualify for copyright protection. (*BellSouth Adver. & Publ'g Corp. v. Donnelley Info. Publ'g, Inc.*, 999 F.2d 1436 (11th Cir. 1993).)

How can you tell if your compilation makes the grade?

The *selection* of the data in a compilation will satisfy the minimal creativity test if the compiler has:

- chosen less than all of the data in a given body of relevant material, regardless of whether it is taken from one or more sources, or
- taken all of the data from several different sources and combined them to form a new work.

For example, there is no selectivity required to compile a list of *all* the people who have telephones in a given geographical area. The compiler of a telephone directory doesn't employ any judgment in deciding who belongs in the directory.

A compiler's *arrangement* or coordination of the data in a compilation will satisfy the creativity requirement as long as the data is ordered into lists or categories that go beyond the mere mechanical grouping of data. Alphabetical, chronological, or sequential listings of data are purely mechanical and do not satisfy the minimal creativity requirement, which is why the alphabetical arrangement of names in a telephone directory is not minimally creative.

Representatives of the Copyright Office have indicated that in their view the following types of compilations will usually fail to satisfy the minimal creativity requirement.

Street address directories, alumni directories, membership lists, mailing lists, and subscriber lists. Where the names and addresses in these types of compilations are arranged in alphabetical or numerical order, and no selectivity was required in determining which names and addresses should be included, they would seem to contain no more creativity than telephone book white pages. Examples include: an alphabetical list of all the Harvard alumni, all the members of the ACLU, or all the subscribers to *Time* magazine; and a mailing list in numerical order according to zip code of all persons who have contributed more than $1,000 to the Republican Party.

Parts lists. An alphabetical or numerical list of *all* the parts in a given inventory clearly fails the creativity test: If the list

---

Making Your Compilation Protectable

There are ways you can help make your compilation satisfy the minimal creativity requirement. If you must compile a list of all of anything, don't simply arrange your data in alphabetical, numerical, or chronological order. For example, if you were compiling a bibliography of every book ever written about the Civil War, you shouldn't simply list every title alphabetically. Instead, you should employ some selectivity by breaking down your bibliography into categories—for instance, books about the causes of the war, Civil War generals, the naval war, and so on. The more judgment you use in arranging your data, the more protectable your compilation.

One of the first post-*Feist* cases dealing with electronic databases illustrates that the more "value-added" features a database publisher provides to users, the more likely the database will be copyrightable. The case involved a computerized database of state trademarks. The state trademark records were themselves in the public domain. However, the publisher added to each trademark record a code indicating the type of mark, modified the state records' description of the mark to conform to standard descriptions, divided the data into separate search fields, and added search indexes to facilitate computer searches of the records. The court held that the publisher's "selection, coordination, arrangement, enhancement, and programming of the state trademark data" satisfied the originality and creativity requirements set forth in the *Feist* decision. (*Corsearch, Inc. v. Thomson & Thomson*, 792 F. Supp. 305 (S.D.N.Y. 1992).) In other words, the database qualified for copyright protection.

is exhaustive, no selectivity is required to compile it; if it is arranged in alphabetical or numerical order, no creativity is required to arrange it.

Genealogies. A genealogy (a table or diagram recording a person's or family's ancestry) consisting merely of transcriptions of public records, such as census or court-house records, or transcriptions made from headstones in a few local cemeteries, are also deemed by the Copyright Office, to lack minimal creativity. On the other hand, the creativity requirement may be satisfied where the creator of a genealogy compilation uses judgment in selecting material from a number of different sources.

The Copyright Office will not register these items unless the applicant convinces the copyright examiner that a minimal amount of creativity was required to select or arrange the information they contain.

De Minimis Compilations

De minimis is Latin for trifling or insignificant. A *de minimis* compilation is one that contains only a few items. Even if a *de minimis* compilation meets the minimal creativity requirement, the Copyright Office will refuse to register it. The Copyright Office considers a compilation of only three items to be clearly *de minimis*.

Copyright Office Regulation

The Copyright Office has issued a regulation providing that works "consisting entirely of information that is common property containing no original authorship, such as ... standard calendars, height and weight charts ... schedules of sporting events and lists or tables taken from public documents or other common sources" are not protectable and may not be registered. (37 C.F.R. § 202.1(d) (1984).) This is certainly true if no creativity is involved in creating such works. But, of course, a table, list, or schedule would be a protectable fact compilation if the selection and arrangement of the information it contained was minimally creative.

Collective Works

Collective works must also meet the minimal creativity and originality requirements. If little or no selectivity and judgment is required to create a collective work, it might not be protectable. For example, an anthology consisting of ten stories in chronological order by the same author who wrote only those ten stories in her entire life would probably not be protectable, because compiling such an anthology would require no selectivity or judgment.

Compilations Containing Protected Expression Receive Greater Protection

An author may add protected expression to a fact compilation or collective work. If original, such expression is protected by copyright just like any other original work of authorship. As a result, if protected expression is included throughout a compilation, it will be much more difficult and risky for users to copy the entire compilation or large chunks of it. Reason: By doing so, they would be copying not only unprotectable facts but the protected expression in the compilation as well.

> EXAMPLE: Robert compiles a bibliography containing the titles, authors, and publishers of every book published in the United States on the Civil War (about 50,000 in all). The bibliography is simply in alphabetical order, so it probably lacks sufficient creativity to be protectable. However, Robert also includes an introduction and annotates some of the selections with explanatory notes. Both the introduction and notes constitute protected expression. Thus, if someone copied the entire bibliography they would be copying protected expression and, therefore, committing copyright infringement. Of course, anyone could still copy the individual bibliographic entries so long as they left the protected expression alone.

Other Protections for Compilations

Given the limitations on copyright protection for compilations and the fact that some compilations might not qualify for any protection, the owners of valuable compilations may wish to find means other than copyright to protect their work. One means might be contract restrictions similar to those employed by the owners of automated databases. For example, books containing fact compilations might be leased to users on terms similar to database licenses. The lease would provide that the user may not copy the compilation without the owner's consent. However, there are many unresolved questions about the enforceability of such contracts. For further information, you should see a qualified copyright attorney.

Preexisting Material in Collective Works Must Be Used Lawfully

Recall that a collective work is a compilation in which the preexisting material consists of separate and independent works that are individually protectable. If such preexisting material is in fact under copyright, it cannot be published as part of a compilation without permission from the owner of the right to reproduce the work (presumably, such permission would have to be paid for).

A compilation author who publishes such preexisting material without permission infringes on the owner's copyright and invites a copyright infringement suit.

> **EXAMPLE:** Assume that Elliot (the compiler of the anthology of the 25 best short stories of the 2010s) obtained permission to republish 24 of the stories but failed to get permission to publish a story written and owned by Tom. Tom is entitled to sue Elliot (and his publisher) for infringing on his exclusive right to reproduce his story.

Permission can take the form of a nonexclusive license to use the material in the collective work, an exclusive license, or even an assignment of all rights in the material. See Chapter 7, "Transferring Copyright Ownership."

Use of Public Domain Material

No permission is necessary if the preexisting material is in the public domain. As discussed in Chapter 4, "What Copyright Protects," public domain material is not protected by copyright; anyone can use it however he or she wishes.

> **EXAMPLE:** Assume that Elliot compiled an anthology of the best short stories of the 1910s (rather than the 2010s). He does not have to obtain permission to use the stories he selected. The copyright in all short stories written in the 1910s expired long ago, and they are all in the public domain.

Use of Material Created by Compiler

A collective work can be created from preexisting material that the collective work author created him- or herself. For example, Elliot could create an anthology of his own best short stories. Of course, in this event, the author would not need to obtain permission to use the material (assuming he still owns the copyright).

Copyright in Preexisting Material Unaffected by Inclusion in Collective Work

The copyright status of the preexisting material used to create a collective work is unaffected by the collective work's existence. Thus, if the preexisting material was in the public domain, it remains in the public domain. If the preexisting material was protected by copyright, such protection continues without regard to the collective work—that is, the duration of copyright protection for the preexisting material remains the same and is unaffected by a transfer of the compiler's rights in his or her compilation.

> **EXAMPLE 1:** Assume again that Elliot compiles an anthology of the best short stories of the 1920s. All the stories in his anthology remain in the public domain. The fact that they were republished in Elliot's anthology does not revive the copyright in the stories.

EXAMPLE 2: Assume instead that Elliot compiles an anthology of the best short stories of the 2010s. All of the stories in the anthology are protected by copyright, so Elliot had to obtain the copyright owners' permission to include the stories in his anthology. The duration of the copyrights in the stories is not affected by the fact that Elliot republished them in his anthology years after they were created. Unless Elliot purchased all or part of the copyrights in the stories, he acquired no ownership rights in them by virtue of their inclusion in his anthology.

Registering Compilations

Fact compilations and collective works can and should be registered. This way, if someone copies the compiler's selection and arrangement, the compiler will be able to obtain statutory damages and attorneys' fees in an infringement suit. (See Chapter 3, "Copyright Registration.")

Initial Copyright Ownership

A work that satisfies the three criteria for copyright protection discussed in Chapter 4 (fixation, originality, and minimal creativity) is protected automatically upon creation. At that same moment, the author (or authors) of the work become the initial owner(s) of the copyright in the work. This chapter is about determining who these authors—and initial owners—are.

It is important to understand who the authors/initial owners are for these reasons:

- Their rights might differ, depending on the nature of their authorship.
- Correct identification of the authors/ initial owners is required to make a valid copyright registration.
- The nature of the authorship affects how long the copyright lasts.

There are several basic ways to author a work and, thereby, become its initial owner:

- An individual may independently author the work.
- An employer may pay an employee to author the work, in which case the employer is an author under the work-made-for-hire rule.
- A person or business entity may specially commission an independent contractor to author the work under a written work-made-for-hire contract, in which case the commissioning party becomes the author.
- Two or more individuals or entities may collaborate to become joint authors.

We discuss each of these types of authorship (and initial ownership) in turn.

Independent Authorship by an Individual

The individual author of a work is the initial owner of its copyright when the work-made-for-hire doctrine doesn't apply and when there is no joint authorship. The individual may exercise any of his or her copyright rights. For example, the author may reproduce and sell the work or authorize others to do so, such as by licensing the rights to a publisher. The author can also transfer ownership in whole or in part to others. (See Chapter 7, "Transferring Copyright Ownership.") An individual copyright owner can do whatever he or she wants with his or her copyright in the United States, being accountable to no one.

Impact of Community Property Laws on Copyright Ownership

In states that have community property laws, property that is acquired while people are married is usually considered to belong to both spouses equally. This means that individual authors who reside in Arizona, California, Idaho, Louisiana, Nevada, New Mexico, Texas, Washington, and Wisconsin may be required to share ownership of their copyrights with their spouses. (See discussion in Chapter 7, "Transferring Copyright Ownership.")

Who Owns Social Media Content?

Every day, millions of people post texts, photos, videos, sound recordings, and other content on social media platforms like Facebook, Twitter, and Instagram. The copyright in such content is owned by the person who creates it (provided it's original). However, whenever you post any content on a social media website, the website automatically obtains a non-exclusive license to use it—pretty much any way it wants. You give the platform this license when you sign up for an account and agree to the platform's terms of use.

Keep this in mind before you post any particularly valuable content on a social media platform. If you create content that you don't want others to use, post it on your own privately run website, not Twitter, Facebook, or another platform. See Chapter 7 for a detailed discussion of nonexclusive licenses.

Works Made for Hire

Not all works are initially owned by the person or persons who actually create them. If you create a protectable work on someone else's behalf, that person (or entity) may be considered the work's author and thereby initially own the copyright in the work, not you. These types of works are called works made for hire.

The owner of a work made for hire is considered to be the author of the work whether the owner is a human being or a business entity, such as a corporation or limited liability company (LLC). As the author, the owner is entitled to register the work, exercise its copyright rights in the work (such as publishing the work or adapting it to a different medium), permit others to exercise these rights, or sell all or part of its rights.

The actual creator of a work made for hire has no copyright rights in the work—the creator may not sell it, publish it, prepare a derivative work from it, or even read it in public. All the creator receives is compensation from the hiring party, whether a salary or another payment.

EXAMPLE: Real estate magnate Donald Frump orders Manny, a longtime employee who serves as Donald's publicist and ghostwriter, to write his autobiography. The resulting book, entitled *The Art of the Steal*, is a worldwide bestseller. It is also a work made for hire. Donald earns $1 million in royalties and sells the film rights for another $1 million. Manny asks Donald for a 10% share of these monies, reasoning that he is entitled to them because he actually wrote the autobiography. Donald refuses but tells Manny he'll give him a $50 a week raise. Manny can take the raise or leave it, but he is not legally entitled to any royalties from the autobiography. As far as the Copyright Act is concerned, Donald is the book's author.

Obviously, it is vitally important for all writers to understand what is and what is not a work made for hire.

Two Different Types of Works Made for Hire

There are probably only two reasons why you or anybody else would go to the trouble of creating a protectable work for another person or entity: (1) You are that person's employee and creating the work is part of your job, or (2) a person or an entity that is not your employer—a magazine, for instance—asks you to create the work for payment or some other remuneration (the Copyright Act calls this specially requesting or commissioning a work).

Let's examine each type of work made for hire.

Works Created by Employees as Part of Their Job

A natural consequence of the employer-employee relationship is that the employer owns whatever it pays an employee to create. It's assumed that an employee agrees to this when taking a job. For example, Ford Motor Company doesn't have to tell assembly line workers they won't own the cars they make or have them sign contracts to this effect. Similarly, an employer doesn't have to tell an employee that the employer will own copyrightable works created on its behalf—the employee is supposed to know this without being told. For this reason,

no written work-made-for-hire contract is required in the employer-employee context.

> **EXAMPLE:** "Scoop" Jackson is hired to be a salaried reporter for the *Yakima Daily News*, which is owned by a privately held corporation. He is required to write stories for the regular online and hardcopy editions of the newspaper as well as post material on the newspaper's blog and Twitter feed. This content will be considered works made for hire, and the *Daily News* will own the copyright to it. The *Daily News* does not have to tell Scoop this and need not draw up a work-made-for-hire agreement for him to sign.

The example above is obvious, but the work-made-for-hire rule is not limited to works written by in-house editorial staffs. The rule extends to anything written by any employee within the scope of employment, including reports, memoranda, letters, email, and websites.

One problem in applying the work-made-for-hire rule in the employer-employee context is determining:

- just who is an employee, and
- exactly when a work is written within the scope of employment.

Who Is an Employee?

The U.S. Supreme Court has held that a person is an employee for copyright purposes if the person on whose behalf the work is done has the *right to control* the manner and means by which the work is created. It makes no difference what the parties call themselves or how they characterize their relationship.

If the person on whose behalf the work is done has the requisite right of control, the person hired is an employee and any protectable work created within the scope of employment is a work made for hire. It also makes no difference whether the control is actually exercised, so long as the *right* to exercise it is present. (*Cmty. for Creative Non-Violence v. Reid,* 109 S. Ct. 2166 (1989).)

If a legal dispute results as to whether the creator of a protectable work was an employee, the courts are supposed to examine a variety of factors to determine whether the requisite degree of control was present in the relationship. Many of these criteria are quite broad, and there are no concrete guidelines as to how they should be applied. As a practical matter, this limited guidance means that judges have great discretion in deciding who is and who isn't an employee for copyright purposes.

Two factors are of prime importance:

- whether the hiring firm pays the worker's Social Security taxes, and
- whether the hiring firm provides employee benefits.

The court held that a part-time computer programmer employed by a swimming pool retailer was not the company's employee for copyright purposes and was therefore entitled to ownership of a program he wrote for the company. The court stated that the company's failure to provide the programmer with health, unemployment, or life insurance benefits, or to withhold Social Security, federal, or state taxes from his pay, was a "virtual admission" that the programmer was an independent contractor. The court stressed that the company could not treat the programmer as an independent contractor for tax purposes and then turn around and claim he was an employee for copyright ownership purposes—he had to be treated the same way for both purposes. (*Aymes v. Bonelli,* 980 F.2d 857 (2d Cir. 1992).)

The moral is this: If you don't pay a worker's Social Security taxes or provide him or her with benefits, you should assume the worker is an independent contractor for copyright ownership purposes.

Given the track record in the courts, you can probably safely assume that a formal salaried employee for whom you pay Social Security taxes and employee benefits would be considered an employee for copyright purposes. However, the rules are ambiguous and given to highly subjective interpretation. When anything short of a formal, salaried employment relationship is involved, there is always a risk it will not be deemed an employment relationship for copyright purposes. This could happen even though you treat such a worker as an employee for tax purposes.

TIP

A person who pays someone else to create a protectable work should not rely on the work-made-for-hire rule outside the context of a formal salaried arrangement. Instead, the person should have the creator transfer to him or her the needed rights. A written agreement must be signed by both parties to accomplish this.

Factors Considered in Determining Employee Status

Here is a list of some of the factors judges are supposed to consider in determining if a person is an employee for copyright purposes. This is not an exclusive list, and no single factor is determinative:

- the skill required to do the work
- the source of tools and materials used to create the work
- the duration of the relationship
- whether the person who pays for the work has the right to assign additional projects to the creative party
- who determines when and how long the creative party works
- the method of payment
- who decides what assistants will be hired and who pays them
- whether the work is in the ordinary line of business of the person who pays for the work
- whether the creative party is in business for him- or herself
- whether the creative party receives employee benefits from the person who pays for the work, and
- the tax treatment of the creative party.

When a Work Is Created Within the Scope of Employment

Not everything an employee writes belongs to the employer. An employee's writings and other copyrightable works are works made for hire only if they are created within the scope of employment. An employee's work is created within the scope of employment only if it:

- is the kind of work the employee is paid to perform
- occurs substantially within work hours at the work place, and
- is performed, at least in part, to serve the employer. (*Bell v. Maloney*, No. 16-1193, 2017 U.S. Dist. LEXIS 111867 (S.D. Ind. July 19, 2017) (quoting Restatement (Second) of Agency § 228).)

Unless an employer and employee agree otherwise, anything an employee writes outside the scope of employment is not a work made for hire. This is so even if the work arises out of the employee's activities on the employer's behalf.

EXAMPLE: Recall our intrepid reporter Scoop Jackson in the example above. Assume that Scoop writes a series of articles for the *Yakima Daily News* exposing unsafe practices in the meatpacking industry. Of course, these articles are works made for hire, the copyright to which are owned by Scoop's newspaper. Scoop also writes a novel on his own time about a reporter who exposes the meatpacking industry. Although the novel is based on Scoop's experiences as an employee-reporter, it is not a work made for hire because it was not created within the scope of his employment—that is, his job duties as a reporter did not include writing fiction.

Works created by an employee outside the scope of employment are automatically owned by the employee. Thus, it is not legally necessary to sign an agreement to this effect. However, an agreement stating that a particular work is not created within the scope of employment can be a very good idea where arguments might later develop about what the scope of employment entails. For this reason, Scoop had his employer sign the document below before he began work on the novel.

An employer and employee are free to agree that the employee will own all or part of the copyright in works created *within* the scope of employment. Such an agreement amounts to a transfer of copyright ownership from the employer to the employee. The employer is still considered the author of the work made for hire. To be effective, the agreement must be in writing and signed by *both* parties.

The agreement can be entered into either before or after the employee creates the work. See Chapter 7, "Transferring Copyright Ownership," for a detailed discussion of transfer agreements.

Are Scholarly Writings Works Made for Hire?

Works created by professors and other scholars employed by universities, colleges, and other academic institutions pose a special problem. Prior to the adoption of the current Copyright Act in 1976, virtually all courts had held that the copyrights in lecture notes, articles, and books written

Letter to the *Yakima Daily News*

March 1, 20xx

Bill Hearst, Publisher
Yakima Daily News
1000 Main St.
Yakima, WA 90002

Dear Bill:

This agreement is to confirm the understanding we've reached regarding ownership of my novel, tentatively titled *You Are What You Eat*.

You acknowledge that my novel will be written on my own time and shall not be written within the scope of my employment with the *Yakima Daily News*.

It is expressly agreed that I shall be the owner of all rights in the novel, including the copyright. Furthermore, the *Yakima Daily News* will sign all papers necessary for me to perfect my ownership of the entire copyright in the work.

If this agreement meets with your approval, please sign below to make this a binding contract between us. Please sign both copies and return one to me. The other signed copy is for your records.

Sincerely,

Scoop Jackson
Scoop Jackson

I agree with the above understanding and represent that I have authority to make this agreement and to sign this letter on behalf of the *Yakima Daily News*.

Bill Hearst
Date: March 2, 20xx

by professors were owned by the professors themselves, not by the universities or colleges that employed them. However, it's unclear whether this special teacher exception to the work-made-for-hire rules is in effect under current copyright law. Because it's unclear, it's wise not to rely on this exception.

So, if we assume there is no teacher exception, are faculty works made for hire? They are if (1) faculty members are employees for copyright ownership purposes, and (2) the materials involved were created within the scope of employment. Unfortunately, there are no court cases to guide us.

To determine whether or not faculty members are employees, generally, one would apply the agency law factors set forth above in "Factors Considered in Determining Employee Status." But even if we apply these facts, there is still no clear answer as to whether the requisite degree of control is present. For example, faculty members typically receive employee benefits and are treated as employees for Social Security tax benefits. These are strong factors showing employee status.

On the other hand, colleges and universities typically do not exercise sufficient control over what professors write for such writings to constitute works made for hire. Although academic institutions may "require" scholars to create scholarly works or risk not being awarded tenure

and other benefits ("publish or perish"), they usually do not dictate what should be written or supervise the writing process itself. The principle of academic freedom is supposed to prevent universities from controlling the ideas expressed in scholarly writings. However, no court has yet decided this question.

Even if we assume that faculty members are employees, it's not clear whether everything they create falls within the scope of employment. Applying the factors set forth above, it would seem that research publications would be within the scope of employment but textbooks would not. Faculty members are not paid by the university to write textbooks, while they are paid to produce research publications, such as scholarly articles and books (again, publish or perish).

However, as a practical matter, the question of whether faculty works are made for hire may be academic (no pun intended). There are two reasons for this. First, and probably most important, academic works usually have little or no economic value, and colleges and universities have no economic incentive to claim copyright ownership in such works. There are few examples of universities stripping faculty members of their copyright ownership.

Second, most colleges and universities now have written copyright ownership policies.

Typically, these policies permit faculty members to retain ownership of works created by their own independent effort—for example, journal articles, research bulletins, monographs, books, plays, poems, and works of art. However, many universities claim sole or joint ownership of works prepared with substantial use of university materials or facilities, administrative materials (such as faculty memos and reports), or materials prepared as part of specially sponsored projects. Some universities claim copyright ownership of computer software.

Where a university policy permits a faculty member to retain copyright ownership of his or her work—which is usually the case—the question of whether the work is a work made for hire does not arise. But, if a university does claim ownership on the basis of a copyright policy, it must be determined if the policy is legally enforceable. It *is* enforceable if the policy is contained in an employment contract signed by the faculty member. However, quite often, there is no formal signed employment contract between the university and faculty member. In this event, a university might claim that copyright ownership is transferred to it by virtue of institutional policies set forth in faculty handbooks or bylaws. Whether such claims would be upheld by the courts is unclear.

The bottom line is that any faculty member should carefully investigate his or her university's copyright policies—preferably before taking the job.

Specially Ordered or Commissioned Works

We've seen above that in the employer-employee context no work-made-for-hire agreement is necessary, and any type of protectable work may be a work made for hire. In contrast, where a person or an entity asks a writer who is not an employee to prepare a protectable work, that work may be a work made for hire only if (1) both parties sign a work-made-for-hire agreement, *and* (2) the work is one of the types of work set out in "Works Made for Hire by Nonemployees," below.

Express Work-Made-for-Hire Contract Required

A specially commissioned work constitutes a work made for hire only if, before the work is created, the commissioning party and the creative party both sign a written contract providing that the work shall be considered a work made for hire. The written agreement is absolutely crucial.

EXAMPLE: Steve hires Sara to write an introduction for his book. Both Sara and Steve sign a contract stating that the introduction will be a work made for hire. When Sara completes the introduction, Steve will be considered its author for copyright purposes.

Freelance Contributions to Magazines and Other Collective Works

The term "freelance writer" usually connotes a self-employed person who contributes articles to newspapers, magazines, and similar publications, whether print or online. Although you might not naturally think of freelance articles as works made for hire, they are if the freelancer and the publication that buys the work both sign a work-made-for-hire agreement.

EXAMPLE: The editor of *The Egoist Magazine* asks Gloria, a freelance writer, if she would be interested in writing an article for the magazine on nightlife in Palm Beach. Gloria says yes. The editor then sends Gloria a letter agreement to sign setting forth such terms as Gloria's compensation and the deadline for the article and its length, and stating that the article shall be a work made for hire. If Gloria signs the agreement, her article will be a work made for hire—that is, the magazine will be the author and initial owner, instead of her.

 TIP

Copyright tip for publishers and editors. Although the Copyright Act gives the publishers of websites, magazines, periodicals, and other collective works the right to use work-made-for-hire agreements with freelance writers, this doesn't mean that they should exercise this right. Some successful freelancers simply refuse to sign work-made-for-hire agreements or will demand extra compensation to do so. Generally, it's wiser—and more supportive of the arts—simply to have the author assign the rights that the magazine really needs and retain any others. For example, if a magazine only really needs the right to publish an article the first time and doesn't care about reprint rights, it should acquire first-time rights from the author and not use a work-made-for-hire agreement.

But, if you insist on using a work-made-for-hire agreement, be sure to:

- Get a full-blown work-made-for-hire agreement signed before the creative person starts work on the project—don't rely on informal go-aheads or engagement letters.
- Include an assignment to you of the creative person's copyright rights in the agreement—this way, if the finished work is for some reason determined not to be a work made for hire, you'll still own all the copyright rights by virtue of the assignment.

Special Rules for California

California law provides that a person who commissions a work made for hire is considered to be the employer of the creator of the work for purposes of the workers' compensation, unemployment insurance, and unemployment disability insurance laws. (Cal. Lab. Code § 3351.5(c); Cal. Unemp. Ins. Code §§ 621, 686.) However, it's unclear how exactly these laws affect the responsibilities and liabilities of persons or entities who commission works made for hire. Neither the California courts nor state agencies have addressed the question. It might mean that the commissioning party has to obtain workers' compensation coverage for the creative party and could be liable for any injuries the person sustains in the course of work. It might also mean that special penalties could be assessed against a commissioning party who willfully fails to pay the creative party any monies due after the person is discharged or resigns.

These potential requirements and liabilities are one reason why it might be desirable for those commissioning work in California to forgo a work-made-for-hire agreement and instead have the creator assign the desired copyright rights to the commissioning party in advance.

Works Made for Hire by Nonemployees

Works made for hire must be created by an employee within the scope of employment, unless they fall into one of the following nine nonemployee categories:
- a contribution to a collective work, such as a magazine, a newspaper article, or an anthology (see Chapter 5, "Adaptations and Compilations")
- a part of a motion picture or another audiovisual work, such as a screenplay
- a translation
- supplementary works, such as forewords, afterwords, supplemental pictorial illustrations, maps, charts, editorial notes, bibliographies, appendixes, and indexes
- a compilation (see Chapter 5)
- an instructional text
- a test
- answer material for a test, and
- an atlas.

Screenplays

Screenplays are among the types of work that are considered to be made for hire if specially commissioned pursuant to a work-made-for-hire agreement. Such agreements are commonly used in the film industry. However, the Writers Guild of America (the screenwriters' union) has entered into collective bargaining agreements with the entertainment industry providing that its members are entitled to retain certain copyright rights in their work-made-for-hire screenplays. The Writers Guild should be consulted about this if a question about copyright ownership of a screenplay arises.

Copyright Tip for Writers

If you sign a work-made-for-hire agreement, you are not considered the author of the work even though you created it. This also means the commissioning party does not have to give you credit for your work. If you want credit, be sure to include in the agreement a provision requiring the commissioning party to give it to you. It should specify the size, type, and placement of your credit.

Supplemental Works

Let's say an author or publisher hires an independent contractor (a nonemployee) to compile an index or bibliography, put together an appendix, take some photographs, or create a few illustrations, maps, or charts to supplement the text. The author or publisher might naturally assume that it will own the copyright in the paid-for work.

But by now, you should know that this will be true only if both parties sign a work-made-for-hire agreement or the independent contractor signs an agreement assigning rights in the work to the author or publisher. If they do neither, the contractor will own the copyright in the work he or she creates. However, the commissioning party will probably be entitled to use the work.

Unsolicited Works Are Not Specially Commissioned Works

A work is specially ordered or commissioned only if it is created at the commissioning party's request. By definition, unsolicited works are not requested and thus cannot be considered specially ordered or commissioned work. This fact cannot be altered by contract.

> EXAMPLE: Archie, a beginning freelance writer, writes an article about a trip he took to Pago Pago and sends it to the Cheap Travel website—a well-known subscription site that routinely publishes freelance submissions. The website accepts the article for publication and sends Archie a contract saying that the work will be a work made for hire. Although Archie's article comes within one of the nine categories of specially ordered works (it is a contribution to a collective work), it is not a work made for hire because it was not written at the website's request. However, if Archie signs the contract, this action will likely be considered a transfer of his copyright in the article to the website.

Work-Made-for-Hire Agreements

As mentioned above, a work created by an independent contractor (a nonemployee) can be a work made for hire only if a written work-made-for-hire agreement is signed by both parties. The law is clear that the parties must agree that the work will be a work made for hire before it is created. But the law is unclear as to whether the work-made-for-hire agreement must be signed before the work is started or can be signed afterwards. One court says it must always be signed beforehand. (*Schiller & Schmidt, Inc. v. Nordisco Corp.*, 969 F.2d 410 (7th Cir. 1992).) But another court ruled that the parties need only verbally agree before the work is begun that it will be a work made for hire and a written agreement may be signed after the work is started or completed. (*Playboy Enters., Inc. v. Dumas*, 53 F.3d 549 (2d Cir. 1995).) The *Playboy* decision applies in New York City where many publishers are located. Even so, it is always advisable to have a signed work-made-for-hire agreement in hand before work is begun, because it might be difficult or impossible to prove you had a verbal agreement with the author that the work would be a work made for hire.

Work-Made-for-Hire Letter Agreement

You don't need to use a long contract for a work-made-for-hire agreement; a short letter or memo can do the job. The letter or memo can be either a paper document with a physical signature or an email or other electronic document with a digital signature. A letter agreement has two advantages: It's easy to draft and is much less intimidating to a creative person than a long contract. If you use a paper agreement, make two copies, sign both, and send them to the creative party to sign. The creative party should keep one signed copy and return the other to you. If you prefer an electronic document or email, each party should receive a digital copy.

Authors Should Be Wary of Work-Made-for-Hire Endorsements on Checks

Authors should carefully examine any checks they receive from magazines, newspapers, publishers, or other sources for whom they have performed freelance work on other than a work-made-for-hire basis. Some unscrupulous publishers add language to their checks or purchase orders stating that the work performed was a work made for hire. Although the legal validity of such a provision on a check is highly questionable, it is not prudent to sign and cash such a check as issued. Instead, either cross out the offending language before cashing the check or return it to the publisher and demand a new check without the work-made-for-hire language. The latter course will result in a delay in your payment but will help make clear to the publisher that your work is not a work made for hire.

FORM

You can download a Sample Work-Made-for-Hire Letter Agreement (and all other forms in this book) from this book's companion page on Nolo.com; see the appendix for the link.

> EXAMPLE: Nastassia writes a nonfiction book and asks Bill, a librarian, to compile an index for it. An index is a supplementary work and one of the nine categories of specially commissioned works. This means the index will be a work made for hire if Nastassia and Bill both sign a work-made-for-hire agreement before Bill starts work. Nastassia could have Bill sign a letter agreement worded like the one shown on the next page.

Standard Work-Made-for-Hire Contract

Some people or companies that hire independent contractors to create works made for hire prefer to use longer agreements in the form of a standard contract. Such agreements typically address a number of issues that have nothing to do with copyright. You may wish to use such an agreement for a particularly complex or expensive project, because it can provide you added protection.

The work-made-for-hire agreement form included in this book covers the following issues not addressed in the short letter agreement discussed below:

- **Writer's independent contractor status.** The agreement includes a lengthy provision designed to show that the writer is an independent contractor, not the hiring firm's employee. (See Clause 6.) This language can be very helpful if the hiring firm is audited by the IRS or a state agency and the writer's employment status is questioned.

  To make it clear that the writer, not the hiring firm, has the right to control how the work will be performed, you need to emphasize the factors the IRS and other agencies consider in determining whether a client controls how the work is done. Of course, a mere recitation without adherence to these understandings won't fool the IRS. Think of this clause as a reminder to you and the writer about how to conduct your business relationship. For a detailed discussion of all the legal issues involved in hiring independent contractors, see *Working With Independent Contractors*, by Stephen Fishman (Nolo).

- **Confidentiality.** If, during the course of his or her work, the writer might have access to your valuable trade secrets—for example, business plans, methods and techniques not known by your competitors, or customer lists—it is reasonable for you to include a nondisclosure provision in the agreement. (See Clause 8.) Such a provision means that the writer may not disclose your trade secrets to others without your permission.

Sample Work-Made-for-Hire Letter Agreement

April 1, 20xx

Bill Brown

2600 State St.

Chicago, IL 60006

Dear Bill:

This letter is to confirm that I have specially ordered or commissioned you to prepare the following work: a two-level alphabetical index for the book entitled *The History of Sex*. The work will be delivered by email in Microsoft *Word* format

This specially ordered or commissioned work shall be completed no later than May 1, 20xx.

You agree that this specially ordered or commissioned work is a work made for hire, and that I, as the person for whom the work is prepared, shall own all right, title, and interest in and to the work, including the entire copyright in the work.

You further agree that to the extent the work is not a work made for hire, you will assign to me ownership of all right, title, and interest in and to the work, including ownership of the entire copyright in the work.

You also agree to execute all papers necessary for me to perfect my ownership of the entire copyright in the work.

You represent and warrant that the work you create or prepare will be original, will not infringe upon the rights of any third party, and will not have been previously assigned, licensed, or otherwise encumbered.

As compensation for your services, I will pay you $2,000 upon satisfactory completion of the work.

Sample Work-Made-for-Hire Letter Agreement (continued)

If this agreement meets with your approval, please sign below to make this a binding contract between us. Please sign both copies and return one to me. The other signed copy is for your records.

Sincerely,

_____

Nastassia Kinsey

I agree with the above understanding.

_____

Bill Brown

Date: _____

Taxpayer ID#: _____

- **No partnership.** It's wise to specify that you and the writer are separate legal entities, not partners or co-venturers. If the writer is viewed as your partner, you'll be liable for the writer's debts and the writer will have the power to make contracts that obligate you to others without your consent. (See Clause 13.)

- **Exclusive agreement.** Business contracts normally contain a provision stating that the written agreement is the complete and exclusive agreement between those involved. This language shows a court or an arbitrator that the parties intended the contract to be their final agreement. And it helps avoid claims that promises not contained in the written contract were made and broken. (See Clause 11.)

- **Choice of law.** It's a good idea for your agreement to provide which state's laws will govern if you have a dispute with the client. Including a choice of law provision is particularly helpful if you and the writer are in different states. There is some advantage to having the law of your own state govern, because your local attorney will likely be more familiar with that law. (See Clause 12.)

- **Assignment and delegation.** As a general rule, either party may assign its rights and delegate its obligations under a contract unless it's expressly prohibited. This means, for example, that the writer could hire someone else to do the work called for in the agreement. If you want to prevent a writer from delegating duties under a work-made-for-hire agreement, you should include a clause prohibiting it without the hiring firm's consent. (See Clause 14.)

- **Arbitration.** One important function of a contract is to provide a means for resolving disputes. As you probably know, court litigation can be very expensive. To avoid this cost, alternative forms of dispute resolution have been developed that don't involve going to court. These include mediation and arbitration.

The work-made-for-hire contract contains a provision requiring the parties to take advantage of these alternate forms of dispute resolution. (See Clause 15.) Under the sample language, the parties must first submit the dispute to mediation. The parties agree on a neutral third person to serve as mediator and help them settle their dispute. The mediator has no power to impose a decision, only to try to help the parties arrive at one.

If mediation doesn't work, the parties must submit the dispute to binding arbitration. Usually, arbitration runs much like an informal court trial without a jury. But the decision maker is an arbitrator rather than a judge. Arbitration is often much faster and cheaper than courts. Parties may be represented by their lawyer, but it's not required.

You should indicate in the mediation/arbitration clause where the mediation or arbitration would occur. You'll usually want it in the city or county where you live or work. If you and the writer live or work a long distance apart, you'll have to agree on a location.

> EXAMPLE: AcmeSoft, Inc., a large software developer, hires Barton Finkle, a freelance translator, to translate the manual for its *AcmeWrite* program into French. A translation is one of the nine categories of specially commissioned works, so the translation can be a work made for hire if both parties sign a work-made-for-hire agreement. AcmeSoft drafts the work-made-for-hire contract shown below for Barton to sign.

FORM

You can download a Work-Made-for-Hire-Agreement (and all other forms in this book) from this book's companion page on Nolo.com; see the appendix for the link.

Agreements With Employees

As discussed above, protectable works created by an employee within the scope of employment automatically become works made for hire. The employee's consent is not required and an express work-made-for-hire agreement is not necessary. Indeed, the employer need not even inform the employee that it will own the copyright in the employee's creations.

However, costly disputes can develop concerning whether a work is created within the scope of employment. For example, an employee who creates a work partly at home outside working hours might claim it is not a work made for hire because the work was done outside the scope of employment.

For this reason, it is a very good idea to have a written agreement describing the employee's job duties, so it will be clear whether a work is created within the scope of employment. It's also wise to include in the agreement a provision assigning (transferring) to you (the employer) the copyright rights in any job-related works that for some reason do not constitute works made for hire.

What Happens When a Work Does Not Satisfy the Work-Made-for-Hire Requirement?

What happens if someone hires another to create a work with the belief that it will constitute a work made for hire, but it turns out that the work-made-for-hire requirements were not satisfied? This situation could occur where a nonemployee signs a work-made-for-hire contract, but the work created did not fall within one of the nine categories of specially commissioned works.

Work-Made-for-Hire Agreement

This Agreement is made between AcmeSoft, Inc. (Client), with a principal place of business at 122 Harr Drive, Portland, Oregon, and Barton Finkle (Writer), with a principal place of business at 1900 Leafy Lane, Ashland, Oregon.

1. Services to Be Performed

Writer agrees to perform the following services: Translation into French of the AcmeSoft user manual for the program *AcmeWrite* 1.0.

2. Deadline

Writer's work must be completed by June 15, 20___ .

3. Payment

In consideration for the services to be performed by Writer, Client agrees to pay Writer as follows: $10,000.

4. Terms of Payment

Writer shall be paid $1,000 upon signing this Agreement and the rest of the sum described above when the Writer completes services and submits an invoice.

5. Expenses

Writer shall be responsible for all expenses incurred while performing services under this Agreement.

6. Independent Contractor Status

Writer is an independent contractor, not Client's employee. Writer's employees or contract personnel are not Client's employees. Writer and Client agree to the following rights consistent with an independent contractor relationship:

- Writer has the right to perform services for others during the term of this Agreement.

- Writer has the sole right to control and direct the means, manner, and method by which the services required by this Agreement will be performed.

- Writer has the right to perform the services required by this Agreement at any place, location, or time.

- Client will not withhold FICA (Social Security and Medicare taxes) from Writer's payments or make FICA payments on Writer's behalf, make state or federal unemployment compensation contributions on Writer's behalf, or withhold state or federal income tax from Writer's payments.

- Writer is ineligible to participate in any employee pension, health, vacation pay, sick pay, or other fringe benefit plan of Client.

- Client shall make no state or federal unemployment compensation payments on behalf of Writer, and Writer will not be entitled to these benefits in connection with work performed under this Agreement.

7. **Intellectual Property Ownership**

To the extent that the work performed by Writer under this Agreement (Writer's Work) includes any work of Authorship entitled to protection under the copyright laws, the parties agree to the following provisions:

- Writer's Work has been specially ordered and commissioned by Client as a contribution to a collective work, a supplementary work, or other category of work eligible to be treated as a work made for hire under the United States Copyright Act.

- Writer's Work shall be deemed a commissioned work and a work made for hire to the greatest extent permitted by law.

- Client shall be the sole author of Writer's Work and any work embodying the Writer's Work according to the United States Copyright Act.

- To the extent that Writer's Work is not properly characterized as a work made for hire, Writer grants to Client all right, title, and interest in Writer's Work, including all copyright rights, in perpetuity and throughout the world.

- Writer shall help prepare any papers Client considers necessary to secure any copyrights, patents, trademarks, or intellectual property rights at no charge to Client. However, Client shall reimburse Writer for reasonable out-of-pocket expenses incurred.

8. Confidentiality

Writer will not disclose or use, either during or after the term of this Agreement, any proprietary or confidential information of Client without Client's prior written permission except to the extent necessary to perform services on Client's behalf.

Proprietary or confidential information includes:

- the written, printed, graphic, or electronically recorded materials furnished by Client for Writer to use

- business plans, customer lists, operating procedures, trade secrets, design formulas, know-how and processes, computer programs and inventories, discoveries, and improvements of any kind, and

- information belonging to customers and suppliers of Client about whom Writer gained knowledge as a result of Writer's services to Client.

Writer shall not be restricted in using any material that is publicly available, already in Writer's possession or known to Writer without restriction, or which is rightfully obtained by Writer from sources other than Client.

Upon termination of Writer's services to Client, or at Client's request, Writer shall deliver to Client all materials in Writer's possession relating to Client's business.

9. Terminating the Agreement

With reasonable cause, either Client or Writer may terminate this Agreement, effective immediately upon giving written notice.

10. Writer's Representations and Warranties

Writer represents and warrants that:

- Writer is free to enter into this agreement.

- Writer will not violate the right of privacy or publicity or infringe upon any copyright or other proprietary right of any other person or entity.

11. Exclusive Agreement

This is the entire Agreement between Writer and Client.

12. Applicable Law

This Agreement will be governed by the laws of the state of Oregon.

13. No Partnership

This Agreement does not create a partnership relationship. Writer does not have authority to enter into contracts on Client's behalf.

14. Assignment

Writer may not assign or subcontract any rights or obligations under this Agreement without Client's prior written approval.

15. Dispute Resolution

If a dispute arises under this Agreement, the parties agree to first try to resolve the dispute with the help of a mutually agreed-upon mediator in the following location: Portland, Oregon. Any costs and fees other than attorneys' fees associated with the mediation shall be shared equally by the parties.

If it proves impossible to arrive at a mutually satisfactory solution through mediation, the parties agree to submit the dispute to binding arbitration in the following location: Portland, Oregon, under the rules of the American Arbitration Association. Judgment upon the award rendered by the arbitrator may be entered in any court with jurisdiction to do so.

Client:

AcmeSoft, Inc.

By: _____

    Minnie Marx

    Vice-President

Date: April 1, 20____

Writer:

_____

Barton Finkle

Date: April 1, 20____

In this event, depending on the exact wording of the agreement, a court could interpret the work-made-for-hire agreement as effecting an assignment of all copyright rights in the work to the hiring party. After all, this is the intended result whenever a work-made-for-hire agreement is signed.

EXAMPLE: Vernon Hill, the president of a large bank, wanted to write a book about his business philosophy. He had his bank enter into an agreement with a publisher, in which the proposed book was characterized as a work made for hire with the bank the author. Hill signed an agreement with the bank stating that the "work is a work made for hire within the meaning of the United States Copyright Law and that the Author [Bank] is the owner of Copyright in the Work."

The book was completed, but relations between Hill and the bank soured and he left. The book was never published. When Hill tried to publish part of the book himself years later, the bank claimed it owned the copyright because it was a work made for hire.

After much litigation, the Court of Appeals held that the work was not a work made for hire. First, the court noted it was unclear whether writing the book was within the scope of Hill's employment. Second, the court determined the work could not be a specially commissioned work because: (a) Hill was not an independent contractor and (b) the book did not fall within one of the categories of specially commissioned works.

However, the court held that the work-made-for-hire agreement constituted an assignment of all of Hill's copyright rights to the bank. The court reasoned that Hill intended to transfer all his copyright rights to the bank when he signed the agreement stating that the book was work made for hire. (*TD Bank N.A. v. Hill*, 928 F.3d 259 (3d Cir. 2019).)

Even if a court decides the hiring party is not entitled to an assignment of the copyright, the hiring party would likely have a nonexclusive license to use the work as intended. This seems only fair, considering that the hiring party paid for the work. A person with a nonexclusive license in a work may use the work but cannot prevent others from using it as well. Nonexclusive licenses may be implied from the circumstances; no express agreement is required. (See the detailed discussion of nonexclusive licenses in Chapter 7, "Transferring Copyright Ownership.")

Assignment of Rights as Alternative to Reliance on Work-Made-for-Hire Rule

Hopefully, it is clear by now that relying on the work-made-for-hire rule can be a risky proposition for the hiring party. Unless the hiring party is dealing with a conventional employee or commissioning one of the nine specially commissioned works discussed in "Specially Ordered or Commissioned Works," above, under an express work-made-for-hire contract, it's impossible to be absolutely sure who will end up owning the copyright in the paid-for work.

The solution to this problem is to have the creator of the work transfer all or part of his or her rights—whatever they are—to the hiring party. As discussed above, this may mean that the creator will still be considered the author and initial owner, but the result will be that the hiring party will end up owning the copyright.

An assignment must be put into effect through a written transfer agreement signed by both parties. The agreement may be signed before or after the work is created. See Chapter 7, "Transferring Copyright Ownership," for discussion of a simple bare-bones assignment agreement and a sample form.

You can also modify the work-made-for-hire agreements by deleting the work-made-for-hire language and instead including a provision like the following:

> You hereby assign to me ownership of all right, title, and interest in and to the Work, including ownership of the entire copyright in the Work. You also agree to execute all papers necessary for me to perfect my ownership of the entire copyright in the work.

EXAMPLE: Mark is writing a book on toxic waste pollution. He hires Sally to take photographs of toxic waste dumps for his book. He has her sign the following assignment letter agreement.

Sample Assignment Letter Agreement

April 1, 20xx

Sally James
200 Beacon Hill
Boston, MA 10000

Dear Sally:

This letter is to confirm that you agree to prepare the following Work: 25 black-and-white photographs of each of the toxic waste dumps on the attached list.

The Work shall be completed no later than May 1, 20xx.

You hereby assign to me ownership of all right, title, and interest in and to the Work, including ownership of the entire copyright in the Work. You also agree to execute all papers necessary for me to perfect my ownership of the entire copyright in the work.

You represent and warrant that the work you create or prepare will be original, will not infringe upon the rights of any third party, and will not have been previously assigned, licensed, or otherwise encumbered.

As compensation for your services, I will pay you $2,000 upon satisfactory completion of the work.

If this agreement meets with your approval, please sign below to make this a binding contract between us. Please sign both copies and return one to me. The other signed copy is for your records.

(continued)

Sincerely,

Mark Anthony

Mark Anthony

I agree with the above understanding.

Sally James

Date: April 2, 20xx

Taxpayer ID#: 123-45-6789

Assignments Can Be Terminated After 35 Years

One possible disadvantage of using an assign-ment of rights as opposed to a work-made-for-hire agreement is that an assignment can be terminated by the author or his or her heirs 35 to 40 years after it is made. (See Chapter 8, "Copyright Duration," for a detailed discus-sion.) However, in most cases, this disadvan-tage is meaningless because very few works have a useful economic life of 35 years.

In addition, a work obtained by an assign-ment from an individual will have a different copyright term than a work made for hire. Works made for hire are protected for 95 years from the date of publication or 120 years from the date of creation, whichever comes first. Works by individuals are pro-tected for the life of the person plus 70 years. (See Chapter 8, "Copyright Duration," for a detailed discussion on how long copyright protection lasts.) Few works have a useful economic life of 70 years, let alone 95 years, so this difference is usually meaningless.

Jointly Authored Works

Things can get even more complicated when two or more individuals create a work that is not a work made for hire. Such a work is normally jointly owned by its creators— that is, each contributing author shares in the ownership of the entire work. A joint author's life is not quite as simple as that of an individual copyright owner. There may be restrictions on what each joint author can do with his or her ownership share, and joint authors must account to each other for any profits they receive from commercial exploitation of the joint work.

When Is a Work Jointly Authored?

A work is jointly authored automatically upon its creation if (1) two or more authors contributed material to the work, and (2) each of the authors prepared a contribution with the *intention* that it would be combined with the contributions of the other authors as part of a single unitary work. We'll refer to such works as joint works.

> EXAMPLE: Peter and Christianne agree to write a biography of Tom Hanks together. Peter writes the chapters covering the first half of Hanks' life, and Christianne writes the remainder. They combine their work to form a single biography of Hanks' entire life. The biography is a joint work by Peter and Christianne.

Authors' Intent Is Controlling Factor

The key to determining whether a work is a joint work is the authors' intent *at the time the work is created*. If the authors intended that their writing be absorbed or combined with other contributions into an integrated unit, the work that results is a joint work. It is not necessary that the authors work together or work at the same time. Indeed, it is not even necessary that they know each other when they create their respective contributions.

> **EXAMPLE:** Paul writes a children's story with the intention that it be combined with a number of illustrations to be created by Jean. Unfortunately, Jean dies before she can create the illustrations. Five years later, Paul meets Mary, a successful artist. Mary reads Paul's story and tells him that she would like to create the illustrations for it. Paul agrees. Mary creates the illustrations. Mary and Paul combine Paul's story and Mary's illustrations into a single integrated work—a children's book. The book is a joint work, co-owned by Mary and Paul. This is so even though Paul had never met Mary when he wrote his story and the story was written years before Mary drew her illustrations. All that matters is that when Paul and Mary created their respective contributions they intended that they be combined with other work to form an integrated whole.

How Much Material Must a Person Contribute to Be a Joint Author?

The respective contributions made to a joint work by its authors need not be equal in terms of quantity or quality. But, to be considered a joint author, a person must contribute more than a minimal amount of work to the finished product. For example, a person who proofreads and makes spelling corrections to a book written by another is not a joint author of that book.

May a Joint Author Only Contribute Ideas?

Most courts require that a person's contribution consist of protectable expression —that is, actual written work—for the person to be considered a joint author. One who contributes ideas or other unprotectable items is not entitled to an ownership interest in the work's copyright unless the parties expressly agree to it, preferably in writing. (See Chapter 4, "What Copyright Protects.")

> **EXAMPLE:** Abe and Zsa Zsa agree to collaborate on a screenplay. Abe conceives a detailed and complex plot for the screenplay, but does no writing himself. Instead, he tells Zsa Zsa the plot and Zsa Zsa uses Abe's ideas to actually write the screenplay. Most courts would hold Zsa Zsa the sole owner of the copyright in the screenplay unless she and Abe had agreed otherwise.

TIP

It is always a good idea for collaborators to have a written agreement setting forth their respective interests in the work to be written. This way, if one contributor is found not to be a joint owner of the work because he or she did not contribute protectable expression to it, that contributor would still be entitled (as a matter of contract law) to the ownership interest stated in the collaboration agreement.

Joint Authors Need Not Be Human Beings

A joint author doesn't have to be a human being. A corporation, a partnership, or another business entity can also be a joint author.

> **EXAMPLE:** Sunnydale Farms, Incorporated, a large corporation that manufactures and sells gardening implements and seeds, agrees to coauthor a book on urban gardens with Ralph, a famous expert on roses. Ralph writes the chapters on growing flowers, while Sunnydale employees write the chapters on growing vegetables. The chapters written by Sunnydale's employees are works made for hire for which Sunnydale is considered the author. The resulting book is a joint work. The joint authors are Ralph and Sunnydale.

Joint Works Compared With Derivative and Collective Works

What happens if the intent to combine contributions into an integrated whole arises after the contributions were created? In this event, the resulting work is not a joint work. Rather, it is either a collective work or a derivative work. It will be a collective work if the respective contributions of the authors were independently created and later simply combined into a collective whole without changing them. It will be a derivative work if the respective authors' contributions are recast, transformed, or adapted to create a new work.

Why It's Important to Know the Difference Between Joint Works and Derivative or Collective Works

Knowing the difference between a joint work and a derivative or collective work is important for these reasons:

- The copyright in a derivative work extends only to the material added to the preexisting material by the derivative work's authors.
- Contributors to a collective work own the copyright only in the material they contributed to the work.
- The authors of a joint work each share ownership in the entire work.

EXAMPLE 1: Assume that Paul in the example above wrote his children's story without any intent that it be combined with illustrations. Acme Publications purchases Paul's entire copyright in the story and decides to publish it with illustrations created by Jean. The resulting work is a collective work—that is, a work in which separately protectable works are combined into a collective whole without making any internal changes to the material. (See Chapter 5, "Adaptations and Compilations," for a detailed discussion of collective works.)

EXAMPLE 2: Art writes and publishes a scientific treatise on quantum theory. Several years later, Art and his colleague Marie decide to produce an updated and expanded version of the work. This revised version of the treatise will not be a joint work, because when Art wrote his original treatise he did not intend to combine it with any other work. Rather, the revised treatise is a derivative work—that is, a work created by transforming the original treatise into a new, revised treatise. (See Chapter 5, "Adaptations and Compilations" for a detailed discussion of derivative works.)

Joint Authors' Collaboration Agreement

A written collaboration agreement is not legally required to create a joint work; an oral agreement is sufficient. However, as Samuel Goldwyn supposedly once said, "A verbal contract isn't worth the paper it's written on." It is vital that collaborators draft and sign a written agreement spelling out their rights and responsibilities. This avoids innumerable headaches later on.

An example of a completed collaboration agreement is provided below. The following discussion focuses on the key provisions in a collaboration agreement, many of which contain blanks you must fill in.

You can download this Collaboration Agreement (and all the other forms in this book) from this book's companion page on Nolo.com; see the appendix for the link.

Collaborator's Contributions

The single most important part of a collaboration agreement is the description of who will perform what work. Think carefully about this before you begin work. Some collaborators write everything together; others work independently and then review and revise each other's first drafts. By far the best practice is to write a detailed outline or synopsis of the work and indicate on it who will write each section. The outline should be attached to the collaboration agreement.

We agree to the division of labor set forth in the ☐ outline ☐ schedule attached to and made part of this agreement. [*Check applicable box*] or

> We agree to the following division of labor:
> _[describe who will do what]_
> _____
> _____ .

Completion Date

Collaborators need to decide on a realistic deadline for completion of the work. They also need to agree on what will happen if the deadline is not met—can it be extended? The following provision allows the collaborators to agree on a new deadline. If they can't agree to a new deadline, they must then decide whether any of the collaborators may complete the work and on what terms. If they can't agree on anything, they have to submit the dispute to mediation and arbitration.

> We shall complete our contributions by _[date]_ or by the date specified in a publishing contract we enter into. If we fail to do so, we may mutually agree in writing to extend the time for completion.
>
> If we fail to agree to an extension, we shall enter into a written agreement as to which of us may complete the Work and on what terms, including what authorship credit and compensation, if any, shall be paid to the collaborator who does not participate in completing the Work. If we are unable to agree, we shall submit our dispute to mediation or arbitration as described below.

Quitting the Collaboration

If one collaborator wants to quit the collaboration, the agreement should provide whether the remaining collaborator(s) can complete the work and, if so, what compensation must be paid to the withdrawing collaborator. The following provision simply leaves it to the collaborators to decide how to proceed if one collaborator wants to quit. If they can't agree, they must submit the dispute to mediation/arbitration.

> If any of us wishes to quit the collaboration before the Work is finally completed and accepted by a publisher, we shall enter into a written agreement setting forth the rights of the withdrawing collaborator, including what authorship credit and compensation, if any, shall be paid to the withdrawing collaborator. If we are unable to agree, we shall submit our dispute to mediation or arbitration as described below.

Ownership

Ownership in the completed work can be divided in any way the collaborators wish. This is so regardless of the quantity or quality of their contributions. Typically, each collaborator is given an equal ownership share—for example, two collaborators would each share an undivided one-half interest in the work; three collaborators would each own a one-third interest; and so forth. The sample agreement in this book provides for equal ownership. Materials a collaborator collects to create the work—for example, tapes or photos—are also jointly owned unless the collaborator paid for them personally.

> We intend that the completed Work shall be a joint work. We shall each be equal co-owners in the copyright in the Work. Materials any of us collect to prepare the Work shall belong to the collaborator who obtains them if acquired at his or her own expense. Otherwise, all materials shall be jointly owned and may be disposed of only upon all the collaborators' written agreement.

However, your ownership interests don't have to be equal. For example, if there were two collaborators, one could be given a greater ownership interest than the other. How to divide your copyright in the work is entirely up to you.

Authorship Credit

How the collaborators' names appear on their completed work is often an important issue. They can be in alphabetical order or any other way. Make sure that whatever you decide is set forth in your agreement to avoid future disputes.

> The Work shall contain the following credit line: [*list authors in the order their names will appear on Work*].

Payments

As with copyright ownership, the income derived from the work can be distributed among the collaborators in any way they desire. This agreement provides two options: an equal distribution or some other arrangement.

> All money accruing from the exploitation of our Work shall be divided equally among us. All contracts we enter into for exploitation of the Work shall provide for equal royalty payments and statements from the payor to each collaborator.

or

> All money accruing from the exploitation of the Work shall be divided as follows: [*describe*] _____ .

Expenses

There are two ways to deal with expenses incurred by the collaborators in creating the work: They can be shared equally, or each collaborator can be required to pay his or her own expenses. You need to decide which approach to take in your agreement by choosing one of the two provisions below.

> All expenses incurred in creating the Work shall be shared equally unless we agree otherwise in writing in advance.

or

> Each of us shall pay our own expenses unless we agree otherwise in writing in advance.

Collaboration Agreement—Page 1

This Collaboration Agreement is made between Nastassia Kinsey whose address is 123 Grub St., Santa Longo, CA; Jack Handy whose address is 1000 Main St., Santa Longo, CA; and Bartleby Crum whose address is 77 Sunset Blvd., Los Angeles, CA.

1. **Description of Work**

   We agree to collaborate to create the following Work: a book-length work with the working title "The History of Sex." The Work will describe how sex evolved from the first primitive life forms to the present day.

2. **Collaborators' Contributions**

   We agree to the division of labor set forth in the outline attached to and made part of this agreement.

3. **Completion Date**

   We shall complete our contributions by April 1, 20____, or by the date specified in a publishing contract we enter into. If we fail to do so, we may mutually agree in writing to extend the time for completion.

   If we fail to agree to an extension, we shall enter into a written agreement as to which of us may complete the Work and on what terms, including what authorship credit and compensation, if any, shall be paid to the collaborator who does not participate in completing the Work. If we are unable to agree, we shall submit our dispute to mediation or arbitration as described below.

4. **Quitting the Collaboration**

   If any of us wishes to quit the collaboration before the Work is finally completed and accepted by a publisher, we shall enter into a written agreement setting forth the rights of the withdrawing collaborator, including what authorship credit and compensation, if any, shall be paid to the withdrawing collaborator. If we are unable to agree, we shall submit our dispute to mediation or arbitration as described below.

5. **Ownership**

   We intend that the completed Work shall be a joint work. We shall each be equal co-owners in the copyright in the Work.

Death or Disability

It may seem macabre to think about, but you need to consider what will happen if one or more collaborators die or become disabled before the work is completed. Can the survivors complete the work? If so, what compensation, if any, should be paid to the disabled collaborator or the deceased collaborator's heirs? The following provision gives the surviving collaborators the right to complete the work themselves or hire someone else to help them do so. After the work is published, the deceased collaborator's estate or disabled collaborator must be paid a pro rata share of the income received from the work. This share is based on the amount of the deceased or disabled collaborator's written contribution to the completed work after deducting expenses incurred by the remaining collaborators in completing the work.

> If any of us dies or becomes disabled before completion of his or her portion of the Work, the remaining collaborator(s) may complete that portion of the Work or hire someone else to do so. The deceased collaborator's estate or disabled collaborator shall be paid a pro rata share of all income received from the Work based on the amount of the deceased or disabled collaborator's contribution to the completed Work after deducting expenses incurred in completing the Work, including any salaries, fees, or royalties paid to another to complete the Work. The remaining collaborator(s) shall have sole authority to enter into contracts or licenses for the Work.

Decision Making

Unless they agree otherwise, joint authors have the right to grant third parties permission to exploit the work on a nonexclusive basis without the other authors' consent. This can lead to chaos if different authors grant nonexclusive licenses of the same rights to different people. It's best that the agreement require that all business decisions be made jointly and that all the collaborators must sign all agreements for publication or other exploitation of the work.

> All editorial, business, and other decisions affecting the Work shall be made jointly by all of us and no agreement shall be valid without all our signatures.

Noncompetition

Collaboration agreements often include noncompetition provisions barring the collaborators from authoring competing works, but that doesn't mean they need to or should. A noncompetition provision can make it difficult or impossible for you or your other collaborators to earn a living. If you want such a provision, it's usually best to limit its duration. You might also want to place other limitations on the restriction— for example, permitting collaborators to write magazine articles on the same topic as the work.

Collaboration Agreement—Page 2

Materials any of us collect to prepare the Work shall belong to the collaborator who obtains them if acquired at his or her expense. Otherwise, all materials shall be jointly owned and may be disposed of only upon all the collaborators' written agreement.

6. **Authorship Credit**

   The Work shall contain the following credit line: Nastassia Kinsey, Jack Handy, and Bartleby Crum.

7. **Payments**

   All money accruing from the exploitation of our Work shall be divided equally among us. All contracts we enter into for exploitation of the Work shall provide for equal royalty payments and statements from the payor to each collaborator.

8. **Expenses**

   All expenses incurred in creating the Work shall be shared equally unless we agree otherwise in writing in advance.

9. **Death or Disability**

   If any of us dies or becomes disabled before completion of his or her portion of the Work, the remaining collaborator(s) may complete that portion of the Work or hire someone else to do so. The deceased collaborator's estate or disabled collaborator shall be paid a pro rata share of all income received from the Work based on the amount of the deceased or disabled collaborator's contribution to the completed Work after deducting expenses incurred in completing the Work, including any salaries, fees, or royalties paid to another to complete the Work. The remaining collaborator(s) shall have sole authority to enter into contracts or licenses for the Work.

10. **Term of Agreement**

    This Agreement begins on the date signed by all parties and shall continue for the duration of the copyright in the Work.

11. **Decision Making**

    All editorial, business, and other decisions affecting the Work shall be made jointly by all of us and no agreement shall be valid without all our signatures.

For a period of _____ years after completion of the Work, none of us shall participate in the preparation of any other work that directly competes with and would significantly diminish the sales of the Work.

[OPTIONAL]

This noncompetition agreement does not apply in the following circumstances: _____ [describe] _____ .

We represent and warrant to each other all of the following:

- Each of us is free to enter into this agreement.
- Our contributions to the Work are original or all necessary permissions and releases have been obtained and paid for.
- None of our contributions to the Work libel, violate the right of privacy or publicity, or infringe upon any copyright or other proprietary right of any other person or entity.

We each agree to indemnify the other(s) for any loss, liability, or expense resulting from the actual breach of these warranties.

Warranties and Indemnities

Virtually all book publishing contracts contain a warranty and indemnity clause in which the authors promise the publisher that their work does not infringe on anybody else's copyright or other rights. If an infringement occurs, the authors are required to indemnify—that is, reimburse—the publisher for the costs involved in defending a lawsuit. This means that if one of your fellow collaborators violates a third person's rights, you could end up liable for the damages. The following provision protects you from this by requiring each collaborator to indemnify the other if he or she commits such a violation.

Assignment and Delegation

The following provision prevents the collaborators from assigning their contract rights or delegating their duties without the other collaborators' written permission. This means, for example, that a collaborator cannot get someone else to do his or her work without the other collaborators' consent.

Collaboration Agreement—Page 3

12. No Partnership

We are collaborators in this single Work. This agreement does not create a partnership relationship.

13. Exclusive Agreement

This is our entire agreement. Any other agreements previously entered into by us are superseded by it.

14. Noncompetition

For a period of two years after completion of the Work, none of us shall participate in the preparation of any other work that directly competes with and would significantly diminish the sales of the Work.

15. Derivative Works

We agree that none of us will incorporate material based on or derived from the Work in any subsequent work without the written consent of the other collaborators.

16. Warranties and Indemnities

We represent and warrant to each other all of the following:

- Each of us is free to enter into this agreement.

- Our contributions to the Work are original or all necessary permissions and releases have been obtained and paid for.

- None of our contributions to the Work libel, violate the right of privacy or publicity, or infringe upon any copyright or other proprietary right of any other person or entity.

We each agree to indemnify the others for any loss, liability, or expense resulting from the actual breach of these warranties.

17. Successors

This agreement shall benefit and bind our heirs, successors, assigns, and personal representatives.

> None of us may assign his or her rights or delegate his or her duties under this agreement without the other collaborators' written consent. However, any collaborator may assign the right to receive royalties or other income from the Work by giving written notice to the other collaborator(s).

Dispute Resolution

One of the most important functions of a collaboration agreement is to provide a means for resolving disputes. As you probably know, court litigation can be very expensive. To avoid this cost, alternative forms of dispute resolution have been developed that don't involve going to court. These include mediation and arbitration.

The following provision requires the collaborators to take advantage of these alternate forms of dispute resolution. You're first required to submit the dispute to mediation. You agree on a neutral third person to serve as mediator and try to help you settle your dispute. The mediator has no power to impose a decision, only to try to help you arrive at one.

If mediation doesn't work, you must submit the dispute to *binding* arbitration. Arbitration is much like an informal court trial without a jury. And arbitrators serve as decision makers rather than judges. Arbitration is usually much faster and cheaper than courts. You may

be represented by a lawyer, but it's not required. You should indicate in the following clause where the mediation or arbitration would occur. You'll usually want it in the city or county where you live. If the collaborators live a long distance apart, they'll have to agree on a location.

> If a dispute arises under this agreement, we agree to first try to resolve it with the help of a mutually agreed-upon mediator in the following location [*list city or county where mediation will occur*]. Any costs and fees other than attorneys' fees associated with the mediation will be shared equally by each of us.
>
> If it proves impossible to arrive at a mutually satisfactory solution through mediation, we agree to submit the dispute to binding arbitration at the following location [*list city or county where arbitration will occur*] under the rules of the American Arbitration Association. Judgment upon the award rendered by the arbitration may be entered in any court with jurisdiction to do so.

Joint Authors' Rights and Duties in the Absence of a Collaboration Agreement

The drafters of the Copyright Act realized that not all joint authors would be prudent enough to enter into written (or even oral) collaboration agreements setting forth their ownership interests, rights, and duties. To

Collaboration Agreement—Page 4

18. Assignment and Delegation

None of us may assign his or her rights or delegate his or her duties under this agreement without the other collaborators' written consent. However, any collaborator may assign the right to receive royalties or other income from the Work by giving written notice to the other collaborators.

19. Applicable Law

This agreement will be governed by the laws of the state of California.

20. Dispute Resolution

If a dispute arises under this agreement, we agree to first try to resolve it with the help of a mutually agreed-upon mediator in the following location: Santa Longo, CA. Any costs and fees other than attorneys' fees associated with the mediation will be shared equally by each of us.

If it proves impossible to arrive at a mutually satisfactory solution through mediation, we agree to submit the dispute to binding arbitration at the following location: Santa Longo, CA, under the rules of the American Arbitration Association. Judgment upon the award rendered by the arbitration may be entered in any court with jurisdiction to do so.

21. Attorneys' Fees

If any legal action is necessary to enforce this agreement, the prevailing party shall be entitled to reasonable attorneys' fees, costs, and expenses in addition to any other relief to which he or she may be entitled.

Signatures:

_____   _____
Nastassia Kinsey   Date

_____   _____
Jack Handy   Date

_____   _____
Bartleby Crum   Date

avoid chaos, they made sure that the act contained provisions governing the most important aspects of the legal relationship between joint authors who fail to agree among themselves how their relationship should operate. You might think of these provisions as similar to a computer program's default settings that control the program when the user fails to indicate settings.

Ownership Interests

Unless they agree otherwise, joint authors each have an undivided interest in the entire work. This is basically the same as joint ownership of a house or other real estate. When a husband and wife jointly own their home, they normally each own a 50% interest in the entire house—that is, they each have an undivided one-half interest. Similarly, joint authors share ownership of all five exclusive rights that make up the joint work's copyright.

Right to Exploit Copyright

Unless they agree otherwise, each joint author has the right to exercise any or all of the five copyright rights inherent in the joint work—meaning, any of the authors may reproduce and distribute the work or prepare derivative works based upon it (or display or perform it). Each author may do so without the other joint authors' consent.

Right to License Joint Work

Unless they agree otherwise, each joint author may grant third parties permission to exploit the work—on a nonexclusive basis—without the other owners' consent. This means that different authors may grant nonexclusive licenses of the same right to different persons!

EXAMPLE: Manny, Moe, and Jack are joint authors of a novel. Manny gives Publisher A the nonexclusive right to publish the book in North America. Moe gives the same right to Publisher B, and Jack to Publisher C. The result, perfectly legal, is that three publishers have the right to publish the book at the same time.

TIP
To avoid the kind of results illustrated in the above example, anyone who purchases an exclusive right in a joint work should require signatures by all the authors. (See Chapter 7, "Transferring Copyright Ownership," for a detailed discussion of copyright transfers.)

Right to Transfer Ownership

Finally, unless they agree otherwise, each author of a joint work may transfer his or her entire ownership interest to another person without the other joint authors' consent. Such person then co-owns the work with the remaining authors. But a joint author can only transfer his or her particular interest, not that of any other author.

EXAMPLE: Sue, Deborah, and Martin are joint authors of a college textbook. Sue decides to transfer her ownership interest to her son, Sam. Since Sue, Deborah, and Martin have not agreed among themselves to restrict their transfer rights in any way, Sue may transfer her interest to Sam without Deborah's or Martin's consent (but Sue could not transfer Deborah's or Martin's ownership interests to Sam without their consent). When the transfer is completed, Sam will have all the rights Sue had as a joint author.

Duty to Account for Profits

Along with these rights, each joint author has the duty to account to the other joint owners for any profits received from his or her use or license of the joint work. All the joint authors are entitled to share in these profits. Unless they agree otherwise, the profits must be divided among the authors according to their proportionate interests in the joint work. (Note, however, that such profits do not include what one author gets for selling his or her share of the copyright.)

EXAMPLE: Bill and Lee are joint authors of a novel. Bill writes a screenplay based on the novel and sells it for $10,000. Lee is entitled to one-half of the $10,000.

It might not seem fair that a joint author who goes to the time and trouble of exploiting the copyright in the joint work by publishing it or creating derivative works based upon it is required to share his or her profits equally with the other joint authors who did nothing. This is still another reason why it's wise to enter into a collaboration agreement.

What Happens When a Joint Author Dies?

Absent a joint tenancy agreement, a deceased joint author's heirs would acquire his or her share in the joint work. The other joint authors do not acquire a deceased owner's share (unless, of course, the deceased owner willed it to them, or the author died without a will and another joint author happened to be a family or blood relation entitled to inherit an interest under the general inheritance laws).

Transferring Copyright Ownership

I n Chapter 6, "Initial Copyright Ownership," we discuss the rights that accompany copyright ownership. Here is a brief recap. An author automatically becomes the owner of a complete set of exclusive rights in any protected expression he or she creates. These include the right to:

- reproduce the protected expression in the physical world or online
- distribute copies of the work to the public by sale, rental, lease, or otherwise
- prepare derivative works using the protected expression (that is, adapt new works from the expression), and
- perform and display the work publicly.

These rights are exclusive because only the owner of one or more particular rights that together make up copyright ownership may exercise it or permit others to do so. For example, only the owner of the right to distribute a book may sell it to the public or permit others—a publisher, for instance—to do so.

With the important exception of self-publishers who reproduce and distribute their work themselves, authors normally profit from their copyrights by selling their rights to publishers or others to exploit. And, except where they publish works that are in the public domain (such as works originally published more than 95 years ago), publishers must acquire the right to reproduce and sell a work from its author or another copyright owner.

The Terminology of Transfers

Several different terms can be used to describe a transfer of copyright ownership rights. Many of these terms are used interchangeably and have no settled legal meaning, but here is how we'll use them in this book:

- Assignment means a transfer of all the exclusive rights that make up a copyright.
- Exclusive license means a transfer on an exclusive basis, of one or more, but less than all, of a copyright owner's exclusive rights.
- Nonexclusive license means giving someone the right to exercise one or more of a copyright owner's rights on a nonexclusive basis. Since this does not prevent the copyright owner from giving others permission to exercise the same right or rights at the same time, it is not a transfer of copyright ownership.

Again, please remember that these definitions are only for the purposes of this discussion. In the real world, it makes no difference if a transfer is called an assignment, a license, a contract, or a grant of rights or is given no label. The effect of an agreement to transfer copyright ownership rights is determined according to the language it contains, not its label.

How Copyright Ownership Rights Are Transferred to Others

A transfer of copyright ownership rights must be in writing and signed by the person who owns the rights being transferred. There are two basic types of copyright transfers: exclusive licenses and assignments. Although these terms are often used interchangeably, there are some differences.

Exclusive Licenses

The term exclusive license is usually used when a copyright owner transfers one or more of his or her rights but retains at least some of them.

> EXAMPLE: Jane writes an article on economics and grants *The Economist's Journal* the exclusive right to publish it for the first time online and in its North American print editions. Jane has granted the *Journal* an exclusive license. Only the *Journal* may publish the article for the first time online and in its North American print editions. But Jane retains the right to republish her article after it appears in the *Journal* and to include it in a book. She also retains the right to create derivative works from it (for example, to expand it into a book-length work), as well as other rights that weren't specifically transferred in the license.

A copyright owner's exclusive rights are almost infinitely divisible. That is, they can be divided and subdivided and licensed to others in just about any way imaginable. In the publishing business, the most common divisions are by language, type of media (hardcover and softcover books, e-books, magazines, film, video, audiotapes, and so on), time, or geography.

> EXAMPLE 1: Jennifer writes a high school math textbook and sells Scrivener & Sons an exclusive license to distribute digital and print editions in the United States only. She then grants MacKenzie Press an exclusive license to sell the book in Canada and Trans-European Publishing Company the right to sell it in all European Union countries.

> EXAMPLE 2: Leo writes a biography and grants Scrivener & Sons the exclusive right to sell it in the United States in hardcover, paperback, and as a digital edition for the Amazon Kindle. He licenses the right to sell a digital edition for the Apple iBook store to AcmeSoft, Inc. He grants all English language rights outside the United States to the British publisher MacCauley & Unwin.

Exclusive Licensee's Rights

The holder of an exclusive license becomes the owner of the transferred right(s). As such, unless the exclusive license provides otherwise, the owner is entitled to sue anyone who infringes on that right during the period of ownership and is entitled to transfer the license to others. The license holder may also record the exclusive license with the Copyright Office; this provides many valuable benefits.

EXAMPLE 3: Martha writes a detective novel. She grants Hardboiled Publications, Inc., the exclusive right to sell the book in all hardcopy and digital editions in the United States and Canada. She then gives Repulsive Pictures the exclusive right to create and distribute a film based on her work; ABC the right to use it for a television series; and Zounds Unlimited, Inc., the right to adapt it into an audiobook.

Can Copyrights Be Transferred by Email?

Can you transfer all or part of a copyright through email? The copyright law says a transfer must be in writing signed by the copyright owner to be valid. An email would not effect a valid transfer unless the electronic signature it contained was deemed to satisfy the signing requirement. Fortunately, Congress has enacted a law called the Electronic Signatures in Global and National Commerce Act (ESIGN for short) providing that electronic signatures are legally valid. (15 U.S.C. § 7001(a).) Courts have held that the ESIGN Act applies to copyright transfers. (*Metro. Reg'l Info. Sys., Inc. v. Am. Home Realty Network, Inc.*, 722 F.3d 591 (4th Cir. 2013).) And the Copyright Office accepts for recordation copyright assignments with electronic signatures.

A signed email can serve as a copyright transfer agreement, so be careful what you put in your emails.

Assignments

If an owner of all the exclusive rights in a copyright simultaneously transfers the entire bundle of rights that make up the copyright to a single person or entity, the transaction is usually called an assignment or, sometimes, an all rights transfer. An assignment must be in writing to be valid.

EXAMPLE: Otto assigns Acme Romances the entire copyright in his romance novel *Love's Lost Languor.* This means that Acme—and only Acme—may publish the work or permit others to do so, or exercise any other part of the bundle of rights that make up the copyright in the work (such as authorizing someone to adapt the book into a screenplay). Otto has relinquished these rights. For all practical purposes, Acme now owns the copyright instead of Otto.

Nonexclusive Licenses Do Not Transfer Copyright Ownership

As mentioned earlier, a nonexclusive license gives someone the right to exercise one or more of a copyright owner's rights, but does not prevent the copyright owner from giving others permission to exercise the same right or rights at the same time. A nonexclusive license is not a transfer of ownership; it's a form of sharing. The most common type of nonexclusive license is one granting an author permission to quote from, distribute, copy, or otherwise use a protected work; such licenses are often called permissions. See Chapter 9, "Using Other Authors' Words," for a detailed discussion and sample permission form.

> EXAMPLE: Tony, an avid parachutist, has written and self-published an e-book on advanced parachuting techniques. He gives the Fresno Parachuting Club permission to publish a copy of the e-book on its blog. Tony retains the right to let others copy and distribute his e-book or may do so himself. Tony has given the club a nonexclusive license to exercise some of his copyright rights in his e-book. The license is nonexclusive because the club cannot prevent Tony from letting others exercise the same rights he has granted to it.

As with exclusive licenses, nonexclusive licenses may be limited as to time, geography, or media or in any other way. They can be granted orally or in writing. The much better practice, however, is to use some sort of writing; this can avoid possible misunderstandings and gives the nonexclusive licensee certain priority rights. It is not necessary to have a formal contract filled with legalese to grant a nonexclusive license. A simple letter or memo is sufficient. Just make sure that you make clear the license is nonexclusive (use the term non-exclusive license) and spell out the terms and conditions of the license—that is, what rights are being licensed, to whom, and for how long.

Nonexclusive Licenses and Social Media

Nonexclusive licenses are used extensively by social media websites, such as Facebook, Instagram, YouTube, and Twitter. To establish an account with such websites, you must agree to their terms of service by checking an online box. These terms invariably require that users grant the website a nonexclusive license to use the content they upload.

Typically, these nonexclusive licenses give the social media websites the right to use uploaded content any way they see fit. The website may do so without paying you, asking you for specific permission, or even informing you.

For example, to obtain a Facebook account, you must agree to terms of service that grant Facebook "a non-exclusive, transferable, sub-licensable, royalty-free, and worldwide license to host, use, distribute, modify, run, copy, publicly perform or display, translate, and create derivative works of your content (consistent with your privacy and application settings)." This license continues until you delete your Facebook account.

Be sure to read the terms of service before you upload any content to any website you don't own. You might wish to refrain from uploading particularly valuable content to Facebook and similar websites. You can always post content on your own privately-owned website without losing your exclusive ownership rights.

First Sale Doctrine

Under what is known as the first sale doctrine, once a copyright owner sells or gives away a copy or copies of a book or another physical manifestation of the copyright, he or she relinquishes all control over that physical copy itself. The purchaser can resell the copy without the copyright owner's permission or, if the purchaser is a library, lend it to the public.

EXAMPLE: Morris self-published 500 copies of a book on do-it-yourself plumbing. He sells all 500 copies of the book to Joe's Hardware Store but does not transfer any copyright rights to Joe's. Joe's is entitled to sell all 500 copies, rent them, give them away, destroy them, or do anything else it wants with them. But, of course, Joe's cannot reproduce the book or exercise any of Morris's other exclusive rights without his permission.

In a 2013 case, the U. S. Supreme Court held the first sale doctrine has no geographic limitations. The case involved a Thai student who came to the United States to study and engaged in a business arrangement with his family in Thailand. They would send him books purchased in Thailand, and he would resell them in the United States market. The student expanded the business and eventually earned $100,000 profit. United States publishers sued the student arguing that the first sale doctrine did not apply to "gray market goods"—lawfully made goods that were imported into (but not made in) the United States. The Supreme Court disagreed and ruled for the student, stating that as long as the copies were lawfully made (under the direction of the copyright holder), there was no requirement that the books be manufactured in the United States. (*Kirtsaeng v. John Wiley & Sons, Inc.*, 568 U.S. 519 (2013).)

Sales of Copies Do Not Transfer Copyright Ownership

Ownership of a copyright and ownership of a material object in which the copyrighted work is embodied—such as a book or an article—are entirely separate things. The sale or gift of a copy or copies of a book, an article, or another protected work does not transfer the copyright owner's exclusive rights in the work. A copyright owner's exclusive rights can be transferred only by a written agreement. For example, a person who buys a copy of a book or manuscript owns that book or manuscript but acquires no copyright rights in the work.

EXAMPLE: Luther, an extremely wealthy and avid book collector, purchases the original manuscript of James Joyce's *Finnegan's Wake* from Joyce's estate. However, Luther does not obtain any copyright rights in the work. Although Luther owns the manuscript, he cannot reproduce and distribute it or exercise any other of the copyright owners' rights in the work without obtaining their permission.

Copyright Transfers Do Not Affect Copyright Duration

Copyright transfers do not affect the duration of the copyright, even if the entire bundle of copyright ownership rights is transferred. See Chapter 8, "Copyright Duration." However, a transfer itself may be limited as to time; that is, it doesn't have to be for the entire duration of the copyright.

> **EXAMPLE:** Margaret grants Green Thumb Publishing the exclusive right to publish her book on gardening in the United States for 20 years. The copyright in the book will last for the rest of Margaret's life plus an additional 70 years. The transfer to Green Thumb has no effect on this. When the 20 years are up, the transferred rights will revert to Margaret or her heirs and will last for the remainder of the copyright term.

Rights Retained by Author After Transfer

A copyright owner who transfers all or part of the bundle of exclusive rights still retains some important rights.

Right to Sublicense Under Exclusive Licenses

Whenever an author or other copyright owner assigns his or her entire bundle of copyright rights to another person or company, that person or company may reassign the copyright to someone else without the original owner's consent. However, this is not necessarily the case when an exclusive license is involved, because an exclusive license only transfers *part* of a copyright owner's rights.

Two federal courts have held that a person or company that receives an exclusive license from an author or other copyright owner may not sublicense—that is, transfer to someone else—the rights it has received unless the license permits it or the copyright owner agrees. (*Gardner v. Nike, Inc.*, 279 F.3d 774 (9th Cir. 2002); *Cincom Sys., Inc. v. Novelis Corp.*, 581 F.3d 431 (6th Cir. 2009).)

These cases have important ramifications for copyright owners and publishers and others to whom they grant exclusive licenses. Unless the license agreement gives them the right to sublicense the work, licensees may be prevented from fully exploiting the work they've licensed. For example, in the *Gardner v. Nike* case cited above, Nike granted an exclusive license to Sony Music Entertainment for a cartoon character named MC Teach. Sony had the exclusive right to use MC Teach in records, TV shows and movies, clothing, and educational materials. Sony then sublicensed to Gardner the right to use MC Teach on educational materials. Nike sued, claiming Sony couldn't sublicense MC Teach without Nike's permission. The court agreed, because the license agreement did not specifically permit such sublicensing. So, Sony was prevented from sublicensing MC Teach to Gardner unless Nike agreed.

Nike was free to withhold such agreement or to demand increased license fees to permit the sublicensing.

Here are some other scenarios where these cases could wreak havoc on licensees' plans:

- A publisher obtains an exclusive license to publish a book in North America. The author retains all other rights. The publishing agreement does not specifically allow the publisher to sublicense its rights in the book. The publisher couldn't sign a license permitting another publisher to produce a Spanish language edition for sale in North America or sell North American book club rights without the author's permission.

- An author obtains an exclusive license to use several photographs in his book. He signs a license with the photographer that says he may use the photos in all editions of the book. But the license agreement says nothing about whether the author can sublicense the photos. When a magazine contacts him to publish an excerpt from the book, the author can't authorize use of the photos in the book unless he obtains the photographer's permission.

- A website buys a series of articles from a freelance writer. The agreement gives the website an exclusive license to use the articles on the Internet. Because the license says nothing about sublicensing, the website cannot license the articles for non-Internet uses—for example,

for publication in print magazines or newspapers.

One way to avoid these issues is to include language in an exclusive license agreement permitting sublicensing. Here's an example:

> [*Name of person or entity receiving license*] may sublicense the rights granted in this agreement.

Alternatively, the person seeking rights can acquire copyright ownership and avoid using exclusive licenses. This can be done through an assignment or, in some cases, use of a work-made-for-hire agreement. (See Chapter 6, "Initial Copyright Ownership.") More and more publishers, newspapers, magazines, and others are utilizing this option of obtaining copyright ownership.

If you would like a middle ground—one where you have some say in sublicensing but you won't interfere in most sublicense agreements—you can soften the effect with a clause in which you withhold consent for sublicenses only for a valid business reason. What's a valid reason? Perhaps the company to which your licensee wants to grant an assignment has a reputation for not paying royalties, or maybe the company is in poor financial shape. You cannot, however, withhold consent for an arbitrary reason, such as someone from the company once treated you rudely. Here's an example:

[*Name of person or entity receiving license*] may not sublicense the rights granted in this agreement without the prior written consent of Licensor. Such consent shall not be unreasonably withheld.

Many exclusive license agreements contain standard boilerplate language stating that the agreement applies to the licensee's "successors and assigns." Whether this language constitutes permission to sublicense is unclear and should not be relied upon.

Nonexclusive Licensees Have No Sublicensing Rights

Those who obtain nonexclusive licenses from copyright owners have no rights to sublicense their rights without the copyright owner's permission. Unlike the *Nike* ruling involving exclusive licenses, above, this rule is settled law throughout the United States.

If you're an author or other copyright owner who grants someone an exclusive license to use your work, you should decide whether to give the licensee the right to sublicense the work. The results of the negotiation might depend on your bargaining power, but you have the legal right to refuse to grant such authority or to demand payment for sublicensing rights.

Statutory Termination of Transfers After 35 Years

A potentially important right retained by authors and their families is the statutory right to terminate transfers of copyright ownership made after December 31, 1977. This right to terminate transfers includes the original grant of rights an author gives to his or her publisher. These statutory termination rights can never be waived or contracted away.

What Rights Can Be Terminated?

Any transfer of copyright rights made by a living author after December 31, 1977 may be terminated. This is so whether the transfer is an assignment of the entire bundle of copyright rights or an exclusive or nonexclusive license of only certain rights. A transfer of a copyright by a will that occurs after an author dies is not subject to statutory termination.

Who Can Exercise the Termination Right?

The statutory termination right may be exercised only by the author of a work or, if the author is dead when the time to terminate arrives, by the author's widow or widower, children (including illegitimate and adopted children), and grandchildren. If an author dies without leaving a surviving spouse or children or grandchildren, the termination right ceases to exist. Note that an author cannot leave termination rights to others in a will. When an author dies, his or her termination rights automatically pass on to a surviving spouse and children and grandchildren, if any. The provisions in an author's will are irrelevant.

The owner of a work made for hire, whether an individual or a business entity, has no statutory termination rights.

> EXAMPLE 1: Sam writes a book in 2000 and signs a publishing contract transferring his entire copyright to Scrivener & Sons that same year. The transfer may later be terminated by Sam or certain family members as described below.

> EXAMPLE 2: Sue writes a book in 2000 and transfers her entire copyright to her boyfriend Bill by a will upon her death in 2001. This transfer may not be terminated by Sue's surviving family.

When Can Transfers Be Terminated?

A transfer of the right to publish (that is, reproduce and distribute) a work may be terminated any time during a five-year period beginning either 40 years after the date of the transfer or 35 years after the date of first publication, whichever is earlier. A transfer of any other rights (for example, the right to adapt a work into a film) can be terminated any time during a five-year period beginning 35 years after the transfer was made and ending 40 years afterwards.

> EXAMPLE: Kelly Stewart signs a contract with Scrivener & Sons on January 1, 1980 to write a novel and grants Scrivener the exclusive right to publish the book in the United States and Canada. The novel, entitled *The Voyeur*, is not published until January 1, 1990. On January 1, 1991, Kelly sells the film rights to her novel to Repulsive Pictures. The publication rights transferred to Scrivener may be terminated by Kelly or her heirs any time between January 1, 2020 and January 1, 2025 (40 to 45 years after the publishing contract was signed). This is earlier than 35 years after the date of actual publication of the book. The film rights transfer to Repulsive may be terminated between January 1, 2025 and January 1, 2031 (35 to 40 years after the transfer was made).

The Copyright Office has created several online tables you can use to calculate your termination period. The tables are available at www.copyright.gov/recordation/termination.html (click on the "When to Terminate" tab).

What Happens After a Transfer Is Terminated?

After a transfer is terminated, the terminated rights revert back to the author if he or she is still alive. If the author is dead, the rights are shared by the author's widow or widower, children, and grandchildren. However, the owners of any derivative works prepared from the work may continue to distribute such works.

EXAMPLE 1: Assume that in 2020 Kelly Stewart terminates the publication rights grant she made to Scrivener & Sons in 1980. This means that Scrivener may not publish any more copies of Kelly's novel without her permission. Kelly may now resell her novel's publication rights to Scrivener or any other publisher or self-publish her novel if she so chooses.

EXAMPLE 2: Assume that it is now the year 2025. Kelly has terminated the film rights transfer she made to Repulsive Pictures back in 1991. Kelly now owns the right to make any new films based upon her novel. However, Repulsive may continue to distribute *Front Window,* a film it produced based on Kelly's novel in 1994; it just can't make any new films from the novel without Kelly's permission.

What Is the Termination Procedure?

A written notice of termination that complies with the statutory requirements must be recorded with the Copyright Office and sent to the owners whose rights are being terminated. Although the termination won't be effective until 35 or 40 years after the transfer, you can serve the notice up to ten years before that. That is:

- For transfers including publication rights, the notice of termination may be served 25 years after publication or 30 years after the transfer was signed, whichever occurs first.

- For transfers not including publication rights, the notice of termination may be served 25 years after the transfer was signed.

Thus, for example, during 2021, a notice of termination may be served to terminate a transfer not involving publication rights made during 1996.

At the very latest, the notice of termination must be served at least two years before the effective date of termination. A notice not recorded by this time will be invalid.

The notice of termination may be written in the form of a letter, including all the following information:

- a statement that the termination is made under 17 U.S.C. § 203
- the name of each person whose rights are being terminated or that person's successor in title, and each address at which service of the notice is being made
- the date the transfer being terminated was made and, if the grant covered the right of publication, the date of publication
- the title of the work and the name of the author(s) and, if possible and practicable, the original copyright registration number
- a brief statement reasonably identifying the transfer to which the notice of termination applies, and the effective date of termination, and
- if the termination is made by the author's heirs, a listing of their names and relationships to that deceased author.

The notice must be served by personal service or first-class mail. Service by mail must be sent to an address which, after a reasonable investigation, is found to be the last known address of the person whose rights are being terminated or his or her heirs or successors. The notice must also be recorded with the Copyright Office before its effective date.

Filing Documents With the Copyright Office

An author or other copyright owner retains the right to file the following documents with the Copyright Office following a transfer of copyright rights.

Supplementary Registrations

Even though the author or another copyright owner no longer owns any copyrights, they may continue to supplement information in the original registration with certain types of new information or changes, according to the procedures discussed in Chapter 3, "Supplementary Registration."

Notice Regarding Contractual Termination or Revocation of Transfer

A copyright owner who transfers ownership of copyright right(s) for a set term (for example, ten years) has the right to notify the Copyright Office when the term has expired, so as to expressly reclaim ownership

on the record. Similarly, an owner who revokes a transfer (due to a breach of the licensing terms or for some other reason) should send a letter to the Copyright Office and have the letter recorded. An example letter is shown below.

January 2, 20xx

Dear Examiner:

My copyright registration #TX 1234657 in the textbook entitled *French for First Graders* was transferred in full to Kiddie Publications for a period of ten (10) years, commencing on January 1, 20xx. This is to notify you that the transfer has terminated and I am the sole owner of copyright #TX 1234567.

Sincerely,

Jacques Paul Jones

Jacques Paul Jones

Moral Rights

In many European and other countries an author automatically retains certain additional rights in his or her work. These are called moral rights (or *droits morals*). Moral rights are rights an author can never transfer to a third party, because they are considered an extension of his or her being. Briefly, they consist of the right to proper credit or attribution whenever the work is published, to disclaim authorship of unauthorized copies, to prevent or call back distribution under certain conditions, and to object to any distortion, mutilation, or other modification of the author's work that is injurious to his or her reputation. The right to prevent colorization of black and white films is an example of a moral right. Moral rights are generally of most concern to visual artists.

The Berne Convention (an international copyright treaty) requires that signatory countries extend these rights to authors. (See discussion in Chapter 11, "International Copyright Protection.") In 1991, Congress amended the Copyright Act to extend certain moral rights to visual artists (see Section 106A of the Copyright Act), but the United States has not granted similar rights to authors.

However, American courts have recognized certain types of rights that are analogous to moral rights, although they might not be referred to as such. For example, any author of a work published in the United States retains the right to have his or her authorship continuously recognized on works that remain true to the original. Conversely, an author retains the right to have his or her name taken off a work that has been substantially changed from the original. These rights do not come from the Copyright Act but rather from the trademark laws, which prohibit misrepresentation of a product's origins. In addition, one court has held that unauthorized changes in a work that are so extensive as to impair its integrity constitute copyright infringement. (See *Gilliam v. Am. Broad. Cos., Inc.*, 538 F.2d 14 (2d Cir. 1976) (granting British comedy group Monty Python an injunction to prevent ABC from airing Monty Python programs that ABC had licensed to broadcast but heavily edited).)

Copyright Transfers Between Freelance Writers and Magazines and Other Periodicals

Now that you have a general understanding of copyright transfer law, let's see how it applies to the relationship between authors and publishers of magazines, newspapers, and similar publications (often called serial publications). Because publishers' and writers' interests differ in these transactions, we'll examine them first from an author's point of view and then from the point of view of a publisher or an editor.

Transfers From the Writer's Point of View

Publishing Jargon

Editors, literary agents, and others in the publishing business have their own jargon to describe an author's copyright rights. An author attempting to sell an article or other contribution to a magazine, a newspaper, or another serial publication is likely to encounter some of the following terms.

Compare to Work-Made-for-Hire Agreements

Magazines and other periodicals are permitted to enter into work-made-for-hire agreements with freelance contributors. Technically, a work-made-for-hire agreement is not a transfer of rights; rather, the employer is considered to be the author of the work. But the practical result is the same as a transfer of all rights: The magazine owns all the rights in the work. The only difference is that an author who makes an all-rights assignment may terminate the assignment after 35 years and retains certain moral rights. Work-made-for-hire agreements are discussed in Chapter 6, "Initial Copyright Ownership."

All world rights. Transfer of all world rights or all rights means that the author assigns all of his or her copyright rights to the magazine or another serial publication. The publication becomes the sole copyright owner. It may publish the work anywhere in the world any number of times, syndicate it, use it in databases, create derivative works from it or permit others to do so, or do anything else it wants with it. The author may not resell the work, create derivative works from it (for example, use it as a chapter in a book), or use it in any other way without the magazine's permission—the author no longer owns the work.

All world serial rights. A transfer of all world serial rights means that the publisher acquires an exclusive license to publish the contribution in newspapers, magazines, and other serial publications throughout the world any number of times for the duration of the copyright term. The author of the article or other contribution may not resell it to any other serial publication anywhere in the world. But the author retains all other rights—for instance, the author may use it as a chapter in a book or sell it for adaptation as a movie or video.

First North American serial rights. A grant of first North American serial rights means that the magazine or other serial publication has an exclusive license to publish the work for the first time in North America (the United States and Canada). Once the work has been published, the author may resell it, create derivative works from it, or do anything else desired with it—he or she owns all the other rights in the work.

Second serial rights. A transfer of second serial rights (or reprint rights) gives a magazine, a newspaper, or another serial publication a *nonexclusive* license to reprint a work once after it has already appeared in another serial publication.

One-time rights. A transfer of one-time rights (also called simultaneous rights) gives the magazine or other publication the right to publish a previously unpublished work once; but, in contrast to a grant of first serial rights (above), the author may sell the work to other publications to appear at the same time. This is a nonexclusive license, rather than an ownership transfer. Newspapers often purchase one-time rights from freelance contributors.

Which Rights Should You Sell?

It is always in a writer's best interests to retain as many rights as possible. Let's examine the consequences of an all-rights grant compared with a grant of first North American rights.

> **EXAMPLE 1:** George writes a short story about a six-year-old's experiences at Christmas. In 2015, he sells all his rights in the story to *Maudlin Magazine* for $750. The story appears in *Maudlin's* December 2015 issue. The story proves to be so popular that *Maudlin* reprints it every December thereafter. Not only that, every year it sells reprint rights to the story to several other magazines and newspapers throughout the country. George gets absolutely nothing from all these reprintings.

> **EXAMPLE 2:** Assume instead that George only sold *Maudlin Magazine* first North American serial rights to his story in 2015. After *Maudlin* printed the story in North America for the first time in December 2015, it had no further rights in the story. George, and only George, could permit *Maudlin* or other magazines and newspapers to reprint it. The income George receives from these reprintings far exceeds the $750 he got from *Maudlin* for the story's initial publication.

TIP
You'll find that many magazines will initially ask for all your rights but will be willing to take less, if you negotiate with them. Don't be afraid to speak up and demand to be treated fairly.

Transfers From a Magazine's Point of View

If you're the editor or publisher of a magazine, periodical, or similar publication, you need to obtain the rights you need from freelancers with the least amount of paperwork and the fewest headaches possible. Be aware that a written agreement is always necessary to purchase an exclusive right from a writer—for example, first North American serial rights.

If you want to be sure a freelancer's piece will appear first or only in your magazine, you must use a written agreement. In the absence of a written agreement, a publisher obtains only a nonexclusive license to publish a freelancer's piece in the magazine or other periodical. Thus, the author can sell it to other magazines (or use it in any other way).

Exclusive first publication rights are of most importance to publishers of national magazines. If you're publishing a newspaper or regional publication, it probably won't matter much if the same piece appears at the same time (or has already appeared) in another periodical in a different part of the country.

Most magazines, especially regional publications, are not interested in resale rights and adaptation rights (such as film rights or the right to include the piece in a book). These rights have value only if there is a market for them; usually, there isn't.

You should develop a transfer agreement form. This may be in the form of a letter or a more formal-looking contract. For sample forms, see the sources listed below in "Transfer Documents." If you're considering using a work-made-for-hire agreement, be sure to read the discussion of work made for hire in Chapter 6, "Initial Copyright Ownership."

Copyright Transfers Between Writers and Book Publishers

Book publishers operate differently from magazines or newspapers.

Publishing Argot

The copyright rights in a book are normally divided into two categories: the primary publication rights and subsidiary (sub) rights.

Primary Publication Right

The exclusive right to publish a work in book form for the first time in the English language is sometimes called the primary right. Publishing agreements vary as to the territory to which this right extends. At a minimum, a U.S. publisher will normally want the exclusive right to publish the work in the United States. The territory is often extended to all countries in which English is spoken; these are called all English language rights. The most expansive possible grant is all-world rights—that is, the right to publish the book in all countries in all languages.

Importance of Foreign Language Rights

The right to translate and sell a book in a foreign language can be very important for some books, such as popular novels, art books, and children's books. These rights are usually sold language by language at international book fairs (such as the Frankfurt (Germany) Book Fair) and by international literary agents.

Book publishers usually obtain the exclusive right to publish a work for the full copyright term, but, in some cases, a shorter period may be involved.

Subsidiary or Sub Rights

All the other copyright rights in a book are called subsidiary or sub rights. These include film, television, radio, and live-stage adaptation rights; the right to publish all or part of the work in a newspaper, a magazine, or another periodical prior to or after book publication; book club publication rights; the right to publish the book in a foreign language or license others to do so; the right to create and distribute nondramatic audio recordings of the work; and the right to publish braille, large-type, and other accessible formats.

Transfers From an Author's Point of View

It is usually in an author's best interest to retain as many rights as possible unless, of course, the publisher pays so much that it makes sense to assign all rights. The more bargaining power an author has, the more rights the author will likely be able to keep. However, it can make good sense to sell subsidiary rights to a publisher in return for a share of the profits (at least 50%), if the publisher is better able to market these rights than the author or the author's agent. A large full-line publisher will often know the subsidiary rights markets well and have the contacts and experience to effectively market an author's sub rights.

Transfers From a Book Publisher's Point of View

It is in a book publisher's best interest to demand an assignment of all rights from the author in return for a royalty and a share of the profits from the sale of the subsidiary rights listed earlier. This gives the publisher the right to sell all the subsidiary rights one by one and keep part of the profits. A 50–50 split of the profits from sub rights sales is common, but other divisions are also used.

Electronic Publishing and Ownership of Electronic Rights

As used in this chapter, electronic rights means the legal right to reproduce, distribute, adapt, and publicly display and perform a work in electronic form. This includes:

- creating electronic versions of written works that can be read online or downloaded from websites such as Amazon.com
- placing all or a substantial part of a work in its original form on magnetic media used directly in computers such as a CD-ROM or DVD-ROM
- reproducing all or a substantial part of a work in its original form in an electronic database like LexisNexis
- adapting a work into a multimedia work, whether distributed online as a mobile application or on a CD-ROM, DVD-ROM, or computer game cartridge, and
- publishing on demand—that is, transferring a digital copy of a work from a publisher's database to a bookstore, which prints it out and sells the consumer the printed copy.

Each of these uses can be regarded as a separate electronic right and dealt with separately in a publishing agreement.

Initial Ownership of Electronic Rights

Electronic rights are no different from any other copyright rights. They are initially owned by a work's author.

Self-employed individuals who create written works alone or with others (the type of people we normally think of as authors) will initially own the electronic and all other copyright rights in their works. (See Chapter 6, "Initial Copyright Ownership.")

The electronic copyright in works made for hire will be initially owned by the employer or hiring party the moment the work is created. The employer or hiring party is the author for copyright purposes, not the person who actually created the work. This includes:

- works created by employees within the scope of their employment, and
- specially commissioned works created by independent contractors under written work-made-for-hire agreements. (See Chapter 6, "Initial Copyright Ownership.")

Because the employer or hiring party using a work-made-for-hire agreement automatically owns all electronic and other copyright rights the moment a work is created, there is no need for them to obtain any additional transfer of rights from the actual creators after the work is completed.

An increasing number of magazines, newspapers, and journals are now using work-made-for-hire agreements with freelance writers in order to obtain all the rights in the work, including electronic rights.

Transfer of Electronic Rights by Individual Authors

With the important exception of self-publishers who reproduce and distribute their work themselves, self-employed authors normally profit from their copyrights by selling their rights to publishers or others to exploit. In today's publishing environment, such sales will typically include the transfer of the author's electronic rights.

When an author sells a book to a publisher, the publishing contract defines which rights the publisher gets and which the author keeps, if any. The right to license a work for use in electronic form is specifically dealt with in the publishing agreement.

Most publishers insist on acquiring all electronic rights along with the right to print the work in book form. However, this is a matter for negotiation, as is how much an author will be paid for such rights. Experienced authors who have agents may be able to retain some or even all electronic rights to a work. Inexperienced authors will likely have difficulty retaining any such rights.

Transfers of Electronic Rights in Freelance Articles

The U.S. Supreme Court held in 2001 that, if a publisher has not acquired electronic rights in writing, permission must be obtained from the author to reproduce a freelance article in an electronic database. (*New York Times Co., Inc., v. Tasini*, 533

U.S. 483 (2001).) The court held that when a freelancer—that is, a nonemployee—contributes an article or other material to a collective work (for example, a newspaper, magazine, periodical, journal, or an anthology or encyclopedia) but does not specifically transfer all or part of his or her copyright rights, the collective work may only use the article or other material in:

- the original version of the collective work—for example, a specific issue or edition of a periodical
- a revision of that specific collective work—for example, later editions of a periodical, such as the final edition of a newspaper, and
- a publication of a later collective work in the same series—for example, a new edition of an encyclopedia or dictionary.

Any other use of the material requires permission from the freelancer.

As a result of the Supreme Court's *Tasini* decision, hundreds of thousands of freelance articles written before the mid-1990s were removed from electronic databases because the databases didn't want to pay for permission to use them. Partly because of *Tasini*, it is now a nearly universal practice for newspapers, magazines, journals, and similar publications to demand that freelancers transfer their electronic rights. This can take one of several forms:

- The freelancer can be required to sign an assignment transferring all his or her copyright rights to the publisher.

- The freelancer can be required to sign a work-made-for-hire agreement—in this event, the publication, not the freelancer, is considered to be the author of the work for copyright purposes. (See Chapter 6, "Initial Copyright Ownership.")
- If less than all rights are being transferred, the freelancer can be asked to specifically transfer electronic rights—a clause transferring such rights needn't be long or complex. A clause like the following will suffice: "Author grants Publisher the right to publish the work through any media deemed appropriate by the Publisher."

More and more publishers are requiring freelancers to transfer all their rights. Of course, this includes their electronic rights.

Ownership of Electronic Rights in Older Works

Modern publishing agreements include specific provisions regarding ownership of electronic rights. However, older agreements might have nothing on the subject, because the technology wasn't known or anticipated at the time. In this event, it can be very difficult to determine who owns the electronic rights. This happened in a case involving the famous writers William Styron, Kurt Vonnegut, and Robert B. Parker. They granted Rosetta Books the right to publish digital versions (e-books) of several of their novels. Several of the books had previously been published by Random House. Random House had signed written contracts for the books providing that it had the exclusive right to "print, publish, and sell the work in book form." Random House claimed this meant it had the exclusive right to publish the works as e-books. Random House sued Rosetta for copyright infringement and lost. The court held that the contract language did not include e-books. The court noted that, in the publishing trade, this clause is generally understood only to grant a publisher the exclusive right to publish a hardcover trade book in English for distribution in North America. (*Random House, Inc. v. Rosetta Books LLC*, 283 F.3d 490 (2d Cir. 2002).)

Paying Authors for Online Uses of Their Works

One difficult problem facing authors and publishers is how to pay authors for online uses of their works. One approach is to form agencies to handle electronic licensing and royalty collection for freelance magazine and newspaper articles. Such collective rights agencies have long been used to license music. At least one such collective rights organization has already been established: the Authors Registry, set up by the Authors Guild and the American Society of Journalists and Authors.

    email: staff@authorsregistry.org

    212-563-6920

    www.authorsregistry.org

As this case shows, interpreting a publishing agreement can be tricky. So, unless the written agreement clearly covers electronic rights, it is wise to seek legal assistance to determine who has the right to publish the work in electronic form.

Transfer Documents

Virtually all book publishers—and many magazines as well—have standard publication agreements they ask authors to sign. Such contracts usually are written by lawyers who have the publisher's best interests in mind, not the author's. If you're an author, be aware that many of the provisions in such agreements normally are subject to negotiation. The topic of author-publisher contract negotiations is beyond the scope of this book. Excellent sources on this topic include:

- *The ASJA Guide to Freelance Writing*, by the American Society of Journalists and Authors, Inc. Contains a recommended standard letter of agreement between a freelancer and a magazine, the ASJA's code of ethics, and chapters on selling books and articles.
- *Negotiating a Book Contract*, by Mark L. Levine (Asphodel Press). Contains a very thorough discussion of publishing contracts.

Sample contracts and useful advice on all aspects of publishing (including finding a good agent) can also be obtained from the following writers' groups:

- The Authors Guild, Inc., 31 East 32nd Street, 7th Floor, New York, NY 10016, 212-563-5904, www. authorsguild.org. The Guild publishes an extensively annotated sample trade book contract available only to Guild members. There is a publication requirement for membership.
- The National Writers Union, 256 West 38th Street, Suite 703, New York, NY 10018, 212-254-0279, www.nwu.org. This national writers' organization has no publication requirement for membership.

Transfer Agreement Must Contain Certain Minimum Provisions

If you encounter a situation where you need to draft your own transfer agreement, there are certain basic requirements that must be satisfied. To be valid, an exclusive license or assignment must be in writing and signed by the owner of the right(s) being transferred. However, in the case of a transfer between an employer and employee, the agreement must be signed by both parties.

A transfer agreement can take many forms. It might be a formal contract, a letter signed by an author, or a signed memorandum. It makes no difference if a transfer agreement is called an assignment, a license, a contract, a grant of rights, or nothing at all.

Whatever a transfer agreement is called, it is important that it be accurate and complete. Listed below are the minimum provisions a transfer agreement normally must contain to be legally binding:

- the names and addresses of the copyright owner and person or entity acquiring the copyright right(s), and
- a description of what rights are being transferred in what work. If the copyright owner is transferring all his or her rights, the following phrase may be used: "John Smith hereby transfers [or assigns] all his right, title, and interest in the novel entitled *Greed* to Mary Jones for the full copyright term." If less than the entire bundle of copyright rights is being transferred, the agreement must clearly state which right(s) are involved.

EXAMPLE 1: Millie, a beginning freelance writer, writes an article on dog training. Desperate to sell her work, Millie grants *Dog's Life Magazine* all world rights. One year after the article is published, Millie contacts *Dog's Life* and asks them to reassign the rights in the article to her so she can use it in a book she's writing on dog training. The *Dog's Life* editor agrees to do so for a nominal sum and tells Millie to send her a transfer agreement to sign. Millie drafts the following copyright assignment.

Copyright Assignment

Dog's Life Magazine, Inc., for value received, grants to Millie Vanilly all right, title, and interest in the copyrightable work described as follows: the article "Dog Dos and Don'ts," published in the Nov. 30, 20xx, issue of *Dog's Life Magazine* at pp. 34-39.

Dog's Life Magazine

_____

Edith Editor
Editor-in-Chief, *Dog's Life Magazine*
April 1, 20xx
100 Park Avenue, New York, NY 10010

_____

Millie Vanilly
March 25, 20xx
10529 Grub St., Marred Vista, CA 90000

FORM

You can download a Copyright Assignment (and all other forms in this book) from this book's companion page on Nolo.com; see the appendix for the link.

EXAMPLE 2: Assume that *Dog's Life Magazine* in the above example refuses to grant Millie the entire copyright in her story. Instead, it agrees to give her only a nonexclusive license to use the story in her book on dog training. This means that *Dog's Life Magazine* retains all other rights in the story and can reprint it or sell it to others. *Dog's Life's* editor drafts the copyright license below for Millie to sign.

Copyright License

Dog's Life Magazine, Inc., for value received, grants to Millie Vanilly an
- ☐ exclusive license
- ☐ nonexclusive license to
  - ☐ reproduce
  - ☐ distribute
  - ☐ create derivative works from
  - ☐ publicly perform
  - ☐ publicly display

the following copyrightable Work: the article "Dog Dos and Don'ts," published in the Nov. 30, 20xx, issue of *Dog's Life Magazine* at pp. 34-39.

Millie Vanilly may sublicense the rights granted in this agreement without *Dog's Life Magazine's* written consent.

This license is made subject to the following terms and conditions: the Work may only be used as part of the book by Millie Vanilly tentatively titled "Dog Training Dos and Don'ts"; however it may be exploited in any language or medium now known or later invented, including, but not limited to, print, microfilm, and electronic media and in translations in all languages.

Dog's Life Magazine

_____

Edith Editor
Editor-in-Chief, *Dog's Life Magazine*
100 Park Avenue, New York, NY 10010
Date: _____

_____

Millie Vanilly
10529 Grub St., Marred Vista, CA 90000
Date: _____

FORM

You can download a Copyright License (and all other forms in this book) from this book's companion page on Nolo.com; see the appendix for the link.

Copies. You should have the transferor sign three original transfer documents: one for him, one for you, and one to record with the Copyright Office.

CAUTION

This section describes the minimum provisions a transfer document must contain to be legally valid. Unlike the examples, most publishing contracts contain many additional provisions that have nothing to do with copyright—for instance, provisions regarding royalties, delivery of manuscript, a warranties and indemnities clause, and many others.

Marriage, Divorce, and Copyright Ownership

Like everybody else, writers and other copyright owners get married and get divorced. A copyright is an item of personal property that must be given to one spouse or the other, or somehow shared, upon divorce. Every state has a set of laws about how property acquired or created by married persons is owned and divided upon divorce. These laws vary greatly from state to state. This section highlights some

basic principles. You'll need to consult an attorney to answer specific questions about how the laws of your state operate.

Copyrights as Community Property

Nine states have community property laws: Arizona, California, Idaho, Louisiana, Nevada, New Mexico, Texas, Washington, and Wisconsin (in all but name). Under these laws, unless they agree otherwise, a husband and wife automatically become *joint owners* of most types of property they acquire during their marriage. Property acquired before or after marriage is separately owned.

A court in the most populous community property state—California—has held that a copyright acquired by one spouse during marriage is community property—that is, is jointly owned by both spouses. (*In re Marriage of Worth*, 195 Cal. App. 3d 768, 241 Cal. Rptr. 135 (1987).) This means that if you are married and reside in California (or later move there), any work you have created while married, or will create, automatically would be owned jointly by you and your spouse *unless you agree otherwise* (see below). This amounts to a transfer of copyright ownership by operation of law.

> EXAMPLE: Emily and Robert are married and live in California. Emily writes a novel. Unless they agree otherwise, Robert automatically acquires an undivided one-half interest in the copyright the moment the work is created.

A court in Louisiana has held that copyrights are not community property in that state. (*Rodrigue v. Rodrigue*, 55 F. Supp. 2d 254 (E.D. La. 1999), (*rev'd on other grounds*, 218 F.3d 432 (5th Cir. 2000).) Courts in the other seven community property states have yet to consider whether copyrights are community property. No one knows whether they will follow California's lead. If you're married and reside in Arizona, Idaho, Nevada, New Mexico, Texas, Washington, or Wisconsin, the most prudent approach is to assume that the copyright in any protectable work you create during marriage is community property. However, check with a family law or copyright lawyer familiar with the laws of your state before taking any action.

The following discussion briefly highlights the effect of according copyrights community property status in California.

Right to Control Copyrights

Normally, *either* spouse is entitled to sell community property (which would include a copyright) without the other's consent. But the profits from such a sale would themselves be community property (that is, jointly owned). The rule is different, however, as to gifts: Neither spouse can give away community property without the other's consent. However, a special provision of California law (Civil Code § 5125(d)) provides that a spouse who operates a business has the primary management and control of that business and its assets. In most cases, a married professional

writer would probably be considered to be operating a business and would therefore have primary management and control over any work he or she creates (the business's assets).

This means that a married professional writer may transfer all or part of the copyright in a work created during marriage without the spouse's consent or signature on any contract. However, the author is legally required to give his or her spouse prior written notice of such transfers (but failure to do so only results in giving the nonauthor spouse the right to demand an accounting of the profits from the transfer).

When a Spouse Dies

Under California law (Probate Code § 201.5), each spouse may will a one-half interest in their community property to whomever they choose; this would include, of course, their interest in any community property copyright. If a spouse dies without a will, the surviving spouse acquires all the deceased spouse's community property.

Division of Copyrights at Divorce

When a California couple gets divorced, they are legally entitled to arrange their own property settlement, jointly dividing their property as they wish. If, however, they can't reach an agreement and submit the dispute to the court, a judge will divide the community property equally. A judge would have many options as how to divide community property copyrights—for example, the judge could award all the copyrights to one spouse and give the other cash or other community property of equal value. If there were, say, ten copyrights of equal value, the judge could give five to one spouse and five to the other; or the judge could permit each spouse to separately administer their one-half interest in all the copyrights.

Changing Marital Ownership of Copyrights by Contract

Property acquired during marriage by California residents does not *have* to be community property. Spouses are free to agree either before or during marriage that all or part of their property will be separately owned. Such an agreement must be in writing and signed by the spouse giving up the community property interest; in some cases, it is desirable for the spouse giving up the interest to consult a lawyer. This is something a husband and wife must discuss and decide on their own; we're not advising you to take any particular action. For detailed discussion, see *Prenuptial Agreements: How to Write a Fair & Lasting Contract*, by Katherine E. Stoner (Nolo).

Equitable Distribution States

All states other than the nine community property states listed above (with the exception of Mississippi) employ equitable distribution principles when dividing property at divorce. Equitable distribution is a principle under which assets (including copyrights) acquired during marriage are divided equitably (fairly) at divorce. In theory, equitable means equal, or nearly so. In some equitable distribution states, however, if a spouse obtains a fault divorce, the guilty spouse may receive less than an equal share of the marital property. Check with a family law attorney in your state for details.

Recording Copyright Transfers With the Copyright Office

The Copyright Office does not make or in any way participate in transfers of copyright ownership. But the office does *record* transfer documents after they have been signed by the parties. When a transfer document is recorded, a copy is placed in the Copyright Offices files, indexed, and made available for public inspection. This is similar to what happens when a deed to a house or other real estate is recorded with a county recorder's office. Recordation of transfer documents is not mandatory, but it results in so many valuable benefits that it is almost always a good idea.

Why Record a Copyright Transfer?

Because a copyright is intangible and can be transferred simply by signing a piece of paper or an electronic document, it is possible for dishonest copyright owners to rip off copyright purchasers.

The Difference Between Recordation and Registration

As described in detail in Chapter 3, copyright registration is a legal formality by which an author or other copyright owner fills out a registration application for a published or unpublished work and submits it to the Copyright Office along with one or two copies of the work. If the copyright examiner is satisfied that the work contains protected expression and the application is completed correctly, the work is registered—that is, assigned a registration number, indexed, and filed in the Copyright Office's records. The copies are retained for five years. Recordation does not involve submitting copies of a work. Recordation simply means that the Copyright Office files a document so that it is available for public inspection. As mentioned above, this can be any document relating to copyright. It can be for a work that is published, unpublished, or even not yet written. A good way to distinguish the two procedures is to remember that written works containing protected expression are registered, while contracts or other documents relating to the copyright in a work are recorded.

EXAMPLE: Carol signs a contract transferring the exclusive right to publish her novel, *The Goniff*, to Scrivener & Sons. Two months later, Carol sells the same rights in the novel to Acme Press. Acme had no idea that Carol had already sold the same rights to Scrivener. Carol has sold the same property twice! As a result, if Scrivener and Acme both publish the book, they'll be competing against each other (and they'll both probably be able to sue Carol for breach of contract, fraud, and other causes of action).

Recordation of transfer documents protects copyright transferees from these and other abuses by establishing the legal priorities between copyright transferees if the transferor makes overlapping or confusing grants. Recordation also establishes a public record of the contents of transfer documents. This enables prospective purchasers of copyright rights to search the Copyright Office's transfer records to make sure that the copyright seller really owns what he or she is selling (this is similar to the title search that a homebuyer conducts before purchasing a house). Finally, recordation of a transfer document for a registered work gives the entire world constructive notice of the transfer; constructive notice means everyone is deemed to know about the transfer, whether or not they really do.

What Can Be Recorded?

Any document pertaining to a copyright can be recorded with the Copyright Office. Of course, this includes any document transferring all or part of a copyright—whether it be an exclusive license or assignment. It also includes nonexclusive licenses, wills, powers of attorney in which authors or other copyright owners give others the power to act for them, and other contracts dealing with a copyrighted work. Notices of termination of older copyrights must be recorded with the Copyright Office.

You can record a document without registering the work it pertains to, but important benefits are obtained if the work is registered. You can even record a document for a work that doesn't exist because it has yet to be written—for example, a publishing contract.

How to Record Transfer Documents (or Other Documents Pertaining to Copyright)

The Copyright Office is in the process of developing an electronic recordation system. However, until this is perfected, you must submit hard copy documents to be recorded.

To record with the Copyright Office a document pertaining to copyright or transferring copyright ownership, you must complete and sign the Copyright Office Form DCS (Document Cover Sheet) and send it to the Copyright Office along with the document and recordation fee. However, use Form TCS (Notice of Termination Cover Sheet) to record notices of termination.

If the work involved hasn't already been registered with the Copyright Office, it should be registered at the same time the document is recorded.

You can fill out the form online at the Copyright Office website (www.copyright. gov/forms) and then print it out for mailing.

The Copyright Office charges a $125 fee to record a transfer document covering one title.

For additional titles, there is an added charge of $60 for each group of up to ten titles—for example, it would cost $185 to record 11 titles, $245 to record 21 titles, and so forth.

The Copyright Office has an electronic recordation fee calculator available at its website (www.copyright.gov/recordation). You need to send all the following to the Copyright Office in one package:

- the original signed Document Cover Sheet and one copy
- the proper recordation fee in a check or money order payable to the Register of Copyrights (unless you have a deposit account), and
- the document to be recorded.

Send your package to:

Library of Congress
Copyright Office–DOC LM 433
101 Independence Avenue SE
Washington, DC 20559-6000

Notices of termination should be sent to:

Copyright Office–Notices of Termination
P.O. Box 71537
Washington, DC 20024-1537

It generally takes the Copyright Office eight months to process basic filings and three months for notices of termination. But you can get an item recorded in a few days by paying a $550 special handling fee. You should receive a Certificate of Recordation from the Copyright Office showing that your transfer document (or nonexclusive license) has been recorded. The original signed transfer document (or nonexclusive license) will be returned with the certificate.

Copyright Duration

Copyright protection doesn't last forever, but it lasts long enough to benefit many people besides the author, potentially including children, grandchildren, great-grandchildren, publishers, agents, and other people and businesses who may have acquired an interest in the copyright.

No matter how many times a copyright is transferred, its duration does not change. The duration is determined by who the original author was and how long he or she lives or, in some cases, by the date the work was created or first published.

When a work's copyright expires, it enters the public domain; in effect, it belongs to everybody. Anyone is free to use it without asking permission, but no one can ever own it again.

Works Created During or After 1978

The great divide in terms of determining a copyright's duration is the date January 1, 1978. The copyright in works created on or after that date usually lasts for the life of the author(s) plus 70 years. Works created before that date have a very different duration.

Single-Author Works: Life Plus 70 Years

As discussed in Chapter 1, "Copyright Basics," copyright protection begins when a

work is created—that is, when it is written down or otherwise fixed in a tangible form. Unless one of the exceptions discussed below applies, the copyright in a work created by a single individual author on or after January 1, 1978 lasts for the life of the author plus an additional 70 years. This means, at the very least, that the copyright in an individually authored work lasts 70 years. And the copyright in a work by a young author could easily last 100 years or more depending, of course, on how long the author lives.

> **EXAMPLE 1:** Bill has a fatal heart attack just as he finishes writing his epic novel on ancient Sparta. The novel's copyright will last for 70 years after Bill's death.

> **EXAMPLE 2:** Natalie completes her own epic novel on ancient Sparta when she is 30 years old. If she ends up living to 80, the copyright in her novel will last for 120 years.

Drafts and Uncompleted Works

Copyright doesn't just protect finished works; it also protects drafts and uncompleted works. Each draft of a work created over a period of time by an individual author is protected for the life-plus-70-year term. A work that is never completed is entitled to the same period of protection.

Works Made for Hire

As discussed in detail in Chapter 6, "Initial Copyright Ownership," a work made for hire is a work created by an employee as part of his or her job or a work that is specially ordered or commissioned pursuant to a written work-made-for-hire contract. The copyright in a work made for hire lasts for 95 years from the date of its *first publication* or 120 years from the date of its *creation*, whichever comes first. (A work is published when it is made freely available to the public; see Chapter 1, "Copyright Basics," for a definition of publish.)

Online Copyright Duration Calculators

Several copyright duration calculators are available online, including the Public Domain Sherpa (www.publicdomainsherpa.com) and Public Domain Slider (http://library copyright.net/resources/digitalslider). However, great care must be exercised when using these calculators. If the data inputted into a calculator is wrong, the answer will be wrong too.

Calculating copyright duration requires a good understanding of basic copyright principles—for example, what constitutes publication, notice requirements, and protection for derivative works. Use of a calculator could give the illusion of a clear answer when, in fact, the copyright status of a work is unclear.

This means that if there were a 30-year delay between creation and publication, the copyright would last for 120 years. For example, if a work made for hire was created in 2000 but not published until 2030, the copyright would expire soonest by using the 120-year-from-creation term—that is, the copyright would expire in 2120. If the 95-years-from-publication term were applied, the copyright wouldn't expire until the year 2125. Any delay between creation and publication of less than 25 years means that the 95-years-from-publication term should be applied, as this would result in the shortest period of copyright protection. For example, a five-year delay would result in a 95-year-from-publication term. But, if creation and publication occur within the same calendar year, as they usually do, the copyright in a work made for hire lasts for 95 years.

Joint-Author Works

As discussed in detail in Chapter 6, "Initial Copyright Ownership," a joint work is a work authored by two or more persons on their own behalf (that is, not a work made for hire). The copyright in a joint work lasts for the life of the last surviving author plus 70 years.

> **EXAMPLE:** Joseph Herodotus and Mary Thucydides write a history of the Persian Gulf War. Herodotus dies soon thereafter. The copyright in the work will last for the rest of Thucydides' life plus 70 more years.

If a work is created by two or more persons under a work-made-for-hire agreement, the 95- or 120-year work-made-for-hire term (discussed above) applies.

> **EXAMPLE:** Two editors employed by Acme Press and two employed by Scrivener & Sons jointly author a book on publishing for their employers. The book is a joint work, co-owned by Acme and Scrivener, but the work-made-for-hire copyright term applies.

Sometimes, a work will be jointly created both by people who work under a work-made-for-hire agreement and people who don't. It's not exactly clear whether the life-plus-70 or work-made-for-hire term should apply in these situations. The Registrar of Copyrights has suggested that the life-plus-70 term should apply, if at least two of the work's creators did not work under a work-made-for-hire agreement. It's likely the courts will adopt this rule.

> **EXAMPLE:** Acme Press has two of its editors collaborate on a book with two freelance writers. The contributions by Acme's editors are works made for hire. The contributions by the two freelancers are not works made for hire. Because two of the authors did not work a under a work-made-for-hire agreement, the life-plus-70 rule should apply according to the Registrar of Copyrights. That is, the copyright in the work would last for the life of the last surviving freelancer plus 70 years.

What if a work is created by one or more people who work under a work-made-for-hire agreement and only *one* person who does not? The Registrar of Copyrights suggests that in this situation whatever copyright term is longer—life-plus-70 or the work-made-for-hire term—should apply.

> **EXAMPLE:** Assume that two editors employed by Acme Press and only one freelance writer write a book together. Again, the editors' contributions are works made for hire, while the freelancer's contribution is not a work made for hire. According to the Registrar of Copyrights, the copyright in the book should last for the longer of the work-made-for-hire terms or 70 years after the freelancer dies.

Anonymous and Pseudonymous Works

Obviously, there is no identified author with an interest in the copyright of an anonymous or pseudonymous work. This makes it impractical to measure the duration of the copyright against the life of the author. As a result, the copyright term follows the work-made-for-hire term—95 years from the date of first publication of an anonymous or pseudonymous work or 120 years from the date of its creation, whichever comes first.

Changing the Term to Life Plus 70 by Making Identity Known to Copyright Office

If the identity of the author of an anonymous or pseudonymous work is officially made known to the Copyright Office before the 95- or 120-year term expires, the copyright term changes to the life of the author plus 70 years (as if the true author's name had been on the copyright to begin with).

Note, however, that the life-plus-70 term won't necessarily be longer than a 95 or 120-year term; it all depends on how long the author lives after the work was published.

Any person who owns all or part of the copyright in a pseudonymous or anonymous work may notify the Copyright Office of the author's true identity. This can be done by registering the work under the author's true name or, if the work has already been registered, by filing a supplementary registration with the Copyright Office. Copyright registration and supplemental registration are discussed in Chapter 3.

Alternatively, it is possible to record (file) a statement with the Copyright Office setting forth the following:

- the name of the person filing the statement
- the nature of the person's interest in the copyright
- the title of the particular work affected, and
- the copyright registration number, if known.

The Copyright Office requires payment of a $125 fee to record the statement. (See Chapter 7, "Transferring Copyright Ownership," for a detailed discussion of how to record documents with the Copyright Office.)

TIP

If an individual author is very ill or rather elderly and not likely to live 25 years after the work is published, the work would probably receive longer copyright protection under the 95-year term for anonymous or pseudonymous works or works made for hire than under the normal life plus 70 years copyright term. The copyright term would also probably last longer if the work was written with a younger collaborator—that is, the copyright would last for 70 years after the last collaborator died. Does this mean that elderly authors should write anonymously or under a pseudonym, or, if possible, characterize their works as works made for hire or write them with youthful collaborators? In most cases, no. Very few works have a useful economic life of more than 70 years. Thus, the life-plus-70 term is usually more than adequate.

End-of-Calendar-Year Rule

All copyright durations run until the end of the calendar year in which they would otherwise expire. For example, the copyright in a work made for hire that was first published in 2000 would expire on December 31, 2095, regardless of what month and day during 2000 it was published. Similarly, if the individual author of a work published in 1979 died in 1980, the copyright in the work would expire on December 31, 2050, regardless of the month and day of his death.

Works Created but Not Published or Registered Before January 1, 1978

With one important exception, works created before January 1, 1978 but not published or registered with the Copyright Office, are subject to the same basic copyright duration rules as those created after January 1, 1978. That is, the copyright lasts for the life of an individual author plus 70 years, or 95 or 120 years (from publication and creation, respectively) for a work made for hire or a pseudonymous or anonymous work.

> **EXAMPLE:** Louisa, a well-known novelist, died in 2000 leaving behind an unpublished manuscript written in 1977. The copyright in the manuscript will last until 2070 (70 years after Louisa's death).

Given the above rule, you'd naturally assume that all unpublished works created by authors who had been dead more than 70 years on January 1, 1978 automatically entered the public domain on that date. However, this did not occur. A special rule provided that the copyright in an unpublished work created before January 1, 1978 could not expire until January 1, 2003, no matter when the author died.

Moreover, if such a work was published between January 1, 1978 and January 1, 2003, the copyright cannot expire before December 31, 2047. This is so regardless of when the author died.

> **EXAMPLE:** Samuel, a Revolutionary War historian, finds an unknown and unpublished diary written by George Washington in 1790. Because the diary was never published (or registered with the Copyright Office), it automatically remained under copyright until December 31, 2002, even though Washington died in 1799.
>
> Samuel had the diary published in 2002. As a result, its copyright was automatically extended until December 31, 2047. The copyright in the diary is owned by whoever inherited Washington's papers, not by Samuel.

Because of these rules, recently discovered unpublished manuscripts by Jane Austen and Mark Twain were protected by copyright in the United States (but no other country). The protection applies even though Austen died in 1817 and Twain in 1910. The works have since been published and will be protected through December 31, 2047.

On January 1, 2003, all unpublished works by all authors who died during 1932 or earlier entered the public domain. On January 1 of every year thereafter, another year's worth of unpublished works also enters the public domain. So, on January 1, 2004, unpublished works by authors who died during 1933 entered the public domain; on January 1, 2005, unpublished works by authors who died during 1934 entered the public domain, and so on.

Determining When Authors Died

All unpublished works by authors who died during 1932 or earlier are in the public domain. If the author is well known, reference works, such as encyclopedias, will probably reveal when (or if) the author died. The website www.biography.com provides this information for over 25,000 people. If the author has a Wikipedia page, it should also contain his or her death date.

In the case of unpublished works made for hire created before 1978 (works created by employees as part of their jobs or works for which a work-made-for-hire agreement was signed), the copyright lasts 120 years from the date of creation. So, all unpublished works made for hire created before 1883 entered the public domain on January 1, 2003. Every year thereafter, another year's worth of works made for hire enters the public domain—for example, on January 1, 2004, all unpublished works

Preventing Unpublished Works From Entering the Public Domain

If you own the copyright in an unpublished work created by an author who died more than 70 years ago, it's too late to save such a work's copyright. It is in the public domain. If you own an unpublished work created by a deceased author whose 70th year after death is approaching, you must publish it no later than the end of that 70th year. For example, if you own an unpublished work by an author who died during 1955, you must publish it by December 31, 2025. If you own an unpublished work by an author who died during 1956 you must publish it by December 31, 2026 and so on. It's not difficult to publish a work for copyright purposes. You don't have to have a publisher distribute it, though this would certainly qualify as publication.

You just have to make copies available to the general public—for example, handing out copies on a street corner would constitute publication.

Does simply placing a work on the Internet constitute publication for copyright purposes? It's unclear, but it might not. Here is one way to definitely publish something by using the Internet. Put up a website (or use a site you already have) with a notice offering to email a copy of the work to anyone who wants one. You can charge for the copy or offer it for free, it makes no difference for publication purposes. The offer to email copies of the work to the general public constitutes a publication for copyright purposes. However, just to be on the safe side, you may want to actually email copies to a few people—four or five is plenty; these can be friends and associates. Keep copies of the emails and the website containing the notice in a safe place.

made for hire created during 1883 entered the public domain; on January 1, 2005, all unpublished works made for hire created during 1884 entered the public domain, and so on. This rule also applies to unpublished pseudonymous and anonymous works.

Works Published or Registered Before January 1, 1978

Determining the copyright term for works created before 1978 can be a complex undertaking. Under the pre-1978 copyright law (called the Copyright Act of 1909), all eligible works enjoyed an initial copyright term of 28 years from the *date of first publication* with a proper copyright notice. Before the end of the first 28 years, the work could be renewed for an additional 28-year term by filing a renewal registration with the Copyright Office. This second term is called the renewal term.

This sounds pretty simple, but things get more complicated. The renewal term for works published before 1978 was extended an additional 39 years to 67 years (28 + 39 = 67), for a total of 95 years of copyright protection (28 + 67 = 95).

Under the law in effect from 1909 through 1992, the renewal term was not automatic. It could be obtained only by filing a renewal registration with the Copyright Office during the 28th year after a work's publication. As you might expect, many authors failed to timely file a renewal for their work. Indeed, only about 20% of all pre-1978 published works were ever renewed.

The renewal requirement resulted in a vast body of work entering the public domain 28 years after publication due to failure to comply with a mere technical formality. Many people found this process unfair, so the law was changed in 1992. The new law made copyright renewals automatic—in other words, the 67-year renewal term was obtained whether or not a renewal registration was filed. Renewal registrations were made purely optional— but the law gives copyright owners who file renewal registrations some important benefits we'll discuss below.

> **CAUTION**
>
> **The 1992 automatic renewal law applies only to works published between January 1, 1964 and December 31, 1977.** Works published during 1923–1963 had to be renewed during the 28th year after publication or they entered the public domain, where they will forever remain (except for works that were first published outside the United States and had their U.S. copyrights restored in 1996—see Chapter 11).

The following sections provide some general rules that will help you decide whether a work published prior to 1978 is still protected by copyright.

Unpublished Works Registered With the Copyright Office Before 1978

Before 1978, authors of some types of unpublished works had the option of registering them with the Copyright Office as unpublished. Such works receive the same copyright term as works published before 1978, with such protection beginning on the date a copy of the registered work was deposited with the Copyright Office.

Not all unpublished works could be registered. The procedure was available only for unpublished lectures and similar works, "dramatic compositions" (plays), musical compositions, "dramatico-musical compositions" (musicals), motion picture screenplays, motion pictures other than screenplays, photographs, works of art, "plastic works" (sculpture and similar works), and drawings. Such items as unpublished writings other than lectures could not be registered, nor could art reproductions or sound recordings. This procedure was not often used except for works that did not qualify as published for copyright purposes, even though they were performed in public or broadcast to the public—for example, plays, screenplays, radio scripts, and teleplays. Copyright Office records must be searched to determine if such works were registered.

If such a registered unpublished work was later published, no new copyright was obtained in the material, and the copyright term for such material was not extended.

Works Published More Than 95 Years Ago

The copyright for any work published in the United States more than 95 years ago has expired—meaning the work is now in the public domain. This is so whether the work was first published in the United States or originally published outside the United States and republished here.

Anyone can use such an expired work without permission or payment, but no one can ever own it.

> **TIP**
> **To determine whether a book or another work was first published more than 95 years ago, simply look at the year shown in the work's copyright notice.** This should be the same year as the year of first publication.

Works Published Less Than 95 Years Ago But Before 1964

Works published less than 95 years ago but before 1964 have already entered the public domain, unless a renewal registration was timely filed with the Copyright Office by the end of the initial 28-year term. If timely filed, the renewal term lasts for 67 years—for a total of 95 years of copyright protection.

EXAMPLE 1: The copyright in a work that was first published in 1932 and timely renewed in 1960 lasts through the end of 2027 (95 years in all).

EXAMPLE 2: The copyright in a work that was first published in 1962 but not timely renewed in 1990 expired on December 31, 1990 (at the end of the initial 28-year term). The work is in the public domain.

How to Determine Whether a Renewal Has Been Timely Filed

As these examples illustrate, it is impossible to know how long the copyright in a work published less than 95 years ago but before 1964 will last, unless you know whether a renewal registration was timely filed. When a book is reprinted after renewal, the copyright notice usually provides this information. Otherwise, you'll need to research the Copyright Office's records to find out if a renewal was timely filed. You can do this research in one of three ways:

- **Have the Copyright Office search its records for you.** They charge $200 an hour for this service, and searches take a minimum of two hours. Unfortunately, it takes the Copyright Office six to eight weeks to conduct a search and report back to you. You can obtain much faster service for less by using a private search firm as described below. The Copyright Office will conduct an expedited search that takes just five business days, but

The 20-Year Public Domain Freeze Is Over

In 1998, Congress passed the Sonny Bono Copyright Extension Act. The act extended the renewal term for pre-1978 published works by 20 years—from 47 years to 67 years. As a result, no new works entered the U.S. public domain due to copyright expiration from 1998 through 2018. This 20-year copyright expiration freeze finally ended in 2019. As of that year, published works again began to enter the public domain due to expiration of their 95-year copyright terms.

On January 1, 2019 all works published during 1923 entered the public domain, including films such as the C.B. DeMille silent version of *The Ten Commandments* and comedies featuring Charlie Chaplin, Buster Keaton, and Harold Lloyd. Literary works by Robert Frost, Aldous Huxley, Sigmund Freud, and Edith Wharton also entered the public domain.

On January 1, 2020, all works published in the United States during 1924 entered the public domain. This included the classic silent film comedies *Sherlock Jr.* and *The Navigator* starring Buster Keaton; George Gershwin's "Rhapsody in Blue"; E. M. Forster's novel *A Passage to India*; and Herman Melville's posthumously published novella *Billy Budd*.

On January 1, 2021, all works published during 1925 enter the public domain, including *The Great Gatsby* by F. Scott Fitzgerald, *The Trial* by Franz Kafka, and *Mein Kampf* by Adolf Hitler.

This process will continue through the year 2039.

this costs a minimum of $1,000. Again, you can obtain faster service for less by using a private search firm.

If you still want the Copyright Office to do your search, you make an online request for a search at the Copyright Office website (www.copyright.gov). At the conclusion of its search, the Copyright Office will issue a written search report, which may be certified for an additional $200 fee. Certified search reports are frequently requested to meet the evidentiary requirements of litigation.

- **Have a professional search firm conduct a search for you.** Several private search firms conduct copyright renewal searches. They usually report back in two to ten working days. For example, CompuMark, the best known of these firms, charges $160 for a renewal search and will report back in three business days. The Durationator Copyright System charges $75 to search a single title.

  Following is a list of copyright search firms:
  - Durationator Copyright System www.durationator.com
  - Government Liaison Services, Inc. www.trademarkinfo.com
  - CompuMark www.compumark.com 800-692-8833

- **Search the Copyright Office records yourself.** This is relatively easy to do for works published during 1950–1963, because the records are available online at the Copyright Office website at www.copyright.gov. But researching works published before 1950 is more difficult, because these records are not available at the Copyright Office website. In the past, it was always necessary to manually search through the *Copyright Office Catalog of Copyright Entries* (CCE)—a monumental series of printed annual catalogs listing and cross-referencing every work registered and renewed by the Copyright Office. The CCE is available to the public at the Copyright Office, located in the James Madison Memorial Building, 101 Independence Avenue SE, Washington, D.C. The CCE can also be found in government depository libraries throughout the country. Fortunately, in-person, manual searches are no longer necessary. All of the 660 CCE volumes have been digitized by the Copyright Office and made publicly available on the Internet Archive (http://archive.org/details/copyrightrecords) with a limited search capability based on the results of optical character recognition (OCR) of the scanned text. A helpful Copyright Office video on how to use these online records is available as a download (mp4 file) at http://copyright.gov/tutorials/records/cce.mp4. Production scanning is also underway for the 40 million catalog card records of registrations recorded from 1871 to 1977. A beta version of this digitized card catalog is available at www.copyright.gov/vcc.

In addition, several private organizations have made the renewal records available online independently of the Copyright Office. For example, Google, Inc., has scanned all 91 volumes of the CCE containing renewal records for books, pamphlets, and contributions to periodicals published from 1923 to 1977 and made them searchable online through Google Books (https://books.google.com/googlebooks/ copyrightsearch.html). The Stanford University Library also created a searchable online database of all the copyright renewals for books published during the period 1923 through 1963 (https://exhibits.stanford.edu/ copyrightrenewals). These records may be searched by title, author, registration date, and renewal date. Also, the Universal Library Project, supported by Carnegie Mellon University, has scanned many of the CCE renewal records and placed digital copies of each page online at a website called the Online Books Page (http://online-books.library.upenn.edu/cce).

Copyright Duration Chart	
Date and Nature of Work	Copyright Term
Published over 95 years ago	The work is in the public domain.
Published less than 95 years ago through 1963 and never renewed	The work is in the public domain.
Published less than 95 years ago through 1963 and timely renewed	95 years from the date of first publication
Published between 1964 and 1977	95 years from the date of publication (renewal term automatic)
Created, but not published or registered, before 1978	Single term of 120 years from creation for unpublished works made for hire, and unpublished or pseudonymous works
Created before 1978 and published 1978–2002	Copyright will expire January 1, 2048.
Created 1978 and later	Life of author + 70 years

RESOURCE

For detailed guidance on how to conduct a copyright renewal search, see *The Public Domain: How to Find & Use Copyright-Free Writings, Music, Art & More,* by Stephen Fishman (Nolo).

Works Published During 1964–1977

The 67-year renewal term begins automatically for works published between January 1,
1964 and December 31, 1977.

> EXAMPLE: Jackie published a novel in 1965.
> The initial 28-year copyright term for the
> book expired on December 31, 1993 (28 years
> after the year of publication). The 67-year
> renewal term began automatically on
> January 1, 1994, whether or not Jackie filed a
> renewal application with the Copyright Office.

However, as discussed below, important
benefits can be obtained in some cases by
filing an optional renewal registration with
the Copyright Office.

Special Rules for Pre-1972 Sound Recordings

Sound recordings created after February 15,
1972 receive the same copyright term as any
other work of authorship. However, sound
recordings created before February 15, 1972
were not protected by federal copyright

law. Rather, they were protected under a
hodgepodge of state laws that varied from
state to state. The federal copyright law
provided that all such state law protections
had to end by December 31, 2067, and all
these works weren't scheduled to enter the
public domain until 2068.

The lack of federal copyright protection
for pre-1972 recordings ended on October 11,
2018 when the Classics Protection and
Access Act (CPA Act)) was signed into law.
(17 U.S.C. § 1401.) The CPA Act provides
pre-1972 sound recordings with a basic
federal copyright term of 95 years from
the year of publication, plus an additional
"transition period" of three to 15 years after
the year of enactment of the CPA Act—in
other words, three to fifteen years after
2018. The transition period is three years
for sound recordings first published before
1923, five years for sound recordings first
published between 1923 and 1946, and
15 years for sound recordings published
between 1946 and 1956. Protection for all
other pre-1972 sound recordings, including
those previously unpublished, expires on
February 15, 2067.

Thus, all sound recordings first published
before 1923 will enter the public domain
on January 1, 2022. Sound recordings first
published between 1923 and 1946 enjoy
100 years of federal copyright protection.
Sound recordings first published between
1947 and 1956 obtain 110 years of
protection. Sound recordings first published
between 1957 and February 15, 1972 are

protected until February 15, 2067. Sound recordings never published before February 15, 1972 enter the public domain on February 15, 2067; this is so even if they are published before that date.

Sound Recordings Created Before February 15, 1972	
Publication History of Work	Copyright Term
First Published Before 1923	Work enters public domain Jan. 1, 2022
First Published 1923–1946	100 years after publication
First Published 1947–1956	110 years after publication
First Published 1957–Feb. 15, 1972	Work enters public domain Feb. 15, 2067
Unpublished before Feb. 15, 1972	Work enters public domain Feb. 15, 2067

Special Rules for Works First Published Outside the United States Before 1978

There are some special rules for works that were first published outside the United States before 1978: They may enjoy a different term of copyright protection and the copyright renewal rules no longer apply to such works.

Copyright Term for Foreign Works

Because of one federal court's peculiar interpretation of the copyright law and the lack of other court decisions on the subject, the copyright duration for works first published before 1978 outside the United States may depend on whether the work involved contained a copyright notice. Copyright notices have never been required for published works in most foreign countries, but they were often used anyway.

A copyright notice valid under U.S. law consists of the © symbol, the word Copyright, or the abbreviation Copr., followed by the publication date and copyright owner's name. However, the date could be left off maps, original works of art and art reproductions, technical and scientific drawings and models, photographs, labels used on products and merchandise, and prints and pictorial illustrations.

Works Published With a Valid Copyright Notice

Any work first published in a foreign country before January 1, 1978 with a copyright notice receives the same copyright term in the United States as works published in the United States during these years (with one big exception, noted below, for works whose copyright was never renewed). The term begins with the year of publication of the foreign work. The copyright terms for such works are as follows:

- Works published before 1923: All these works received a 75-year U.S. copyright term and, therefore, are all in the public domain in the United States.

- Works published 1923–1963: The vast majority of these works received a 95-year copyright term, dating from the year of publication with a copyright notice. Note that many works published during 1923–1963 used to be in the public domain in the United States because their U.S. copyrights were not renewed with the U.S. Copyright office during the 28th year after publication. However, most foreign works published during 1923–1963 that were never renewed had their U.S. copyright protection restored in 1996 and are protected for a full 95 years. But a few foreign works didn't qualify for copyright restoration and are still in the public domain in the United States. These are primarily works that were in the public domain in their home countries as of January 1, 1996. Also, works by Americans first published outside the United States during 1923–1963 are not eligible for copyright restoration. Thus, for example, photographs of Marilyn Monroe by an American photographer that were initially published in a British newspaper in 1962 with a copyright notice and not timely renewed 28 years later were not eligible for restoration. As a result, the photos were in the U.S. public domain. (*Barris v. Hamilton*, 51 U.S.P.Q. 2d 1191 (S.D.N.Y. 1999).) (See Chapter 11 for a detailed discussion of restoration of copyrights in foreign works.)

- Works published 1964–1977: Any work first published outside the United States during the years 1964 through 1977 with a copyright notice receives a 95-year copyright term, from the date of publication with notice. This means that the earliest any foreign work published between 1964 and 1978 will enter the public domain in the United States because of copyright expiration is January 1, 2060.

Works Published Before 1978 Without a Copyright Notice

Many works first published outside the United States did not contain copyright notices, because they were not required in the country of publication. Should these works be treated any differently than works first published outside the United States with a notice? One federal court—the Ninth Circuit Court of Appeals—has answered this question "yes." However, this court's rulings apply only in the western United States, and it's possible other courts in other parts of the country may disagree. As a result, it's possible for a work first published outside the United States before 1978 without a copyright notice to be in the public domain in some states and still under copyright in others!

The Rule in the Western United States

Federal courts in the Ninth Judicial Circuit —which covers the states of Alaska, Arizona, California, Hawaii, Idaho, Montana, Nevada, Oregon, and Washington—have determined that works first published outside the United States without valid copyright notices should not be considered as having been published under the U.S. copyright law in effect at the time. (*Twin Books Corp. v. Walt Disney Co.*, 83 F.3d 1162 (9th Cir. 1996).) Because these works are viewed as unpublished for American copyright purposes, they receive the same copyright term as unpublished works: They are protected for the life of the author and for 70 years after his or her death.

EXAMPLE: The artists Pierre-Auguste Renoir and Richard Guino created a series of sculptures that were first published in France in 1917 without a copyright notice. In 2003, the owner of the sculptures filed a copyright infringement suit in Arizona against a company that was selling bronze copies of them without permission. Under the Ninth Circuit rule, which applied in Arizona, the sculptures did not acquire U.S. copyright protection when published outside the United States, and they were also not in the U.S. public domain. The district court concluded that such works receive the copyright term applicable to unpublished works, which lasts for 70 years after the death of the last surviving author. Renoir died in 1919, but Guino lived until 1973. Thus, the court held that the copyright for the sculptures lasted until January 1, 2043. (*Société Civile Succession Richard Guino v. Beseder, Inc.*, 414 F. Supp. 2d 944 (D. Ariz. 2006).)

However, there is an important exception to this rule: If the work was later republished before 1978 with a valid copyright notice, whether in the United States or abroad, it received the same term of U.S. copyright protection as if it were first published in the United States that year. These copyright terms are listed in the previous section.

EXAMPLE: The children's book *Bambi: A Life in the Woods*, by Felix Salten, was originally published in Germany without a copyright notice in 1923. It was then republished in Germany with a copyright notice in 1926. The 1926 publication triggered the 95-year copyright term provided for U.S. works published at this time. This means *Bambi* won't be in the public domain in the United States until 2022. Had *Bambi* not been republished with a copyright notice, it would have been protected for 70 years after Salten died. (*Twin Books Corp. v. Walt Disney Co.*, 83 F.3d 1162 (9th Cir. 1996).)

The Rule in the Rest of the United States

Most copyright experts don't agree with the decision reached by the Court of Appeals in the *Twin Books* case. They believe there should be no difference in copyright terms for works published in the United States or abroad. Although the court's ruling is a binding legal precedent that all trial courts located in the Ninth Circuit must follow, courts in other parts of the country are not required to follow it and likely won't. Thus, for example, if the case involving the Renoir sculptures discussed in the above example had been filed in New York instead of Arizona, it is likely that the New York federal district court would have held that the sculptures were in the U.S. public domain, because they were published before 1923. However, to date, no court outside the Ninth Circuit has ruled on this issue, so no one can be absolutely certain what courts outside the Ninth Circuit will do.

What You Should Do

So what should you do? Unless you're certain that the work involved will not be used or made available in any of the states that make up the Ninth Circuit (which notably includes California), the only prudent course is to follow *both* the Ninth Circuit's ruling and the rule that most experts believe should be used.

Under this approach, a work first published outside the United States without a copyright notice before 1978, and never republished before 1978 with valid notice, would be treated as in the public domain only if (1) the author has been dead more than 70 years (the same rule as for unpublished works); *and* (2) the work was first published more than 95 years ago (the same rule as for works published outside the United States with a valid notice).

EXAMPLE: Assume that Pierre-Auguste Renoir created a sculpture which was first published in France without notice in 1917 and never republished with notice. The work would be in the public domain under the Ninth Circuit's ruling because Renoir died in 1919—more than 70 years ago; and, because the work was first published more than 95 years ago, it would be in the public domain under the rule likely to be followed in the rest of the country. Thus the work is in the public domain in the entire United States.

Duration of Copyright in Adaptations (Derivative Works)

As discussed in detail in Chapter 5, "Adaptations and Compilations," a derivative work is a work that transforms or adapts previously existing material into a new work of authorship. A good example is a screenplay based on a novel. The copyright in a derivative work published before 1978 lasts for 95 years from publication if timely renewed and 28 years if not. The copyright in a derivative work created on or after January 1, 1978 lasts for the life of the author plus 70 years, unless it's a work made for hire or a pseudonymous or anonymous work as discussed above. The creation of a derivative work has no effect on the duration of the copyright in the preexisting material it incorporates.

EXAMPLE: Barbara writes a screenplay in 2020 based on a novel published by Art in 1980. The copyright in the novel will expire 70 years after Art dies. The copyright in the screenplay will expire 70 years after Barbara dies.

It is quite common for the copyright in the preexisting material to expire long before the copyright in a derivative work based upon it. In this event, others can use the preexisting material to create their own derivative works, or for any other purpose, without asking permission from the owner of the derivative work or anyone else. But others cannot use the material added to the preexisting work by the creator of the derivative work.

EXAMPLE: Leslie purchases the right to create a play based on a novel published by Burt in 1932. She publishes the play in 2020. The copyright in the novel was timely renewed in 1960. Thus, copyright protection for the novel will last until 2037, while the copyright in Leslie's play will last for the rest of her life plus 70 years. After 2037, anyone may write their own play based upon Burt's novel, because it is in the public domain. But, in doing so, they could not copy from Leslie's play without her permission.

Termination of Transfers of Renewal Term Rights in Pre-1978 Works

As discussed above, works first published or registered before 1978 originally had an initial 28-year copyright term and a second 28-year renewal term. However, the renewal term was extended twice: First, it was extended an additional 19 years to 47 years in 1978; it was then extended by an additional 20 years to 67 years in 1998. This means the owner(s) of the renewal term ownership rights in a pre-1978 work would enjoy 67 years of copyright protection provided the work was timely renewed.

A pre-1978 work's initial and renewal terms are considered to be completely separate. An author may transfer all or part of his or her copyright ownership rights during the work's renewal term. Such a transfer can be made any time before a work's renewal term actually begins. Indeed, before 1978, authors typically transferred their renewal term rights to their publishers and others when they first sold their work. This meant that, in most cases, publishers and other transferees—not authors or their families—would be entitled to the additional 39 years of copyright protection created by extending the renewal term to 67 years.

The whole purpose of having a renewal term was to give authors and their families a second chance to market their work. Thus, it did not seem fair that publishers should benefit from the extra 39 years added to the renewal term. To prevent this, a special provision of the Copyright Act gives authors or their heirs the right to get those extra 39 years of copyright ownership back by terminating pre-1978 transfers of renewal term rights.

EXAMPLE: Art published a novel in 1952. His publishing contract contained a provision by which he transferred to his publisher his publication rights in the novel for the renewal term. Art's publisher timely filed a renewal application with the Copyright Office in 1980. The renewal term will last for 67 years, until 2047. However, Art or his surviving family can terminate the renewal rights transfer Art made to his publisher in 1952 and get back the publication rights in the novel for the last 39 years of the renewal term—that is, from 2008 until 2047.

By far, the best known instance of the exercise of this termination right involves the comic book hero Superman. In 2008, the widow and daughter of Jerome Siegel, one of the two original creators of Superman, successfully used the termination provision to terminate Siegel's 1938 transfer of all his copyrights rights in the original *Superman* comic to Marvel Comics for $130. However, the heirs of Superman's co-creator, Joe Shuster, were unable to terminate his transfer to Marvel, because Schuster's sister had negotiated a new agreement in 1992, and therefore, this new agreement superseded and replaced the pre-1978 grant. (*Larson v. Warner Bros. Ent., Inc.*, 504 Fed. Appx. 586 (9th Cir. 2013).)

The copyright law now gives authors or their heirs two separate chances to get back ownership of their works for all or part of the extra 39 years of copyright protection.

Works Published Less Than 61 Years Ago

A transfer of renewal rights may be terminated at any time during the five-year period beginning 56 years from the date that the work was first published. For example, a renewal rights grant for a work published in 1965 may be terminated any time between January 1, 2021 and December 31, 2026. You should think of this period as a five-year window of opportunity during which you can get back the last 39 years of copyright ownership.

Works Published More Than 61 Years Ago

What if the time period for terminating renewal rights transfers as set forth above has expired and the author or heirs failed to exercise their termination rights? All is not lost. In this event, the author or heirs or executor can terminate the renewal rights transfer for the last 20 years of the 95-year copyright term. To do so, they must act any time during 75 to 80 years after the work was first published. This is a second window of opportunity to get back copyright ownership.

EXAMPLE: Agnes published a novel in 1945. The publishing contract contained a provision transferring her renewal term rights to her publisher. Agnes could have terminated the renewal term transfer by acting during 2001–2006, but she failed to do so. However, Agnes or her heirs or executor can still terminate the transfer as to the last 20 years of the novel's 95-year copyright. To do so, they must act sometime during 2020–2025—that is, 75–80 years after the novel was first published.

What to Do

A termination of a pre-1978 transfer of renewal term rights can be accomplished by the author or by the author's widow or widower, children, or grandchildren. If none of these individuals are living, the termination may be accomplished by the executor or administrator of the author's estate or by the author's personal representative or trustee.

If you are the author of a pre-1978 work that still has value more than 50 years after publication, or the widow, widower, child, or grandchild of such an author, you or other family members should consult a copyright attorney some time during the 56th year after publication. The attorney will be able to determine if a terminable transfer of renewal term copyright ownership rights was made and, if so, help you take the necessary procedural steps to terminate it.

If more than 61 years have elapsed since the work was first published and the renewal rights transfer was never terminated, then calendar a new date—75 years after the work's publication—and see an attorney then.

The Copyright Office has created several online tables you can use to calculate your termination period. They are at www.copyright.gov/recordation/termination.html (click on the "When to Terminate" tab).

Using Other Authors' Words

To quote is not necessarily stealing.
Quotation can be vital to the fulfillment of
the public-enriching goals of copyright law.
—Judge Pierre N. Leval

Introduction

This chapter is about using other authors' words. Sooner or later, almost all of us feel the need to quote, closely paraphrase, digitally or physically copy, or otherwise use what others have written. Here are some **examples**:

- Nancy, a book reviewer, quotes several passages from a novel in the context of a published book review.
- Phil, a historian and biographer, quotes from several unpublished letters and diaries written by his subject.
- Regina copies several paragraphs from an online news article in her blog.
- Sylvia, a poet, quotes a line from a poem by T.S. Eliot in one of her own poems.
- Kay, a librarian, makes a **photocopy** of the library's only remaining copy of Stephen King's latest bestseller.
- Arnold, a high school teacher, makes 30 copies of a newspaper article to distribute to his class.

Some of these uses are lawful without obtaining the permission of the owner of the copyrighted material; others would constitute copyright infringement absent the copyright owner's consent. The purpose of this chapter is to enable you to know when permission is and is not required.

Three-Step Analysis to Determine If Permission Is Required

To determine whether you need to obtain permission to use any given item, you need to answer the following three questions. If the answer to all three is yes, you need permission; otherwise, you don't.

Are You Taking an Author's Expression?

You only need permission to use an author's expression—that is, the particular sequence of words an author writes down or otherwise fixes in a tangible form to express his or her ideas, explain facts, and so on. Ideas and facts themselves are in the public domain, freely available for all to use. This idea-expression dichotomy is discussed in detail in Chapter 4, "What Copyright Protects." Review that chapter to determine whether what you want to use is expression. If you're sure it isn't, you don't need permission to use it. If there's any doubt in your mind, however, assume that it is expression and go on to the next question. (Of course, photocopying another author's work always constitutes a taking of that person's expression.)

Is the Author's Expression Protected by Copyright?

Not all expression is protected by copyright. Much is in the public domain and may be used freely without seeking anyone's permission. All expression contained in works for which copyright protection has expired is in the public domain. This includes any work published over 95 years ago and works published less than 95 years ago through 1963 that have not been timely renewed. Review the discussion of copyright duration and renewal in Chapter 8, "Copyright Duration."

Codification of Fair Use Privilege

The fair use privilege was originally created by judges in the 19th century. It was subsequently made a part of the Copyright Act when it was enacted in 1976. Section 107 of the act provides that:

"The fair use of a copyrighted work ... for purposes such as criticism, comment, news reporting, teaching, ... scholarship, or research, is not an infringement of copyright. In determining whether the use made of a work in any particular case is a fair use the factors to be considered ... include:

1. the purpose and character of the use, including whether such use is of a commercial nature or is for nonprofit educational purposes;
2. the nature of the copyrighted work;
3. the amount and substantiality of the portion used in relation to the copyrighted work as a whole; and
4. the effect of the use upon the potential market for, or value of, the copyrighted work."

In addition, certain types of expression are not entitled to copyright protection at all; this includes, for example, works by U.S. government employees, titles and short phrases, and certain blank forms. (See Chapter 4, "What Copyright Protects," for a detailed discussion.)

If the expression is protected by copyright, go on to the next question.

Does Your Intended Use of the Protected Expression Go Beyond the Bounds of Fair Use?

You do not need permission to use other authors' protected expression if your use constitutes a fair use. However, permission is required where the intended use of the expression goes beyond the bounds of fair use. The fair use privilege is discussed in detail below. If, after reading that discussion, you decide that your intended use of expression protected by copyright is not a fair use, you must seek permission to use it. The mechanics of seeking permission are discussed in Chapter 13.

Introduction to the Fair Use Privilege

As we discussed in Chapter 1, the purpose of the copyright laws is to advance the progress of knowledge by giving authors an economic incentive to create new works. Authors and their heirs are automatically granted the exclusive right to reproduce, adapt, perform, and display their works for at least 70 (and usually more) years; they are, in effect, granted a monopoly over the use of their work.

Copyright Office Fair Use Index

In a laudable effort to help the public understand the fair use rules, the Copyright Office has compiled an online Fair Use Index. It contains detailed summaries of some of the most notable court decisions involving fair use, going back to 1846. Reading these summaries, which are searchable by type of work involved, can help you understand how courts apply the complex fair use rules. The Fair Use Index can be found at www.copyright.gov/fair-use.

However, there are situations where strict enforcement of an author's monopoly would hinder, rather than promote, the growth of knowledge. An obvious example is that of a researcher or scholar whose own work depends on the ability to refer to and quote from prior scholars' work. No author could create a new work if first required to repeat the research of every author who had gone before.

Of course, scholars and researchers could be required to bargain with each copyright owner for permission to quote from or refer to prior works. But this would likely prove so onerous that many scholars would hunt for another line of work, and the progress of knowledge would be greatly impeded.

Can Fair Use Apply Where Permission Is Denied?

If you ask a copyright owner for permission to use his or her work and the owner refuses, can you then use it without permission on the grounds of fair use? The Supreme Court has said yes: "If the use is otherwise fair, no permission need be sought or granted. Thus, being denied permission to use a work does not weigh against a finding of fair use." (*Campbell v. Acuff-Rose Music, Inc.*, 114 S. Ct. 1164 (1994).) This means that even though you're certain that your intended use is fair, you can go ahead and seek permission for the use from the copyright owner because you want to avoid the possibility of expensive litigation. If the copyright owner proves to be unreasonable and withholds permission, you can then go ahead and use the material on the basis of fair use. But, of course, the copyright owner could still sue you. If the use really was fair, you would win the suit even though you had unsuccessfully sought permission.

To avoid these types of results, the fair use privilege was created. Pursuant to the fair use rule, an author is permitted to make *limited* use of a prior author's work without asking permission. All authors and other copyright owners are deemed to give their automatic consent to the fair use of their work by others. The fair use privilege is perhaps the most significant limitation on a copyright owner's exclusive rights.

When Is a Use a Fair Use?

Determining whether the fair use privilege applies in any given situation is not an exact scientific process. Rather, it requires a delicate balancing of all the factors discussed below. Probably the most useful rule for fair use is this variant of the golden rule: "*Take not from others to such an extent and in such a manner that you would be resentful if they so took from you.*" (Joseph McDonald, *Non-Infringing Uses*, 9 Bull. Copyright Soc'y 466 (1962).)

The following four factors must be considered to determine whether an intended use of an item constitutes a fair use:

- the purpose and character of the use
- the nature of the copyrighted work
- the amount and substantiality of the portion used, and
- the effect of the use upon the market for the copyrighted work.

Not all these factors are equally important in every case, but all are considered by the courts in deciding whether a use is fair. Moreover, the factors often interact with each other. For example, the more transformative the intended use, the less significance that may be given to other factors that could otherwise weigh against a finding of fair use, such as commercialism. So keep that in mind when making your own fair use analysis.

The Purpose and Character of the Use

First, the purpose and character of your intended use must be considered in determining whether it is a fair use. The test here is to see whether the subsequent work merely serves as a substitute for the original or "instead adds something new, with a further purpose or different character, altering the first with new expression, meaning, or message." (*Campbell v. Acuff-Rose Music, Inc.*; also see "Can Fair Use Apply Where Permission Is Denied?" above.) The Supreme Court calls such a new work transformative.

This is a very significant factor. The more transformative a work, the less important are the other fair use factors, such as commercialism, that may weigh against a finding of fair use. Why should this be? It is because the goal of copyright to promote human knowledge is furthered by the creation of transformative works. "Such works thus lie at the heart of the fair use doctrine's guarantee of a breathing space within the confines of copyright." (*Campbell v. Acuff-Rose Music, Inc.*)

Following are very typical examples of transformative uses where preexisting expression is used to help create new and different works. These types of uses are most likely to be fair uses:

- **criticism and comment**—for example, quoting or excerpting a work in a review or criticism for purposes of illustration or comment
- **news reporting**—for example, summarizing an address or article, with quotations, in a news report, and
- **research and scholarship**—for example, quoting a passage in a scholarly, scientific, or technical work for illustration or clarification of the author's observations.

Fair Use Checklist

You can use the following Fair Use Checklist to help determine if your intended use is a fair use. See the appendix for directions on how to download a copy of this form.

Name of Copyrighted Work: _____

Proposed Use: _____

Amount of Work to Be Used: _____

Prepared by: _____ Date: _____

1. Purpose and Character of the Use

Favoring Fair Use

☐ Teaching (including multiple copies for classroom use)

☐ Research

☐ Scholarship

☐ Nonprofit educational institution

☐ Criticism

☐ Restricted access (limited to students or other appropriate group)

☐ Parody

☐ Transformative or productive use (changes the work for new utility)

☐ News reporting

☐ Comment

Opposing Fair Use

☐ Commercial activity

☐ Profiting from the use

☐ Entertainment

☐ Bad-faith behavior

☐ Denying credit to original author

2. Nature of Copyrighted Work

Favoring Fair Use

☐ Published work

☐ Factual or nonfiction based

☐ Important to favored educational objectives

☐ Portion used is not central or significant to entire work

Opposing Fair Use

☐ Unpublished work

☐ Highly creative work (art, music, novels, films, plays)

☐ Fiction

3. Amount of Proposed Use

Favoring Fair Use

☐ Small quantity

☐ Portion used is not central or significant to entire work

☐ Amount is appropriate for favored educational purpose

Opposing Fair Use

☐ Large portion or whole work used

☐ Portion used is central to or "heart of the work"

4. Effect of Proposed Use on Market for Copyrighted Work

Favoring Fair Use

- ☐ User owns lawfully purchased or acquired copy of original work
- ☐ One or few copies made
- ☐ No significant effect on the market or potential market for copyrighted work
- ☐ No similar product marketed by the copyright holder
- ☐ Lack of licensing mechanism

Opposing Fair Use

- ☐ Could replace sale of copyrighted work
- ☐ Significantly impairs market or potential market for copyrighted work or derivative
- ☐ Reasonably available licensing mechanism for use of the copyrighted work
- ☐ Affordable permission available for using work
- ☐ Numerous copies made
- ☐ You made it accessible on the Web or in another public forum
- ☐ Repeated or long-term use

Although not really transformative, photocopying by teachers for classroom use can also be a fair use, because teaching also furthers the knowledge-enriching goals of the copyright laws.

Note that the uses listed above, with the possible exception of news reporting, are primarily for nonprofit educational purposes. Although some money might be earned from writing a review or scholarly work, financial gain is not usually the primary motivation—disseminating information or otherwise advancing human knowledge is.

If permission were required for these socially helpful uses (presumably for a fee), it is likely that few or no reviews or scholarly works would be written; neither the authors nor publishers of works that earn such modest sums could afford to pay for the necessary permissions. (News organizations perhaps could afford to pay for permissions, but requiring them to do so in all cases would inevitably impede the free flow of information and might also violate the free press guarantees of the First Amendment of the Constitution.)

In contrast, an author or publisher of a work written primarily for commercial gain usually can afford to pay for permission to use others' protected expression. It also seems inherently fair to require the author or publisher to do so. In the words of one court, fair use "distinguishes between a true scholar and a chiseler who infringes a work for personal profit." (*Wainwright Sec., Inc. v. Wall St. Transcript Corp.*, 558 F.2d 91 (2d Cir. 1977).)

For these reasons, the fact that a work is published primarily for private commercial gain weighs against a finding of fair use. For example, using the line, "You don't need a weatherman to know which way the wind blows" (from Bob Dylan's song "Subterranean Homesick Blues") in a poem published in a small literary journal would probably be a fair use. But using the same line in an advertisement for raincoats probably would not be.

However, the fact that a writer's primary motive is commercial does not always mean the writer can't exercise the fair use privilege. If the other fair use factors are in the writer's favor, the use may be considered a fair use. This is particularly likely where the use benefits the public by furthering the fundamental purpose of the copyright laws: the advancement of human knowledge.

EXAMPLE: The authors of an unauthorized popular biography of Howard Hughes quoted from two *Look* magazine articles about Hughes. All three fair use rules were satisfied. Only a small number of words were quoted, and the authors had provided proper attribution for the quotes. In addition, the copyright owner of the articles (who turned out to be Hughes himself) had no intention of using the articles in a book, so the use was not a competitive use. A court held that the quotations qualified as a fair use. Although the biography had been published primarily to earn a profit, it also benefited the public. The court stated that "while the Hughes biography may not be a profound work, it may well provide a valuable source of material for future biographers (if any) of Hughes or for historians or social scientists." (*Rosemont Enters., Inc. v. Random House, Inc.*, 366 F.2d 303 (2d Cir. 1966).)

It is even possible for an advertisement to constitute a fair use of protected expression if it serves the public interest as well as the advertiser's commercial interests. For example, a vacuum cleaner manufacturer was permitted to quote in an advertisement from a report in *Consumer Reports* comparing various vacuum cleaners (and concluding that the manufacturer's model was the best) because the advertisement significantly increased the number of people exposed to the Consumers Union's evaluations. The advertisement served the public interest by disseminating helpful consumer information. (*Consumers Union of United States, Inc. v. General Signal Corp.*, 724 F.2d 1044 (2d Cir. 1983).) The same rationale probably applies to the widespread practice of quoting from favorable reviews in advertisements for books, films, plays, and so on. However, as a general rule, you should always seek permission to quote protected material in an advertisement.

The Nature of the Prior Work

As we discussed in Chapter 4, "What Copyright Protects," to preserve the free flow of information, less copyright protection is given to factual works (scholarly, technical, scientific works, and so on) than to works of fancy (novels, poems, plays, and so on). This is particularly true where there are only a few ways to express the facts or ideas in a factual work, and the idea or fact and its expression are deemed to merge. Thus, authors have more leeway in using material from factual works than from fanciful ones, especially where it's necessary to use extensive quotations to ensure the accuracy of the factual information conveyed.

Use of Unpublished Materials

The extent to which unpublished materials, such as letters and diaries, may be quoted without permission is a controversial copyright issue.

EXAMPLE: Anthony, a well-known film historian, finds an unpublished letter written in 1990 by a famous Hollywood director who died in 2020. May Anthony quote from the letter in a book he's writing about the film industry without obtaining permission from the letter's copyright owners (presumably, the director's descendants and heirs)? The answer is maybe, maybe not.

When it comes to fair use, unpublished works are inherently different from published works. Publishing an author's expression without having been authorized to do so infringes upon the author's right to decide when and whether a work will be made public. Obviously, this factor is not present with published works, and the Supreme Court has held that the fact that a work is unpublished weighs heavily against a finding of fair use. (*Harper & Row Publishers, Inc. v. Nation Enters.*, 471 U.S. 539 (1985).)

This in itself was not surprising. However, in a pair of highly controversial decisions out of New York (where most major publishers are located), a federal circuit court went much further than the Supreme Court and indicated that the unauthorized use of unpublished materials can *never* be a fair use. In the first case (*Salinger v. Random House, Inc.*, 811 F.2d 90 (2d Cir. 1987)), the court prohibited a well-known literary biographer from quoting or closely paraphrasing in a biography of J.D. Salinger from 44 unpublished letters written by Salinger, which the biographer had discovered in university research libraries. In the other case (*New Era Publ'ns Int'l v. Henry Holt & Co., Inc.*, 873 F.2d 576 (2d Cir. 1989)), the court held that, but for a legal technicality, it would have been impermissible for an author to quote without permission from L. Ron Hubbard's unpublished writings in a highly critical Hubbard biography.

Attribution Does Not Make a Use Fair but Should Always Be Provided

Some people have the mistaken idea that they can use any amount of material so long as they give the author credit, whether in a footnote or by mentioning the title of the book after a quotation. This is simply not true. Providing credit for a quotation will not in and of itself make the use of the quote a fair use. For example, if you quote an entire chapter from another author's book without permission, your use wouldn't be considered fair even if you give that author credit.

On the other hand, it is always a good idea to provide attribution for quoted or paraphrased material. There are two reasons for this.

First, the copyright law makes it illegal to remove "copyright management information" if you know it will induce or facilitate copyright infringement. Copyright management information incudes a work's title, the author's name, and the copyright notice. It appears that copyright management information may be removed where a work is copied on the grounds of fair use, but it's a good idea to include such information anyway—this prevents even the possibility of being sued for removing such information. (For a detailed discussion of liability for removing copyright management information, see Chapter 10, "Copyright Infringement.")

Second, it is likely that a judge or jury would look with disfavor on an author who attempts to pass off the words of others as his or her own and then has the nerve to cry "Fair use!" when sued for copyright infringement. Judges might be inclined not only to find that the use is not a fair use but also to impose particularly heavy damages in an infringement suit. If you quote someone else's work, always give that person credit. Quoting with attribution is a very good hedge against getting sued or losing big, if you are sued.

These decisions had a definite chilling effect on publishers. In some cases, books that quoted letters were rewritten to omit the quotations. And suits against other biographers were filed.

As you might expect, publishers, authors' groups, biographers, historians, and others in the literary community were highly critical of these two federal circuit decisions out of New York, arguing that they enabled the heirs of well-known figures to control how scholars and others can use their unpublished writings, effectively creating a class of widow or widower censors.

After a two-year fight, the fair use provision in the Copyright Act was amended in 1992 to make clear that the fact that a work is unpublished does not act as an absolute bar to a finding of fair use. Section 107 of the Copyright Act now states: "The fact that a work is unpublished shall not itself bar a finding of fair use if such finding is made upon consideration of all ... [four] fair use factors."

This amendment to the Copyright Act was intended to return the law to where it was before the controversial New York federal court decisions discussed above. The fact that a work is unpublished weighs against fair use, but it is a hurdle that can be overcome in some cases. An important case decided before the amendment became law illustrates how the law works today. In this case, a biographer's unauthorized use of a modest amount of material from unpublished letters and journals by the author Richard Wright was found to be a fair use. The court held that, although the unpublished status of the material weighed against fair use, the other three fair use factors all were in the biographer's favor. (*Wright v. Warner Books, Inc.*, 953 F.2d 731 (2d Cir. 1991).)

TIP

In deciding whether your unauthorized use of unpublished material could be a fair use, focus first and foremost on the impact of your use on the value of the material. J.D. Salinger's literary agent testified at trial that Salinger could earn as much as $500,000 if he published his letters. Thus, if a biographer were permitted to publish portions of his most interesting letters first, it could have cost Salinger substantial royalties. This could not be a fair use. But you might be able to use unpublished material if it would not cost the copyright owner anything. For example, quoting a few lines from a letter written by an unknown and long-dead Civil War veteran might constitute a fair use where the letter itself has little or no intrinsic value to the veteran's heirs.

Fair Use of Out-of-Print Works

The drafters of the Copyright Act and the Supreme Court have suggested that a user might have more justification for reproducing a work without permission if it is out of print and unavailable for purchase through normal channels. (*Harper & Row Publishers, Inc. v. Nation Enters.*, 471 U.S. 539 (1985).) Thus, most courts give users more leeway when they copy or otherwise make use of out-of-print works. But this does not mean that any amount of material from out-of-print works may be used without permission.

The Amount and Substantiality of the Portion Used

The more material you take, the more likely your work will serve as a substitute for the original and adversely affect the value of the copyright owner's work—making it less likely that the use can be a fair use. However, contrary to what many people believe, there is no absolute word limit for fair use. For example, it is not always okay to take one paragraph or less than 200 words. Copying 12 words from a 14-word haiku poem wouldn't be fair use. Nor would copying

200 words from a work of 300 words likely qualify as a fair use. However, copying 2,000 words from a work of 500,000 words might be fair. It all depends on the circumstances—for example, it may be permissible to quote extensively from one scientific work to ensure the accuracy of another scientific work.

The *quality* of the material you want to use must be considered as well as the quantity. The more important it is to the original work, the less likely is your use a fair use. For example, in one famous case, *The Nation* magazine obtained a copy of President Gerald Ford's memoirs prior to their publication. The magazine published an article about the memoirs in which only 300 words from Ford's 200,000-word manuscript were quoted verbatim. The Supreme Court held that this was not a fair use because the material quoted, dealing with Ford's pardon of former President Nixon in the wake of the Watergate scandal, was the "heart of the book ... the most interesting and moving parts of the entire manuscript." (*Harper & Row Publishers, Inc. v. Nation Enters.*, 471 U.S. 539 (1985).)

An author of a work consisting primarily of a prior work—particularly the heart of the work, with little added or changed—will likely not be successful in invoking the fair use privilege.

 TIP

Although there is no legally established word limit for fair use, many publishers act as if there were one and require their authors to obtain permission to quote more than a specified number of words (ranging from 100 to 1,000 words). You should always ask your publisher about such requirements and seek to obtain any necessary permissions as soon as possible. See Chapter 13 for more information.

The Effect of the Use on the Market for, or Value of, the Prior Work

The fourth fair use factor is the effect of the use upon the potential market for, or value of, the copyrighted work. You must consider not only the harm caused by your act of copying, but whether similar copying by others would have a substantial adverse impact on the potential market for the original work.

Because fair use is an affirmative defense to copyright infringement, it is up to the defendant (the copier) in an infringement case to show there is no harm to the potential market for the original work—which can be difficult. The more transformative the subsequent work (meaning, the more it differs from the original and is aimed at a different market), the less likely it will be deemed to adversely affect the potential market for the original.

For example, a court found fair use where the authors of a scholarly study of the artist Pablo Picasso used photos of his paintings from a 1932 catalog. The out-of-print catalog was available only through art auctions and sold for as much as $100,000, while the study went for $150 per volume and was sold as a reference work for libraries and academic institutions. The court found that the two works did not compete with each other because of their "disparate markets and wildly different price points." (*de Fontbrune v. Wofsy*, 409 F. Supp. 3d 823 (N.D. Cal. 2019).)

But if you want to use an author's protected expression in a work of your own that is similar to the prior work and aimed at the same market, your intended use will probably be deemed to adversely affect the potential market for the prior work. This weighs against a finding of fair use.

> EXAMPLE 1: Nick, a golf pro, writes a book on how to play golf. Not a good putter himself, he copies the chapter on putting from a how-to golf book written by Tiger Woods (one of the greatest putters in golf history). Because Nick intends for his book to compete with and hopefully supplant Woods's, this use would likely not be a fair use, particularly given the large amount of copying. In effect, Nick is trying to use Woods's protected expression to eat into the sales of Woods's own book.

> EXAMPLE 2: Ophelia, a historian, writes a study of women's roles in Elizabethan England. Working under extreme deadline pressure, somehow she unconsciously quotes or closely paraphrases many important passages in a groundbreaking study of the topic written by Horatio ten years before. Ophelia intends for her book to compete with and hopefully supplant Horatio's prior work. Ophelia's use of Horatio's material is likely not a fair use.

> EXAMPLE 3: Suzy writes a guide to Social Security aimed at retirees. She borrows several charts and graphs from a prior work on the same subject aimed at the same market. This copying is likely not a fair use.

Effect of Use on the Market for Derivative Works Must Be Considered

Because the effect of the use on the potential market for the prior work must be considered, the effect on the market for derivative works based on the original must also be analyzed. As discussed in detail in Chapter 5, "Adaptations and Compilations," a derivative work is one that is based upon or recast from a prior work. One good example of a derivative work is a play or screenplay based on a novel. A finding that a work has a negative impact on the market for derivatives of an original work weighs against fair use.

EXAMPLE: A group of artists created a book called *Oh, the Places You'll Boldly Go!*—a "mash-up" of the Dr. Seuss classic *Oh, the Places You'll Go!* and *Star Trek*. The estate of Dr. Seuss sued the artists for copyright infringement. The court held there was no fair use. This was so even though the work was sufficiently transformative to be a fair use and did not supplant the market for the original Dr. Seuss works. The court noted that the Seuss estate had an extensive literary licensing program. Although the estate had not licensed any mash-ups of same type as *Boldly*, there was a potential market for them. Thus, allowing an unlicensed mash-up could have an adverse impact on the market for derivative works based on the Seuss works. (*Dr. Seuss Enters., L.P. v. ComicMix LLC*, 256 F. Supp. 3d 1099 (S.D. Cal. 2017).)

Fair Use Online

The fair use privilege applies in the online digital world just as it does in the offline analog world. The fair use factors discussed above must be applied to any intended online use. The more transformative the use, the more likely the online use will be considered a fair use.

Examples of Fair Use Online

We've seen above that news reporting, criticism, and comment are all classic examples of fair use. Thus, a fair use was found when a nonprofit organization posted a newspaper article about police discrimination on its website. The court reasoned that the nonprofit's use was transformative because its purpose was to educate the public about discrimination issues. (*Righthaven, LLC v. Jama*, No 2:10-CV-1322 JCM, 2011 WL 1541613 (D. Nev. Apr. 22, 2011).) Similarly, a court held it was fair use when a user of an online political forum posted a five-sentence excerpt from a newspaper article with a link back to the newspaper's website. The court held that the use was quantitatively small and did not cause the newspaper financial harm. (*Righthaven, LLC v. Democratic Underground, LLC*, 791 F. Supp. 2d 968 (D. Nev. 2011).)

And, in a celebrated case, fair use was found to apply when someone leaked internal emails from Diebold Election Systems revealing flaws in Diebold's e-voting machines, and the emails were republished on numerous websites. The court declared that "[t]he email archive was posted … [to] inform … the public about the problems associated with Diebold's electronic voting machines. It is hard to imagine a subject the discussion of which could be more in the public interest." (*Online Policy Group v. Diebold, Inc.*, 337 F. Supp. 2d 1198 (N.D. Cal. 2004).)

No Fair Use Found

On the other hand, there was no fair use where a website called Free Republic posted verbatim complete copies of news stories from dozens of news sources, including the *Los Angeles Times* and *Washington Post*. Free Republic argued that the postings were a fair use because the website's users were allowed to comment on the news stories. But the court rejected that stance, ruling there was little transformative about copying the entirety of news articles, and the wholesale copying of articles was not necessary in order for users to be able to comment on them. Moreover, posting the articles fulfilled (at least to some extent) demand for the original works, diminishing the newspapers' ability to sell and license them. Finally, the fact that Free Republic posted the articles to help attract donations also weighed against a finding of fair use. (*Los Angeles Times v. Free Republic*, 54 U.S.P.Q.2d 1453, 1455-56 (C.D. Cal. 2000).)

There was also no fair use where Scientology critic Dennis Erlich posted the entirety of many writings by Scientology founder L. Ron Hubbard onto an Internet newsgroup. Although the postings were done for the purpose of criticism and comment, the court found that the use was not transformative because (1) Erlich copied entire works and, (2) unlike the typical critic, he added little new expression to them. (*Religious Tech. Ctr. v. Netcom On-Line Communications Servs, Inc.*, 923 F. Supp. 1231 (N.D. Cal. 1995).)

What About Social Media?

The fact that work of authorship has been placed on a social media platform like Twitter or Facebook does not mean that it can be freely used, especially for commercial purposes. For example, a photographer who posted on Twitter photos he took of the aftermath of the 2010 Haiti earthquake successfully sued a news agency for copyright infringement, after the agency copied and distributed the photos to subscribers without permission. The photographer was awarded $1.2 million in damages. (*Agence France Press v. Morel*, 769 F. Supp. 2d 295 (S.D.N.Y. 2011).) Although the fair use defense was not raised in this case, the use of the photos very likely did not constitute a fair use because (1) the entire works were used, (2) the use was commercial, (3) the use was not transformative, and (4) the use had a clearly harmful effect on the potential market for licensing the photos.

Similarly, there was no fair use where CNN, TMZ, and several other media companies copied a photo of Donald Trump posted on Instagram by a guest at a wedding at President Trump's New Jersey golf course. The court rejected the theory that the use was transformative simply because the photographer took the photo for personal, not commercial, use. (*Otto v. Hearst Commc'ns, Inc.*, 345 F. Supp. 3d 412 (S.D.N.Y. 2018).)

Note, however, social media websites like Facebook do have a nonexclusive license to make use of content posted by users (see Chapter 7). But this license does not extend to others, such as news organizations.

Fair Use and the Photocopy Machine

Individual photocopying of one copy of an article from a magazine or periodical or small portion of a book for personal use—not as part of a business activity—probably constitutes a fair use.

Making multiple copies of anything, or copying entire books or other works you get from libraries or friends to avoid having to buy them, probably isn't a fair use. However, there is no practical way for copyright owners to enforce their copyright rights against individual photocopiers. There are no copyright police stationed at photocopy shops.

Photocopying for commercial purposes or to promote business activities is likely not a fair use, particularly if multiple copies of a work are made. For example, a group of seven major publishers obtained a $510,000 judgment against one duplicating business for copying excerpts from books without permission, compiling them into "course packets," and selling them to college students. (*Basic Books, Inc. v. Kinko's Graphics Corp.*, 758 F. Supp. 1522 (S.D.N.Y. 1991).)

What about photocopying scientific and technical journal articles and similar materials for research purposes? Also, not a fair use. Example: Employee researchers of the oil giant Texaco systematically copied entire technical and scientific journal articles to save the material for research purposes. The journals sued Texaco for copyright infringement. The court held that this type of wholesale archival copying was not a fair use, because it was not transformative or productive—that is, Texaco's employees were just making exact copies of articles, not creating anything new. The copying was done simply to save Texaco money on subscriptions and licensing fees. The court said that Texaco should either obtain licenses from the Copyright Clearance Center or a similar organization or buy more subscriptions for its researchers. (*Am. Geophysical Union v. Texaco, Inc.*, 60 F.3d 913 (2d Cir. 1994).)

Copying by Teachers

Copying by teachers for scholarly or classroom use is generally favored as a fair use, because it is done for nonprofit educational purposes. However, if taken to extremes, such copying would destroy the market for educational materials. In an effort to strike a balance among the needs of teachers and publishers and authors, a set of guidelines for teacher photocopying was agreed upon by representatives of author-publisher and educational organizations and unofficially endorsed by the congressional committee that drafted the Copyright Act.

Technically, the guidelines do not have the force of law, but it is highly unlikely that any court would hold that copying by a teacher within the guidelines did not constitute a fair use.

TIP

The guidelines establish *minimum* fair use standards for teachers. It is possible that teacher photocopying that exceeds the guidelines could be considered a fair use as well. In one case, for example, a court held that 70 instances of copying copyrighted books and posting them on a university's e-reserve system were not infringing because of fair use and for other reasons. The court viewed the Copyright Office's 1976 Guidelines for educational fair use as a minimum, not a maximum, standard. The court then proposed its own fair use standard: (a) 10% of a book with fewer than ten chapters or of a book that is not divided into chapters, or (b) no more than one chapter or its equivalent in a book of ten or more chapters. (*Cambridge Univ. Press v. Becker*, 863 F. Supp. 2d 1190 (N.D. Ga. 2012).)

The guidelines may be summarized as follows.

Single Copies

A teacher may make *one copy* of the following items for purposes of scholarly research, or use in teaching or preparing to teach a class:

- a chapter from a book (but not an entire book)
- an article from a periodical or newspaper
- a short story, short essay, or short poem, whether or not from a collective work, such as an anthology, and
- a chart, graph, diagram, drawing, cartoon, or picture from a book, periodical, or newspaper.

Multiple Copies for Classroom Use

A teacher may also make multiple copies of the items listed above (not to exceed more than one copy per pupil in the course) provided that the following are true:

- The amount of material copied is sufficiently brief.
- The copying is done spontaneously.
- The cumulative effect test is met.
- Each copy includes a notice of copyright.

Brevity

There are strict numerical limits as to how many words may be copied, but these limits may be stretched so that copies don't end with an unfinished line of a poem or an unfinished prose paragraph.

Poetry. Multiple copies may be made of a completed poem of 250 words or less that is printed on not more than two pages or up to 250 words from longer poems.

Prose. Multiple copies may be made of (a) a complete article, story, or essay of less than 2,500 words; (b) an excerpt of 500 words from works that are between 2,500 and 4,999 words long; and (c) an excerpt up to 1,000 words or 10% of the work, whichever is less, from longer works.

Illustrations. Multiple copies for classroom use may be made of one chart, graph, diagram, drawing, cartoon, or picture contained in a book or periodical issue.

Special works. The guidelines also include a category called "special works." No one is exactly sure what a special work is.

However, it appears that special works include works of poetry or prose of less than 2,500 words intended for children that combine language with illustrations. Such special works may not be copied in their entirety. Only an excerpt of up to two published pages and containing not more than 10% of the words in the text may be reproduced.

Spontaneity

The idea to make the copies must come from the teacher him- or herself, not from school administrators, the board of education, or any other higher authority. Moreover, the idea to make the copies and their actual classroom use must be so close together in time that it would be unreasonable to expect a timely reply to a request for permission from the publisher or copyright owner.

> **TIP**
>
> **It usually takes at least a month or two for a publisher to respond to a permission request.** Thus, the spontaneity requirement will probably be met where the copies are used in class less than a month after they are made. But, of course, this rule wouldn't apply if the material is included in a curriculum prepared prior to the start of the school term.

Cumulative Effect of Copying

The copying must not have an undue cumulative effect on the market for the copyrighted work. This test is met so long as the following are true:

- The copying is for only one course in the school where the copies are made.
- Not more than one short poem, article, story, or essay or two excerpts from longer works are copied from the same author, nor more than three from the same anthology or other collective work or periodical volume during one class term.
- There are no more than nine instances of such multiple copying for one course during one class term.

The limitations on the number of articles that can be copied does not apply to copying from newspapers, current news periodicals, and current news sections of other periodicals.

Copyright Notice

A copyright notice must be included on all copies made. This can easily be accomplished by copying the page in the work where the copyright notice appears. If this is not done, the notice must be added to the copies. It should be in the exact same form as on the original work.

Photocopy Charges

Finally, the teacher's students may not be charged more than the actual cost of making the photocopies.

Prohibited Copying

Even if all the requirements listed above are satisfied, multiple copies may not be made to substitute for the purchase of books, publisher's reprints, or periodicals; to create anthologies or compilations; or to substitute for or replace "consumable" works, such as workbooks, exercises, standardized tests, test booklets, and answer sheets.

In addition, the same teacher may not copy the same item from term to term. Thus, for example, it was not a fair use for a teacher to use the same photocopied materials for three successive school terms. (*Marcus v. Crowley,* 695 F.2d 1171 (9th Cir. 1983).)

Electronic Copies

Making electronic copies of copyrighted works for classroom use—for example, making them available on a course website —can be a fair use, but not if the copying goes too far. This was illustrated when Georgia State University (GSU) allowed its professors to make digital copies of excerpts from a number of publishers' research-based monographs. The excerpts were made available through GSU's electronic reserves system to students enrolled in courses for which the readings were assigned, thus functioning much like an online course pack. Cambridge University Press and other publishers filed suit. Fair use was found in those cases where the amount copied was less than one whole chapter or fewer than 50 pages and less than 10% of the work. (*Cambridge Univ. Press v. Patton,* 769 F.3d 1232 (11th Cir. 2014).) When making electronic copies for classroom use, the guidelines for photocopying by teachers should generally be followed.

Copying by Libraries and Archives

Fair use analysis becomes difficult when copying by libraries and archives is involved. Such institutions play a vital role in preserving and disseminating knowledge. Yet, if they were permitted to engage in unfettered copying, the market for all written works would be reduced and authors' economic incentives to create new works would be diminished.

Congress has determined that certain types of unauthorized copying by libraries and archives must be permitted whether or not it would constitute a fair use under the standards discussed above.

There are two separate exemptions available for libraries and archives: The first exemption gives libraries and archives the right to make up to three physical or digital copies of any work for certain purposes. The second exemption allows copies to be made only of those works that have entered the 75th year of their copyright term.

Copying for Archival or Replacement Purposes or at User's Request

Books or other written works often are lost or become worn out. Replacing them may be difficult where the work is out of print. In this event, can a library make a new copy itself without obtaining permission from the copyright owner? Library users often ask librarians to photocopy articles from a periodical. Can a library legally make the copy? The answer to both questions may be yes if the following special exemption applies.

Which Libraries and Archives Can Benefit From Special Exemption?

The exemption applies to all nonprofit libraries and archives—for example, municipal libraries, university and school libraries, and government archives. However, a library or an archive need not be nonprofit to qualify. A library or an archive owned by a profit-making enterprise or proprietary institution may qualify for the exemption so long as the copying itself is not commercially motivated. This means that a profit may not be earned from the copies themselves—for instance, they could not be sold for a profit—but the information contained in the copies may be used to help a company make a profit-making product. For example, the exemption might be claimed by research and development departments of chemical, pharmaceutical, automobile, and oil companies; the library of a private hospital; and law and medical partnership libraries.

However, if the library or archive is not open to the general public, it must be open at least to persons doing research in the specialized field covered by the library collection who are not affiliated with the library or its owner. This requirement eliminates many libraries and archives owned by private companies that are open only to employees.

When Does the Exemption Apply?

The special exemption may be claimed only if all of the following are true:

- The library or archive owns the work as part of its collection.
- No more than three physical or digital copies of the work are made at one time.
- No charge is made for the copying beyond the costs of making the copy.
- The copies contain the same copyright notice that the work itself contains; if the work contains no notice, a legend must be included in the copies stating that the work may be protected by copyright.

So long as these requirements are met, it is permissible for a library or an archive to make an authorized photocopy of a work under the following four circumstances.

Archival reproductions of unpublished works. Up to three copies of any unpublished work may be made for purposes of preservation or security or for deposit for research use in another library or archive. The work may be photocopied or otherwise physically reproduced, or digital copies may be made. However, if the work is digitally copied, the digital copies may not be made available to the public outside the library or archive premises. This means the digital copies could only be read on computers at the library or archive. They may not be placed on a network that people outside the library can access or the Internet. But first, the library or archives must make a reasonable effort to purchase an unused replacement at a fair price. This will always require contacting commonly known trade sources in the United States and, in the normal situation, the publisher or other copyright owner (if the owner can be located at the address listed in the copyright registration) or an authorized reproducing service as well.

Replacement of lost, damaged, or obsolete copies. A library or an archive may also make up to three physical or digital copies of a published work that is lost, stolen, damaged, deteriorating, or stored in an obsolete format. A format is considered obsolete when the device necessary to read the work is no longer manufactured or is no longer reasonably available in the commercial marketplace. As with unpublished works, if digital copies are made, they may not be made available to the public outside the library or archive premises.

Library user requests for articles and short excerpts. A library or an archive may make one copy (it doesn't have to be a facsimile) of an article from a periodical or a small part of any other work at the request of a library user or at the request of another library on behalf of a library user, provided that the following are true:

- The copy becomes the property of the library user.
- The library has no reason to believe the copy will be used for purposes other than private study, scholarship, and research.

- The library displays a copyright notice at the place where reproduction requests are accepted. (For the form of this notice and other regulations regarding it, see 37 C.F.R. § 201.4 (1988).)

Library user requests for entire works. A library or an archive may also make a copy (it doesn't have to be a facsimile) of an entire book or periodical at a library user's request (or at the request of another library on behalf of a library user) if the library determines after reasonable investigation that a copy cannot be obtained at a reasonable price, either because the work is out of print or for some other reason. The same type of investigation must be conducted as for replacement of lost or damaged copies (above). In addition, the same good-faith and posting requirements must be met as for reproduction of articles and short excerpts (above).

No Multiple Copies

The library and archive exemption extends only to isolated and unrelated reproductions of a single copy. It does not authorize related or concerted reproduction of multiple copies of the same material, whether at the same time or over a period of time. This is so whether the copies are intended for one individual or a group. For example, if a college professor instructs his or her class to read an article from a copyrighted journal, the school library would not be permitted to reproduce copies of the article for the class.

No Systematic Copying

Systematic copying is also prohibited. This means that a library or an archive may not make copies available to other libraries or groups of users through interlibrary networks and similar arrangements in such large quantities so as to enable them to substitute the copies for subscriptions or reprints that they would otherwise have purchased themselves. The National Commission on New Technological Uses for Copyrighted Works (CONTU) has developed the following guidelines as to how much copying is permissible:

- Within any calendar year, one library or archive may obtain from another library or archive not more than five copies of any factual article or articles from a single periodical published less than five years previously. The five-copy limitation applies even if each copy is of a different article or from a different issue. All that matters is that all the articles came from the same periodical and were published not more than five years before the copies are made.
- A library or an archive may not obtain from another library or archive more than five copies of material other than factual periodical articles from any given work within any calendar year.
- If the requesting library or archive has on order or in its collection the item that it wants copied, but it does not have the item in its possession at the time and cannot reasonably repossess the item at the time, the copy made at its request will not count toward the maximum number of permissible copies.
- A library or an archive may not satisfy another library's or archive's request for copies unless the request is accompanied by a representation that the request conforms with these guidelines.
- Every library or archive must keep on file each request for copies it made to other libraries or archives.

Photocopying Beyond the Scope of the Exemption

Unauthorized copying that is not covered by, or goes beyond the limits of, the special exemption is permissible only if it is a fair use under the more flexible fair use factors discussed above.

Photocopying by Library Patrons

Many libraries refuse to make copies for patrons. Instead, they simply install coin-operated machines for patrons to use themselves. A library or an archive is not liable for unsupervised use of photocopy machines on its premises provided that a proper warning notice is displayed. For the form of this notice and other regulations regarding it, see 37 C.F.R. § 201.4 (1988).

Copying Works Over 75 Years Old

In 1998, the Sonny Bono Copyright Term Extension Act extended the copyright term for works published before 1978 from 75 to 95 years. The act also included a new exemption for libraries and an archives. Under this exemption, a library, an archive, or nonprofit educational institution functioning as a library or an archive may reproduce, display, or perform in physical or digital form for purposes of preservation, scholarship, or research a copy of a work that has entered the last 20 years of the 95-year copyright term. As of 2021, works in the last 20 years of their copyright term would include all works published during 1927 through 1945.

However, three requirements must first be met. Following a reasonable investigation, the library or archive must have determined all of the following:

- The work is not subject to normal commercial exploitation—that is, cannot be purchased from the publisher or booksellers.
- A copy of the work cannot be obtained at a reasonable price.
- The copyright owner of the work has not filed a notice with the Copyright Office that either of the first two conditions cannot be met (see below).

The exemption does not apply to unpublished works and may only be claimed by libraries or archives themselves, not by people who use them.

TIP

The majority of works first published in the United States before 1964 are in the public domain because their copyrights were never renewed. Such works may be copied freely for any purpose. Therefore, libraries and archives should first check to see if an old work they want to copy has been renewed before bothering to investigate whether this exemption applies. Note, however, that most works first published outside the United States before 1964 didn't have to be renewed. (See Chapter 8 for detailed discussion.)

Notice to Libraries and Archives

Copyright owners who own works in their last 20 years of copyright protection are allowed to file a notice with the Copyright Office stating that the work is subject to normal commercial exploitation or that a copy can be obtained at a reasonable price. If such a notice is filed, a library or an archive may not utilize the exemption discussed here.

The Copyright Office has created a form for this purpose called Form NLA. You can download a digital copy from the Copyright Office's website at www.copyright.gov/forms/nla.pdf. However, the Copyright Office will not send you a hard copy of the form. Form NLA may be filed any time during a work's last 20 years of copyright protection. The notice must be accompanied by a $50 fee for the first work covered and an additional $20 for each additional work covered by the notice. Include a check payable to the

Register of Copyrights. The notice and fee should be sent to:

Library of Congress
Copyright Office
101 Independence Avenue SE
Washington, DC 20559-6000
Attn: NLA

The Copyright Office says that the notice must be filed more than once during the last 20 years of the work's copyright life. However, it has yet to decide how often.

The notice must be signed under penalty of perjury. This means that if you claim in the notice that the work you own is subject to normal commercial exploitation or can be obtained at a reasonable price, it must be true. Don't lie in order to prevent libraries from making free copies of your work.

The Copyright Office will place the information contained in all the notices it receives in its online database called the COHD file. This may be searched online through the Copyright Office website at www.copyright.gov. Before relying on this exemption, a library or an archive should search this database to see if a notice has been filed covering the work or works the library wants to copy.

Other Fair Uses

Fair use is not limited just to quotations and photocopying. Discussed below are some other types of uses that may be fair uses.

Parody

A parody is a work of fancy that ridicules another, usually well-known, work by imitating it in a comic way. For example, the bestselling novel *Fifty Shades of Gray* has spawned many parodies, including *Fifty Shades of Alice in Wonderland*, a cookbook called *Fifty Shades of Gravy*, and a Jewish-themed *Fifty Shades of Oy Vey*.

To parody a work, it is usually necessary to use some of the original work's expression, so that readers will be able to recognize what's being parodied. However, it is rarely possible to get permission to parody or satirize someone else's work. Thus, parodies can exist only because of the fair use doctrine. Recognizing this, courts have historically held that parody and satire deserve substantial freedom, both as entertainment and as a form of social and literary criticism.

In a seminal decision involving a parody of the song "Pretty Woman" by the rap group 2 Live Crew, the Supreme Court strongly reaffirmed the view that a parody, like other comment and criticism, may be a fair use. Indeed, the court held that even a commercially distributed parody of a well-known song can constitute a fair use. To determine whether any parody is a fair use, all four fair use factors discussed above, must be weighed.

The Supreme Court, in *Campbell v. Acuff-Rose Music, Inc.*, 114. S. Ct. 1164 (1994), gave specific guidance on how the fair use factors should be evaluated in a parody case.

Parody: *Gone With the Wind*

When is a work a parody and when is it not? Cases involving Dr. Seuss and the book *Gone With the Wind* show just how difficult it can be to know for sure. One thing is certain, though: If a court decides a work isn't a parody, the fair use defense will fail.

In the Dr. Seuss case, two authors wrote a book called *The Cat NOT in the Hat! A Parody by Dr. Juice.* The book told the story of the O.J. Simpson trial through poems and sketches similar to those in the famous *The Cat in the Hat* children's stories by Dr. Seuss. The work was narrated by Dr. Juice, a character based on Dr. Seuss, and contained a character called "The Cat NOT in the Hat." The story begins in Brentwood:

> *A happy town*
> *Inside L.A.*
> *Where rich folks play*
> *The day away*
> *But under the moon*
> *The 12th of June*
> *Two victims flail*
> *Assault! Assault!*
> *Somebody will go to jail!*
> *Who will it be?*
> *Oh my! Oh me!*

The owners of the copyrights in Dr. Seuss sued for copyright infringement. The authors claimed that their work was a fair use of the Dr. Seuss stories because it was a parody. They argued that by applying Dr. Seuss's style to adult subject matter their work commented on the "naiveté of the original" Dr. Seuss stories as well as on society's fixation on the O.J. Simpson trial.

The court disagreed. It said that a parody was a "literary or artistic work that imitates the characteristic style of an author or a work for comic effect or ridicule." *The Cat NOT in the Hat!* didn't qualify because the authors' poems and illustrations merely retold the Simpson tale. Although they broadly mimicked Dr. Seuss's characteristic style, they did not hold it up to ridicule or otherwise make it an object of the parody. The court opined that the authors used the Seuss characters and style merely to get attention or avoid the drudgery of working up something fresh. It upheld an injunction that barred Penguin Books from distributing 12,000 books it had printed at an expense of $35,000. (*Dr. Seuss Enters., L.P. v. Penguin Books USA, Inc.,* 109 F.3d 1394 (9th Cir. 1997).)

Four years later, the exactly opposite result was reached by another court in a case involving the legendary Civil War novel *Gone With the Wind.* The book, called *The Wind Done Gone,* chronicles the diary of a woman named Cynara, the illegitimate daughter of a plantation owner, and Mammy, a slave who cares for the owner's children. Without obtaining permission from the copyright owner of *Gone With the Wind,* the author of *The Wind Done Gone* copied the prior book's characters, famous scenes and other elements from the plot, and dialogue and descriptions. The Margaret

Parody: *Gone With the Wind* (continued)

Mitchell estate sued both the publisher and author for copyright infringement.

The court held that *The Wind Done Gone* was protected by the fair use privilege, and thus the Mitchell estate could not obtain a court order halting its publication. The court concluded that *The Wind Done Gone* was a parody. The court held that a work is parody "if its aim is to comment upon or criticize a prior work by appropriating elements of the original in creating a new artistic, as opposed to scholarly or journalistic, work." *The Wind Done Gone* satisfied this test because it was a specific criticism of and rejoinder to the depiction of slavery and the relationships between blacks and whites in *Gone With the Wind*. (*Suntrust Bank v. Houghton Mifflin Co.,* 268 F.3d 1257 (11th Cir. 2001).)

The difference between these cases seems to be that the court didn't like *The Cat NOT in the Hat*, while it did like *The Wind Done Gone*. The *Cat* court said that authors' claim that their work commented on the naiveté of the Dr. Seuss stories was "pure shtick" and "completely unconvincing." In contrast, the *Wind* court said the book was "a critical statement that seeks to rebut and destroy the perspective, judgments, and mythology of *GWTW*." Subjective decisions like these show why it can be so hard to predict if a parody is a fair use or not.

Market Effect on Derivative Works Must Be Considered

The effect of a parody on the market for derivative works based on the original must also be considered. As discussed in Chapter 5, "Adaptations and Compilations," a derivative work is a work based on or recast from an original, such as a play or screenplay based upon a novel. The right to license derivative works is one of a copyright owner's most important rights. A parody may itself be a derivative work of the original it parodies. But the effect of a parody on the market for other parodies of the original need not be considered. This is because in the real world copyright owners hardly ever license parodies of their work. In other words, it is only necessary to consider the effect of a parody on the potential market for derivative works other than other parodies of the original. Again, where the copying is slight, the market effect on derivative works is also slight.

EXAMPLE: William writes a one-act play that parodies the best-selling novel *The Bridges of Madison County*. In deciding whether the play is a fair use, a court must consider the effect the play has on the potential market for other plays based on the novel. But the court need not consider whether the play affects the market for other parodies of the novel, because the novel's author is unlikely to license parodies of his work.

Purpose and Character of the Use

The Supreme Court stated that the heart of any parodist's claim of fair use is that an author's preexisting work needed to be copied in order to create a new work that, at least in part, comments on or criticizes the prior author's work. However, a self-proclaimed parodist who copies a prior work merely to get attention or to avoid the drudgery in working up something fresh has a weak claim to fair use.

Does it matter that a parody might be seen to be in bad taste? The Supreme Court said no. All that matters is that the work can reasonably be perceived to contain a parodic element—in other words, it comments on or criticizes the original work in some way. Whether a parody is in good or bad taste does not matter to fair use.

The fact that a parody was commercially motivated weighs against a finding of fair use but is not determinative by itself.

The Nature of the Copyrighted Work

Expressive works of fancy like novels and plays are generally given greater copyright protection than more utilitarian factual works like newspaper accounts or scientific works. However, the Supreme Court stated that because parodies almost always copy publicly known expressive works, this fair use factor is not helpful "in separating the fair use sheep from the infringing goats."

The Amount and Substantiality of the Portion Used

To be effective, a parody must take enough material from the prior work to be able to conjure it up in the reader's or hearer's mind. To make sure the intended audience will understand the parody, the parodist usually has to copy at least some of the most distinctive or memorable features of the original work. Once enough has been taken from the original work to assure identification, how much more is reasonable to take will depend on the extent to which the work's overriding purpose and character is to parody the original. However, a parody composed primarily of an original work with little new material added is not likely to be considered a fair use.

Effect of the Use on the Market for the Prior Work

A finding that a parody has a detrimental effect on the market for, or value of, the original work weighs against fair use. However, the Supreme Court stated that a parody generally does not affect the market for the original work because a parody and the original usually serve different market functions. A parody is particularly unlikely to affect the market for the original where the copying is slight in relation to the parody as a whole.

But what if a parody is so scathing or critical of the original work that it harms the market for it? Does this weigh against fair use? The Supreme Court answered this question with a resounding no. Biting criticism is not copyright infringement, even if it effectively destroys a work both artistically and commercially.

> **TIP**
>
> **Applying these fair use factors is a highly subjective exercise.** One judge's fair use might be another's infringement. A parody will probably be deemed a fair use so long as:
>
> - The parody has neither the intent nor the effect of fulfilling the demand for the original.
> - The parodist does not take more of the original work than is necessary to accomplish the parody's purpose (the more recognizable the original work, the less needs to be taken to parody it).

- The original work is at least in part an object of the parody (otherwise there would be no need to use it).

Calligraphy

A single copy reproduction of a copyrighted work by a calligrapher for a single client is a fair use. Likewise, a single reproduction of excerpts from a work by a student calligrapher or teacher in a learning situation would be a fair use of the copyrighted work.

Copying for the Blind

The making of a single Braille copy or tape recording of a copyrighted work by an individual as a free service for blind persons would probably be considered a fair use. But making multiple copies or tapes for commercial purposes would not be.

Copyright Infringement: What It Is, What to Do About It, How to Avoid It

Previous chapters have discussed the steps an author or other copyright owner must take to give his or her work maximum protection under the copyright laws. Now we explore how these protections are enforced. This subject is referred to as "copyright infringement."

When a copyright dispute arises, there are often several self-help steps a copyright owner can take. These generally amount to telling the infringer to stop the infringing activity or pay for the infringement. When push comes to shove, however, there is only one remedy with teeth in it. This is to ask a federal court to order the infringing activity halted and award a judgment for damages. Because this type of litigation is procedurally complex, an attorney skilled in copyright litigation is required.

This chapter is not intended as a substitute for a good copyright attorney. Rather, its aim is to:

- help you recognize when copyright infringement has occurred
- suggest some steps an author or other copyright owner can take to deal effectively with infringement without resorting to lawyers and the courts
- tell you what to expect in the event of a court action
- help you estimate what damages and other types of court relief are potentially available to you in an infringement suit
- introduce some ways to defend against infringement charges, and
- tell you how to protect yourself from infringement claims.

What Is Copyright Infringement?

In Chapter 1, "Copyright Basics," we described a copyright as a bundle of five exclusive rights. These include the right to reproduce, distribute, prepare derivative works based upon, perform, and display a protected work. Subject to important exceptions discussed below, these rights cannot be exercised by anybody but the copyright owner unless the owner's permission is obtained. If copyright rights are exercised without the owner's permission, the copyright is said to be infringed.

Infringement of written works usually involves the unauthorized exercise of a copyright owner's exclusive rights to reproduce the work and prepare derivative works based on it. In plain English, this means the unauthorized *copying* of the work. This chapter focuses on infringement due to copying. However, be aware that performing a play, publishing an unauthorized copy, or reciting a written work in public also constitutes copyright infringement—unless the copyright owner's permission is obtained.

There are many ways to copy a written work. An infringer might copy another's work by means of a computer, scanner, photocopy machine, or other mechanical device. Or an infringer might do it the old-fashioned way—by transcribing verbatim or paraphrasing protected material into a work of his or her own. The latter type of copying need not even be done consciously to constitute infringement. A person who unconsciously copies from memory a work after having read it can be a copyright infringer, but the penalties imposed on such a person would usually be less than those for a person who consciously and willfully copied another's work.

The Difference Between Plagiarism and Copyright Infringement

Many people believe that plagiarism and copyright infringement are the same thing. Not so: A plagiarist is a person who poses as the *originator* of words he or she did not write, ideas he or she did not conceive, or facts he or she did not discover. For purposes of plagiarism, the material stolen need not be protected by copyright. In contrast, a copyright infringer is a person who makes unauthorized use of material protected by copyright. Absent protection, there can be no infringement. Moreover, infringement can occur even though the infringer gives proper credit to the author of the protected expression. Of course, some infringers also take credit for the work they copy; they are both plagiarists and infringers.

EXAMPLE 1: Louis, a professor of French, translates a novel by the obscure 19th century French novelist Jean Valjean and publishes it under his own name. The novel is in the public domain, thus Louis has not committed copyright infringement. He is, however, a plagiarist, because he has posed as the originator of the novel.

EXAMPLE 2: The publisher Scrivener & Sons publishes a paperback version of Stephen King's latest bestseller without his permission. Scrivener has infringed on King's copyright by publishing his book without permission, but it has not committed plagiarism because it has not posed as the author of the book.

EXAMPLE 3: Dr. Jekyl, a biophysicist at a leading university, copies a paper written by one of his colleagues and publishes it under his own name in a scientific journal. Because the colleague's paper was protected by copyright, Dr. Jekyl is both a plagiarist and copyright infringer.

How to Avoid a Plagiarism Charge

To avoid charges of plagiarism, authors of scholarly works (histories, biographies, legal and scientific treatises, and so on) must always give proper credit to the sources of their ideas and facts, as well as any words they borrow. Authors of less serious works, how-to books for example, should always attribute quotations, but may not always need to give credit for ideas and facts they borrow (authors of such works should discuss this with their publishers). It is neither customary nor necessary for authors of works of fancy, such as novels and plays, to credit the sources of their inspiration, whether other works of fancy, newspaper accounts, or histories. But they should, of course, give proper attribution for direct quotations.

A plagiarist cannot be sued for copyright infringement if all he or she takes are unprotected ideas or facts or words that exist in the public domain. There is no legal requirement to provide attribution when public domain works are copied and placed into new works. (*Dastar Corp. v. Twentieth Century Fox Film Corp.*, 123 S. Ct. 2041 (2003).) But publishing contracts usually contain a provision, called a warranties and indemnities clause, by which the author promises that the work submitted to the publisher is not in the public domain. So a plagiarist could be sued by a publisher for breach of contract or possibly fraud. And, aside from the possible legal consequences, being accused of plagiarism is usually not good for one's career. College professors and journalists have been fired because of plagiarism.

How to Know Whether You Have a Valid Infringement Claim

If you come away with nothing else from this chapter, remember this: *The fact that another person's work is similar to your own does not necessarily mean that he or she has committed copyright infringement.* Infringement occurs only if all three requirements discussed below are present:

- ownership of a work protected by a valid copyright
- actual copying of the work by the alleged infringer (remember, this chapter focuses on infringement by copying; infringement of other exclusive copyright rights is also possible), and
- improper use of the work's protected expression by the alleged infringer.

We discuss each element below. Where it's clear you have a valid infringement claim, it may be possible to settle the matter without the aid of an attorney as discussed below. However, if you're not sure whether you have a valid claim, get professional help. How to find a competent copyright lawyer is discussed in Chapter 14, "Help Beyond This Book."

A Work Protected by Copyright

The question of infringement does not even arise unless the work allegedly infringed is protected by copyright. This means that the work must meet the three prerequisites for copyright protection discussed in detail in Chapter 4, "What Copyright Protects." The work must be:

- **fixed in a tangible medium of expression.** You cannot sue anyone for copying words you have spoken but never written down or otherwise fixed in a tangible form.
- **independently created.** The material allegedly infringed upon must have been independently created. You cannot sue someone for copying words that were copied from others.

- **minimally creative.** The work you believe has been infringed upon must have been the product of a minimal amount of creativity. You probably will not be able to successfully sue someone for copying a recipe, an alphabetically organized directory, or similar items.

Timely Registration Creates Presumption of Validity

So long as your work is registered within five years of the date of first publication, it is presumed to be protected by a valid copyright and the person(s) named in the registration certificate are presumed to be the copyright owner(s). This presumption is one of the greatest benefits of copyright registration. It means that you do not have to go to the time and trouble of proving that your work is original (which can be very hard to prove) or that you actually wrote it. Rather, it's up to the alleged infringer to try to prove that the work was not original or that your copyright is invalid for some other reason.

Actual Copying by the Alleged Infringer

Second, it must be clear that the alleged infringer actually copied your work. In some cases, there might be witnesses who saw the alleged infringer copy the work (the infringer may have had a collaborator), or the infringer might even admit it. However, an up-front admission of copying is unusual. More typically, copyright infringement—like adultery—usually happens behind closed doors, and the participants rarely admit their involvement. For this reason, copying is usually established not through direct evidence such as witnesses or admissions, but by showing two things:

- access by the infringer, and
- that the works, or parts of them, are substantially similar.

If these elements proven, copying is *inferred*, because no other reasonable explanation for the similarities exists.

Access

To prove access, you must show that the alleged infringer had access to your work— that is, the opportunity to view it. The fact that your work has been made generally available to the public through publication is sufficient to establish access. Placing a work online is also usually enough to establish access. In the case of unpublished works that have never been made available online, however, access must be shown in different ways. One way would be to show that the alleged infringer had contact with a third person—for instance, an editor—who possessed a copy of your manuscript. But in the absence of such contacts, you're going to have a hard time convincing anyone that the alleged infringer had access to your unpublished work.

Substantial Similarity

Here, you must prove that your work and the work by the alleged infringer are so similar that copying must have occurred. Assuming the alleged infringer had access to your work, you must compare the similarities between your work and the infringer's to see if copying might reasonably be inferred. But keep in mind that similarity does not always mean that copying has occurred.

We would all like to think that no one else has ever had the same thoughts or feelings or dreams as we have had. But, in sad fact, this is simply not the case. We are not unique. As usual, Oscar Wilde said it best: "The brotherhood of man is not a mere poet's dream: It is a most depressing and humiliating reality." As a result, it's not only common that two or more people will have the same ideas at the same time and express them in similar ways—it's often inevitable.

To rule out the operation of factors that might give rise to similarity without copying—such as those listed below in "Similarity Is Not Always Due to Copying" —your work and the alleged infringer's must be so similar that these factors are not a rational explanation. Courts call this level of similarity "substantial similarity."

You don't need to engage in a hyper-critical textual analysis to determine whether substantial similarity exists. Simply compare both works from all angles and ask

Similarity Is Not Always Due to Copying

The late copyright attorney Alexander Lindey, in his classic study *Plagiarism and Originality* (1952), identified the following 14 causes, other than copying, why two works may be similar:

- the use, in both, of the same or similar theme
- the fact that commonplace themes carry commonplace accessories
- the use, in both works, of stereotypes or stock characters
- the fact that both employ the same well-weathered plot
- the limited number of plots generally
- the presence, in both, of hackneyed ingredients, episodes, devices, symbols, and language
- the fact that both authors have drawn on the world's cultural heritage or cast their works in the same tradition
- the imperatives of orthodoxy and convention
- the impact of influence and imitation
- the process of evolution
- the dictates of vogue or fashion
- the fact that both authors have stolen from the same predecessor
- the fact that both have made legitimate use of the same news item, historical event, or other source material, and
- the intervention of coincidence.

Making Lists of Similarities

It might be helpful to draw up a list of similarities you discover between your work and another work you think might be infringing. You can then show the list to a copyright lawyer, who might even have the list admitted into evidence if a lawsuit results. Here's a small portion of such a list prepared by the producers of the original *Star Wars* film who successfully claimed that their work was copied by the creators of the television movie *Battlestar Galactica*:

- The central conflict of each story is a war between the galaxy's democratic and totalitarian forces.
- In *Star Wars*, the young hero's father had been a leader of the democratic forces, and the present leader of the democratic forces is a father figure to the young hero. In *Battlestar*, the young hero's father is a leader of the democratic forces.
- An entire planet, central to the existence of the democratic forces, is destroyed in both stories.
- The heroine in both stories is imprisoned by the totalitarian forces.
- A friendly robot, who aids the democratic forces, is severely injured (*Star Wars*) or destroyed (*Battlestar*) by the totalitarian forces.
- There is a scene in a cantina (*Star Wars*) or casino (*Battlestar*), in which musical entertainment is offered by bizarre, nonhuman creatures.

yourself whether the average reader would conclude that the author of the later-created work copied from the first.

Of course you should look for similarities in wording, but other similarities might also help establish copying. In the case of a work of fancy, such as a novel or play, compare such aspects of the works as their themes, plots, characters, settings, moods, paces, and writing styles. For a factual work, such as a history or biography, similarities in the facts, structure, and organization of the works might help indicate copying.

What Judges and Juries Actually Do in Infringement Cases

Judges and juries normally do not engage in a hypercritical line-by-line analysis of the works in question to determine if a defendant's paraphrasing or copying of a prior work's total concept and feel constitutes infringement. Rather, they simply ask themselves whether the average intended reader of the works would regard them as substantially similar. This is not a scientific process. It's based mostly on a judge or jury's gut impressions and sense of fairness. If the judge or jury thinks that the alleged infringer has done something wrong, they will usually find him or her guilty of copyright infringement.

💡 **TIP**
Publishers of certain types of works, particularly directories and other fact compilations, sometimes deliberately insert minor errors in their work to help prove copying. If the alleged infringer's work contains the same errors, copying must have occurred.

Improper Use of Protected Expression

The fact that the alleged infringer in all likelihood copied from your work will get you through the courthouse door but is not enough to establish infringement. The final and most important element of infringement is that the alleged infringer has copied your work's *protected expression*. As discussed in detail in Chapter 4, "What Copyright Protects," a work's protected expression consists of the author's independently created word sequences and the selection and arrangement of material. Everything else, including the ideas and facts the work expresses, is in the public domain, free for all to use.

There are four levels or degrees of copying of protected expression that can constitute copyright infringement:

- verbatim copying of *all* of a work's protected expression
- verbatim copying of *part* of a work's expression

- paraphrasing a work's protected expression, and
- copying a work's total concept and feel or fundamental essence.

Verbatim Copying of an Entire Work

The most obvious type of copyright infringement occurs when an entire book, story, or article is copied verbatim (or nearly so) without the copyright owner's permission. No one can doubt that infringement has occurred when virtually every word in the alleged infringer's work is the same as yours. Indeed, when there is this much copying, many courts dispense with the need to show access; instead they presume it.

EXAMPLE 1: Sally writes a short story and gives *The New Zorker* magazine permission to publish it once. Three months later, she discovers that *The Plagiarist's Review* has republished her story without asking her permission (she had retained all her other copyright rights in the story). The *Review* has clearly infringed upon Sally's copyright in her story.

EXAMPLE 2: Lou publishes an online subscription newsletter on trends in the publishing world. He discovers that one of his subscribers has made electronic copies of the newsletter available to the general public on its website. This is also verbatim copying and infringes Lou's copyright.

Partial Verbatim Copying

Far more common than verbatim copying of an entire work, especially where such factual works as biographies, histories, and how-to books are involved, is verbatim (or near verbatim) copying of only a portion of a work's protected expression, whether a few lines, paragraphs, pages, or chapters. This kind of copying constitutes copyright infringement only if a substantial amount of protected expression is taken.

How much is substantial? There is no definite answer. Verbatim copying of 300 or 400 words would usually be considered substantial enough to constitute infringement. However, it is possible for less copying to be infringement if the material taken is of great value or highly original. For example, infringement was found where the defendant copied 12 sentences from Martin Luther King's "I Have a Dream" speech in an advertising pamphlet for funeral accessories. (*Martin Luther King, Jr., Ctr. for Social Change, Inc. v. Am. Heritage Prods.*, 508 F. Supp. 854 (N.D. Ga. 1981), *rev'd on other grounds*, 694 F.2d 674 (11th Cir. 1983).)

Paraphrasing

In the infringement context, paraphrasing means making alterations in an author's words instead of copying them verbatim. Whether done consciously (to make it appear copying has not occurred) or unconsciously, paraphrasing constitutes copyright infringement if there is a substantial amount of it. If this were not so, an infringer could get away with infringement simply by making minor changes in an original work's wording.

However, this type of close paraphrasing must be contrasted with changing an author's protected expression to such an extent that there are no recognizable similarities in the prior and subsequent works' expression. In the words of one court, "copying so disguised as to be unrecognizable is not copying." (*See v. Durang,* 711 F.2d 141 (9th Cir. 1983).)

In some cases, it can be very difficult to tell whether a work's protected expression has been paraphrased or an alleged infringer has merely taken the ideas and facts in the work and put them in his or her own words, which because of the merger doctrine (Chapter 4, "What Copyright Protects"), coincidence, and others factors, happen to be similar to the prior work's. It can be difficult to predict in such cases whether a judge or jury would conclude that infringement has occurred. (See "Paraphrasing Self-Test" below.)

Copying a Work's Total Concept and Feel

The final type of copying that can constitute infringement—and the most difficult to detect and prove—is unauthorized copying of a work's total concept and feel. This type of copying is often claimed to be present in infringement cases involving such works of fancy as novels, plays, and poems. "Total concept

Paraphrasing Self-Test

Compare the following passages taken from actual published works and decide for yourself whether the author of the second passage infringed upon the protected expression in the first passage. We also tell you what the courts decided.

Passage in first created work	Passage in subsequent work	How the courts ruled
Surprisingly, the newborn is a remarkably capable organism from the moment he begins to breathe. He can see, hear, smell, and he is sensitive to pain, touch, and change in position. The only sense modality which may not be functioning immediately at birth is taste, but even this sense develops rather quickly.	From his first breath, the child is remarkably well-equipped for life. He can see, hear, smell, touch and feel pain. All his senses, except taste, are operating immediately, and even taste develops rapidly.	Infringement. The court was probably swayed by the fact that there were over 400 examples of this type of paraphrasing from the prior work. (*Meredith Corp. v. Harper & Row, Publishers*, 378 F. Supp. 686 (S.D.N.Y. 1974).)
And second, he says that likely to aid comparisons this year was the surprisingly limited extent to which Fiber Division's losses shrank last year.	The second development likely to aid comparisons this year was the surprisingly limited extent to which the Fiber Division's losses shrank last year.	Infringement. This was just one of dozens of passages in financial reports that were closely para-phrased in a financial newspaper. (*Wainwright Sec. v. Wall St. Transcript Corp.*, 558 F.2d 91 (2d Cir. 1977).)
Ohm's Law is a very important law which you must learn. R = E/I where R = resistance in ohms E = pressure in volts I = current in ampheres.	Ohm early in the 19th century discovered that the ratio of the pressure to the current in a given circuit is constant. This is the fundamental law of the flow of electrical currents. R = E/I where R = resistance in ohms E = pressure in volts I = current in ampheres.	Infringement. The court was probably swayed by the fact that there were over 400 examples of this type of paraphrasing from the prior work. (*Meredith Corp. v. Harper & Row, Publishers*, 378 F. Supp. 686 (S.D.N.Y. 1974).)

Paraphrasing Self-Test (continued)		
Passage in first created work	**Passage in subsequent work**	**How the courts ruled**
[A]s the Lord commanded he lifted up the rod and smote the waters of the river and all the waters that were in the river were turned to blood. And the fish that were in the river died; and the river stank; and the Egyptians could not drink the waters of the river; and there was blood throughout all the land of Egypt.	In accordance with the directive previously received from higher authority, he caused the implement to come into contact with the aquifer, whereupon a polluting effect was perceived. The consequent toxification reduced the conditions necessary for the sustenance of aquatic vertebrates below the level of continued viability. Olfactory discomfort standards were substantially exceeded, and potability declined. Social, economic, and political disorientation were experienced to an unprecedented degree.	No infringement. Okay, we cheated. This is a made-up example that no court has or ever could rule on. The first passage is from Exodus in the King James Version of the Old Testament, which is in the public domain. However, even if the passage was protected by copyright, it's not likely that anyone would conclude that the second passage infringed upon it. Although we would never advise anyone to write this badly, the second passage (taken from Richard C. Wydick, *Plain English for Lawyers*, 66 Cal. L. Rev. 727 (1978)) is a good example of an author's taking the facts in a prior work and putting them into his or her own words.
Ellen, Julia, and Rachel will be here on Tuesday; they'll stay for two days. Don't know what will happen when they get here. I'm hoping for peace and quiet.	Early in 1960, Wright wrote to Margrit de Sabloniere that Ellen, Julia, and Rachel would be arriving for a two or three day visit. Wright said that he did not know what would happen when they arrived but that he was hoping for peace and quiet.	No infringement. The author of an unauthorized biography of Richard Wright paraphrased these lines from an unpublished letter by Wright. The court held there was no infringement because the paraphrasing constituted "straightforward factual reportage" of the "most basic and banal factual matter," not Wright's protected expression. (*Wright v. Warner Books, Inc.*, 748 F. Supp. 105 (S.D.N.Y. 1990).)

Paraphrasing Self-Test (continued)		
Passage in first created work	**Passage in subsequent work**	**How the courts ruled**
He looks to me like a guy who makes his wife keep a scrapbook for him.	[Salinger] had fingered [Wilkie] as the sort of fellow who makes his wife keep an album of press clippings.	Infringement. The author of an unauthorized biography of J.D. Salinger paraphrased these lines from an unpublished letter by Salinger. The court characterized the biographer's passage as a close paraphrase of highly original expression. (*Salinger v. Random House, Inc.*, 811 F.2d 90 (2d Cir. 1987).)

and feel" is one term courts use to describe a work's fundamental essence or overall pattern. It consists of the *totality* of all the elements an author selects and combines to form a single work of authorship. Total concept and feel includes a novelist's selection and combination of themes, setting, stock characters, scenes, situations, literary devices, writing style, and plot. This type of infringement protects an author's selection and combination of individual elements that are not separately protected by copyright. (See Chapter 4, "What Copyright Protects.")

Remember: A work's overall pattern or fundamental essence must be copied for there to be infringement. If only a few of a work's unprotectable elements themselves are similar—for instance, stock characters, situations, or plots—there is no infringement. Most authors who bring total concept and feel suits lose their cases for this reason.

EXAMPLE: Reyher published a children's story derived from an old folk tale about a child who becomes separated from her mother. To strangers, the child describes her mother as the most beautiful woman in the world. When she is finally reunited with her mother, the mother turns out to be homely in appearance. A story with an almost identical plot was subsequently published in a children's magazine. There was no verbatim copying or paraphrasing. Reyher sued the magazine for copyright infringement, claiming that her story's total concept and feel had been copied. Reyher lost. The court held that although the two stories had the same plots and similar situations, they differed in almost every other way, including the setting, theme, characterization, and mood. Thus the two works' total feel was not the same. (*Reyher v. Children's Television Workshop*, 533 F.2d 87 (2d Cir. 1976).)

Remember too that a work's fundamental essence or total concept or feel must be *original*—that is, independently created—to be protected. The less originality involved in selecting and combining a work's constituent elements, the less copyright protection it will receive. For example, works of fancy that are written according to tried-and-true formulas—for example, Gothic romances, Westerns, police shoot-'em-ups, and buddy movies—are accorded less protection than highly original works of art containing uncommon themes, characters, or plots.

When Copying Protected Expression Is Excused

In some cases, authors are allowed to copy other authors' protected expression without permission. This might occur through operation of the merger doctrine (legalese for situations where there are only a few ways to express an idea or fact) or where the copying constitutes a fair use of the protected expression.

Unavoidable Copying: The Merger Doctrine

Sometimes an author has no alternative but to copy or paraphrase another author's words. This situation occurs where there is just one way, or only a few ways, to adequately express a particular idea or fact. In these cases, the idea or fact and the way it's expressed are deemed to merge and the

expression—the first author's words—is given very limited copyright protection or no protection at all. The merger doctrine applies mainly to factual works such as histories, biographies, and scientific treatises, rather than to works of fancy such as novels, plays, and poems. This is because, by their very nature, facts provide their own limitation of how they can be described, while the ideas present in fictional works can almost always be written in new and different ways.

As a result of the merger doctrine, in some cases verbatim copying or close paraphrasing of even a substantial number of words from a factual work may not constitute infringement. See Chapter 4, "What Copyright Protects."

Fair Copying: The Fair Use Privilege

Copying of protected expression will also be excused where it constitutes a fair use of the material. The fair use privilege applies primarily in situations where an author quotes or otherwise uses a limited amount of protected expression for scholarly, educational, or other nonprofit purposes. See Chapter 9, "Using Other Authors' Words."

Self-Help Remedies for Copyright Infringement

Assuming you have a valid infringement claim, you might be able to obtain a satisfactory resolution of an infringement claim on your own. Depending on the circumstances, simply sending the alleged infringer and his or her publisher(s) (who are also liable for any infringement; see below) a cease and desist letter may do the trick. This sort of letter serves several functions simultaneously:

- It lets the infringer know that you believe he or she is infringing on your copyright.
- It establishes a date for your discovery of the infringement. This is important for purposes of the statute of limitations on copyright infringement lawsuits discussed below.
- It tells the infringer you intend to stop him or her.
- It gives the alleged infringer a chance to explain his or her conduct and perhaps offer a satisfactory compromise before you spend a lot of money initiating a lawsuit. Even if you're sure you're right, it doesn't hurt to listen to the other person's story. In addition, by giving the infringer a chance to respond, you might find out a lot about how he or she plans to defend a court action if you choose to bring one.

Contents of a Cease and Desist Letter

A cease and desist letter should normally include:

- your contact information
- the name of your work, date of first publication, and copyright registration number if the work was registered

- the nature of the activity you believe to be an infringement of your copyright
- a demand that the infringer cease and desist from the activity and pay you for any damages you've sustained, or if the infringement is not still going on, simply pay your damages, and
- a request for a response within a stated time period.

Your letter can threaten legal action, but you're probably wiser not to at this stage. The specter of imminent legal action is likely to make the other person paranoid, defensive, and unwilling to cooperate. It might also send him or her straight to a lawyer.

When you draft your letter, remember that you may end up wanting to use it in court. Accordingly, avoid being nasty, cute, tentative, or overly dramatic.

Cease and desist letters should be sent by certified mail, return receipt requested. If the infringer refuses to accept your letter, arrange to have it delivered personally by someone who isn't involved in the dispute and who'll be available to testify that the letter was delivered. You might have to hire a process server to deliver the letter, if you don't know anyone who can do it for you.

EXAMPLE 1: Sally, a freelance writer, discovers that *The Plagiarist's Review* has reprinted without her permission an article she wrote and published several years ago and to which she retains all the copyright rights. Sally sends the magazine's editor the letter shown below.

January 1, 20xx

Editor in Chief
The Plagiarist's Review
100 Copycat Lane
New York, NY 10000

Dear Sir:

I recently became aware that your magazine published in its November 20xx issue an article entitled "Old Ideas in New Bottles." I originally wrote this article in January 2020, and it was first published in June 2020 in *The Patawamee Magazine*.

I own all of the rights in this article. Because I never authorized you to reprint the article in your publication, it follows that you infringed upon my copyright by doing so.

This letter is to demand that you immediately cease and desist from selling any copies of *The Plagiarist's Review* containing the infringing article. In addition, I demand to be reasonably compensated for the use of my article in the copies that have already been sold.

Please respond to this letter by January 15, 20xx.

Very truly yours,

Sally Bowles
Sally Bowles

February 28, 20xx

President
Copycat Press
100 Grub Street
Boston, MA 10001

Dear Sir:

I recently discovered that three chapters, totaling 130 pages, from my Ph.D. dissertation, entitled *The French Chamber of Deputies, 1932–1940*, have been copied nearly verbatim in your recently published title *All of French History*, by Professor S.T. Cole. Enclosed is a copy of the chapters in question along with a copy of the dissertation's title page; note the copyright notice in my name. The dissertation was registered with the Copyright Office on July 15, 20xx; the registration number is TX123456.

I do not know Professor Cole, have never been contacted by him, and never gave him or anyone else permission to use material from my dissertation, to which I own all the copyright rights.

This letter is to demand that you immediately cease and desist from selling any copies of *All of French History* containing the material from my dissertation. In addition, I demand that I be compensated for the use of my dissertation in the copies that have already been sold.

Please respond to this letter by March 15, 20xx.

Very truly yours,

James C. McCarthy
James C. McCarthy

cc: Professor S.T. Cole
    Department of Humanities, Elite College
    Marred Vista, CA 90000

For more samples, check out the thousands of cease and desist letters at the Lumen database (https://lumendatabase.org).

EXAMPLE 2: James obtained his Ph.D. in French history four years ago. His Ph.D. dissertation, entitled *The French Chamber of Deputies, 1932–1940*, was microfilmed and made available to researchers in various research libraries around the country. James timely registered the dissertation with the Copyright Office. He discovers that three chapters of his dissertation have, without his permission, been copied almost verbatim in a new textbook on French history "written" by Professor Cole and published by Copycat Press. James sends the letter shown below to Copycat Press and a copy to Professor Cole.

Responses to Cease and Desist Letters

What happens after the alleged infringer receives your letter typically depends on the nature of the infringer and the infringing conduct. Hopefully, it will be possible for you to work out a reasonable solution, such as making the infringement legal through a license under which you're paid an agreed-upon fee for the use of your work (see Chapter 7, "Transferring Copyright Ownership") and getting the infringer to stop future infringements. The fee, of course, is subject to negotiation. It should include a penalty for the inconvenience the infringer caused you—probably at least 50% more than you would have charged had the infringer asked you for permission to use your work in the first place.

Any compromise settlement should be in writing and signed by all the parties.

EXAMPLE 1: Sally Bowles in the example above agreed to grant *The Plagiarist's Review* a retroactive, nonexclusive license to publish her article. In return, the *Review* promised to print a correction in a future issue stating that she was the author of the article; it also promised to publish and pay for two new articles by Sally in upcoming issues. Sally felt that was better than just getting a one-time payment for the unauthorized use of her old article.

She sends the compromise settlement letter shown below.

EXAMPLE 2: Because James, the author of the dissertation *The French Chamber of Deputies, 1932–1940* in Example 2, above, had timely registered his dissertation with the Copyright Office, he might be entitled to substantial statutory damages if the case went to court. Accordingly, Copycat Press agreed to pay James $3,000 to settle the matter (this was 50% more than James would have charged had Copycat asked him for permission to use his work in the first place). In return, James agreed to release Copycat Press from liability for infringing on his work. James was not able to reach a settlement with Professor Cole, who denied copying from James's dissertation. James decided to pocket the money and forget pursuing his case against Cole.

James sent Copycat Press the letter shown below.

Compromise Settlement Letter for Example 1

Felix Franklin
Editor-in-Chief
The Plagiarist's Review
123 Copycat Lane
New York, NY 10000

Dear Mr. Franklin:

This letter embodies the terms of our settlement of the outstanding dispute arising from publication of the article "Old Ideas in New Bottles" in the November 20xx issue of *The Plagiarist's Review*:

1. Sally Bowles hereby retroactively grants *The Plagiarist's Review* a nonexclusive license to reprint her article "Old Ideas in New Bottles" in its November 20xx issue.

2. *The Plagiarist's Review* promises to print a prominently placed correction in its March 20xx issue, in words approved by Sally Bowles, informing its readers that Sally Bowles was the author of the article "Old Ideas in New Bottles" that ran in the November 20xx issue and that her name had been left off the article in error.

3. *The Plagiarist's Review* also promises to publish the following articles by Sally Bowles at its customary fee no later than December 20xx:
   - an approximately 2,000-word article tentatively entitled "What to Do If You're Accused of Plagiarism," and
   - an article of approximately 1,500 words on the subject of marketing freelance writing.

Sally Bowles
_____   _____
Sally Bowles   Date

_____   _____
Felix Franklin, Editor-in-Chief   Date
The Plagiarist's Review

Compromise Settlement Letter for Example 2

Lisa Bagatelle
President
Copycat Press
100 Grub Street
Boston, MA 10001

Dear Ms. Bagatelle:

This letter embodies the terms of our settlement of the outstanding dispute arising from Copycat Press's publication of the book *All of French History* by Professor S.T. Cole:

1. Copycat Press will pay James McCarthy the sum of $3,000 as compensation for the unauthorized use of material from his Ph.D. dissertation entitled *The French Chamber of Deputies, 1932–1940*.

2. Copycat Press promises not to use any of James McCarthy's work, including material from his Ph.D. dissertation, in the future without his authorization. This includes reprintings and new editions of *All of French History* and other works.

3. James McCarthy agrees that this completely settles the matter in dispute between James McCarthy and Copycat Press, and releases Copycat Press from any further liability for publication of material from *The French Chamber of Deputies, 1932–1940*, by Copycat Press.

James McCarthy
_____   _____
James McCarthy   Date

_____   _____
Lisa Bagatelle, President   Date
Copycat Press

Overview of Copyright Infringement Lawsuits

If you can't satisfactorily resolve the matter yourself (perhaps with a short consultation with a copyright lawyer), you have two alternatives: Forget about it or hire a lawyer and bring an infringement suit in federal court. The following is an overview of the nuts and bolts of a copyright infringement suit. It is intended to give you a general idea of what you can expect from copyright litigation, not as a substitute for further research or a consultation with an experienced copyright attorney. See Chapter 14, "Help Beyond This Book," for a guide to further research and ways to find a copyright attorney.

Who Can Sue

A person or an entity who files an infringement suit is called the plaintiff. The plaintiff must be someone who owns the copyright rights at issue or is entitled to receive royalties from them. This will typically be the author or the publisher to whom the author has sold some or all of his or her rights to the work.

> EXAMPLE: Manuel writes a biography of Alexander Hamilton and sells his reproduction and distribution rights to Scrivener & Sons. Leslie copies a substantial portion of Manuel's book in her own published biography of Hamilton. Both Manuel and Scrivener are entitled to sue Leslie for copyright infringement of the exclusive rights to reproduce and distribute the work.

Work Must Be Registered With Copyright Office

Before a plaintiff can file a copyright infringement lawsuit against anyone, either: (1) The work involved must be registered with the Copyright Office, or (2) the Copyright Office must refuse to register the work after the copyright owner submitted a complete application. The U.S. Supreme Court says it is not sufficient to merely file your registration application with the Copyright Office. Registration must either be completed or refused before suit may be filed. (*Fourth Estate Pub. Benefit Corp. v. Wall-Street.com, LLC*, 139 S. Ct. 881 (2019).) While it is not necessary to register before the infringement occurred, if you do so (or within 90 days of publication), you can obtain statutory damages of $750 to $150,000 per infringed work. A registration application normally takes months for the Copyright Office to process, but expedited registration is available if you pay a substantial, extra fee. See Chapter 3 for a complete guide to copyright registration.

Deciding who does and doesn't own derivative rights in a work in the context of a copyright infringement action is often complex. For example, an author may transfer film rights to one person or entity, television rights to another, and foreign language translation rights to still others. And, unless prohibited in the original transfer of rights, the derivative rights may be further transferred and divided—for example, the entity that buys the TV rights may transfer Japanese TV rights to someone else. Often, an author who transfers all or part of his or her derivative rights retains the right to receive part of the total fee (often a royalty) from their exploitation.

> **EXAMPLE:** Manuel sells the worldwide television adaptation rights to his Hamilton biography to the Founders Channel in return for $100,000 and a 5% share of the profits from the film. Acme Productions produces an unauthorized television documentary for Canadian television based on Manuel's biography and quotes substantial portions of Manuel's words. Both Manuel and Founders may sue Acme. However, because it would get most of the recovery from a suit against Acme, Founders would likely carry the ball in this situation— that is, Founders' attorneys would do most of the work and Manuel would simply join along as a plaintiff.

Liability for Removing Copyright Management Information

In 1998, Congress created a new legal basis for suing copyright infringers. The Digital Millennium Copyright Act (DMCA; 17 U.S.C. §§ 1202, 1203) makes it illegal to remove "copyright management information" from copyrighted works and gives copyright owners the right to sue for damages people who do so. The right to sue under the DMCA is in addition to any rights they may already have to sue such people for copying their works.

The main intent behind the law was to prevent infringers from removing copyright notices and other ownership information from material placed in the online world. Thus, several courts have held that the law applies only to copyright notices that function as a part of an automated copyright protection or management system or that are digitally placed on a copyrighted work. (*IQ Group, Ltd. v. Wiesner Publ'g, LLC*, 409 F. Supp. 2d 587 (D.N.J. 2006).) For example, one court held that the law did not apply to copyright notices placed on fabric designs. (*Textile Secrets Int'l, Inc. v. Ya-Ya Brand Inc.*, 524 F. Supp. 2d 1184, 1192-93 (C.D. Cal. 2007).) However, other courts have disagreed with this view and held that the statute applies to all types of copyright notices. For example, a court held that the law was violated when someone removed a handwritten copyright notice from architectural plans and falsely claimed to be the copyright owner of the plans. (*Fox v. Hildebrand*, No. CV 09-2085 DSF, 2009 U.S. Dist. LEXIS 60886 at *2, 5-8 (C.D. Cal. July 1, 2009).)

What Is Copyright Management Information?

Copyright management information includes:
- the title and other information identifying the work
- a work's copyright notice
- the author's name and any other identifying information about the author
- the copyright owner's name and any other identifying information about the owner
- any terms and conditions for use of the work, and
- identifying numbers or symbols on the work referring to any of the above information or Internet links to such information.

What Can't You Do With Copyright Management Information?

The law makes it illegal to do any of the following if you know or have reasonable grounds to know that it will induce, facilitate, or conceal a copyright infringement:
- intentionally remove or alter any copyright information
- distribute, import for distribution, or publicly perform a work whose copyright management information has been removed or altered without permission from the copyright owner or legal authority

- provide false copyright management information, or
- distribute or import for distribution a work containing false copyright management information.

For example, it is illegal to remove the copyright notice from a digital work and then copy and place it online without the copyright owner's permission.

Penalties for Violations

Any person injured by a violation of the law may sue the violator for damages and seek to obtain a court injunction ordering the violator to stop distributing the work from which the copyright management information was removed, altered, or falsified. Such a suit may be brought in addition to any suit for copyright infringement the person may have against the violator.

> EXAMPLE: John is the author and copyright owner of an article about online business strategies that was published on a national magazine's website. He discovers that the article has been copied and placed on another website without his or his publisher's permission. John's name, the title of the article, the publisher's name, and the copyright notice were removed from the materials before they were placed online. John can sue the national magazine (the owners of the website) for copyright infringement because the magazine illegally copied and distributed his article. He can also sue the magazine for removing the copyright management information from

his work: his name, book title, copyright notice, and publisher's name. He can obtain damages for both violations—copyright infringement and illegal removal of copyright management information. Ordinarily, both legal claims would be joined in a single lawsuit brought by John against the national magazine.

If the suit is successful, the injured person may obtain from the court an award of its actual monetary damages or may instead ask for statutory damages. Such statutory damages range from a minimum of $2,500 to a maximum of $25,000 per violation. It's up to the court to decide how much to award within these limits. If the defendant is a repeat offender—has violated the law two or more times within three years—the court may increase the damage award up to three times. The court may also award the injured person attorneys' fees and court costs.

However, the court may reduce the damages or not award any damages at all if the offender convinces the judge that he or she was not aware and had no reason to believe that his or her acts constituted a violation. In addition, the court may not award damages against a nonprofit library, an archive, or an educational institution if the court finds that it was not aware and had no reason to believe that its acts constituted a violation.

A person or company that willfully violates the law for commercial advantage or private financial gain may be criminally prosecuted by the U.S. Justice Department. Criminal penalties are steep: A first-time offender can be fined up to $500,000 and imprisoned up to five years. But nonprofit libraries, archives, and educational institutions are not subject to criminal prosecution.

Exceptions for Fair Use and Public Domain Works

There are some situations where it is permissible to remove copyright management information without the copyright owner's permission.

First, the law provides that such an action is permissible if permitted by law. One case where the law may permit removing copyright management information is when material is copied on the grounds of fair use. The fair use privilege permits people to copy portions of copyrighted works without obtaining permission from the copyright owner under certain circumstances. (See Chapter 9 for a detailed discussion of fair use.) In some cases it might not be possible or convenient to include copyright management information when a work is copied on the grounds of fair use—for example, when creating a parody of a copyrighted work. In this event, its removal would likely not be considered a legal violation.

Although the law doesn't explicitly say so, it doesn't apply to works that have entered the public domain. Such works can be freely copied and altered in any way. Because no one owns a public domain work, no harm is done by removing copyright management information.

Finally, law enforcement, intelligence, and other government agencies are permitted to alter or remove copyright management information in order to carry out lawful investigative, protective, information security, or intelligence activities.

Criminal Prosecutions for Infringement

Willful copyright infringement for financial gain has long been a federal crime, punishable by imprisonment, fines, or both. However, as a practical matter, the federal authorities rarely bothered to prosecute copyright infringers. They just didn't view copyright infringement as a high-priority crime justifying allocation of limited law enforcement resources. The U.S. Department of Justice's view has since changed, at least with regard to infringement of computer software—an activity software publishers claim costs them billions of dollars every year. The Justice Department and FBI have been actively going after software pirates.

In the best-known case of its kind, the U.S. Attorney attempted to prosecute an MIT student who set up a computer bulletin board to dispense copyrighted software for free. The case was ultimately dismissed because the infringer didn't earn any money from his actions. (*United States v. LaMacchia*, 871 F. Supp. 535 (D. Mass. 1994).)

In response to this defeat, Congress amended the copyright law to permit criminal prosecutions of those who commit copyright infringement, even if they don't do so for financial gain. Although the law, called the No Electronic Theft Act (17 U.S.C. § 506; 18 U.S.C. § 2319), was specifically intended to deal with software piracy on the Internet, it is so broadly written it could apply to other types of infringement as well.

Two different types of copyright infringement can now result in criminal liability. Let's examine both in turn.

Willful Infringement Not for Financial Gain

First, it is a federal crime to willfully reproduce or distribute by electronic or any other means one or more copyrighted works with a total retail value of $1,000 or more within any 180-day period. This act constitutes a crime even if the infringer earns no money or other financial gain from the infringement.

There is a sliding scale of penalties that can be imposed against people convicted of violating this law:

- If the copyrighted works involved have a total retail value of more than $1,000 but less than $2,500, a violator can be imprisoned for up to one year or fined up to $100,000 or both.
- If the offense consists of the reproduction or distribution of ten or more copies of one or more copyrighted works with a total retail value of $2,500 or more, the violator can be imprisoned for up to three years and fined up to $250,000. Prison time can be increased to six years in the case of a second offense.

This provision was specifically designed to apply to people who use the Internet or electronic bulletin boards to copy and distribute pirated software, but who don't charge users for the copies or otherwise financially benefit from the infringement.

Willful Infringement for Financial Gain

The criminal penalties increase if a person willfully commits copyright infringement for financial gain. "Financial gain" includes receipt, or expectation of receipt, of anything of value, including the receipt of other copyrighted works.

If fewer than ten unauthorized copies are made or the copied works have a retail value of less than $2,500, violators can be imprisoned up to one year or fined up to $100,000 or both.

If the offense consists of reproducing or distributing during any 180-day period, at least ten copies of one or more copyrighted works, with a retail value of more than $2,500, violators can be jailed for up to five years or fined up to $250,000 or both. Prison time can be increased to ten years in the case of a second or subsequent offense.

Who Is Liable for Infringement?

Although a primary goal might be simply to stop a publisher from selling any more copies of an infringing work, you are also entitled to collect damages from those liable for the infringement. As discussed in Chapter 3, "Copyright Registration," if you timely registered your work, you may elect to receive special statutory damages and attorneys' fees, which is an important right when your actual damages are very small or difficult to prove.

Who may be liable for such damages and fees? Quite simply, *everybody* who participates in or contributes to copyright infringement. This might include not only the author of the infringing work but also its initial publisher and other publishers who reprint it, the publisher's printer, and even the bookstores that sell the work. Such persons or entities are liable regardless of whether they actually know that the work they published, printed, or sell infringes on another person's copyright. Moreover, corporate officers and employees—such as editors employed by publishing companies—actively involved in the infringement may be held *personally liable* along with their employers. Any person who is sued for copyright infringement is called the defendant.

How Much Time You Have to Sue: Statute of Limitations

There are strict time limits—called statutes of limitations—on when copyright infringement suits may be filed. If you fail to file in time, the infringer may be able to have your suit dismissed, even though you have a strong case. In cases where you have not discovered the infringement fairly promptly after it has occurred, statute of limitations questions can be tricky. It's wise to see a knowledgeable copyright lawyer about the proper application of the limitations period to your particular case.

Multiple Infringements or Just One Within Three Years?

A factor complicating the three-year period has to do with situations in which repeated acts of infringement occur over a long period of time—for example, where a book containing infringing material is sold over a period of years. Is each sale of the book a separate infringing act? Or do all the sales together constitute one infringing act? Courts disagree with each other on this question.

EXAMPLE: Acme Press begins to sell a book containing infringing material in January 2013. Carl, the copyright owner, finds out about the infringement that same year but doesn't do anything about it. However, Acme continues to sell the book through January 2021, when Carl finally decides to file suit. Most courts would permit Carl to obtain damages only for the losses he incurred due to the sales that occurred within three years before he filed suit. However, some courts would permit him to recover damages from January 2013, because they view all the sales of the infringing works as part of one "continuing wrong." (See *Taylor v. Meirick*, 712 F.2d 1112 (7th Cir. 1983); *Gaste v. Kaiserman*, 669 F. Supp. 583 (S.D.N.Y. 1987).)

The general rule is that an infringement suit must be filed within three years after the date the copyright owner should reasonably have discovered the infringing act occurred. In some cases, it can reasonably take a copyright owner a long time to discover that the infringement took place, especially where the infringer attempted to conceal the act of infringement. Moreover, the three-year period starts to run anew every time there is a fresh infringement upon a work. For this reason, if more than three years have passed since the infringing work was first published, don't jump to the conclusion that your suit is barred by the statute of limitations.

EXAMPLE: In 2016, several professors at Esoterica College have Pinko's Copyshop photocopy portions of Bill's biography for inclusion in class materials for courses on Middle Eastern history. Bill doesn't discover this until 2021. If a court views the five-year delay as reasonable, Bill will be able to bring an infringement suit against Pinko's.

What You Can Get If You Win: Remedies for Copyright Infringement

Once you've proven the elements of infringement, the next step is to establish what remedies you're entitled to. The potential remedies include:

- **Injunctive relief.** This typically consists of a court order requiring the infringer to stop publishing the infringing work and destroy all remaining copies.

- **Actual damages and infringer's profits.** The plaintiff is entitled to be compensated for the value of lost sales (often difficult to prove) and for other losses resulting directly from the infringement. The plaintiff is also entitled to collect the amount of the defendant's profits from the infringement over and above the amount the plaintiff is awarded for his or her lost profits.
- **Statutory damages.** If the plaintiff's work was timely registered and he or she so chooses, the plaintiff is entitled to receive special statutory damages provided in the copyright law (statute) instead of actual damages and other economic damages.
- **Attorneys' fees.** A copyright owner can also get attorneys' fees. Again, timely registration is required.

We'll examine each remedy in turn. Again, this isn't a complete description of the legal procedures involved but is designed to give you an overview of the available remedies.

Injunctive Relief

An injunction is a court order telling someone to stop doing something. In a copyright infringement action, the order usually is simply for the defendant to stop the infringing activity. An injunction is commonly a quick, effective remedy because, in many cases, it is possible to get positive action from the court long before the actual trial is held to decide who wins.

Indeed, it is possible for a plaintiff to ask the court for a temporary restraining order (TRO)—a type of injunction— almost immediately without notifying the defendant or holding a formal court hearing. A TRO may last ten days at most. A hearing with all parties must then be held on whether the judge should issue a preliminary injunction. A preliminary injunction operates between the time it is issued and the final judgment in the case (basically, the duration of the court case). This interim court order is available when it appears likely to a federal judge, on the basis of written documentation and a relatively brief hearing at which the lawyers for each side present their view of the dispute, that the plaintiff:

- will most likely win the suit when the trial is held, and
- will suffer irreparable injury if the preliminary injunction isn't granted.

Ordinarily, irreparable injury is presumed to exist where someone infringes upon a copyright owner's exclusive rights. (*Apple Comput., Inc. v. Franklin Comput. Corp.*, 714 F.2d 1240 (3d Cir. 1983).)

If the judge grants the preliminary injunction, the plaintiff must post a bond in an amount determined by the judge. If the injunction is later found to have been wrongfully granted, the defendant can collect from the bond the damages and costs he or she incurred due to the injunction.

Once a preliminary injunction is granted, it remains in effect pending a further determination of whether infringement occurred at the formal trial. In theory, a trial will probably be held one or two years later. But, in fact, the parties often fashion a settlement based on the results of the preliminary injunction hearing.

> **EXAMPLE:** Nolo sued another publisher for publishing and distributing a book infringing on Nolo's title, *Dog Law,* by Mary Randolph. Nolo and Randolph were able to obtain a preliminary injunction from a federal judge barring the publisher from distributing any more copies of its book. A settlement was reached soon thereafter. The whole process took just three months from the date suit was filed.

If a settlement is not reached and a full-scale trial occurs, the same issues as those raised in the preliminary injunction hearing will be litigated in more detail. If the plaintiff again prevails, the preliminary injunction will be converted into a permanent one, either including the same terms and orders or different ones, depending on what the plaintiff proves at trial. If the plaintiff loses, the preliminary injunction (if one was granted) will be dissolved and the defendant can go back to doing what it was doing before, plus be compensated for the consequences of the lawsuit out of the bond.

Damages

If you win a copyright infringement suit, you usually have the right to collect money (called damages) from the infringer. As mentioned, if your work was timely registered with the Copyright Office, you will be entitled to choose between collecting actual damages and special statutory damages.

Actual Damages and Infringer's Profits

Actual damages are the lost profits or other losses sustained as a result of the copyright infringement. In other words, actual damages are the amount of money that the plaintiff would have made but for the infringement. This may include compensation for injury to the plaintiff's reputation due to the infringement and for lost business opportunities (often difficult to prove)—for example, a lost opportunity to sign a publishing contract to write a sequel to a novel because an infringing novel hurt its sales. To obtain actual damages, the plaintiff must prove in court that the alleged losses actually occurred. Business records and witnesses (often including the plaintiff him- or herself) must be presented to substantiate the plaintiff's actual losses.

As stated above, the plaintiff is also entitled to recover the amount of the defendant's profits from the infringement to the extent they exceed the plaintiff's recovery for lost profits.

EXAMPLE: The plaintiff is awarded $10,000 for lost sales due to the defendant's infringement. The defendant earned $15,000 in profits from the infringement. The plaintiff is entitled to $5,000 of the defendant's profits.

To establish the defendant's profits, the plaintiff is required only to prove the infringer's gross revenue from the infringing work. The defendant's business records would usually be presented for this purpose. The defendant must then prove what its actual net profit from the infringement was—that is, the defendant must produce records or witnesses to show the amount of expenses deductible from the infringing work's gross revenues (such as printing and distribution costs) and the amount of profit, if any, attributable to the noninfringing material in the defendant's work (often difficult to prove).

Statutory Damages

Statutory damages are set by the copyright law and require no proof of how much the loss was in monetary terms. However, as discussed in Chapter 3, "Copyright Registration," statutory damages are available only if the work was timely registered—that is, before the infringement began or within three months of publication. Statutory damages are awarded at the discretion of the judge or jury and don't depend on having to prove a loss in any specific amount due to the infringement. Statutory damages fall within the following range:

- Absent a finding that the infringer acted either willfully or innocently, between $750 and $30,000 for all the infringements by a single infringer of a single work, no matter how many infringing acts there were. If multiple separate and independent works were infringed, statutory damages may be awarded for each work.
- If the court finds that the infringer acted *willfully*—that is, knew he or she had no legal right to the material, but took it anyway—the judge may increase the amount of statutory damages up to $150,000. An infringer is presumed to have acted willfully if he or she provided false contact information to a domain name registry to register, renew, or maintain a domain name used in connection with the infringement.
- But if the court finds that the infringer acted *innocently*—that is, used the copyrighted material sincerely believing he or she had the right to do so—the judge has discretion to award as little as $200. However, if the work to which the infringer had access contained a valid copyright notice, the infringer may not claim to have acted innocently. As discussed in Chapter 2, "Copyright Notice," this is why it is always a good idea to include a valid copyright notice on your work (even though a notice is not legally required for works published after March 1, 1989).

Because the actual damages (the owner's lost profits and other provable losses) caused by an infringement are often small, statutory damages can far exceed actual damages where the infringer acted willfully. In some cases, courts have awarded millions of dollars in statutory damages. For example, *Playboy Magazine* was awarded $3,737,500 in statutory damages where an infringer copied 7,475 *Playboy* photographs onto its website. *Playboy* got $500 for each copied photo. (*Playboy Enter's, Inc. v. Sanfilippo*, No. 97–0670–IEG (LSP), 1998 WL 207856 (S.D. Cal. Mar. 25, 1998).

A plaintiff who is eligible for both actual and statutory damages may choose which kind to receive at any time, up to and during the trial. Your decision will depend on the facts of your particular case and should, of course, be made in conjunction with your attorney.

Destroying the Infringing Works

Another civil remedy for copyright infringement consists of an impound and destroy order from the court. This order tells the sheriff or marshal to go to the infringer's place of business (or wherever the infringing material is located) and impound (take into custody) any infringing works. Impoundment can happen at any time after the suit has been filed. If the plaintiff wins, the court may order the sheriff to destroy the infringing material.

Attorneys' Fees and Costs

If your suit is successful and you timely registered your copyright, the court may also order the defendant to pay your attorneys' fees and some costs of going to court. However an award of fees and costs is not required. It's up to the judge to decide whether to make such an award and how much it should be (the amount must be reasonable). The criteria some courts use to decide whether to award attorneys' fees include whether the defendant acted in bad faith or unreasonably or was otherwise blameworthy. Many courts will be especially likely to award fees to a plaintiff whose actions helped to advance the copyright law or defend or establish important legal principles.

The cost of bringing an infringement suit can be very high—easily tens of thousands of dollars. If for no other reason than to have the opportunity of recovering your attorneys' fees should you have to bring an infringement suit, you should always timely register your work with the Copyright Office.

> **TIP**
>
> **The cost of bringing an infringement suit can be very high, easily tens of thousands of dollars.** If for no other reason than to have the opportunity of recovering your attorneys' fees should you have to bring an infringement suit, you should always timely register your work with the Copyright Office.

If the plaintiff loses the suit, the court has discretion to award the defendant all or part of his or her attorney's fees. In determining whether to award attorney's fees to defendants, the courts must use the same criteria as for awards to plaintiffs. (*Fogerty v. Fantasy, Inc.*, 114 S. Ct. 1023 (1994).)

What to Do If You're Accused of Infringement

What should you do if you're accused of copyright infringement? First, see how serious the claim is. If it's minor—for example, an author validly claims that you have quoted a bit too much of his or her work, used an illustration, or reprinted an article without permission—the matter can usually be settled very quickly for a few hundred dollars, certainly less than $1,000. This kind of thing happens all the time in publishing. There is no need to see a lawyer (who'll probably charge you at least $250–$500 per hour) to deal with this type of minor annoyance. Have the author sign a letter releasing you from liability in return for your payment.

On the other hand, if you receive a letter or email from an author or author's attorney alleging a substantial claim—for example, that a book you're publishing to great success is an unauthorized derivative work and its sale should be halted immediately—it's probably time to find a copyright lawyer. If, even worse, you are served with a complaint (a document initiating a lawsuit), you must

act quickly, because you might have as little as 20 days to file an answer (response) in the appropriate court. If you don't respond in time, a judgment can be entered against you. Finding a lawyer is discussed in Chapter 14, "Help Beyond This Book."

However, even if the case is serious, don't despair. The fact is, many infringement suits are won by the defendant, because either the plaintiff did not have a valid claim to begin with or the defendant had a good defense. This section is not a substitute for a consultation with an experienced attorney; rather, it is designed to give you an idea of some of the things you need to discuss when you see an attorney.

Defenses to Copyright Infringement

Even if there are substantial similarities between the plaintiff's work and your work, you will not necessarily be found guilty of infringement. The similarities might simply be the result of coincidence; in which event, there is no liability. But even direct copying from the plaintiff's work might be excused if it constitutes a fair use or there is another valid defense.

Possible defenses to an infringement action include many general legal defenses that often involve where, when, and how the lawsuit was brought, who was sued, and so on. We obviously can't cover all of this here. This section is limited to outlining the major defenses that are specific to copyright infringement actions. Again, if you find yourself defending a serious copyright infringement action, retain a qualified attorney!

Fair Use

Authors are allowed to copy other authors' protected expression if the copying constitutes a fair use of the material. Fair use is a complete defense to infringement. See Chapter 9, "Using Other Authors' Words."

The Independent Creation Defense

As discussed in Chapter 4, "What Copyright Protects," copyright protection does not prevent others from independently developing works based on the same idea or explicating the same facts. If you can convince the judge or jury that you created your work independently, not by copying from the plaintiff, you will not be held liable for infringement. In effect, you would try to prove that any similarities between your work and the plaintiff's are purely coincidental. Such coincidences are not at all uncommon.

The one sure way to show independent creation is for you to prove that your work was created before the plaintiff's. If your work was registered before the plaintiff's, this will be easy to prove.

EXAMPLE: Marilyn claims that Jack turned her novel into a screenplay without her permission and sues him for infringement. Jack had deposited a copy of the allegedly infringing screenplay with the Copyright Office one year before Marilyn published her novel. Jack can prove independent

creation simply by submitting a certified copy of his deposit into evidence.

In the case of unregistered works, you would have to present other evidence showing when the work was created, such as witnesses who saw you write it or dated notes and drafts.

What if the plaintiff's and your works were created at about the same time or you can't prove when you created your work? In this event, it is very difficult, if not impossible, to prove independent creation. This is because the alleged copying need not be done consciously for the plaintiff to win. Unconscious copying also constitutes infringement (although the damages imposed may be smaller than for conscious, willful copying). Your quandary, then, is how to prove you didn't unconsciously copy from the plaintiff's work. About the best you can do in this situation is show that you created similar works in the past without copying and you had no need to copy from the plaintiff's work. The judge or jury just might believe you.

 CAUTION
Never assert independent creation or any other defense if it's not true. If your defense is based on lies, you'll most likely lose anyway and possibly anger the judge or jury. As a result, you could end up being far more severely punished than you otherwise might have been and possibly prosecuted for perjury, a felony.

Statute of Limitations

A plaintiff can't wait forever to file an infringement suit. A copyright infringement lawsuit must be filed within three years after the date that the infringement reasonably should have been discovered by the plaintiff. The three-year period starts to run anew every time there is a fresh infringement upon a work; but each infringement is actionable only within three years of its occurrence. These rules are tricky, but if the plaintiff waited too long to file suit, the defendant might be able to have the case dismissed. However, it's possible for an infringement lawsuit to be brought long after an allegedly infringing work was first created. For example, the Supreme Court permitted a screenwriter who claimed that the movie *Raging Bull* infringed on a screenplay he wrote in 1963 to wait 18 years after the film was released before filing a copyright infringement lawsuit because the film continued to be distributed. (*Petrella v. Metro-Goldwyn-Mayer, Inc.*, 572 U.S. 663 (2014).)

Material Copied Was in the Public Domain

If the material you allegedly copied is in the public domain, it can be used by anyone for any purpose. As discussed in detail in Chapter 4, the public domain includes:

- the ideas and facts contained in protected works
- the ideas, facts, and expression contained in works that don't qualify for copyright protection because they do not constitute original, fixed, minimally creative works of authorship
- works that might otherwise qualify for protection but are denied it, such as works by government employees, certain blank forms, titles, and short phrases, and
- works for which copyright protection has expired.

Remember, however, that so long as the plaintiff's work was registered within five years after creation, it is presumed to be protected by copyright. This presumption for the plaintiff means that you will bear the burden of proving the work was really not protected.

The Use Was Authorized

In some cases, the alleged infringer isn't an infringer, but a legal transferee. For example:

- The infringer might legitimately claim to have received a license to use the plaintiff's work, and the work the plaintiff claims to infringe on his copyright falls within that license. Example: Author A orally tells Author B he can copy his work, then later claims never to have granted the permission.
- Conflicting or confusing licenses or sublicenses are granted and the defendant claims to be the rightful owner of the right(s) in question.
- A transferee wasn't restricted in making further transfers and transferred the copyright to individuals unknown to the original owner.

Several examples of lawful transfers are presented in Chapter 7, "Transferring Copyright Ownership." If any of these transferees were sued, they would have a good defense—that is, their use was lawful.

Other Defenses

Some of the other possible defenses to copyright infringement include such things as:

- the notion that if the plaintiff is guilty of some serious wrongdoing him- or herself—for example, falsifying evidence—the plaintiff cannot complain about your alleged wrongs, or
- the idea that the copyright owner knew of your acts and expressly or impliedly consented to them.

Public Domain Status of Foreign Work

Certain foreign works that you may have thought were in the public domain because of failure to comply with U.S. copyright formalities, such as using a copyright notice or filing a copyright renewal, are no longer in the public domain. Copyright in many of these works was automatically restored on January 1, 1996 as a result of United States' adherence to the GATT Agreement. However, you may have special rights if you used such foreign material before 1996. (See Chapter 11, "International Copyright Protection.")

Deciding Whether to Settle or Fight

If a substantial claim is involved, the decision whether to settle the case or fight it out in court should be made only after consulting an attorney who is familiar with the facts of your particular case. However, in making this decision you need to carefully weigh the following factors:

- the likelihood the plaintiff will prevail
- how much the plaintiff is likely to collect after a win
- the costs of contesting the case, not only in terms of money, but time, embarrassment, and adverse publicity, and
- how much the plaintiff is willing to settle for.

If the plaintiff clearly does not have a valid claim, you might be able to have the suit dismissed very quickly by filing what's called a summary judgment motion. Under this procedure, the judge examines the plaintiff's claims and decides whether there is any possibility the plaintiff could prevail if a trial were held. If not, the judge will dismiss the case. Of course, you must pay a lawyer to file a summary judgment motion, but if successful, it will cost far less than taking the case to trial. Moreover, the court might be willing to award you all or part of your attorneys' fees, which is especially likely if the plaintiff's suit was clearly frivolous.

On the other hand, if the plaintiff does have a valid claim, paying an attorney to fight a losing battle will only compound your problems. Valid claims should be settled whenever possible. A plaintiff who was able to obtain a preliminary injunction from a federal judge probably has a valid claim.

How to Protect Yourself From Copyright Infringement Claims

The only way you can absolutely prevent others from accusing you of copyright infringement is never to write and publish anything. However, there are some less drastic steps you can take to help protect yourself from infringement claims:

- First and foremost, always get permission to use other authors' protected expression, unless your intended use clearly constitutes a fair use. (See Chapter 9, "Using Other Authors' Words.") If you're not sure whether or not you need permission, consult a copyright attorney.
- Date and keep your notes and drafts; these might help you to prove that your work was created independently from the plaintiff's.
- Promptly register your finished work with the Copyright Office; registration conclusively establishes the date of creation of the material you deposited with your application. If you're extremely worried about being sued for infringement, it may even be worthwhile to register your unfinished drafts.

- If you're an editor for a magazine or publishing company, always promptly return manuscripts you reject. Nothing arouses a writer's suspicions more than having a publisher keep a rejected manuscript and then later publish a similar work by another writer. If you already have another writer working on the same or similar idea, let the author of the rejected material know about it.
- Film and television producers and others in the entertainment industry who receive unsolicited submissions should either: (1) have an established policy of returning unsolicited manuscripts unopened, or (2) refuse to read them unless the author signs a release absolving the reader from liability for infringement.

Copyright Infringement Online

Copyright infringement occurs every second in the online world, particularly on the Internet, which isn't controlled or supervised by anybody. Many online users have the mistaken idea that any work available online can be freely copied, distributed, and otherwise used without permission.

The problem of unauthorized copying of copyrighted works is not new. Ever since the perfection of the photocopy machine, books, articles, and other printed works have been copied and distributed without permission from, or payment to, the copyright owners. The introduction of the fax machine made it even easier to deliver photocopies over long distances.

However, there are important limitations on distribution of unauthorized photocopies: Copy quality degrades with each generation; photocopying large amounts of work can be time-consuming, expensive, and inconvenient; and a copied document is still in the same format as the original and can be easily identified as a copyrighted work.

None of these limitations exist for digital copies. Perfect digital copies can be made easily, cheaply, and quickly, over and over again. Digital copies do not degrade. It is easy to disguise the origins of a digital copy by making simple format changes that require only a few keystrokes. And digital copies are easy to distribute: A copy can be posted on the Internet and easily copied by any number of users anywhere in the country or across the world.

Indeed, unauthorized copying is so ubiquitous on the Internet that some have declared that copyright is dead. However, to paraphrase Mark Twain, the reports of copyright's death are greatly exaggerated. The fact is that the copyright laws have never prevented private individuals from making unauthorized copies. What copyright has done and will continue to do, even in the online era, is deter the big players from stealing others' work.

For example, because they're afraid of being sued for infringement, publishers are seeking permission from their authors to reproduce the authors' preexisting works online and are also making sure that publishing agreements for new works address electronic rights. For the same reason, copyrighted photos and other materials have been removed from the Internet when copyright owners complained. And an entire website on Elvis Presley was removed when the Presley estate complained that the site violated the estate's copyright and other intellectual property rights.

Who's Liable for an Infringement?

As discussed above, anyone who directly exercises any of a copyright owner's exclusive rights without permission is guilty of copyright infringement unless there is a legal excuse, such as fair use. You'll be liable, for example, if you download a protected work from the Internet and publish it in a book or on website, a CD-ROM, or online storage medium without permission.

EXAMPLE: A software publisher called Wizardware downloaded from the Internet several sample "cities" created and uploaded by players of the computer game *Sim City*. Wizardware published the cities on a CD-ROM. Maxis Corporation, owner of *Sim City*, sued Wizardware for copyright infringement, claiming that Maxis owned the artwork the players used to create the cities, along with the computer code that was included in the CD-ROM. The judge ordered Wizardware to stop manufacturing and selling the CD-ROM and impounded all existing copies, until a trial could be held. (*Maxis Inc. v. Wizardware Group, Inc.*, No. 3:95-CV-04045 (N.D. Cal. 1996).)

If you're liable for infringement, a court can order you to stop the infringing activity, destroy any copies you've made, and pay the copyright owner damages—whether or not you knew the work you infringed upon was protected. The fact you didn't know a work was protected might affect the damages you'll be required to pay but will not relieve you of liability for infringement.

However, you don't have to infringe on someone's work yourself to be liable. A person who induces, causes, or helps someone else commit copyright infringement can be held liable as a contributory infringer. For example, you could be liable for contributory infringement if you permit someone else to use your computer and modem to transmit unauthorized copies of a work.

What about companies that provide access to the Internet (often called Internet service providers or ISPs)? Obviously, an ISP will be liable for infringement where it or its employees actively engage in the infringement—that is, copying, distributing, or displaying a copyright owner's works without permission.

However, a far more important question is whether ISPs are liable when they don't actively participate in the infringement, and instead, one of their subscribers or users commits the infringement. Most courts have held that an ISP is liable for copyright infringements committed by its subscribers only if either of the following is true:

- The ISP knew about, or should have known about, the infringing activity and induced, caused, or contributed to the infringing actions.
- The ISP had the right and ability to control the infringer's acts and received a direct financial benefit from the infringement.

EXAMPLE: Dennis Erlich, a former member of the Church of Scientology, uploaded copyrighted Scientology material onto the Internet using the ISP Netcom to obtain Internet access. The church sued both Erlich and Netcom for copyright infringement. The court held that Netcom was not liable for direct copyright infringement because it did not directly participate in copying and posting the church materials on the Internet. All Netcom did was operate as an ISP. Moreover, Netcom did not receive a direct financial benefit from the alleged infringement because it only charged Erlich a flat fee for Internet access. This meant that Netcom could be held liable for Erlich's acts only if it knew about them and induced, caused, or materially contributed to Erlich's allegedly infringing conduct. (*Religious Tech. Ctr. v. Netcom On-Line Commc'n Serv. Inc.*, 907 F. Supp. 1362 (N.D. Cal. 1995).)

Under normal copyright infringement rules, an ISP or other entity that provides access to the Internet will likely not be held liable for subscribers' or users' infringing conduct where the ISP only passively transmitted or stored the allegedly infringing material at the user's direction, provided that the ISP didn't know or have reason to know about the infringement or receive a direct financial benefit from it. However, an ISP could become liable where it directly participates in the infringement, directly benefits from it financially, or looks the other way when it should have reasonably suspected that a subscriber or user was committing infringement. These are the *normal* copyright rules. In 1998, Congress enacted a law giving ISPs special relief from liability from copyright infringements committed by their subscribers or users and for certain other common Internet activities. (See the detailed discussion in the following two sections.)

Internet service providers should delete any infringing material they become aware of or terminate the accounts of users who commit infringement. User agreements should also prohibit users from engaging in illegal activities, including copyright infringement, and provide that the user will indemnify (repay) the operator for claims resulting from such conduct.

Internet Service Providers' Safe Harbor for Copyright Infringement Liability

It has been difficult or impossible for copyright owners to enforce their rights against individual online infringers because (1) individual infringers can be hard to find, and (2) they often have no money to pay any damages. As a result, copyright owners

have frequently sued ISPs instead—that is, the companies that provided access to the Internet and stored and transmitted the allegedly infringing material.

The threat of such lawsuits greatly concerned ISPs and led them to lobby hard for Congress to enact a special law exempting them from liability for online copyright infringements by their subscribers or users under certain circumstances. This law, known as the Digital Millennium Copyright Act (DMCA), took effect in 1998 (17 U.S.C. §§ 1201-1205, 1301-1332). Among its many provisions are "safe harbors" exempting ISPs from liability for monetary damages resulting from copyright infringements by their users. The safe harbors also exempt ISPs from liability for common Internet practices, such as caching, that could raise infringement issues.

The basic intent of the DMCA safe harbors is to codify into law the holding of the *Religious Technology Center* case discussed in the previous section—that an ISP cannot be held liable for copyright infringement where it acts as a passive automatic conduit for Internet users but does not know about or actively participate in the alleged infringement.

However, to qualify for the safe harbor exemptions, a number of complex requirements must be complied with. (See "What ISPs Must Do," below.)

These safe harbor rules are lengthy and complex, but they are important—not just to ISPs but copyright owners as well. If you believe someone has committed copyright infringement by placing your copyrighted material online without your consent, the rules might bar you from suing the ISP the infringer used to access the Internet. This may make it effectively impossible for you to obtain damages, because the actual infringer may have no money or assets. On the other hand, the rules give you a very powerful tool to have the ISP remove the infringing material without your having to go to court.

What ISPs Must Do

The safe harbor rules are complex and lengthy. Fortunately, it isn't necessary to understand them all in detail to qualify. Here's all an ISP must do to qualify for the safe harbor exemptions:

- Designate an agent to whom copyright owners may send notices of claimed infringement; this involves filling out a simple form and sending it to the Copyright Office and posting the information on its website.
- Adopt a policy that repeat copyright infringers will have their accounts terminated and let subscribers know about it.
- Designate someone to deal with notices of claimed infringement from copyright owners; prompt action will be required.

If you're a person who uses the Internet to post or email copyrighted material, the safe harbor rules could impact you greatly as well. Your ISP might remove material you've posted because someone claims it's infringing. Such removal can occur without any court hearing or other legal process, and you might have no legal remedy against the ISP.

What to Do If Someone Infringes Your Work Online

If you discover that someone has copied your work and placed it online, you have some powerful self-help weapons at your disposal to get the infringing work removed. You should take a three-step approach:

- Make sure a copyright infringement has actually occurred.
- Send a cease and desist email to the infringer demanding that the work be removed.
- If the work isn't removed, send DMCA notices to the infringer's Internet hosting company, search engines, and others.

Step 1: Make Sure Infringement Has Occurred

First things first: You need to be certain that copyright infringement has actually occurred. (See the first sections of this chapter for a detailed discussion of what constitutes copyright infringement.) Keep in mind that not all copying is copyright infringement—some types of copying qualify as a fair use (see Chapter 9) and some things are not protected by copyright at all, such as facts and ideas (see Chapter 4). Both the person you accuse of infringement and the ISP can sue you for damages if you knowingly misrepresent—that is, lie—that copyright infringement has taken place.

Discovering Online Infringers

You can use search engines like Google to attempt to discover whether someone is copying your work online. There are also various services that employ sophisticated software to do this for you automatically. These include:

- Copyscape (www.copyscape.com)
- Stop Web Pirates (www.stopweb pirates.com), and
- Maverickeye (www.maverickeye.de).

In one case involving online content, a company was required to pay more than $125,000 in damages after attempting to use the DMCA takedown procedure to remove content (internal emails about faulty voting machines) whose unauthorized online distribution the court found to be protected by fair use. Accordingly, if you are not sure whether material available online infringes your copyright, you should contact an attorney. (*Online Policy Group v. Diebold, Inc.*, 337 F. Supp. 2d 1198 (N.D. Cal. 2004).)

Step 2: Send Cease and Desist Email

If you are sure your work has been infringed, send a cease and desist email to the copier demanding that they remove your work and stop infringing on your copyrights. You'll often be able to find contact information for the infringer at the website where your work appears. If not, check out the website's WHOIS information at https://whois.icann.org.

This email is very similar to the cease and desist letter discussed earlier in this chapter. Give the infringer 24 to 48 hours to remove your content or otherwise respond.

EXAMPLE: Jill actively maintains a blog called "Wage Slave No More" (nowageslave. com) that provides advice to self-employed people. She discovers that a lengthy article from the blog has been reposted verbatim without her permission on a website called NerdAdvice.com. She sends the following email to the site's email address:

Subject Line: Cease and Desist Notice to NerdAdvice.com

To whom it may concern:

I am the copyright owner of the article entitled "How the Self-Employed Can Save Money on Taxes," published on my blog at www.nowageslave.com/1043828. All content on nowageslave.com, including the article "How the Self-Employed Can Save Money on Taxes," is copyrighted under U.S. law, and unauthorized duplication is illegal.

Your website NerdAdvice.com has illegally copied the entire text of my article. The infringing work appears at the following location on your website: www.nerdadvice.com/103984.html. A screenshot taken from this URL is attached to this email as Exhibit 1.

I demand that you immediately remove the article from your website and cease and desist all further unauthorized copying of my copyrighted content. If you do not remove my content within 48 hours of receipt of this email, I will file takedown notices against you under Section 512 of the Digital Millennium Copyright Act (DMCA) with your hosting provider, search engines, and others. I will also pursue all appropriate legal remedies against you for copyright infringement. Under 17 U.S.C. Section 504, the consequences of copyright infringement include statutory damages between $750 and $30,000 per work, at the discretion of the court, and damages of up to $150,000 per work for willful infringement.

For nowageslave.com,

Jill Johnson

Step 3: Send DMCA Takedown Notices

If the infringer does not respond adequately to your cease and desist email or can't be found, you should send a Notice of Claimed Copyright Infringement (commonly called a DMCA takedown notice) to the infringer's ISP, as well as to Internet search engines, such as Google, and possibly others as well.

Using this notice and takedown procedure is not mandatory. You can always forgo it and go straight to court and file a copyright infringement lawsuit against the infringer or ISP. But it's usually wise to take these initial self-help steps first. Filing a DMCA takedown notice is not difficult and can easily be accomplished by any copyright owner without paying a lawyer. If the notice is successful and the ISP removes the infringing material or disables access to it, there will often be no need to file an expensive court action. If the infringing material is removed by the ISP, you will still have the right to sue the infringer for damages, but in this event, the ISP will not be liable for damages.

Takedown Notice to ISP

ISPs are companies and institutions that provide people with Internet access and host websites and other materials on the Internet. The ISP is usually not the infringer, but rather the conduit through which the infringer has accessed the Internet. If it is not clear which ISP the alleged infringer uses, check the domain name registration records for the website where the infringing material is found. You can do this at: www.networksolutions.com/whois/index.jsp or www.whoishostingthis.com.

Most ISPs have designated an agent to receive DMCA takedown notices (doing so is required to qualify for the safe harbor from copyright infringement liability discussed above). The ISP is supposed to post this information at its website. The Copyright Office also maintains a centralized online directory of designated agent contact information for public use at www.copyright.gov/dmca-directory.

Draft and sign a Notice of Claimed Copyright Infringement and send it to the agent. The notice must:

- identify the copyrighted work you claim was infringed (if the infringement involves many different works at a single online site, you can include a representative list rather than listing each one)
- identify the online site where the alleged infringement has occurred and identify specifically what material on the site you claim is infringing (include copies, if possible); if a link is involved, it must be identified
- give the name and contact information for the person signing the notice
- state that the information in the notice is accurate and that the complaining party "has a good-faith belief that use of the material in the manner complained of is not authorized by the copyright owner, its agent, or the law"

- state, under penalty of perjury, that the signer of the notice is authorized to act on behalf of the copyright owner of the material claimed to have been infringed, and
- be signed with either a physical or electronic signature.

Different ISPs have different policies about how you should format your DMCA takedown notice. Be sure to read and follow the requirements of the ISP involved. The notice can be either emailed or sent by postal mail to the ISP.

FORM
You can download a Notice of Claimed Copyright Infringement (and all other forms in this book) from this book's companion page on Nolo.com; see the appendix for the link.

If the notice is in compliance with the rules, the ISP must decide whether to remove or disable access to the allegedly infringing material. The ISP does not have to remove or disable access to such material; but, if it does so, the safe harbor will apply. Moreover, the ISP is immune from all legal liability for removing or disabling access to the material—meaning that neither the subscriber nor user nor anyone else can sue it for doing so. This is so even if it turns out that the material complained of was not infringing.

The law imposes no specific time limit on how quickly the ISP must act. It simply says the ISP must act "expeditiously" (quickly). If the ISP does remove or disable access to the allegedly infringing material, it must "promptly" notify the subscriber or user of the action. The ball then enters the subscriber's court.

Takedown Notice to Google and Other Search Engines

You can request that Google and other search engines remove the infringing page from their search results by filing DMCA takedown notices using the same procedure described above for ISPs. You can send a DMCA takedown notice to Google through the following URL after logging in to your Google Account: www.google.com/webmasters/tools/dmca-notice.

Other Takedown Notices

You should check the infringer's website to see if it is earning advertising revenue from your content—for example, by selling Google Adwords. You can discover if the infringer is using Adwords or Yahoo/Bing Ads at www.semrush.com, and if so, you can contact those companies at:

- Google Adwords: https://support.google.com/legal/troubleshooter/1114905, and
- Bing/Yahoo Ads: https://about.ads.microsoft.com/en-us/resources/policies/copyright-infringement.

User's Counter-Notification

An ISP's subscriber or user doesn't have to take the removal of the material lying down. If the user believes that the material is not infringing or has been mistakenly identified, it can take action to have the material put back by the ISP, Google, and others to whom you sent a takedown notice. To do this, the user must send the ISP a counter-notification. The counter-notification must:

- identify the allegedly infringing material and give its Internet address
- state, under penalty of perjury, that the material was removed or disabled by the ISP as a result of mistake or misidentification of the material
- state that the user consents to the legal jurisdiction of the federal district court in the judicial district where the user's address is located; or, if the user lives outside the United States, consents to jurisdiction in any federal district court where the ISP may be sued
- state that the user agrees to accept service of legal process from the copyright owner or other person who signed the Notice of Claimed Copyright Infringement
- give the user's name and contact information for the person signing the notice, and
- be signed with either a physical or electronic signature.

The counter-notification can be either emailed or sent by postal mail to the ISP's designated agent.

 FORM
You can download a counter-notification (and all other forms in this book) from this book's companion page on Nolo.com; see the appendix for the link.

Upon receipt of a counter-notification satisfying the above requirements, the ISP must "promptly" send the copyright owner or other person who sent the Notice of Claimed Copyright Infringement a copy of the counter-notification and inform such person that the ISP will replace the removed material or stop disabling access to it in ten business days (not counting weekends or holidays).

The ISP must replace the removed material or stop disabling access to it not less than ten or more than 14 business days after it received the user's counter-notification, unless the copyright owner brings a court action as described below.

By sending a counter-notification, the user in effect forces the copyright owner to put up or shut up. The copyright owner will have to go to court and convince a judge that it's likely that a copyright infringement has occurred. If the copyright owner doesn't want to go to court, the ISP will have to replace the removed material or stop disabling access to it.

Copyright Owner's Response to Counter-Notification

If the subscriber sends the ISP a counter-notification, you can forget about getting the infringing material removed or disabled without having to go to court. Instead, you will have to file a copyright infringement lawsuit against the subscriber in federal court and ask the court to grant you an injunction ordering the subscriber to stop the infringing activity on the ISP's system. To obtain such an injunction, you'll have to convince the court that it is likely that the subscriber has committed copyright infringement.

If you don't want the ISP to put the material back or stop disabling access to it, you'll have to act quickly. Access to the material will have to be restored by the ISP no more than 14 business days after the subscriber sent it the counter-notification. It is possible, however, to obtain an injunction very quickly. (See above for a detailed discussion of injunctions in copyright infringement cases.)

To file your lawsuit, you'll have to know the subscriber's or user's identity. The DMCA contains a procedure allowing you to subpoena the ISP and require it to give you this information.

Use of Licenses to Prevent Infringement

A license gives someone permission to do something. For example, when your state issues you a driver's license, it gives you permission to drive a car. Copyright owners can give others permission to use their works by granting licenses. (See Chapter 9.)

Licenses are often used in the online world. For example, the owners of commercial computer databases like LexisNexis limit access to users who sign license agreements and agree to pay access fees. Such agreements often attempt to regulate the way users deal with online materials. For example, they may forbid users from transferring digital copies of such material to others.

A user doesn't necessarily have to physically sign a license for it to be enforceable. Online licensing agreements are likely enforceable where access to an online service, website, or electronic database is made available only after users are given the opportunity to read the agreement. Such licenses are likely not enforceable, however, where the user is not allowed to read it before being given access to protected material.

Some copyright experts assert that license restrictions that go beyond what the copyright laws allow might be unenforceable, because the federal copyright laws preempt (take precedence over) state contract laws. Under this view, for example, a license restriction that attempted to do away with a user's fair use rights would be unenforceable.

However, the seminal court case on this issue takes the opposite view, holding that licenses can restrict the use even of information in the public domain. Matthew Zeidenberg bought a CD-ROM containing business telephone listings from ProCD.

He downloaded the listings to his computer from the CD-ROM and made them available on the Internet, attaching a search program he created himself. Zeidenberg did not commit copyright infringement, because phone listings are in the public domain. (See Chapter 5, "Adaptations and Compilations.") However, he did violate the terms of a shrink-wrap license agreement that came with the CD-ROM. Such license agreements, which were commonly included inside software and CD-ROM packages, typically bar purchasers from copying, adapting, or modifying the work. The court held that the shrink-wrap license was an enforceable contract. Since Zeidenberg violated the license, he was liable to ProCD for damages. (*ProCD, Inc. v. Zeidenberg*, 86 F.3d 1447 (7th Cir. 1996).) Most courts have followed this court decision since 1996. Thus, you should assume any license you agree to will be legally enforceable.

Technological Solutions to Infringement

If copyright ceases to be an important way for content providers to protect their works, it will likely be because highly effective technological solutions to infringement will be found. This includes the use of encryption schemes—that is, translating digital works into unreadable gibberish as the military does with secret messages. Users would be able to decrypt and read a work only after paying a fee to the copyright owner.

Copyright owners are fearful that infringers might devise means of circumventing their anti-infringement technological measures —for example, devise means of "cracking" encryption codes. The DMCA includes a complex provision designed to prevent this. Following is the briefest possible overview of this statute.

Illegal Uses

It makes it illegal for anyone to make, import, or sell devices or services whose primary purpose is to circumvent technological measures used to prevent unauthorized access to or copying of a work. Subject to several exceptions, it also makes it illegal for anyone to obtain *access* to a work by circumventing any technological measure (such as encryption) that effectively controls access to the work.

Exemptions in Statute

Exempt from the access prohibition are nonprofit libraries, archives, and educational institutions that wish to gain unauthorized access to works solely to make a good-faith determination of whether to acquire a copy. Exemptions are also given for law enforcement, intelligence, and other government activities; bona fide encryption research; security testing; and cases where the technological measure or work it protects is capable of collecting personal identifying information about online users.

Exemptions by Regulation

In addition, the Copyright Office is allowed to enact a regulation exempting certain classes of works from the statute's anti-circumvention provisions. This regulation expires after three years, at which time the Copyright Office must review it and determine whether to extend it for another three years or adopt a new regulation. The current regulation, exempting several classes of works, was adopted on October 28, 2018 and will expire on October 28, 2021. It permits the following:

- literary works distributed electronically —that is, e-books—for use with assistive technologies for people who are blind, visually impaired, or have other impairments
- computer programs that operate the following types of devices to

allow connection of a used device to an alternative wireless network ("unlocking"): smartphones, tablets, mobile hotspots, and wearable devices (e.g., smart watches)

- computer programs that operate the following types of devices to allow the device to interoperate with or to remove software applications ("jailbreaking"): smartphones, tablets and other all-purpose mobile computing devices, smart TVs, and voice assistant devices
- computer programs (other than video games) for the preservation of computer programs and computer program-dependent materials by libraries, archives, and museums
- computer programs that control motorized land vehicles, including farm equipment, for purposes of diagnosis, repair, and modification of the vehicle
- motion pictures (including television programs and videos):
  - for educational uses by college and university faculty and students
  - for educational uses by K-12 instructors and students
  - for educational uses in massive open online courses (MOOCs)
  - for educational uses in digital and literacy programs offered by libraries, museums, and other nonprofits
  - for nonfiction multimedia e-books
  - for uses in documentary films and other films where the use is in parody or for a biographical or historically significant nature
  - for the provision of captioning and/ or audio description by disability services offices
  - for uses in noncommercial videos.
- computer programs for purposes of good-faith security research
- video games for which outside server support has been discontinued, to allow individual play by gamers and preservation of games by libraries, archives, and museums (as well as necessary jailbreaking of console computer code for preservation uses only)
- computer programs that operate 3D printers to allow use of alternative feedstock, and
- literary works consisting of compilations of data generated by implanted medical devices and personal monitoring systems.

Penalties

Penalties for DMCA violations are the same as for removal of copyright management information. (See above.)

For a detailed understanding of this incredibly complicated statute, you'll need to read the law. A copy of the DMCA is available at: www.govinfo.gov/content/pkg/FR-2018-10-26/pdf/2018-23241.pdf.

International Copyright Protection

There is no single body of international copyright law. Each country has its own copyright law that applies within its own borders. However, through a series of international treaties, almost all nations have agreed to give each other's citizens the same copyright protection they afford to their own citizens. If you take the correct procedural steps, your copyright will be protected in virtually every country in the world.

We'll first examine copyright protection outside the United States for works by American citizens or permanent residents, and then turn to copyright protection within the United States for foreign citizens or nationals.

International Protection for U.S. Citizens and Nationals

The protection afforded to written works by the U.S. copyright laws ends at the United States borders. The extent of the protection given to work by Americans outside the United States is governed by international treaties. The United States and almost all other countries of the world have signed a series of international treaties—the most important of which is the Berne Convention. International copyright protection for works by U.S. citizens and permanent residents largely depends on the rights granted by these international treaties.

The Berne Convention

The world's first major international copyright convention was held in Berne, Switzerland, in 1886. The resulting agreement was called the Berne Convention for the Protection of Literary and Artistic Works or the Berne Convention for short. The Berne Convention is the most important international copyright treaty with the highest standards of protection. Almost all countries belong to the Berne Convention.

In a nutshell, Berne member countries agree that literary, artistic, and scientific works, including all types of writing, are protected in the following ways.

Principle of National Treatment

Every country that has signed the Berne Convention must give citizens or permanent residents of other Berne countries at least the same copyright protection that it affords its own nationals; this is known as national treatment. As a U.S. citizen or permanent resident, any protectable work of yours is entitled to national treatment in every country that has signed the Berne Convention.

EXAMPLE: Carl, an American citizen and resident, publishes a biography of Czar Ivan the Terrible in 2020. One year later, while browsing in a London bookstore he discovers a condensed version of his book published under another author's name by a British publisher. Because the United States and United Kingdom have both signed the Berne Convention, if Carl sues the British publisher and author for copyright infringement in the British courts, he will be entitled to the same treatment as any British subject who brings this suit.

No Formalities

No formalities, such as notice and registration, may be required for basic copyright protection. However, some countries offer greater copyright protection if a copyright is registered or carries a particular type of notice. For example, in Japan and Canada, registration provides a means of making your work a public record and can be helpful in case of an infringement action. Other countries have certain procedural requirements that must be followed before foreign works may be distributed within their borders, such as customs rules, censorship requirements, or other regulations. Compliance with these types of formalities should be taken care of by a foreign agent hired by the author's publisher or the author or author's agent.

Minimal Protections Required

Every Berne country must offer a minimum standard of copyright protection in their own country to works first published or created by nationals of other Berne countries. This protection must include:

- **Copyright duration of at least the author's life plus 50 years.**
- **The granting of moral rights to the author.** Moral rights are rights an author can never transfer to a third party because they are considered an extension of his or her being. Briefly, they consist of the right to claim authorship, to disclaim authorship of copies, to prevent or call back distribution under certain conditions, and to object to any distortion, mutilation, or other modifications of the author's work injurious to his or her reputation. The right to prevent colorization of black-and-white films is an example of a moral right. Moral rights are generally of most concern to visual artists.
- **Some provision allowing for fair dealing or free use of copyrighted works.** This includes material used in quotations for educational purposes, for reporting current events, and so forth. (In the United States, this is called fair use, and it is discussed in detail in Chapter 9, "Using Other Authors' Words.")

Copyright Term for U.S. Works in Berne Countries

Under the Berne Convention, copyright protection must be granted for at least the life of the author plus 50 years. However, member countries can provide longer copyright terms if they wish. For example, most European countries now have a copyright term of life plus 70 years—the same as in the United States for works published after 1978. You can find a useful chart listing the copyright terms of all the nations of the world at https://en.wikipedia.org/wiki/List_of_countries%27_copyright_lengths.

Application of the Berne Convention to Works Created Before March 1, 1989

The United States was a latecomer to the Berne Convention; it did not join until March 1, 1989. The Berne Convention does not apply to a work first published in the United States before that date unless the work was also published in a Berne country at the same time (that is, within 30 days of each other). This is called simultaneous publication. Before 1989, American publishers commonly had their books published simultaneously in the United States and Canada or Great Britain (both Berne countries) so that they could receive the protection of the Berne Convention. This fact was usually indicated on the same page as the work's copyright notice.

GATT

In late 1994, the United States signed the General Agreement on Tariffs and Trade (GATT). GATT is a massive international treaty signed by 117 countries dealing with almost all aspects of international trade. For our purposes, what is most important about GATT is that it includes a special agreement on intellectual property called Trade Related Aspects of Intellectual Property Rights (TRIPS for short). TRIPS requires each member country to agree, at a minimum, to enact national copyright laws giving effect to the substantive provisions of the Berne Convention discussed above. However, moral rights, which are generally not recognized in the United States, were expressly left out of TRIPS. This means that the United States cannot be subject to GATT dispute settlement procedures over the scope of moral rights.

TRIPS requires all GATT member countries to provide meaningful penalties for copyright infringement. These must include injunctive relief (including preliminary injunctions that can be obtained to stop infringing activities before trial) and adequate monetary damages. In addition, member countries must adopt procedures for excluding infringing goods at their borders upon application by U.S. or other copyright owners to their customs services.

GATT also includes mechanisms for settlement of country-to-country disputes regarding implementation of these requirements through the World Trade Organization, an international agency based in Geneva and similar to the World Bank. Special GATT remedies (for example, withdrawal of tariff concessions) may be imposed for violation of GATT rules.

The WIPO Treaty

The United States has signed yet another international copyright treaty. This one was sponsored by the World Intellectual Property Organization (WIPO), a United Nations agency based in Geneva, Switzerland. The treaty is called the WIPO Copyright Treaty (WCT).

The Berne Convention was last revised in 1979, and neither it nor the Universal Copyright Convention (UCC, the other principal international copyright treaty created in 1952) specifically provided for copyright protection for digital works or computer software. The WCT was drafted in 1996 to help fill this gap. It was signed by the United States in 1996 and has been signed by most other major industrial nations.

The WCT requires member countries to enact copyright laws giving effect to the substantive provisions of the Berne Convention. But perhaps the most important aspect of the WCT is that it requires member countries to give copyright protection to works in digital form. This means, for example, that unauthorized copying of material placed on a website can constitute

copyright infringement. The WCT also requires member countries to provide effective legal remedies against anyone who removes or alters rights management information from digital works—that is, electronically stored information about who owns the copyright in the work. The U.S. copyright law was amended in 1998 to comply with these requirements.

Protections in Countries Not Covered by Conventions

There are a handful of countries that have not signed any of the copyright treaties discussed above and that are not a party to trade agreements such as GATT.

These countries have no copyright relations with the United States and provide no protection for U.S. authors' works. These countries include Eritrea, Ethiopia, Iran, Iraq, and San Marino.

Bringing Infringement Suits in Foreign Countries

If your work is infringed upon by a person or an entity in a foreign country, the first thing to do is consult with an experienced American copyright attorney. Even if the infringement occurred in another country, you might be able to sue the infringer in the United States. In this event, an American court would apply the copyright law of the foreign country, not American law. If you have to file suit abroad, you'll need to hire a copyright attorney in the foreign country involved to represent you. Your American copyright attorney should be able to refer you to an experienced copyright lawyer in the country involved.

Before you go to the expense of filing suit, however, be sure to have your attorney explain to you what remedies (for instance, monetary damages, injunctions) you will be entitled to if the suit is successful. Remember, you'll only be entitled to the same treatment that a citizen of the country involved would receive.

Although the United States has been urging other nations to take copyright infringement more seriously than they have in the past, some (particularly developing) countries still do not impose meaningful penalties on infringers. This means it might not be economically worthwhile to bring infringement suits against infringers in some countries.

Protection in the United States for Non-U.S. Citizens

We now examine copyright protection in the United States from the point of view of non-U.S. citizens.

Foreign Works Entitled to U.S. Copyright Protection

The following works by non-U.S. citizens or permanent residents are entitled to full U.S. copyright protection.

Works First Published in the United States

Any work first published in the United States is entitled to full copyright protection in the United States, no matter what country the author is a citizen of or lives in.

> **EXAMPLE:** Kim, a citizen and resident of South Korea, first publishes a book of poetry in the United States. His book is entitled to full U.S. copyright protection.

Works First Published in Treaty Countries

A work is also entitled to full copyright protection in the United States if it is first published in a country that has signed any of the following international copyright treaties:

- the Berne Convention
- the Universal Copyright Convention
- the GATT Agreement
- the WIPO Copyright Treaty, or
- a bilateral (country-to-country) copyright treaty with the United States.

Almost every country in the world has signed one or more of these treaties, including every major industrialized country. As a result, almost all works published in foreign countries are entitled to full U.S. copyright protection.

> **EXAMPLE 1:** Pierre, a French citizen and resident, publishes a book in France. Because France signed the Berne Convention, the work is entitled to full U.S. copyright protection.

EXAMPLE 2: Pierre, a French citizen, first publishes his work in Vietnam. The work is entitled to U.S. copyright protection because Vietnam is a treaty country.

Unpublished Works

All *unpublished* works are fully protected under U.S. copyright law, no matter what country they were created in.

EXAMPLE: Maria, an Argentinian citizen and resident, creates an unpublished opera. The work is entitled to full U.S. copyright protection.

Foreign Works Not Entitled to U.S. Copyright Protection

A handful of countries have not signed any of the international copyright treaties. These are:

Eritrea	Iraq
Ethiopia	San Marino
Iran	

A work published in any of these countries by a citizen or resident of any of these countries is not entitled to U.S. copyright protection—that is, it is in the public domain.

EXAMPLE: Omar, an Iraqi citizen and resident, publishes a book in Iraq. Because Iraq is one of the few countries that has signed none of the copyright treaties, Omar's work is not protected by U.S. copyright.

However, application of the rules described in the previous section shows that a work by a citizen or permanent resident of one of these outcast countries is protected under U.S. copyright law if it is:

- *first* published in the United States, or
- *first* published in a treaty country, or
- is unpublished.

EXAMPLE 1: Assume that Omar's book in the example above was first published in the United States. Even though Omar is an Iraqi citizen and resident, his book is entitled to full U.S. copyright protection.

EXAMPLE 2: Assume instead that Omar's book was first published in France. It is entitled to full U.S. copyright protection because it was first published in a treaty country.

EXAMPLE 3: Jaleh, an Iranian citizen, has created an unpublished screenplay. The screenplay is entitled to full U.S. copyright protection: It's protected for the rest of her life plus 70 years. This is so, even though the United States has no copyright relations with Iran.

For copyright protection purposes, a work is first published in the United States or a treaty country if it was published in such a country either before or within 30 days after it was published in a nontreaty country.

EXAMPLE: Achmed, a citizen and resident of Afghanistan, published in Afghanistan a book on mountain climbing. Two weeks later, the book was also published in India. For copyright purposes, Achmed's book was first published in a treaty country (India) and is entitled to full U.S. copyright protection.

The copyright status of the following countries is unclear—in other words, no one is sure what protection, if any, works published in these countries are entitled to in the United States:

Nauru	Republic of South Sudan
Palau	Somalia

Compliance With U.S. Copyright Formalities

It is not necessary for a non-U.S. citizen to place a valid copyright notice on published work or register it with the U.S. Copyright Office to obtain copyright protection in the United States. Indeed, unlike the case with U.S. citizens, a non-U.S. citizen need not register a work first published abroad before filing suit in the United States for copyright infringement. However, as discussed in Chapter 2, "Copyright Notice," and Chapter 3, "Copyright Registration," extremely important advantages are gained under U.S. copyright law if a published work contains a valid copyright notice and a published or unpublished work is registered with the Copyright Office. Therefore, notice and registration are strongly advised for all foreign authors.

Restoration of Copyrights Under GATT Agreement

The GATT TRIPS Agreement required that U.S. copyright law be rewritten to restore U.S. copyright protection for certain foreign works that:

- were published in the United States, and
- entered the public domain in the United States because certain copyright formalities were not complied with.

The U.S. copyright law was rewritten to implement this provision, and works meeting the law's requirements had their copyright automatically restored. In other words, these works are no longer in the public domain.

The intent of the law was to put the United States in compliance with the Berne Convention, which never required formalities like a copyright notice or renewal to obtain copyright protection. Foreign authors who failed to comply with these unique U.S. copyright formalities were forgiven and granted a full term of U.S. copyright protection. Unfortunately, U.S. citizens did not receive this same treatment; copyright in their public domain works was not restored. The U. S. Supreme Court upheld the constitutionality of these restoration provisions, holding that it was permissible for Congress to allow some works that fell in the public domain to be "born again" with copyright protection. (*Golan v. Holder*, 565 U.S. 302 (2012).)

This was a major change in U.S. copyright law that affected not only the authors and copyright owners of the affected works, but also U.S. citizens who thought the works were in the public domain and used them without seeking permission.

Which Works Lost U.S. Copyright Protection

Works created by citizens or residents of countries other than the United States entered the public domain in the United States if any of the following were true:

- They were published in a foreign country between January 1, 1978 and March 1, 1989 without a valid copyright notice or were published in the United States any time before March 1, 1989 without a valid notice.
- They were published in the United States or a foreign country before January 1, 1964, but the copyright was never renewed by filing a renewal application with the U.S. Copyright Office during the 28th year after publication. (See Chapter 8, "Copyright Duration.")
- They were published in the United States before January 1, 1978, but were not registered with the U.S. Copyright Office within six months after the Register of Copyrights notified the copyright owner that registration and deposit must be made.

It's impossible to say how many works were ever published in the United States before 1989 without a valid copyright notice. It's likely most works that were deemed valuable at the time did have a notice. However, notices were often left off works that were viewed as not very valuable or of only temporary interest—postcards, for example.

It's likely that, by far, the largest category of restored foreign works are those published before 1964 for which no renewal notice was filed during the 28th year after publication. The Copyright Office estimates that only about 15% of pre-1964 published works were ever renewed. The 15% that were renewed probably include a large proportion of those pre-1964 works with continuing economic value. However, mistakes were frequently made and many noteworthy works were never renewed.

Copyright was also restored in works that received no copyright protection in the United States, because they were first published in countries with which the United States had no copyright relations at the time of publication. You might be surprised to know that as recently as 1973, the United States had no copyright relations with the Soviet Union. Works published before 1973 in the Soviet Union were in the public domain in the United States. Copyright in such works has now been restored provided they are still under protection in Russia or the other nations that made up the now-defunct Soviet Union. Probably most significant among these works are those by Soviet composers, such as Prokofiev and Shostakovich.

Which Works Had Copyright Restored

U.S. copyright was restored only in those works:

- that had at least one author who was a citizen or resident of a country other than the United States that is a member of the Berne Copyright Convention or World Trade Organization (a GATT member), has signed the WIPO Copyright Treaty, or has a copyright treaty with the United States—which includes almost all the countries of the world
- that, if published, was first published in one of the countries described above (not necessarily the same country as the author's), but not published in the United States within 30 days following the foreign publication, and
- whose copyright protection had not expired as of January 1, 1996 under the copyright laws of the foreign country.

In almost all foreign countries, copyrights for most types of works last for the life of the author plus 70 years. If the author of the foreign work died in 1925 or earlier, the work did not qualify for copyright restoration in the United States.

You need to know the copyright term of the foreign author's country and when the author died to know if the work was in the public domain in its home country on January 1, 1996, the date the automatic copyright restoration for foreign works took effect.

Copyright Restored Automatically

Copyright restoration for all foreign works meeting the above requirements occurred automatically on the date the copyright parts of the GATT Agreement became effective: January 1, 1996. These works receive the same term of copyright protection in the United States they would have enjoyed had they never entered the public domain.

> **EXAMPLE:** In 1950, Thames Press, a British publisher, published in Great Britain a novel called *Sticky Wicket,* by the English writer John Jones. Thames failed to file a renewal registration for the book in 1978, and as a result, it entered the public domain in the United States on January 1, 1979. However, the U.S. copyright in the book was automatically restored by the GATT Agreement, effective January 1, 1996. This automatic restoration occurred, because: (1) The work was written by a British subject and was first published in Great Britain (a Berne member), and (2) the British copyright on the book had not expired as of 1995 (British copyrights last for the life of the author plus 70 years). The book receives the same term of copyright protection in the United States it would have enjoyed had a renewal been timely filed—95 years from the date of publication. The novel will be protected by copyright in the United States until December 31, 2045.

Who Owns Restored Works

The U.S. copyright in a restored work is initially owned by the author as defined by the law of the country of origin, not U.S. law. If the author died before GATT's effective date, ownership is determined under the inheritance laws of the author's country. Disputes concerning initial ownership of restored foreign copyrights are to be determined by U.S. federal courts applying the law of the country of origin.

If the author at any time assigned, licensed, or otherwise transferred all or part of his or her copyright rights, the transfer is supposed to be given effect according to the terms of the agreement. Disputes concerning copyright transfers must be resolved in U.S. state courts applying U.S. law.

Copyright Protection in Canada

Canada's copyright law is similar, though not identical, to that of the United States. Canada is a member of all the major copyright conventions discussed above. Thus, U.S. citizens enjoy the same copyright protection in Canada as do Canadian citizens and vice versa.

Works Protected by Copyright

The requirements for copyright protection in Canada are essentially the same as in the United States. Protection begins automatically the moment you create an original work of authorship. Canadian law protects:

- all types of written works, such as books, pamphlets, poems, and other works consisting of text, including computer programs
- dramatic works, such as films, videos, plays, and screenplays
- musical compositions
- paintings, sculpture, drawings, graphics, and other artwork
- photographs, films, and videos
- architectural works, and
- all types of recordings.

As in the United States, copyright protection does not extend to ideas or facts, only to the way they are expressed by a particular author. Nor does copyright protect individual words, titles, short phrases, slogans, or blank forms.

Scope of Copyright Rights

The rights of a copyright owner in Canada are virtually the same as in the United States. The owner has the exclusive right to:

- reproduce all or a substantial part of the protected work
- publish the work
- perform the work in public—for example, to perform a play in public or display in public an artistic work created after June 7, 1988, and
- adapt the work—for example, to convert a novel into a screenplay, translate a work into another language, or record an audiobook.

Canadian Government Works Protected by Copyright

Unlike in the United States where works of the federal government are generally in the public domain, Canadian government works are generally protected by what is called Crown copyright. However, permission is not required to reproduce Canadian government works for personal or public noncommercial purposes or for cost-recovery purposes, unless:

- otherwise specified in the material you wish to reproduce, or
- you plan to revise, translate, or adapt the work.

Public noncommercial purposes mean a distribution of the reproduced information either for your own purposes only or for a distribution at large whereby no fees whatsoever will be charged.

Permission is always required when the work being reproduced will be distributed for commercial purposes.

Permission to reproduce other Canadian government documents must be obtained from the department or agency that created the work. Contact points for permissions from all the Canadian government's departments and agencies can be found at http://publications.gc.ca/site/eng/ccl/index.html.

As in the United States, the copyright owner may transfer or license any of these rights to others.

Under Canadian law, all authors also have certain moral rights which are stronger than in the United States. No one is allowed to distort, mutilate, or otherwise modify an author's work in a way that is prejudicial to his or her honor or reputation. In addition, the author's name must be included on the work.

Moral rights belong only to the creator of a work; they cannot be sold or transferred to anyone else. However, authors may waive their moral rights when they sell their work. Moral rights exist for the same length of time as copyright and pass to an author's heirs, even if they do not inherit ownership of the copyright itself.

Copyright Duration

The basic copyright term in Canada is the life of the author plus 50 years. If a work has more than one author, the copyright lasts for 50 years after the last author's death. All copyright terms last until the end of the year in which the author dies and then continue for an additional 50 calendar years. However, the term of the copyright depends on the nature of the work.

Longer Canada Copyright Terms

In 2020, Canada signed the United States–Mexico–Canada Agreement. This trade agreement requires Canada to extend its basic copyright term to life plus 70 years and life plus 75 years for sound recordings. This change had not been implemented when this book went to press.

Photographs

The term of protection for photographs depends on the author. There are three possible terms of protection:

- When the author is a natural person (as opposed to a business entity, such as a corporation), the copyright lasts for 50 years after the author dies.
- If the author of a photograph is a corporation, the copyright lasts 50 years after "the making of the initial negative or plate from which the photograph was derived or, if there is no negative or plate, of the initial photograph."
- If the majority of voting shares in a corporate owner are owned by a natural person who would have qualified as the author of the photograph, the copyright lasts 50 years after the photographer dies.

Before 1994, photographs had a copyright term of 50 years after creation of the original negative. Under a special transitional rule, a 50-year term is provided for photographs first created between January 1, 1994 through December 31, 1998.

Films and Videos

Canadian copyright differentiates between films (including videos) that do and do not have a dramatic quality—that is, "in which the arrangement or acting form or the combination of incidents represented give the work a dramatic character." Films with dramatic quality are protected for the life of the author plus 50 years.

Works that don't have a dramatic quality would include, for example, most home movies. If such a film or video is published within 50 years of creation, it is protected for 50 years from the date of publication. If it was not published within that 50-year period, it is protected for 50 years from the year of creation.

Sound Recordings, Broadcasts, and Performances

The copyright in a sound recording lasts for 50 years from the end of the year in which the original master copy or tape was created. The copyright in a broadcast lasts for 50 years after the initial broadcast. The copyright in a performer's performance lasts for 50 years after the performance is first fixed or, if it is not fixed, 50 years after it is performed.

Canadian Government Works

Works created by Canadian federal and provincial government employees are protected by Crown copyright. Copyright in these works lasts for 50 years from the year of publication. Copyright in unpublished government works is perpetual. However, anyone may, without charge or request for permission, reproduce laws enacted by the government of Canada and decisions and reasons for decisions of Canadian federal courts and administrative tribunals. The copier must exercise due diligence to ensure the accuracy of the materials reproduced and that the reproduction is not represented as an official version.

Unknown Authors

The copyright in a work written by an anonymous or pseudonymous author lasts for either 50 years after publication or 75 years after creation, whichever is shorter. However, if the author's identity becomes known, the copyright will last for 50 years after the author dies. The same terms apply to joint anonymous or pseudonymous authors, except that if one or more of the authors' identities becomes known, the copyright lasts for 50 years after the last of such known authors dies.

Posthumous Works

A posthumous work is a work that was under copyright when its author died but was not published before the death. The duration of the copyright in these works depends upon their date of creation. For such works created after July 25, 1997, the term of copyright protection is the normal life-of-the-author-plus-50-year term. However, any of three different terms may apply if the work was created before July 25, 1997:

- If the author died and the work was subsequently published, performed, or delivered before July 25, 1997, the copyright lasts for 50 years after such publication.
- If the author died during the period from 1927 through 1997 and the work was not published, performed, or delivered before July 25, 1997, the copyright lasts until January 1, 2048.
- If the author died before 1927 and the work was not published before July 25, 1997, the work is in the Canadian public domain.

Copyright Ownership

Canadian copyright ownership rules are very similar to those in the United States. Any work of authorship created by an employee within the course of employment is automatically owned by the employer unless there is an agreement to the contrary.

Works created by independent contractors —that is, nonemployees—are owned by the contractor, not the hiring firm, unless there is an express or implied agreement transferring ownership to the hiring firm. For example, a work contributed by a freelance writer to a magazine is owned by the writer unless there is an agreement to the contrary.

Limited Fair Use Rights

One major difference between the United States and Canada is in the area of fair use. Canada has no "fair use" as such. Instead, it has what is called "fair dealing." Fair dealing is much more limited than fair use in the United States. It allows people such as critics, reviewers, and researchers to quote from other authors' works without obtaining permission, but only for purposes of private study, research, or criticism. In the case of a published review, criticism, or newspaper summary, the user is required to give the source and the author's name, if known.

Recent amendments to the Canadian copyright laws establish a major new right to copy on the part of libraries, archives, and nonprofit educational institutions. Under these new amendments, nonprofit libraries, archives, and museums are permitted to:

- make copies of published or unpublished works that are not commercially available in a medium and quality that meets their users' needs, in order to maintain or manage their permanent collections
- reproduce an entire article in a newspaper or magazine, if the edition is at least 12 months old at the time of copying and the copy is used for private study or for research purposes, and
- make a single copy of an article from a scientific, technical, or scholarly periodical at any time.

In addition, nonprofit educational institutions will be permitted to reproduce copyrighted materials for the purpose of instruction, tests, or examinations.

Copyright Notice

No copyright notice is required for works published in Canada, and no legal benefits are obtained from having one. However, it's still advisable to include a notice on any work that might be distributed outside Canada, especially if it will be seen or used in the United States.

Copyright Registration

Copyright registration is completely optional. Unlike in the United States, it is not necessary to register to file a copyright infringement suit in Canada. The benefits of registration are much more limited than in the United States. A person who registers a work in Canada receives a registration certificate from the Canadian Copyright Office. The certificate serves as evidence that your work is protected by copyright and that you—the person registered—are the owner. This means that in the event of a legal dispute, you do not have to prove ownership; the burden is on your opponent to disprove it. This will prove modestly beneficial if you ever sue someone for copyright infringement in Canada. It can be particularly helpful if you need to obtain a quick court injunction against a copyright pirate to stop an infringing activity.

How to Register

Each separate work must be separately registered. There is no group registration for a number of works, as is allowed in the United States. The registration process is very easy. You merely fill out an extremely simple application and send it to the Canadian Copyright Office with the required fee. Unlike in the United States, you are *not* required to deposit a copy of your work.

You can register online by filling out an electronic application form and paying the fee by credit card. Or, you can download the application and mail it in. For detailed guidance, visit the Canadian Intellectual Property Office website at www.cipo.ic.gc.ca.

Registration Fee

The fee for registration is $50 in Canadian dollars if the application is submitted online; $65 if it is not. Registration is valid for as long as the copyright for the work exists. Once you register your copyright, you do not have to pay any additional fees to maintain or renew it.

Additional Information

The Canadian Copyright Office has produced a very useful Guide to Copyright that can be accessed at the Canadian Intellectual Property Office website at www.cipo.ic.gc.ca. There, you can also obtain copies of the Canadian Copyright Act and Rules.

There is an excellent one-volume guide to Canadian copyright law called *Canadian Copyright Law*, by Lesley Ellen Harris (Wiley).

Information about all forms of intellectual property in Canada may be found on the website maintained by the Canadian Intellectual Property Office at http://cipo.gc.ca.

Marketing Your Work in Foreign Countries

If you are sharing ownership of foreign rights with your publisher, the publisher usually markets them through foreign agents with which it has established relationships and at international book fairs (the Frankfurt International Book Fair being the most important). If you have retained all your foreign rights and have an agent, the agent will market your foreign rights through foreign subagents.

If you've retained your rights and don't have an agent, you need to retain one. You can use an American agent who has contacts with foreign subagents or directly contact agents in the particular countries in which you wish to sell your rights. The latter course will save you money, because you'll only have to pay a commission to the foreign agent, not to an American agent as well. The publication *International Literary Marketplace* lists British and other foreign agents.

Copyright and Taxation

This chapter provides an overview of federal taxation for writers who create copyrighted works. It is for self-employed writers—that is, writers who create their works on their own, not as employees. It focuses on tax issues of particular interest to writers, especially deducting writing expenses and the hobby loss rule.

RESOURCE

If you handle your taxes yourself, you'll need to obtain a more detailed book specifically on taxation. Many books are available including *Deduct It! Lower Your Small Business Taxes,* by Stephen Fishman (Nolo) and *Home Business Tax Deductions: Keep What You Earn,* by Stephen Fishman (Nolo). The IRS also has free publications on every conceivable tax topic. Some of the most useful include:

- Publication 334, *Tax Guide for Small Business*
- Publication 505, *Tax Withholding and Estimated Tax*
- Publication 937, *Employment Taxes and Information Returns*
- Publication 533, *Self-Employment Tax,* and
- Publication 535, *Business Expenses.*

You can obtain these and all other IRS publications from the IRS's website at www.irs.gov.

Writers' Income Tax Deductions

Charles, a freelance writer, has been working on a book on international terrorism for the last two years. In the course of his research and writing, he has incurred substantial expenses. This year, these included:

- $3,000 in travel and hotel expenses for trips to the Middle East and Europe to interview subjects for the book
- $2,000 for a portable computer
- $2,000 in home office expenses, and
- $3,000 for payments to a research assistant.

These amounted to $10,000 in writing expenses for the year. Naturally, Charles would like to know if he can use these expenses to help reduce his tax burden—that is, he wants to know if he can deduct his expenses.

A tax deduction is an expense or the value of an item that you can subtract from your gross income (all the income you earn) to determine your taxable income—the amount you earn that is subject to taxation. The more deductions you have, the lower your taxable income and the less tax you pay.

Is Writing a Hobby or Business?

Can Charles deduct his writing expenses? The answer is, "It depends." To determine whether or how an expense can be deducted, it is first necessary to figure out how Charles's writing activities should be characterized for tax purposes—as a hobby or a business.

Tax Savings From Deductions

Only part of any deduction will end up as an income tax savings—for example, a $5,000 tax deduction will not result in a $5,000 saving. To determine how much income tax a deduction will save you, you need to know your marginal tax bracket. This is the tax bracket in which the last dollar you earn falls and it's the rate at which any additional income you earn would be taxed. To determine how much tax a deduction will save you, multiply the amount of the deduction by your top tax bracket. For example, if your top tax bracket is 24%, you will save $24 in income taxes for every $100 you are able to claim as a deductible business expense (24% × $100 = $24).

The income tax brackets are adjusted each year for inflation. For the current brackets, see IRS Publication 505, *Tax Withholding and Estimated Tax*.

In addition, you may deduct your business expenses from your state income tax. State income tax rates vary, but they average about 6%. (Alaska, Florida, Nevada, South Dakota, Texas, Washington, and Wyoming don't have state income taxes.)

If you earn income from your business, you can also deduct most of your expenses for self-employment tax purposes. The self-employment tax rate is about 15.3% on net self-employment income up to the Social Security tax cap ($137,700 in 2020).

Adding all this together, you'll see the true value of a business tax deduction. For example, if you're in the 24% federal income tax bracket, your effective self-employment rate is about 13.4% because you deduct half of these taxes from your income tax. Thus, a tax would be worth as much as 24% + 13.4% + 6% = 43.4%. So you could end up deducting about 43.4% of the cost of your business expenses from your state and federal taxes. If, for example, you buy a $1,000 computer for your business, you'll save a whopping $434 in taxes. In effect, the government is paying for almost half of your business expenses. This is why it's so important to take all the business deductions to which you're entitled.

Writing as a Hobby

The worst of all possible tax worlds is for your writing activities to be deemed a hobby by the IRS. Because hobbies are not businesses, hobby writers cannot take the tax deductions to which businesspeople are entitled. However, for decades hobbyists were allowed to deduct their hobby-related expenses up to the amount of income the hobby earned during the year. Hobby expenses were deductible as a personal miscellaneous itemized deduction on IRS Schedule A. This meant these expenses could be deducted only by hobby writers who itemized their personal deduction, and only if, and to the extent, they exceeded 2% of the hobby writer's adjusted gross income (total income minus business expenses and a few other expenses). While not a very generous deduction, it was better than nothing. Unfortunately for hobby writers, the Tax Cuts and Jobs Act (Pub. L. No. 115-97) completely eliminated the itemized deduction for hobby expenses, along with all other miscellaneous itemized deductions. The prohibition on deducting these expenses is in effect for 2018 through 2025, meaning hobby writers may not deduct any expenses they incur from writing during these years. But hobby writers still have to report and pay tax on any income they earn from their writing hobby! The only exception is that hobbyists may deduct from their hobby income the cost of goods they sell or the cost of materials and supplies they use to make things they sell. (Treas. Reg. 1.183-1(e).) For example, a hobby writer who self-publishes a book may deduct from any writing earnings the cost of paper, printing, and other book production expenses. The miscellaneous itemized deduction for hobby expenses is scheduled to return in 2026.

EXAMPLE: Assume that Charles's writing activities were deemed a hobby by the IRS. His $10,000 in annual expenses would not be deductible from any income he earned from his hobby. But he is required to pay income tax on any money he earned from the hobby.

You don't need to understand all this in great detail. Just be aware that a finding by the IRS that your writing activities are a hobby will be a tax disaster. The only good thing about being a hobbyist is that you don't have to pay self-employment taxes on hobby income. Writers who are in business do have to pay such taxes.

For tax purposes, a hobby is any activity you engage in primarily for a reason other than to earn a profit—for example, to have fun, pass the time, get famous, please your spouse (or avoid your spouse), or any other reason. Or, to put it another way, if your primary motive for writing is to earn a profit, it is not a hobby. How do you show the IRS that your motive for writing is to earn a profit? You must actually earn a profit or, at least, act as if you want to earn profits. This is explained in detail below.

If you *want* writing to be a hobby, not a business, that's perfectly fine. There's no law that says a writer has to be in business. Writing is a wonderful hobby.

Writing as a Business

If being deemed a mere hobbyist is the worst thing that can happen to you tax-wise, being viewed as a businessperson is the best. Businesspeople are the pampered pets of the tax code, receiving the best possible tax treatment.

If writing qualifies as business and, like most independent writers, you are a sole

Net Operating Losses

Sometimes a writer's losses are so great that they will exceed his or her total income for the year. For example, assume that Charles earned only $15,000 in total income, while incurring $20,000 in currently deductible writing expenses for the year. He would have a net loss for the year of $5,000 ($15,000 – $20,000 = –$5,000). Such a loss is called a net operating loss or an NOL, for short.

Although it might not be pleasant to lose money over an entire year, having an NOL can result in important tax benefits.

You may be able to "carry a loss back"—that is, apply your NOL to past tax years by filing an application for refund or amended return. This option enables you to get a refund for all or part of the taxes you paid in prior years. Losses incurred 2018 through 2020 can be carried back five years. Those incurred 2017 and earlier could be carried back two years. However, the Tax Cuts and Jobs Act eliminated all NOL carrybacks for 2021 and later. Losses for these years can only be carried forward—that is, deducted in future years.

The calculations involved in determining how much you can deduct from prior years' income can be complicated. Tax preparation programs like *TurboTax* aren't designed to handle NOLs, so it's wise to let a tax professional help you determine your NOL.

For more information on NOLs, refer to IRS Publication 536, *Net Operating Losses (NOLs) for Individuals, Estates, and Trusts*. You can obtain this and all other IRS publications from the IRS Internet site at www.irs.gov.

---

proprietor, you list all your writing business expenses and income on IRS Schedule C, *Profit or Loss From Business*. You deduct your writing business expenses from writing business income. You pay tax only on your net business income (gross business income minus business expenses).

EXAMPLE: Assume that Charles earned $20,000 from writing for the year, and that his $10,000 in expenses qualified as current business deductions. He would deduct his $10,000 expenses from his $20,000 writing income on his Schedule C, leaving $10,000 in net writing business income subject to taxation (both income and self-employment taxes).

If, as is the case with many writers, your writing expenses exceed your writing income or you have no writing income at all, you will have a net loss from writing for the year. You can usually deduct this business loss from all the income you earn for the year, whatever the source—for example, from your salary or investment income—thereby reducing your taxable income for the year.

EXAMPLE: Assume that Charles earned no money from writing for the year, but still incurred $10,000 in annual expenses that could be currently deducted. He would have a net loss from writing of $10,000. He can deduct his $10,000 writing loss from all his income for the year, which was $50,000 in interest and investment income and salary from a part-time teaching job. So, instead of having to pay income tax on $50,000 in income, he only had to pay it on $40,000 ($50,000 – $10,000). This $10,000 deduction ends up saving Charles $3,500 in federal and state income tax for the year—$3,500 he would not have had were he not engaged in the business of writing.

How to Show the IRS Writing Is a Business

It should be clear by now that writers who qualify as businesspeople get the best tax treatment. Two main factors are considered by the IRS in determining whether writing is a business:

- Your primary motive for writing must be to earn a profit.
- You must engage in writing continuously and regularly over a substantial time period.

The IRS has established two tests to measure these factors. One is a simple mechanical test that asks whether you've earned a profit in three of the last five years. The other is a more complex test based on whether you behave like a business.

Note that the IRS applies these tests only if your tax returns are audited. In other words, you might mistakenly presume that writing is a business, only to learn four or five years later that the IRS has a different opinion. In that case, you would be disallowed any improper deductions made during those years and required to pay any miscalculated taxes and penalties. The cost can be quite expensive, and for that reason, we strongly recommend that you bolster your position as a business by reviewing this chapter.

Profit Test

You usually don't have to worry about the IRS labeling writing as a hobby if you earn a profit from it in any three of the last five years. If your venture passes this test, the IRS must presume it is a business. This doesn't mean the IRS can't claim your writing is a hobby, but it shifts the burden to the IRS to prove it is a hobby. In practice, the IRS usually doesn't attack ventures that pass the profit test unless it's clear the numbers have been manipulated just to pass it.

You have a profit when the taxable income from an activity is more than the deductions for it. You don't have to earn a big profit to satisfy this test, and there is no set amount or percentage of profit you need to earn.

EXAMPLE: Tom began to work on a new book in 2015. He earned no income from writing during 2015–2016 and therefore had no profits from writing for those years.

He published the book in 2017. Due to his royalty income from the book, he earned a profit from writing during 2014 through 2019. As of 2020, he had earned a profit during three of the last five years. Thus, in 2020, the IRS must presume writing is running a business for Tom.

Unfortunately, a great many writers can't satisfy the profit test. It may take far more than five years before you see any money at all from writing, let alone turn a profit.

IRS Form 5213

The IRS has a form called Form 5213, *Election to Postpone Determination as to Whether the Presumption Applies That an Activity Is Engaged in for Profit.* If you file this form, the IRS must wait an extra year before it can determine whether you've shown a profit under the profit test. This might sound like a good deal, but it isn't. Don't file this form. Doing so only alerts the IRS that you should be audited on the hobby loss issue. For this reason, almost no one ever files Form 5213.

Behavior Test

If, like many writers, you can't satisfy the profit test, you can still show you're running a business by passing the behavior test. However, you'll have to work hard to show that you are trying your darndest to make money from writing.

Under the behavior test, the IRS looks at the following "objective" factors to determine whether you are behaving as if you honestly believe you will earn a profit from writing.

Do you act like you're in business? If you act like you're running a business, you likely want to earn a profit. Among other things, acting like a business means you keep good books and other records and otherwise carry on your writing activities in a businesslike manner.

Do you have expertise? It would look pretty odd to the IRS if, for example, a person claimed to be writing a book on nuclear physics but had no educational background or other expertise in the field. Such a person would not seem to be serious about earning money. On the other hand, a person who had a degree in physics or had writing credits in the field would appear to be serious about earning a profit from writing about physics. If you lack the necessary expertise, you should acquire it through study or by consulting with experts in the field.

Do you write regularly and continuously? You can work part-time at writing and still be in business. As a general rule, the more time and effort you put into writing, the more likely it will appear you want to earn a profit.

Do you have a good track record? Having a track record of success in other businesses in the past—whether or not related to writing—helps show your present writing activities are a business.

Have you earned at least some profits? Even if you can't satisfy the profit test, earning at least occasional profits helps show you're in business.

How big are your profits? Earning only small or occasional yearly profits while having large losses or a large investment in an activity tends to show a lack of a profit motive. On the other hand, earning a substantial profit one year after years of losses helps show you are in a business. After all, writers often earn little or nothing for many years in the hope of a big payday down the road when their work is published or otherwise sold.

Are you rich? The IRS figures you likely have a profit motive if you don't have a substantial income from sources other than writing. After all, you'll need to earn money from your writing to survive. On the other hand, substantial income from sources other than writing might indicate a lack of a profit motive. This factor is never determinative by itself.

Are you having too much fun? Finally, activities that are inherently fun or recreational are less likely to be engaged in for profit than those that are not fun. Writing is often viewed as a "fun" activity by the IRS—particularly where the writer does a substantial amount of pleasurable traveling as part of the writing process. This means, for example, that a writer who claims a trip to Paris as a writing business expense because the novel is set in Paris will have a harder time showing a profit

motive than an accountant or a computer programmer who never leaves a cubicle.

Passing the IRS Behavior Test

The first three factors listed above—acting like a business, having expertise, and expending time and effort—are by far the most important. Studies have shown that no taxpayer who has satisfied these factors has ever been found not to have a profit motive. If you take the following steps, you'll have a good chance of passing the test. Most importantly, in order to show that you carry on your writing activities in a business-like manner:

- **Keep good business records.** Keeping good records of your expenses and income from writing is the single most important thing you can do to show you're in business and want to earn a profit. Without good records, you'll never have an accurate idea of how you stand financially. Lack of records shows you don't really care if you make money or not. You don't need an elaborate set of books. A simple record of your expenses and income will suffice. See *Working for Yourself,* by Stephen Fishman (Nolo), for a detailed discussion of record keeping for self-employed people.

- **Persistently try to sell your work.** Writers who are in business ordinarily try to sell their work—they don't write solely for enjoyment. Authors who fail to make systematic sales efforts will usually be found to be hobbyists. Keep a record of where you submit your work and save all acceptance and rejection letters or other letters or email you receive from publishers or editors.

- **Legally protect your writings.** Any original writing is automatically protected by copyright the moment it is written down or otherwise recorded. However, you can obtain additional legal benefits by registering your works with the Copyright Office. Registering is inexpensive and easy to do and helps to show you're a serious businessperson. (See Chapter 3 for a detailed discussion of copyright registration.)

- **Keep a separate checking account.** Open up a separate checking account for your writing business. This will help you keep your personal and business expenses separate—another factor that shows you're running a business.

- **Get business stationery and cards.** It might seem like a minor matter, but obtaining business stationery and business cards shows you think you are in business. Hobbyists ordinarily don't have such things. You can inexpensively create your own stationery and cards yourself using off-the-shelf software products.

- **Get online.** Most writers who are serious about earning money from their work have a website, blog, or some other type of online presence to market their writing, themselves, or both (their "brand"). Lack of an online presence indicates that you're not really interested in earning a profit from your writing activity.

- **Join professional organizations and associations.** Join and participate in writer's organizations and associations—for example, the National Writers Union or Authors Guild.

- **Create a business plan.** It is also helpful to draw up a business plan with forecasts of revenue and expenses. For detailed guidance on how to create a business plan, see *How to Write a Business Plan*, by Mike McKeever (Nolo).

- **Have or get expertise.** If you lack all the expertise you need to be a successful writer, develop it by attending educational seminars and similar activities or consulting with experts. Keep records to show your attempts to gain expertise—for example, notes documenting your attendance at a writing seminar.

- **Work steadily.** People who run a business ordinarily work continuously and regularly. They don't work one day and then do nothing for the next six months. So, you can't write one short article a year and claim that writing is a business.

You don't have to work full-time on writing to show you have a profit motive, but you should work steadily rather than sporadically. This can be an important factor in an IRS determination. Long ago, the IRS ruled that a person who writes only one book as a sideline and never revises it would not be considered to be in business. In contrast, an author who prepares new editions of a book from time to time, writes other books and materials, and lectures professionally would likely be viewed as being in business. (Rev. Rul. 55-385.)

Keep a log showing the time you spend writing; this doesn't have to be fancy—you can just mark down the time you spend on your calendar. If you're audited, this documentation will show how hard you've been working.

Writers Who Failed the Behavior Test

Following are real-life examples of writers who failed the behavior test. These examples help show how the IRS and courts apply the test:

- **The author who never sold a book.** Bradley, a social services caseworker, worked part-time at writing for over 17 years. He set up an office in a room in his home and wrote fiction. However, he only submitted one manuscript, a novel called *The Glass Mask*, to a publisher. It was rejected, and he never attempted to get it published elsewhere. The only money he ever made from writing was $700 his mother paid him to write her biography. The IRS claimed Bradley was a hobby writer, and the court agreed. The court said his failure to make systematic efforts to sell his work showed he engaged

in writing "essentially for personal pleasure," not to make a profit. (*Sherman v. Commissioner*, T.C. Memo. 1989-269, 57 T.C.M. (CCH) 599.)

- **The engineer's complaint.** Bert, an intermittently employed electrical engineer, wrote various articles in his spare time. These articles were not on the subject of engineering, but on such topics as his hatred of the IRS and his problems with his mother. He wrote 44 such articles over a three-year period and managed to get five published— unfortunately, for free. Although Bert claimed to have spent substantial time writing, the tax court held that he was a hobbyist. Bert failed to keep adequate books and records, and the court found that his articles didn't appear to be written with the purpose of earning money from publication. Rather, his diatribes resembled diary entries or served as a means for him to let off steam about the income tax system. (*Bert v. Commissioner*, T.C. Memo. 1989-503, 58 T.C.M. (CCH) 144.)

Writers Who Passed the Behavior Test

The following writers passed the behavior test, even though they earned no profit from their writing during the time in question:

- **The struggling playwright.** Eleanor supported herself as a Hollywood screenwriter and freelance book and article writer for 28 years. Following her marriage, she continued to write magazine articles but started devoting more of her writing time to plays, which she sent to agents and producers. She lost money from these activities for eight out of 12 years. The IRS audited her and claimed that, although she had once been a professional writer, playwriting was merely a money-losing hobby she engaged in after her marriage. Eleanor appealed to the tax court and won. The court was impressed by the businesslike manner that Eleanor managed her playwriting. She spent two to four hours a day writing in her office, a 20' x 20' room located in the same building as her apartment but on a separate floor. She kept a separate bank account in which she deposited income from her writing activities and from which she paid expenses connected with her writing. She was a long-time member of the American Society of Journalists and Authors, the Dramatists' Guild and Authors' Leagues, and the American Federation of Television and Radio Actors. This all led the court to believe that Eleanor wrote her plays to earn a profit and was therefore in business. (*Howard v. Commissioner*, T.C. Memo. 1981-250, 41 T.C.M. (CCH) 1554.)

- **The freelancer with great expectations.** Seymour, a veteran writer with many articles and screenplays to his credit, spent almost a whole year in New York researching D.W. Griffith's papers at the Museum of Modern Art. He used this research to write an article on Griffith for *Film Culture Magazine* and also signed a contract to write a book on the pioneer film director. Seymour earned no money from the article but was to be paid a royalty for the sales of his book. The IRS objected when Seymour deducted his travel expenses for the time he spent in New York, claiming he was not in business during that time. The tax court disagreed and held that Seymour was in business because he had a good-faith expectation of earning a profit from his book once it was published. (*Stern v. United States*, 71-1 U.S.T.C. (CCH) P9375, 1971 WL 354 (Mar. 26, 1971).)

Types of Expenses Writers May Deduct

Virtually any writing expense you incur is deductible as long as it is:

- ordinary and necessary
- directly related to your writing business, and
- for a reasonable amount.

An expense that satisfies these requirements is deductible whether your writing activity qualifies as a business or hobby, subject to the limitations on deductions for hobbies noted above.

Ordinary and Necessary

An expense qualifies as ordinary and necessary if it is common, accepted, helpful, and appropriate for your writing business. An expense doesn't have to be indispensable to be necessary; it need only help your business in some way, even in a minor way. It's usually fairly easy to tell if an expense passes this test.

> EXAMPLE 1: Bill, a freelance writer, is writing a book about ancient Athens. He hires a research assistant and pays her $50 an hour. This is clearly a deductible business expense. Hiring research assistants is a common and accepted practice among professional writers. The assistant's fee is an ordinary and necessary expense for Bill's writing business.

> EXAMPLE 2: Bill, the freelance writer, visits a masseuse every week to work on his bad back. Bill claims the cost as a business expense, reasoning that avoiding back pain helps him concentrate on his writing. This is clearly not an ordinary or customary expense for a freelance writer, and the IRS would not likely allow it as a business expense.

Expense Must Be Related to Your Business

An expense must be related to your writing business to be deductible, meaning you must use the item you buy for your business in some way. For example, the cost of a personal computer is a deductible business expense if you use the computer to write freelance articles.

You cannot deduct purely personal expenses as business expenses. The cost of a personal computer is not deductible if you use it just to play computer games. If you buy something for both personal and business reasons, you may deduct the business portion of the expense. For example, if you buy a smartphone and use it half the time for business calls and half the time for personal calls, you can deduct half the cost of the phone as a business expense.

However, the IRS requires you to keep records showing when the item was used for business and when for personal reasons. One acceptable form of record would be a diary or log with the dates, times, and reason the item was used. This kind of record keeping can be burdensome and might not be worth the trouble if the item isn't very valuable.

To avoid having to keep such records, try to use items either only for business or only for personal use. For example, if you can afford it, purchase two computers and use one solely for your writing and one for playing games and other personal uses.

Deductions Must Be Reasonable

There is usually no limit on how much you can deduct, so long as it's not more than you actually spend and the amount is reasonable. Certain areas are hot buttons for the IRS—especially travel and meal expenses. The IRS won't allow such expenses to the extent it considers them lavish.

Also, if the amount of your deductions is very large relative to your income, your chance of being audited goes up dramatically. One analysis of almost 1,300 tax returns found that you are at high risk for an audit if your business deductions exceed 63% of your revenues. You're relatively safe so long as your deductions are less than 52% of your revenue. If you have extremely large deductions, make sure you can document them in case you're audited.

Writer's Brothel Expenses Not Deductible

Vitale, a retired federal government budget analyst, decided to write a book about two men who travel cross-country to patronize a legal brothel in Nevada. To authenticate the story and develop characters for the book, he visited numerous legal brothels in Nevada by acting as a customer for prostitutes. He kept a detailed journal describing his experiences at the brothels, including the dates (and sometimes the hours) of his visits, the prostitutes he met, and the amount of cash he paid each one. He wrote and published the book, called *Searchlight, Nevada*, and later claimed a deduction of $3,480 on his tax return for cash payments to prostitutes. The tax court found that writing was a business for Vitale, although he had yet to earn a profit from it. However, it denied the deduction for prostitutes, declaring that the expenditures were "so personal in nature as to preclude their deductibility." (*Vitale v. Commissioner*, T.C. Memo. 1999-131, 77 T.C.M. (CCH 1869.)

Common Deductions for Writing Businesses

Expenses that self-employed writers may deduct from their income tax commonly include:

- commissions paid to literary agents
- legal and accounting fees
- marketing expenses, including expenses for an author website
- permissions fees
- bank fees for a writing business bank account
- costs of renting or leasing vehicles, equipment, and other property used in your business
- depreciation of business assets
- education expenses—for example, the cost of attending writing seminars or classes
- expenses for the business use of your home
- fees you pay to people you hire to help your writing business—for example, payments to a research assistant or the cost of hiring a publicist to help you promote a book
- health insurance for yourself and your family
- insurance for your business—for example, liability and business property insurance
- office expenses, such as office supplies
- office utilities
- postage
- professional association dues
- books needed for your writing business

- repairs and maintenance for business equipment, such as a photocopier or fax machine
- retirement plan contributions
- software purchased for your writing business
- subscriptions to business-related publications, and
- travel and meal expenses.

When to Deduct Expenses

Some expenses can be deducted all at once; others have to be deducted over a number of years. It all depends on how long the item you purchase can reasonably be expected to last—what the IRS calls its useful life:

- **Current expenses.** The cost of anything you buy for your writing business that has a useful life of less than one year must be fully deducted in the year it is purchased. This includes, for example, rent, telephone and utility bills, photocopying costs and postage, and other ordinary business operating costs. Such items are called current expenses.
- **Capital expenses.** Certain types of costs are considered to be part of your investment in your business instead of operating costs. These are called capital expenses. In the past, most long-term assets had to be depreciated over several years—anywhere from three to 39, depending on the asset.

However, changes in the tax law the last few years enable most writers to currently deduct in a single year most long-term assets they purchase, such as computers, office furniture, and books. The IRS de minimis safe harbor allows such items to be currently deducted if they cost no more than $5,000, while IRC Section 179 enables up to $1,020,000 in personal property to be deducted in a single year. Also, a 100% bonus depreciation is available through 2022 to deduct the full cost of personal property—the one exception being real estate. The cost of commercial real estate must be deducted over 39 years.

Writers Need Not Capitalize Short-Term Expenses

In the past, writers had it tough tax-wise, because they were required to capitalize all costs they incurred while creating their works. This meant they had to deduct them over several years as sales occurred. However, the tax law was changed in 1988 to provide a special exception to these capitalization rules for writers or other creative individuals. (I.R.C. § 263A(h).) Writers may now deduct costs, other than some capital expenses as described above, in the year incurred.

Taxation of Copyright Income

Virtually any income you earn from writing—that is, creating copyrighted written works—is subject to federal income taxation. Federal income taxation applies whether your income takes the form of a set fee for an article or a royalty based on sales. Virtually all freelance writers are cash-basis taxpayers. This means they must pay tax on their earnings only when they are actually received, not when promised. Thus, for example, if a publisher promises to pay you a $100,000 advance when you submit a completed manuscript, you'd have to pay tax on the advance only when it was paid to you.

Prizes and awards (cash or noncash) given to writers are also taxable income. Scholarship and fellowship grants are excluded from taxable income only to the extent they are used for tuition and course-related fees, books, supplies, and equipment at a qualified educational institution.

Income Reporting

How do the folks at the IRS find out how much you've earned from writing? Easy … publishers tell them. Any magazine, website, publisher, or other enterprise or person that pays you $600 or more by check, cash, or direct deposit during the year as a nonemployee writer must complete a Form 1099-NEC reporting the payments. The payer must file a copy of the 1099 with:

- the IRS
- your state tax office, if your state has income tax, and
- you.

To make sure you're not underreporting your income, IRS computers check the amounts listed on your 1099s against the amount of income you report on your tax return. If the amounts don't match, you have a good chance of being billed for underpaying your taxes.

Publishers and others need not file a 1099 form if you've incorporated your business and the publisher pays your corporation, not you personally.

In addition, payers need not file a 1099-NEC if you are paid electronically by a third-party payment service—for example, through online payment services like PayPal. However, PayPal and other third-party payment services must report the payments they make to you on IRS Form 1099-K, if you receive payments of more than $20,000 per year and have 200 or more transactions.

You should receive all your 1099s for the previous year by January 31 of the current year. Check the amount of compensation listed as paid to you in each 1099 against your own records to make sure they are consistent. If there is a mistake, contact the payer immediately and request a corrected 1099. You don't want the IRS to think you've been paid more than you really were. You don't have to file your 1099s with your tax returns. Just keep them in your records.

Self-Employment Taxes

In addition to income taxes, you'll also have to pay Social Security and Medicare taxes on the profit you earn from your writing business. These taxes are called self-employment or SE taxes. You must pay SE taxes if your net yearly earnings from your writing business are $400 or more. When you file your annual tax return, you must include IRS Form SE, showing how much SE tax you were required to pay. However, SE taxes need only be paid by writers who are in business—not by hobby writers. For more information on SE taxes, see IRS Publication 533, *Self-Employment Tax.*

Capital Gains vs. Ordinary Income

As you are probably aware, the IRS taxes your income as either capital gains or ordinary income. The top capital gains tax rate (as of 2020) is 20%, compared with 37% for ordinary income. (Note: Capital assets held for less than one year are taxed at ordinary income rates.) This means that writers with higher incomes could pay substantially lower taxes if they were allowed to treat the money they receive from the sale of a copyright as a long-term capital gain rather than as ordinary income.

Capital gains treatment is available only when you sell a capital asset—this commonly includes such things as real estate, stocks, and bonds. Logically, there would seem to be no reason why a copyright shouldn't also be treated as a capital asset. Unfortunately, Congress disagrees. A special provision of the tax law bars writers from obtaining capital gains treatment on money they earn from the sale of copyrighted works they create themselves. A person who is given ownership of a copyrighted work by an author is also denied capital gains treatment. (I.R.C. § 1221(a)(3).) However, a person who inherits a copyrighted work from a deceased author may be entitled to capital gains treatment when he or she sells the work. Consult with a tax expert if you're in this situation.

Paying Your Taxes

When you're a self-employed writer—not employed to write—no income tax is withheld from your compensation and you don't receive a W-2 form. Instead, you must pay all your income and Social Security taxes to the IRS yourself in the form of periodic payments known as estimated taxes. You must pay estimated taxes if you're a sole proprietor and expect to owe at least $1,000 in federal tax for the year on your writing business income.

> **EXAMPLE:** Joe expects to earn a profit of $10,000 from his writing business this year. He is in the 24% tax bracket, so he will owe $2,400 in taxes. Thus, he has to pay estimated taxes during the year.

There is one exception to this rule: If you paid no taxes last year, you don't have to pay any estimated tax this year no matter how much tax you expect to owe. But this is true only if you were a U.S. citizen or resident for the year and your tax return for the previous year covered the whole 12 months.

Moreover, if, in addition to being a self-employed writer, you hold a job and have taxes withheld from your paychecks by your employer, you need not pay estimated tax if the amount withheld is at least equal to the lesser of:

- 90% of your total tax due for the current year, or
- 100% of the tax you paid the previous year (110% if you earned over $150,000).

If the amount you currently have withheld from your paychecks does not meet the above test, you might be able to avoid having to make estimated tax payments by asking your employer to take more tax out of your earnings. To do this, file a new Form W-4 with your employer. Keep in mind that if you don't have more withheld each month (and make your own quarterly estimated tax payments instead), you'll have more control over your cash flow.

Estimated tax must ordinarily be paid in four installments, with the first one due on April 15, the next June 15, then September 15, and finally January 15. However, you don't have to start making payments until you actually earn income from your writing business. If you don't receive any income by March 31, you can skip the April 15 payment. In this event, you'd ordinarily make three payments for the year, starting on June 15. If you don't receive any income by May 31, you can skip the June 15 payment as well, and so on.

 RESOURCE

See IRS Publication 505, *Tax Withholding and Estimated Tax,* **for a detailed explanation of estimated taxes.** You can download it from www.irs.gov or obtain a copy by calling the IRS at 800-TAX-FORM or visiting your local IRS office.

Obtaining Copyright Permissions

This chapter covers how to get permission to use text—whether from a book, magazine, newspaper, newsletter, website, or journal. The following sections will help you identify the company or person who owns the rights to the text (the "rights holder") and offers suggestions for how to make your permissions request. It also discusses special situations that occur when using text from interviews, speeches, or print publications. At the end of the chapter, you'll find two sample text permission agreements: a short-form agreement and a longer, more detailed agreement.

RESOURCE

This chapter is adapted from material from *Getting Permission*, **by Richard Stim (Nolo).**

CAUTION

Confirm whether permission is necessary. No permission is required if the text you want to use is in the public domain. And, many uses of text are allowed without permission under the fair use privilege. The public domain is discussed in Chapter 4, and fair use is discussed in Chapter 9.

Start With the Copyright Clearance Center

Start your quest for permission with the Copyright Clearance Center (CCC) at www.copyright**.com** (not www.copyright **.gov**). The CCC has nothing to do with the U.S. Copyright Office and is not part of the government. It is a privately run online permissions broker, which funds itself by taking a cut of the permissions and license fees users pay to use content licensed through the CCC's service.

The CCC has drastically simplified the process of obtaining text permissions. By using the CCC, you can avoid having to search for or contact the copyright owner directly. Instead, you need only identify the book, journal, or magazine article and complete an online form.

If the work is part of the CCC's online database, you can usually obtain permission within one or two days (sometimes immediately) and pay for the rights you need by credit card. Acting as the agent and broker for publishers and authors, the CCC allows you to pick and click your way through millions of works, including books and journal and magazine articles.

Publishers set the fees with these permission brokers. For example, a national newspaper, via CCC, charges $400 to reprint an article in a book and $600 to reprint an article in a national magazine. These prices are similar to those for permissions granted without the use of the CCC's service—but if you wish to comparison shop, you can contact the copyright owner directly following the suggestions below.

The CCC's online procedure is often far easier than the traditional system of locating and calling a publisher, negotiating permission, and signing a written agreement. If a service does not represent a publisher—that is, the publisher's works are not designated in the database—you may still use the service to inquire about the use of works on your behalf.

The CCC represents over 10,000 print publishers, including *The New York Times* and *The Wall Street Journal*, which makes its website a good place to start your permissions search. Through the CCC, you can obtain permission for:

- **Photocopying.** This includes photocopy permissions for newspaper and magazine articles, books, journals, research reports, or other published documents.

- **Email.** CCC grants rights to email an online article or PDF file.

- **Electronic uses.** CCC allows you to post digital content on your corporate website, intranet, and extranet.

- **Printouts.** CCC facilitates your ability to print out Web-based and other digital content onto paper and overhead slides.

- **Republication.** CCC permits you to republish content in a newsletter, book, or journal.

- **Digital rights.** CCC grants rights to scan printed material into digital form when an electronic version is not readily available.

To use the CCC's service, visit the website (www.copyright.com) and create an account (most likely you'll want a pay-per-use account and not an annual subscription). Complete the registration, and you will be directed how to start using your pay-per-use account. There's a helpful online search page in which you can choose the type of permission wanted and search for the publication by title, publisher, ISBN, author, or editor. When you find the material you're seeking, CCC will provide you with the terms for licensing or, if necessary, provide you with a direct contact to the rights holder to negotiate

Creative Commons Licenses

Many content owners, especially those who place their work on the Internet, provide advance permission for the public to make free use of their work by employing one of several open content licenses developed by the Creative Commons, a nonprofit corporation whose goal is "to cultivate a commons in which people can feel free to reuse not only ideas, but also words, images, and music without asking permission—because permission has already been granted to everyone." Since its founding in 2001, the Creative Commons has become a worldwide phenomenon with over 140 million webpages subject to Creative Commons licenses and search engines dedicated to finding Creative Commons-licensed content on the Internet.

These licenses were developed to "let authors, scientists, artists, and educators easily mark their creative work with the freedoms they want it to carry."

Copyright owners may choose among one of the following six types of licenses that allow varying degrees of permission-free use of the work involved.

Attribution (CC BY)

"This license lets others distribute, remix, adapt, and build upon your work, even commercially, as long as they credit you for the original creation. This is the most accommodating of licenses offered. Recommended for maximum dissemination and use of licensed materials."

Attribution-NoDerivs (CC BY-ND)

"This license lets others reuse the work for any purpose, including commercially; however, it cannot be shared with others in adapted form, and credit must be provided to you.

Attribution-Noncommercial-Share Alike (CC BY-NC-SA)

"This license lets others remix, adapt, and build upon your work non-commercially, as long as they credit you and license their new creations under the identical terms."

Attribution-Share Alike (CC BY-SA)

"This license lets others remix, adapt, and build upon your work even for commercial purposes, as long as they credit you and license their new creations under the identical terms. This license is often compared to "copyleft" free and open source software licenses. All new works based on yours will carry the same license, so any derivatives will also allow commercial use. This is the license used by Wikipedia, and is recommended for materials that would benefit from incorporating content from Wikipedia and similarly licensed projects."

Attribution-Noncommercial (CC BY-NC)

"This license lets others remix, adapt, and build upon your work non-commercially, and although their new works must also acknowledge you and be non-commercial, they don't have to license their derivative works on the same terms."

Creative Commons Licenses (continued)

Attribution-Noncommercial-NoDerivs (CC BY-NC-ND)

"This license is the most restrictive of our six main licenses, only allowing others to download your works and share them with others as long as they credit you, but they can't change them in any way or use them commercially."

Creative Commons-licensed material placed on the Internet is supposed to contain a Creative Commons logo consisting of two Cs within a circle. Clicking on the logo or a plain text hyperlink sends the user to a page on the Creative Commons website that contains a "Creative Commons deed"—an easy to read, brief description of the license. The deed, in turn, contains a hyperlink that sends the user to a copy of the complete version of the license, referred to as "legal code." For more information about Creative Commons licenses, refer to https://creativecommons.org/licenses.

---

terms. The latter functionality is triggered when CCC handles some, but not all, rights for a certain publisher. In other cases, CCC might contact the rights holder for you and get back to you in a few days with a quote. Much of CCC's permission process is channeled through the CCC automated service, Rightslink (www.rightslink.com).

If you're having trouble at any point in the CCC's process, the site has FAQs and a useful demo to help you.

Permissions Departments

Many publishers have permissions departments or a person who handles reprints, permissions, and clearances. Information about the permissions department is usually found on or near the copyright page of a book or in a magazine or journal's masthead page. Online magazines and book publishers' websites generally include copyright and permissions information on the introductory webpage (the index or home page).

Are You Under Contract to Write a Book?

Have you signed a contract to write an article or book? Publishing contracts usually indicate who has responsibility for obtaining permission for anything you use in your article or book, either the author (you) or the publisher. Your publishing contract may also specify the language to be used in any permission agreement you obtain. Inquire whether your publisher has its own permission form you can use.

If the book, magazine, or journal contains no specific information about permissions, direct your inquiries to the "Permissions Department" at the publisher's main business address, usually listed in the first or last few pages of a publication.

Locating Publishers

Contact information for publishers can usually be found on their websites, which can be located through a Google search. Information on book publishers is also available in online and print publications, such as *Books in Print* (www.booksinprint.com), *Literary Market Place* (www.literarymarketplace.com), and *International Literary Market Place* (www. literarymarketplace.com). *Writer's Market* (Writer's Digest Books, www.writersdigest. com) provides a list of U.S. book publishers, as well as publishers of magazines, journals, and greeting cards. For small press information, try Dustbooks.com (www.dustbooks. com). If you're looking for information on academic publishers, check out the Association of American University Presses directories, published by the University of Chicago Press (www.press.uchicago.edu).

For information on locating periodical publishers, try an online search or consult *The National Directory of Magazines* and *The Standard Periodical Directory*, both published by Oxbridge Communications (www.mediafinder.com), or review *Ulrich's International Periodicals Directory* (http:// ulrichsweb.serialssolutions.com).

When There Is More Than One Publisher

Different publishers may print the same book in different versions. For example, one book might be published first in hardcover, later published in paperback by a different publisher, and then published outside the United States in a foreign language by yet a third publisher. Articles might be printed in magazines and then reprinted in digests or books by different publishers.

In cases of multiple publishers, you must find out who controls the right to reprint the work in another publication (known as reprint rights). The person or company who controls a work's reprint rights is known as the primary rights holder. Often, the first publisher is the primary rights holder. In the case of a book, this is usually the hardcover publisher. You can find the name of the hardcover publisher by searching an online bookstore such as Amazon (www.amazon.com) or Barnes & Noble (www.barnesandnoble. com) using the title or author of the book.

If the hardcover publisher tells you that it does not have the right to reprint the work, ask if the publisher knows whom you should contact. If the publisher doesn't know, contact the author. (Contacting and negotiating with authors is discussed below.)

Also, keep in mind that the primary rights holder might control rights in only one country. If you intend to reproduce a work outside that country, you might need to seek additional permission.

For example, one rights holder may have the right to publish a work in the United

States, another in Great Britain, and yet another in Canada. If the work for which you're seeking permission will be distributed in the United States, Great Britain, and Canada, you will need permission from all three rights holders. The primary rights holder can often lead you to foreign rights holders. If not, information about foreign publishers can be located in the publication *International Literary Market Place*.

Contact the Author

If the publisher doesn't own the rights you need, it might be able to put you in contact with the author by forwarding your request to the author or, if the author is deceased, to the author's estate. For privacy purposes, it's unlikely that the publisher will give you the author's address or phone number.

You might be able to locate an author using public sources, such as the Authors Registry (www.authorsregistry.org), which maintains a directory of authors and will search for one or two names, usually free of charge. Information about over 1,000 non-fiction writers may be found through the American Society of Journalists and Authors (www.asja.org).

Also, the University of Texas (http://norman.hrc.utexas.edu/watch) maintains a searchable database entitled WATCH (Writers, Artists, and Their Copyright Holders). This database contains the names and addresses of copyright holders or contact persons for authors and artists whose works are housed in libraries and archives in North America and the United Kingdom. The WATCH database also contains limited information on whether an author's or artist's copyrighted work has entered the public domain.

Educational Copying and Coursepacks

Some types of copying for educational purposes are allowed without requiring permission. However, this does not extend to the wholesale copying of articles for classroom use in coursepacks. The Copyright Clearance Center (CCC) (www.copyright.com) has a special program that assists educators in obtaining permission to include works in both paper and electronic coursepacks.

If the rights for the text are owned by two or more authors, you will need to obtain permission from only one of them—provided that your use is nonexclusive and for U.S. or North American rights. Nonexclusive means that other people can use the text for the same purpose as you. If you obtain permission from one of several coauthors, your permission agreement should include a statement that the rights holder has the authority to grant the rights in the agreement. For example, include a statement like "Licensor warrants that it has the right to grant permission." (This language is included in the sample licenses at the end of this chapter.) This provision places you in a better legal position if a dispute arises over your right to use the material.

Regional Rights Versus Foreign Language Rights

The territory in which a publication is distributed and the language in which it is published involve two separate rights. In other words, reprint rights are sold language by language and territory by territory. When dealing with U.S. publishers, unless you specifically ask for reprint rights in a foreign language, you will only be given the right to reprint the work in English in the territory specified. This means, for example, that acquiring "world" rights is not the same as acquiring rights in all languages. Rather, it means you have the right to publish the work in English throughout the world.

Be specific in your requests and permission agreements, and keep your fees low by asking for only the rights you need. If your work will only be published in English, don't ask for foreign language rights. For example, if your magazine is distributed primarily in the United States and Canada, you probably only need one-time North American rights: the right to publish the work one time in the United States and Canada in English.

However, if you print a French language edition for Canadian readers, you would need one-time North American rights and French language rights.

Distributing Photocopies at Work Might Be an Infringement

Many businesses attempt to save money by copying an article from a journal, periodical, or book and distributing it to employees or outside clients without seeking permission. Such unauthorized copies can be made electronically through email, on a company website, or by photocopying. Though common, such copying is a violation of copyright law if done without permission. (See Chapter 9, "Using Other Authors' Words.")

Permission to copy and distribute materials can be acquired directly from the publisher or from the Copyright Clearance Center (www.copyright.com). The CCC provides individual-permission services (as well as "repertory" or "blanket" licensing services), including an automated transactional reporting service called "RightsLink." In some cases, a business can obtain an annual blanket license that permits unlimited copying from the CCC's collection of 1.75 million works. These blanket licenses are based on the type of industry and the number of employees for whom photocopies will be made. For example, law firms might pay a blanket license fee of $150 per year for each professional employee.

For details on copying for educational purposes, see "Educational Copying and Coursepacks," above.

You will need permission from all of the coauthors in any of the following cases:

- You want to use the text on an exclusive basis—meaning you are the only person who can use the text for a specific purpose.
- You want to use the text on a worldwide, nonexclusive basis—because some countries require consent of all co-owners even for nonexclusive uses.
- You want to use the text for a commercial purpose, to sell a service or product—for example, you want to include a quotation from a book in an advertisement (but simply using the text in a book or an article you're writing for money is not considered to be a commercial purpose).

Special Situations

Finding rights holders for certain types of text, such as interviews, letters, and speeches, can prove a little tricky. Below are suggestions for getting permission to use these types of works, as well as unpublished and out-of-print texts.

Interviews

If you want to use an interview from a magazine or book, contact the publisher of the book or magazine. To use a written transcript of an interview from a radio or television show, contact the network or station that originally aired the show. For interviews first published on a website, contact the owner of the site, usually indicated on the bottom of the home or index page.

If you seek permission to use a transcript of a television or radio interview, most stations have permissions departments that will furnish you a printed version. Sometimes you can download interview transcripts from the station's website. If you want to use the actual audio or audiovisual recording of an interview, you will need to obtain the consent of the person or company who recorded the material, often the radio or television station that initially broadcast it.

If the publisher, website owner, or television or radio station is not the rights holder and cannot lead you to the rights holder, try to locate the interviewer through one of the author resources listed earlier in this chapter.

On occasion, determining the rights holder of an interview can get messy. In some cases, such as celebrity interviews, the interview subject might have placed restrictions on the use of interview material. In other situations, the interview subject may seek to prevent republication of the interview, claiming copyright ownership of his or her responses. A publication might write to you stating the following: "We are unable to grant your request because our publication holds no rights to the reuse of this material. Quotations that appear within the text remain proprietary to the speaker."

Unfortunately, sometimes a publication will provide you the interview text even if they don't own the rights to it. If you reprint the text, the interview subject could sue you for unauthorized reproduction of his or her remarks. To deal with this possibility, when seeking permission to reprint an interview, ask if there is a written consent by the interview subject on file and, if so, ask for a copy. If there is no release, ask if the rights holder is willing to sign a written assurance that it has the authority to grant the rights you need. Such a document should state: "Licensor warrants that it has the right to grant permission." This will not shield you from liability as effectively as a signed release from the interview subject, but it does provide you with some legal protection. If the interview subject later files a lawsuit, you will have a stronger case against the licensor (the rights holder) for breach of the written assurance it gave you. If you are still worried about whether you have the right to reproduce the interview, your only option is to seek a release from the interview subject.

Letters

The writer of a letter is usually the owner of the copyright in the letter. However, there are two exceptions to this rule: Letters written by employees within the course of employment are owned by the employer, and letters written by federal employees within the course of employment are in the public domain.

Don't assume that the recipient of the letter owns the rights you need. The recipient owns only the physical letter itself. For example, the owner of a letter written by Elvis Presley could sell the physical letter itself, but only the Estate of Elvis Presley could grant rights to reproduce the text of the letter. And don't assume you can use an unpublished letter, no matter how old, without permission. Review the section below, on unpublished works, first.

Speeches

Not all speeches are protected by copyright. Copyright law protects a speech only if it is written down or recorded ("fixed") and if the writing or recording was done with the speechwriter's permission. If a speaker improvises a speech and his or her words are not written down or recorded with his or her authority, the speech has no copyright protection. Both criteria, fixation (recording) and authorization, are necessary. If the text of a speech is not fixed with the authorization of the speaker, you are free to use it without violating copyright law.

Determining Whether a Speech Has Been Published

If a speech is protected by copyright, it is important to determine whether the text of the speech has been published, because works that have not been published enjoy longer periods of copyright protection. Giving a speech or lecture in public does not amount to "publication." Legally, publication occurs only when copies of the speech or lecture are distributed to the public.

This rule was fortified in a case involving Martin Luther King, Jr.'s, "I Have a Dream" speech. A federal court of appeals ruled that Reverend King's 1963 performance of the speech to 200,000 people (and simultaneous broadcast over radio and television) did not amount to publication of the speech. (*Estate of Martin Luther King, Jr., Inc. v. CBS, Inc.*, 194 F.3d 1211 (11th Cir. 1999).)

Who Owns the Copyright?

If a speech is written down before it's given, the author usually owns the copyright (assuming the author also delivered the speech—see below for rules on ghostwriters). However, if the speech was written as part of an employment obligation—for example, a speech written by the president of Apple Computer for a shareholders' meeting—the author's employer owns the speech. If the speech was written by a federal government employee as part of his or her employment—for example, a speech by the Secretary of the Treasury to Wall Street investors—it is in the public domain. If the speech was ghostwritten—written by someone other than the speaker—the ghostwriter owns

the rights, unless the ghostwriter was the speaker's employee or transferred the rights to the speaker (or someone else) under a written agreement.

If the speech was given extemporaneously (improvised, not written down in advance) but recorded with the speaker's permission, the author/speaker usually owns the copyright in the speech itself, the same way as if it was written down (as described above). But, the recording of the speech belongs to the people who recorded it— for example, a TV station news crew or a newspaper reporter. A video, film, or sound recording of a speech is a copyrighted work in its own right, owned by the person who made the work. However, a verbatim, written transcription of the speech—made, for example, by a newspaper reporter at the scene—is not separately copyrightable, because the author/speaker owns the speech (but not the recording of it).

If the speech was recorded, you'll need to obtain permission from both the author/speaker and the recorder of the speech to use the recorded copy of the speech. The same rule holds true whenever you want to use a sound recording, film, or video of a speech, instead of the written text.

If you cannot locate the speaker, contact the organization that sponsored the event. Often you can find the full text of a speech reprinted on the Internet, so a search engine may help you locate the rights holder.

Orphan Works

One problem that constantly bedevils people who want to obtain permission to use copyrighted works is when the copyright owner cannot be identified or located. This is particularly common for older works with little economic value. Such works are often called "orphan works." The Copyright Office completed two studies of the problem in 2006 and 2015 and issued two reports ("Report on Orphan Works" (2006), "Orphan Works and Mass Digitization: A Report of the Register of Copyrights" (2015), available at www.copyright.gov).

The Copyright Office has recommended the enactment of legislation to protect users of orphan works from copyright infringement lawsuits. Under the proposal, a person who uses an orphan work without permission would have to pay no more than "reasonable compensation," if the work's owner later surfaces and complains, provided that such user (1) performed a good-faith search to identify and locate the owner before the work was used, (2) filed a Notice of Use with the Copyright Office, (3) provided attribution to the copyright owner, if reasonable under the circumstances, and (4) included a (yet-to-be-devised) orphan works symbol with any distribution, display, or performance of the work. To date, this proposed legislation has not been enacted by Congress.

Out-of-Print Works

Just because a book or magazine is out of print does not mean that its copyright has run out. Your use, without permission, may still amount to an infringement. Therefore, if you intend to use text from an out-of-print publication, start by contacting the publisher. A good way to find the name of the publisher is through online bookstores, such as Amazon and Barnes & Noble, which have extensive listings of out-of-print books and publishers.

Locating the copyright owner of out-of-print works becomes more complicated if the publisher no longer exists. Authors often own the rights to their out-of-print works because publishing contracts often return rights to the author if the publisher stops selling the book. If your search for the publisher and author leads to dead ends, you will have to perform more extensive copyright research or hire a copyright search firm to determine the current owner.

If you're not sure whether a book is out of print, try consulting *Books in Print* (www.booksinprint.com). This massive online database is searchable (for a hefty subscription fee). You may be able to access it for free through a local or college library.

Unpublished Text

As with an out-of-print work, do not assume that an unpublished work is free to use. The rules regarding copyright

Titles and Short Phrases May Be Protected Under Trademark Law

Titles and short phrases are not protected under copyright law. Despite their public domain status, names, titles, and short phrases can be protected under trademark laws. A trademark is any word, photograph, or symbol that is used to identify specific products or services.

Permission is not required to use a trademark in any of the following cases:

- Your use is for informational or editorial purposes—for instance, you use the trademark as part of an article or story.
- Your use is part of accurate comparative product statements.

You do need to obtain permission in these cases:

- Your use is commercial and likely to create confusion among consumers.
- Your use is commercial and reflects poorly on or "tarnishes" the trademark.
- You modify the trademark.

Take, for example, the slogan "Just Do It." Because the phrase does not qualify for copyright protection, you can use it in a song lyric, movie, or book. However, because Nike has a trademark for the phrase, you cannot use it in a manner that is likely to confuse consumers into thinking that you are associated with Nike or that tarnishes Nike's reputation.

protection for unpublished works depend on if and when the author died and, in the event the work was ultimately published, the date of publication. (See Chapter 8 for a detailed discussion of copyright duration for unpublished works.)

As you can imagine, it can be quite difficult to locate copyright owners for unpublished works, because there is no publisher to contact. Copyright Office records might help, if the unpublished work was registered. Determining ownership for unpublished works is especially difficult if the author is deceased and the author's estate or heirs are hard to track down. The WATCH database (https://norman.hrc.utexas.edu/watch) might help you track down the author of an unpublished work.

ISBNs and ISSNs

ISBNs (International Standard Book Numbers) and ISSNs (International Standard Serial Numbers) identify books and magazines and are sometimes required when seeking permission. ISBNs are used for books; ISSNs are used for magazines, journals, newsletters, and other serial publications. These numbers can be found on or near the title or copyright page or near the publication's UPC bar code. Because several numbers can be printed on the bar code, look for the number preceded by either "ISSN" or "ISBN."

Using Text From Advertisements

Text in advertisements is usually owned by the corporate sponsor of the advertisement. However, in some cases it may be owned by the advertising agency or publication that prepared the ad. To locate an ad agency or corporate advertiser, try using an online search engine or *The Standard Directory of Advertising Agencies* (www.redbooks.com).

When You Can't Find the Rights Holder

If you've used the techniques discussed in this chapter and cannot find the person or business whose permission you need, you have a few options. You could try to delve deeper into copyright records at the Copyright Office. These records might help you determine who owns the work currently, because many copyright transfers are recorded with the Copyright Office.

The Copyright Office's renewal records will reveal if the publisher has failed to renew the copyright in the work—which puts the work in the public domain if it was published in the United States less than 95 years ago but before 1964. Chapter 8 offers guidance on the three most common methods of searching Copyright Office records: hiring a search firm, paying the Copyright Office to do the search for you, or searching the Copyright Office records using the Internet.

If you still cannot locate the rights holder, it may be time to consider using the material without permission. As you might imagine, this poses risks. If the rights holder finds out about your use, you (or your publisher) could receive an email or letter from the rights holder or an attorney demanding that you stop using the material (known as a cease and desist letter).

Before you use any material without permission, you should answer two questions:

- How likely is it that the rights holder will see your work?
- What is your potential legal liability if you are subject to a claim of copyright infringement?

Giving Credit Where It Is Due

Your permission agreement will detail your obligation to include a written credit for the author or publisher. Make sure the credit is correct as required in your permission agreement. This is a serious subject between you and the rights holder. Unless otherwise required under your permission agreement, you can group credits together on the copyright page. For example:

- "Elvis's Toothbrush" originally appeared in *Meet the Stars* © 2019, by Missy Laws. Reprinted by permission of Ross Books.
- "You Can Collect Toilet Paper" originally appeared in *Antique and Collecting Magazine* © 2021, by Harriet L. Rinker. Reprinted by permission of the author.

Likelihood of Discovery

The likelihood that the author or rights holder will discover your unauthorized use depends on the extent of the distribution of your work and the popularity of the rights holder's work. For example, if you use an excerpt from an obscure writer's work in a book that sells under 2,000 copies, the odds are in your favor that the writer will not learn of your use. On the other hand, if you use a well-known quote from a famous play in an article for a major magazine that has millions of readers online and off, your use has a much greater chance of being discovered. The more likely it is that the rights holder will see your use of the copyrighted work, the more caution you should take in proceeding without the owner's permission.

Potential Liability

When using material without authorization, there is always a risk and potential liability—meaning responsibility under the law for which you may have to pay money damages. The amount of risk depends on several factors, described below. Generally, if you can show that you made a good-faith effort to search for the copyright owner, you will probably only have to pay the rights holder the standard fee within the trade for a similar use. However, there are exceptions to this general rule. A disgruntled copyright owner may refuse to grant permission and insist that you halt distribution of your work. Alternatively, a copyright owner may demand an exorbitant payment and drag you into court.

Consider the following risk factors when proceeding without permission:

- **The investment in the project using the copyrighted work.** The more money spent on your project, the greater the risk in the event that you must halt publication. It might not be worth risking a $100,000 project for the sake of using one unauthorized illustration.
- **The diligence of your copyright search.** The more diligently you searched, the less risk. A thorough search demonstrates that you acted in good faith and could demonstrate that it's not possible to locate the copyright owner.
- **The nature of your work and how easy it would be to remove the offending portion.** If it is easy for you to remove the unauthorized material from your work, less risk is involved. For example, a photo posted on a website can be easily removed, while one printed in a book cannot be removed without wasting any remaining inventory and reprinting the whole thing.
- **The nature of the copyrighted portion and how easy it is to replace.** Although not as important as the other factors, your risk analysis should incorporate how hard it will be to replace the material in the event that you must remove it.

What Does "Publication" Mean?

Publication occurs for copyright purposes when the copyright owner, or someone acting with the copyright owner's authority, distributes one or more copies of the work to the general public or offers the work for distribution, public display, or public performance. Copies do not need to be sold for publication to occur—they can be leased, rented, loaned, or even given away, so long as the work has been made available to the general public.

Publication does *not* occur when:

- Copies of the work are made but not distributed.
- The text of the work is performed publicly (for example, a speech is presented).
- The text of the work is displayed (for example, in a slide presentation or on television).

A "limited publication" is also not considered a publication. A limited publication occurs if copies are distributed only to:

- a selected group of people
- for a limited purpose, and
- without the right of further reproduction, distribution, or sale.

For example, it is not a publication when an author sends copies of a manuscript to several publishers seeking publication.

EXAMPLE: Jim publishes a newsletter for seafood restaurants and wants to use material from a cookbook entitled *Steamed Eels*, published in 1977. Jim was unable to locate the publisher; his letters to the publisher were returned with a notice that the company had moved with no forwarding address. Jim later learned from a distributor that the publisher had gone bankrupt in 1983. Jim paid the Copyright Office to perform a search, which turned up only an address for the author who died in 1986. Jim wrote to the author's last known address, but his letter was returned as undeliverable. Jim searched on the Internet for people with the same last name as the author and posted requests for information at several cooking websites. Jim documented this search and then researched the standard fee for a similar text license. Based on this, Jim proceeded to use the material without permission, citing *Steamed Eels* and its author in his work. In the event that the copyright owner turns up, Jim is prepared to pay a reasonable fee for using the work. Jim's risk is relatively low because his search was very diligent and, given the obscurity and relatively low value of the work he's copying, the financial risk for infringement is low.

When weighing risk factors, consider the expense and aggravation of the two worst-case scenarios: litigation and halting distribution of your work:

- **Litigation.** Any "wronged" party can file a lawsuit regardless of the merits of their claim. A frivolous lawsuit can drag on for months, and the attorneys' fees can amount to several thousand dollars. Even worse, a lawsuit based on a nonfrivolous claim (one in which there is a reasonable basis for the claim) could proceed for years, and your attorneys' fees can soar into the tens of thousands of dollars.

- **Halting distribution.** If a copyright owner forces you to halt distribution, you face losing the money spent on the printing or distribution of the work, as well as the additional expenses to reprint and redistribute it. In addition, your costs might include recovery of unsold copies from distributors, notification to purchasers, and loss of revenue from advertisers. (See Chapter 10 for a detailed discussion of copyright infringement.)

Negotiating Text Permission and Fees

Obtaining permission to use text involves a four-step process:

1. First, you must clearly and specifically identify what material you want to use and how to use it

2. Next, you must send a permission request letter to the publisher or rights holder.

3. Then you and the publisher or rights holder must negotiate a permission fee, if any.

4. Finally, you must get a signed permission agreement. Your permission request letter or email could work as the agreement, or you might need to draft a separate permission agreement. Alternatively, the publisher or other rights holder might have a permissions form to use.

Make a Request to the Rights Holder

After you identify the material and rights you need, you should send a letter or email to the rights holder requesting permission to use the material. Your permission request letter or email should provide all of the details about the text you want to use, how you expect to use it, and the permission you seek.

Keep Your Rights Request Simple

Most text permission requests are for the right to reproduce all or part of a work. For example, say you want to reproduce text in your magazine or on your website. If that's all you need, keep your rights request short and simple.

EXAMPLE: Chris wants to reprint a newspaper column on his website. The request he sends is basically as follows: "I am creating a website for the Association of Barking Dog Observers (ABDO) and would like to post the January 20, 2020, Dave Barry column at our site for one month. I would like to know how much it would cost to post this column. Also, I would appreciate it if you could fax or email me a sample permission agreement."

There are two different types of request letters or emails you can use:

- One type of request letter/email simply informs the rights holder of your needs and anticipates that you and the rights holder will later complete and sign a separate permission agreement.

- The other type of request letter/email serves as both a request and a simple permission agreement for your use of the material. The copyright owner reviews the request and gives you permission by signing and returning the letter. If an email is used, the copyright owner prints it out, signs it by hand, and returns a physical or scanned copy to you. This approach is recommended for simple requests to reproduce text.

The second type of letter—that serves as both a request and an agreement—is discussed later in this chapter. This section looks at a basic permission request letter that contemplates that the parties will negotiate and sign a separate permission agreement letter. You'll find a sample Copyright Permission Request Letter below.

Whichever type of request letter you use, include a copy of the text that you wish to reproduce with your letter.

FORM

You can download a Copyright Permission Request Letter (and all other forms in this book) from this book's companion page on Nolo.com; see the appendix for the link.

Negotiate Permission Fees

Next you'll need to work out how much you'll have to pay for the rights you've requested. The publishing industry does not have standard rates for using text. Some magazine and newspaper publishers use fixed rates for common permission situations and can furnish you with what is known as a rate card listing such fees. In other instances, the owner won't be able to assess the fee until after reviewing your request. Below, we've summarized some fee information.

Using Text in a Book

The fees for using text in a book are commonly affected by:

- the number of copies to be printed: Pricing is often calculated at print runs of 5,000, 10,000, and 100,000 copies.

- whether the work will be distributed in electronic and audiobook editions

- the price of the book

- territorial and language rights: World rights can cost double or triple the cost of U.S. rights alone. A rights holder may charge 25% more for permission to reprint in a second language.

- the duration of the use: Will it be limited to a term of years or for the entire life of the work?

- whether the use is for a nonprofit purpose

- placement of the text within the book: For example, a half-column quote placed at the beginning of a chapter or book might result in a higher fee, and

- whether the licensed material will be used in related products, such as custom editions, abridgements, or teacher editions.

Generally, you should expect to pay anywhere from $100 to $400 for use of text in a book, depending on the size of the print run and your rights request. By way of example, one national magazine charges $100 per column of text (there are three full columns to a standard page) for use in a book with a print run over 5,000 copies, and $125 for print runs over 100,000. Sometimes, the fees might seem high. For example, a professor who sought to use four lines from a poem by Emily Dickinson was quoted a fee of $200 by a university press. (Note: Because of copyright rules regarding unpublished works, not all of Dickinson's work is in the public domain.)

Using Text on Your Website

The fees for website uses are evolving—meaning nobody is quite sure how much to charge. The fees are affected by:

- the extent of advertising on the website
- whether the site is intended primarily to provide information to the public (sometimes referred to as an "editorial" purpose). The rights holder might want to know whether the purpose of the site is to provide information or sell products or services.
- whether the organization sponsoring the site is a nonprofit

- the number of visitors to the site per day, and
- whether the text will be used in a print publication as well as the website. For example, will you use the text in a magazine and on the magazine's website?

A national magazine may charge between $100 and $500 to allow you to post an article on a website, with higher fees being charged for popular commercial sites—for example, posting a review of a movie at a high-traffic Hollywood studio website. Many publishers limit the length of time for these permissions to one year or less.

Minimizing Fees

It's possible to get fees lowered or avoid them entirely by doing any combination of the following:

- seeking a one-time nonexclusive use, as long you are not planning to write future editions or different versions of your work
- narrowing your permission request. The narrower your request, the less you might have to pay. For example, don't ask for "worldwide rights, all languages" if you only need "United States rights, English."
- acquiring multiple items from one publisher. Often, you can reduce your per-item fee by licensing more than one work from the same publisher.
- paying up front. You may be able to lower the fee by offering to pay up front instead of waiting 30 or 60 days.

Copyright Permission Request Letter

Dear Ms. Hitchcock:

I am writing to you about your article, "Why I Hate Surround Sound." *New Audio Magazine* informed me that you were the owner of rights in the article. I'm writing a book entitled *DDA: Death to Digital Audio*, and I'd like to use an abridged version of your article in the book. The details are as follows:

> Title of Your Article (the "Selection"): "Why I Hate Surround Sound"
> Author: Michelle Hitchcock
> Source of Article: *New Audio Magazine*
> Volume, Issue, ISSN: Vol 23, No. 6, ISSN 1099-8722
> Number of Pages: 4

My intended use of the Selection is as follows:

> Title (the "Work"): *DDA: Death to Digital Audio*
> Publisher: Cumberland Books
> Type of Publication: Book (trade paperback)
> Rights Needed: (1) the right to shorten or modify the Selection (I'll send you a copy of the abridged version for your approval); and (2) the nonexclusive right to reproduce the Selection in all editions of the trade paperback book, *DDA: Death to Digital Audio*.
> Estimated First Print Run: 6,000
> Expected Price: $12.95
> Projected Published Date: January 20xx

I'm seeking these rights for myself and my publisher, Cumberland Books, and for any company that might acquire my rights to the book in the future. Please review this request and let me know the terms for licensing rights as well as the required credit. Once you let me know, I can prepare a permission agreement. Thank you very much.

Sincerely,

Roberta Weston

Roberta Weston

Execute a Permission Agreement

Once the rights holder has agreed to grant permission and you've agreed on a fee, you need to complete and sign a written text permission agreement. There are two ways you can go about this:

- You can convert your permission request letter into a permission agreement (a "permission letter agreement").
- You can draft and execute a detailed permission agreement that should suffice for most text-licensing situations (a "permissions agreement").

This section provides samples of each.

Sample Permission Letter Agreement

This short-form agreement is similar to those used by many magazines. As a variation on the permission request letter above, it is intended for authors and publishers who only want to reprint text, whether in printed form or on a website. This approach—turning the request letter into an agreement—is recommended if your request is simple and you have agreed upon the terms. For example, if you want to include several paragraphs from an essay on your website, newsletter, or book, this form should be sufficient.

Does the Agreement Have to Be in Writing?

Unless you have an "exclusive" agreement, (see Chapter 7, "Transferring Copyright Ownership"), your license or permission agreement does not have to be in writing to be valid. A nonexclusive oral permission may be enforceable as long as it qualifies as a contract under general contract law principles. However, there are limits on oral agreements. For example, in most states, an oral agreement is valid for only one year. Also, it can be very difficult to prove that an oral agreement exists, not to mention to prove its terms. Because of these limitations, do not rely on an oral licensing or permission agreement—get it in writing.

What If the Copyright Owner Furnishes the Permission Agreement?

Many publishers' permissions departments and other copyright owners will provide their own permission agreements. Read such an agreement carefully. If it contains provisions you can't understand, ask the publisher to explain them or seek legal help.

FORM
You can download a Text Permission Letter Agreement (and all other forms in this book) from this book's companion page on Nolo.com; see the appendix for the link.

Instructions for Permission Letter Agreement

If you use this form, you don't need a separate request letter (as discussed in the previous section). Complete the agreement as if you were preparing the worksheet or a request letter. Below are some additional explanations for various sections:

- At the end of the *Licensor Information* section, the provides a space where the licensor (the person from whom you are requesting permission) can indicate if he or she does not own the rights you are seeking. If this section is filled in, the licensor cannot grant you the necessary permission, so you will need to obtain permission from whomever the licensor indicates in the blank.
- It is possible that the licensor will want to grant rights only for a specific print run or for a specific period of time. Or, the licensor may not want to grant you permission to transfer the rights to someone else. In this event, modify the grant to reflect these requests—for example, strike the language regarding "successors, licensees, and assigns."

- It's possible that you will want more rights than are granted in this letter agreement. For example, you might need rights for all foreign translations and derivative rights and you might want these rights in all media. If you want a broader grant of rights, you can use the Licensor's Approval of Request language below to replace the language in the agreement above. Be aware that the licensor might object to such a broad grant, causing a delay in the permissions process.

Licensor's Approval of Request
I warrant that I am the owner of rights for the Selection and have the right to grant permission to republish the materials as specified above. I grant to Licensee and Licensee's successors, licensees, and assigns the nonexclusive worldwide right to adapt and republish the Selection in all languages, in all editions of the Work, and in all versions derived from the Work in all media now known or hereafter devised.

TIP
Make the process convenient for the copyright owner. When sending your permission letter agreement, always enclose a stamped, self-addressed envelope for the licensor's convenience.

Text Permission Letter Agreement

To _____ ("Licensor"):

I am writing to you to request permission to use the following material.

Licensor Information

Title of Text (the "Selection"): _____

Author: _____

Source publication (or product from which it came): _____

If from a periodical, the ISSN, volume, issue, and date. If from a book, the ISBN:

_____

If from the Internet, the entire URL: _____

Number of pages (or actual page numbers) to be used: _____

If you are not the copyright holder or if worldwide rights must be obtained elsewhere, please indicate that information: _____

Licensee Publication Information

The Selection will appear in the following publication(s) (the "Work"): _____

_____

Title: _____

Name of publisher or sponsor ("Licensee"): _____

Author(s): _____

Type of publication: _____

If print publication, estimated print run: _____

If print publication, projected publishing date: _____

If print publication, expected price: $_____

If website, the URL: _____

If website, estimated monthly hits: _____

If website, the posting date: _____

Rights needed: _____

Text Permission Letter Agreement (continued)

Fee

Licensee shall pay a fee of $ _____ to Licensor at the following address:

_____

upon publication of the Work or within 6 months of executing this agreement, whichever is earlier.

Credit

A standard credit line including your company name will appear where the Selection is used. If you have a special credit line you would prefer, indicate it below:

_____

Samples

Upon publication, Licensee shall furnish _____ copies of the Work to Licensor.

Signed by Licensee: _____

Name: _____

Title: _____

Address: _____

Date: _____

Licensor's Approval of Request

I warrant that I am the owner of rights for the Selection and have the right to grant the permission to republish the materials as specified above. I grant to Licensee and Licensee's successors, licensees, and assigns the nonexclusive worldwide right to republish the Selection in all editions of the Work.

Permission Granted by: _____

Signed by Licensor: _____

Name: _____

Title: _____

Address: _____

Date: _____

Sample Permission Agreement

The permission agreement on the next page is intended for authors and publishers who are negotiating for more than basic reproduction rights—for example, assembling an anthology of short stories, assembling contributions for an encyclopedia, or acquiring multiple or foreign rights to reproduce a work:

- In the introductory paragraph, insert the names of the licensor (the party who owns the material) and the licensee (you or the person who is seeking permission).
- In the Licensor Information and Licensee Publication sections, fill in the blank spaces.
- In the Grant of Rights section, complete the grant to reflect the rights that you have negotiated.
- Complete the Territory section to reflect the regions in which you have acquired rights—the World, the United States, Canada, or whatever region you have agreed upon. For more help, review Chapter 8.
- In the Fees section, check the appropriate boxes and complete the information.
- Complete the Credit and Samples section per your agreement with the licensor.
- A warranty is a contractual promise made by the licensor. Some licensors do not want to make promises, particularly promises that the work does not infringe any third parties' copyright or other rights. You might have to modify the Warranty section or strike it entirely if the licensor objects.

 FORM

You can download a Text Permission Agreement (and all other forms in this book) from this book's companion page on Nolo.com; see the appendix for the link.

Text Permission Agreement

_____ ("Licensor")
is the owner of rights for certain textual material defined below (the "Selection").
_____ ("Licensee") wants to
acquire the right to use the Selection as specified in this agreement (the "Agreement").

Licensor Information

Title of Text (the "Selection"): _____

Author: _____

Source publication (or product from which it came): _____

If from a periodical, the ISSN, volume, issue, and date. If from a book, the ISBN:

_____

If from the Internet, the entire URL: _____

Number of pages or actual page numbers to be used: _____

Licensee Publication Information

The Selection will appear in the following publication(s) (the "Work"): _____

_____

(check if applicable and fill in blanks)

☐ book—title: _____

☐ periodical—title: _____

☐ event handout—title of event: _____

☐ website—URL: _____

☐ other—title: _____

Name of publisher or sponsor: _____

Author(s): _____

Estimated date(s) of publication or posting: _____

Estimated number of copies to be printed or produced (if a book, the estimated
first print run): _____

If for sale, the price: $ _____

If copies are free to attendees of a program, the cost of program: _____

If a website, the average number of visitors per month: _____

Text Permission Agreement (continued)

Grant of Rights

Licensor grants to Licensee and Licensee's successors and assigns, the: (*select one*)

☐ nonexclusive

☐ exclusive

Right to reproduce and distribute the Selection in: (*select all that apply*)

☐ the current edition of the Work

☐ all editions of the Work

☐ all foreign language versions of the Work

☐ all derivative versions of the Work

☐ all media now known or later devised

☐ promotional materials published and distributed in conjunction with the Work

☐ other rights _____

Territory

The rights granted under this Agreement shall be for _____

_____ (the "Territory").

Fees

Licensee shall pay Licensor as follows: (*select one and fill in appropriate blanks*)

☐ **Flat Fee.** Licensee shall pay Licensor a flat fee of $_____ as full payment for all rights granted. Payment shall be made:

    ☐ upon execution of this Agreement

    ☐ upon publication

☐ **Royalties and Advance.** Licensee agrees to pay Licensor a royalty of _____ % of net sales. Net sales are defined as gross sales (the gross invoice amount billed customers) less quantity discounts and returns actually credited. Licensee agrees to pay Licensor an advance against royalties of $_____ upon execution of this Agreement. Licensee shall pay Licensor within 30 days after the end of each quarter. Licensee shall furnish an accurate statement of sales during that quarter. Licensor shall have the right to inspect Licensee's books upon reasonable notice.

Text Permission Agreement (continued)

Credit and Samples

(check if applicable and fill in blanks)

☐ **Credit.** All versions of the Work that include the Selection shall contain the following statement: _____

☐ **Samples.** Upon publication, Licensee shall furnish _____ copies of the Work to Licensor.

Warranty

Licensor warrants that it has the right to grant permission for the uses of the Selection as specified above and that the Selection does not infringe the rights of any third parties.

Miscellaneous

This Agreement may not be amended except in a written document signed by both parties. If a court finds any provision of this Agreement invalid or unenforceable, the remainder of this Agreement shall be interpreted so as best to effect the intent of the parties. This Agreement shall be governed by and interpreted in accordance with the laws of the State of _____. This Agreement expresses the complete understanding of the parties with respect to the subject matter and supersedes all prior representations and understandings.

Licensor _____   Licensee _____

By: _____   By: _____

Name: _____   Name: _____

Title: _____   Title: _____

Address: _____   Address: _____

Date: _____   Date: _____

                                         Tax ID # _____

Help Beyond This Book

Hopefully, this book provides a good basic background on most aspects of copyright of interest to writers. Additional general information can be obtained for free from the Copyright Office. The Copyright Office publishes a series of pamphlets (called circulars) on many copyright topics. You can download digital copies of all the circulars from the Copyright Office website at www.copyright.gov.

If you have any questions that aren't answered by this book, a two-step process is suggested. First, take a look at one or more intensive background resources. These might contain all the information you need. If not, access the primary copyright resources: the copyright statutes, regulations, and case law.

RESOURCE

Recommended reading. Use *Legal Research: How to Find & Understand the Law*, by Stephen Elias and the Editors of Nolo (Nolo), or another basic legal research guide, to help you understand legal citations, how to use a law library, and understand what you find there.

Intensive Background Resources

Following are some recommended resources on copyright law. You can find others in your law library's catalog.

Treatises, encyclopedias, and so on. The most authoritative sources on copyright are two legal treatises: *Nimmer on Copyright* and *Patry on Copyright*. These are multivolume works that contain detailed and thorough discussions of virtually every legal issue concerning copyright. They're available in many university libraries and law libraries.

Each point is supported by exhaustive citations to the relevant legal decisions, sections of the copyright statutes, and Copyright Office regulations where appropriate. By using such resources, you can find citations to the primary copyright materials of interest to you. You should note, however, that such treatises tend to discuss only the *law* of copyright. You will find no how-to discussions. That's why you bought this book.

For the serious copyright student, an excellent one-volume resource is *Copyright: Cases and Materials*, by Robert A. Gorman, Jane C. Ginsburg, and R. Anthony Reese, used to teach law students. It contains the text of virtually every important copyright court decision, the copyright law and other primary materials, excerpts from law review articles, commentary by the authors (nationally recognized authorities on copyright), and other useful materials.

If you're in need of a highly detailed discussion of the public domain—things that are not protected by copyright—refer to *Copyright and the Public Domain*, by Stephen Fishman (Law Journal Press).

If you are interested in copyright protection in the United States for works by foreign authors, or protection in other countries for works by Americans, the best starting point for your research is *International Copyright,* by Paul Goldstein and Bernt Hugenholtz (Oxford University Press).

Copyright Law Reporter. For the most recent information available on copyright, consult the *Copyright Law Reporter,* a monthly service published by Wolters Kluwer. It contains the full text or summaries of recent copyright-related court decisions and relevant discussions of new developments in copyright law. You can find this expensive resource in law libraries.

Law review articles. If you have a very unusual copyright problem that is not covered by *Nimmer, Patry,* or other books on copyright law, or a problem in an area in which the law has changed very recently, the best sources of available information can be articles appearing in scholarly journals called law reviews. You can find citations to all the law review articles on a particular topic by looking under "Copyright" in the *Index to Legal Periodicals* or *Current Law Index.* A key to the abbreviations used in these indexes is located at the front of each index volume. Substantial collections of law reviews are usually found only in large public law libraries or university libraries.

Forms. If you need sample agreements or other forms, consult *Lindey on Entertainment, Publishing and the Arts,* by Alexander Lindey and Michael Landau (Thomson Reuters). The first volume of this four-volume work contains sample forms on every aspect of publishing.

Copyright Office on the Internet

The Copyright Office has a very helpful website (www.copyright.gov). You can read and download frequently requested Copyright Office circulars, announcements, and the most recent proposed and final Copyright Office regulations. You can also read the Compendium of U.S. Copyright Office Practices—a mammoth guide to Copyright Office registration procedures and the copyright law in general.

You can search Copyright Office records, including original and renewal registrations from 1978 to the present.

Primary Source Materials on Copyright

Here's where to go for information straight from a court or regulatory body.

CAUTION

If you attempt legal research yourself, be aware that interpreting statutes and cases can be difficult without legal training and a specific background in the area being researched. Before you act on anything you find in the law library, consult with a knowledgeable attorney.

Statutes. The primary law governing all copyrights in the United States is the Copyright Act of 1976. The Copyright Act is located in Title 17 of the United States Code. A copy of the Copyright Act can be found on the Copyright Office website (www.copyright.gov). On the next page, you'll find a guide listing the sections of Copyright Act.

Regulations. The U. S. Copyright Office has issued regulations that implement the copyright statutes and establish the procedures that must be followed to register a work. These regulations can be found on the Copyright Office website at www.copyright.gov.

Court decisions. There are several ways to find court decisions on a particular legal issue. As mentioned above, intensive background sources, such as *Nimmer on Copyright,* the *Copyright Law Reporter,* and law review articles, contain many case citations. In addition, the United States Code Annotated and United States Code Service both cite and briefly summarize all the decisions relevant to each section of the Copyright Act of 1976. These are located just after each section of the act. You can do free online searches of the full text of court decisions using Google Scholar (https://scholar.google.com). Searches using keywords like "copyright" or "copyright infringement" will yield many relevant cases.

Finding a Copyright Lawyer

Copyright law is a highly specialized field, and copyright attorneys know the area better than other lawyers. If you don't know of a good copyright attorney, you might be able to find one through your publisher, your literary agent, or other writers you know. Writers groups are also an excellent source of referrals to copyright attorneys, and many such groups can be found in the publication *Literary Market Place* (www.literarymarketplace.com).

In addition, attorneys in many cities throughout the country operate volunteer legal aid groups that help artists and writers resolve their legal problems. These groups usually work like this: You'll be asked to pay a small fee to be interviewed by a paralegal or other nonattorney volunteer. If your gross household income is below a specified level (the exact amount varies among the legal aid offices), and you have a problem that requires legal assistance, you will be referred to an attorney who will represent you free of charge (except for direct out-of-pocket expenses such as filing fees, photocopying, long-distance phone calls, and so forth). However, even if you earn too much to qualify for free legal assistance, these groups should be able to refer you to an experienced copyright attorney.

You don't have to use the legal aid group located nearest to where you live. If you don't qualify for free assistance from the

Copyright Act Citation Guide—Title 17 of the United States Code

To avoid numerous footnotes, we have not provided extensive citations to the Copyright Act in the text. Listed below are all the sections of the Copyright Act that have been discussed in this book.

Subject Matter and Scope of Copyright

Sec. 101	Legal definitions of compilation, work made for hire, derivative work, and other copyright terms; works covered by Berne Convention
Sec. 102	General definition of what is protected by copyright
Sec. 103	Extent of protection for compilations and derivative works
Sec. 104	Effect of author's national origin; impact of Berne Convention
Sec. 104A	Copyright renewal
Sec. 105	No copyright in U.S. government works
Sec. 106	Copyright owners' five exclusive rights
Sec. 107	Fair use privilege
Sec. 108	Photocopying by libraries and archives
Sec. 109	First sale rule
Sec. 110	Performances and displays not constituting infringement

Copyright Ownership and Transfer

Sec. 201	General ownership provisions
Sec. 202	Ownership of copyright distinct from ownership of material object
Sec. 203	Termination of transfers and licenses
Sec. 204	Execution of transfers
Sec. 205	Recordation of transfers

Copyright Duration

Sec. 301	Copyright Act preempts other federal and state laws
Sec. 302	Post-1977 works
Sec. 303	Works created but not published before 1978
Sec. 304	Pre-1978 works
Sec. 305	Year-end termination rule

Notice, Deposit, and Registration

Sec. 401	Notice requirements in general
Sec. 403	Notice for works containing U.S. government works
Sec. 404	Notice for contributions to collective works
Sec. 405	Omission of notice
Sec. 406	Error in name or date
Sec. 407	Deposit requirements
Sec. 408–410	Copyright registration
Sec. 411	Registration as prerequisite to infringement suit
Sec. 412	Registration as prerequisite to statutory damages and attorneys' fees

Copyright Infringement and Remedies

Sec. 501	What constitutes copyright infringement
Sec. 502–505	Remedies for infringement
Sec. 506	Criminal liability
Sec. 507	Statute of limitations on infringement suits

group nearest you, a group in a different part of the country might have a higher income-eligibility requirement that you're able to meet. California Lawyers for the Arts has no means test at all. The only drawback to using these volunteer groups is that it usually takes about three to five weeks for a volunteer attorney to get around to helping you.

Paying an Attorney

If you don't qualify for, or are unable to obtain, free legal assistance, you'll quickly discover that experts don't come cheap. Most copyright attorneys charge $250 to $500 per hour. Unless you are wealthy or own a very valuable work, any copyright infringement action is likely to cost more than you can afford to pay out of your own pocket. Filing a case and obtaining a settlement without trial can easily cost $30,000. Taking a copyright infringement case to trial can cost hundreds of thousands of dollars.

However, if your work was timely registered and you win your suit, the judge has discretion to order the defendant to pay your attorneys' fees. The amount of such an award is completely up to the judge; the only restriction is that the award be reasonable. If you have a good case and the defendant can afford to pay such fees and damages, an attorney might agree to take your case on a contingency basis—that is,

collect his or her fees from any damages or fees that the court ultimately awards if your suit is successful.

What about defendants in copyright infringement suits? If you are sued for infringement and prevail at trial, the judge can order the losing plaintiff to pay all or part of your attorneys' fees. In the past, many courts would award such fees to a defendant only if they found that the plaintiff's suit was frivolous or brought in bad faith. But these courts would not require this in making fee awards to plaintiffs. In 1994, the Supreme Court held that this approach was incorrect and that fees must be awarded to plaintiffs and defendants in an evenhanded manner. In other words, the same criteria must be applied to both plaintiffs and defendants. (*Fogerty v. Fantasy, Inc.*, 114 S. Ct. 1023 (1994).)

Intellectual Property Lawyers

Copyright is part of a larger specialty known as intellectual property law, which also includes patents and trademarks. Many lawyers who advertise as intellectual property lawyers can competently handle all three types of cases. But some are primarily patent attorneys who don't put much effort into the copyright side of their practice. If you are shopping for a copyright lawyer, do your best to find someone who specializes primarily in copyrights.

The criteria some courts use to decide whether to award attorneys' fees to the winning side include whether the losing party's suit was frivolous or brought in bad faith, or whether the losing party otherwise acted unreasonably. Many courts will be especially likely to award fees to a prevailing party whose actions helped to advance the copyright law or defend or establish important legal principles.

Copyright and contract information hotline. The New York Volunteer Lawyers for the Arts (www.vlany.org) operates a hotline that authors and artists may call to obtain answers to questions on copyright and publishing contracts. The phone number is 212-319-2787, ext. 1; call between 10 a.m. and 6 p.m. Eastern time, Monday through Friday.

At least 28 states have organizations that provide legal services and information to the arts community at a reduced rate. You can find links to their websites at https:// en.wikipedia.org/wiki/ Volunteer_Lawyers_ for_the_Arts.

How to Use the Downloadable Forms on the Nolo website

Get Forms, Updates, and More at
***The Copyright Handbook's* Companion Page**

You can download all of the forms in this book at *The Copyright Handbook*'s companion page on Nolo's website (free for readers of this book) at:

www.nolo.com/back-of-book/COHA.html

In addition, when there are important changes to the information in this book, we'll post updates at the companion page, as well as podcasts from the author, Stephen Fishman.

This book comes with forms and downloadable files that you can access online at:

www.nolo.com/back-of-book/COHA.html

To use the files, your computer must have specific software programs installed. Here is a list of types of files provided by this book, as well as the software programs you'll need to access them:

- **RTF.** You can open, edit, print, and save these form files with most word processing programs such as Microsoft *Word*.
- **PDF.** You can view these files with Adobe *Reader*, free software from www.adobe.com.

Editing RTFs

Here are some general instructions about editing RTF forms in your word processing program. Refer to the book's instructions and sample agreements for help about what should go in each blank:

- **Underlines.** Underlines indicate where to enter information. After filling in the needed text, delete the underline. In most word processing programs you can do this by highlighting the underlined portion and typing CTRL-U.
- **Bracketed and italicized text.** Bracketed and italicized text indicates instructions. Be sure to remove all instructional text before you finalize your document.
- **Optional text.** Optional text gives you the choice to include or exclude text. Delete any optional text you don't want to use. Renumber numbered items, if necessary.
- **Alternative text.** Alternative text gives you the choice between two or more text options. Delete those options you don't want to use. Renumber numbered items, if necessary.
- **Signature lines.** Signature lines should appear on a page with at least some text from the document itself.

Every word processing program uses different commands to open, format, save, and print documents, so refer to your software's help documents for help using your program. Nolo cannot provide technical support for questions about how to use your computer or your software.

> **CAUTION**
> In accordance with U.S. copyright laws, the forms provided by this book are for your personal use only.

List of Forms

The following files are RTFs:

Form Name	File Name
Work-Made-for-Hire Agreement	Agreement.rtf
Copyright Assignment	Assignment.rtf
Collaboration Agreement	Collaboration.rtf
Copyright License	Copyright.rtf
Counter-Notification in Response to Claim of Copyright Infringement	Counter.rtf
Work-Made-for-Hire Letter Agreement	Letter.rtf
Notice of Claimed Copyright Infringement	Notice.rtf
Copyright Permission Request Letter	Permission.rtf
Text Permission Agreement	TextAgreement.rtf
Text Permission Letter Agreement	TextLetter.rtf
Fair Use Checklist	FairUse.rtf

The following files are PDFs:

Form Name	File Name
Form NLA	nla.pdf
Form NLA/CON	nlacon.pdf

Index

NOLO *Save 15% off your next order*

Register your Nolo purchase, and we'll send you a
coupon for 15% off your next Nolo.com order!

Nolo.com/customer-support/productregistration

On Nolo.com you'll also find:

Books & Software

Nolo publishes hundreds of great books and software programs for consumers and
business owners. Order a copy, or download an ebook version instantly, at Nolo.com.

Online Forms

You can quickly and easily make a will or living trust, form an LLC or corporation,
apply for a provisional patent, or make hundreds of other forms—online.

Free Legal Information

Thousands of articles answer common questions about everyday legal issues,
including wills, bankruptcy, small business formation, divorce, patents,
employment, and much more.

Plain-English Legal Dictionary

Stumped by jargon? Look it up in America's most up-to-date source for
definitions of legal terms, free at Nolo.com.

Lawyer Directory

Nolo's consumer-friendly lawyer directory provides in-depth profiles of lawyers all
over America. You'll find information you need to choose the right lawyer.

COHA14